Real A+ College
Term
Papers

Real College Term Papers

ARCO

MACMILLAN • USA

First Edition

Copyright © 1999 by Mark Alan Stewart

Macmillan Reference USA
A Pearson Education Macmillan Company
1633 Broadway
New York, NY 10019-6785

An Arco Book

Manufactured in the United States of America

10 9 8 7 6 5 4 3 2 1

Library of Congress Number: 98-83025

ISBN: 0-02862876-4

TABLE OF CONTENTS

ACKNOWLEDGEMENTS

The editors gratefully acknowledge the follow individuals and firms for contributing their A+ college term papers to this book:

Collegiate Care

The Paper Store, Inc.

Eva Anda

Gabrielle Carbaugh

Chris Coretto

Patrick Cunningham

Peter Dahan

Joellen Estrada

David Haans

John Lopez

Greg Nicholson

Suene Mozako

Sarah Piantanida

Roberto Rosas

John Rosenkrantz

Catherine Rubenstein

Susan Storrie

Guy Tabler

CREDITS

Some of the information contained in Part I of this book is adapted from the following sources:

MLA Handbook for Writers of Research Papers (Fourth Ed.), by Joseph Gibaldi. The Modern Language Association of America, New York, 1995.

Publication Manual of the American Psychological Association (Fourth Ed.). American Psychological Association, Washington, DC, 1994.

How to Write a Term Paper, by Cynthia Keyworth. ARCO Publishing, Inc., New York, 1983.

20 Questions for the Writer: A Rhetoric with Readings (Sixth Ed.), by Jacqueline Berke and Randal Woodland. Harcourt, Brace, Jovanovich, New York, 1997.

INTRODUCTION

Real A+ College Term Papers was designed from the ground up to provide you with the information you *really* need for that dreaded term paper assigment that's hanging over your head. Not only does this book provide a cut-to-the-chase overview of how to put together a great term paper, it also *shows* you how—with 50 A+ term papers from every academic area. By studying these papers, you'll learn what themes, approaches, and writing styles actually work, and you'll be able to refine your own paper so that it, too, becomes an A+ masterpiece. So stop bugging your older brother and sister to see their old college papers for inspiration; you've got everything you need right here!

About Part I of This Book

Part I guides you step-by-step through the term-paper process—from brainstorming and researching to writing, revising, and proofreading. Keep in mind as you read Part I, particularly Chapter 3, that our guidelines for formatting your paper and for citing outside material are intended only as highlights of the "specs" required by the two most widely used term paper "style sheets":

▶ The MLA (Modern Language Association) style

▶ The APA (American Psychological Association) style

IMPORTANT: Do *not* rely solely on our overview of these styles; always consult the official *MLA Handbook for Writers of Research Papers* or the *Publication Manual of the American Psychological Association* (depending on your instructor's preference) for correct citation and formatting. See Chapter 3 for details about these official publications.

About Part II of This Book

Part II consists of 50 A+ term papers, some written by real college students like you, others written by professional writers. Preceding each paper you'll find a brief description of the paper's topic, along with a brief comment about what sets this paper apart from the crowd as an A+ paper.

Each paper in Part II conforms to one of the following three style sheets for college term papers:

▶ MLA in-text citation form (and *Works Cited* or *Works Consulted* list)

▶ MLA endnote citation form

▶ APA in-text citation form (and *References* list)

Immediately preceding each paper we've noted which style the paper employs. As you examine each paper in Part II, keep in mind that we've omitted the following formatting elements, which your instructor will probably require:

- ▶ Separate title page and abstract page (required by the APA style sheet)

- ▶ Running head (which normally appears at the top of each page of a term paper)

- ▶ Page break preceding the bibliographical information (the MLA and APA style sheets both call for this information to begin on a new page)

Also keep in mind that we've added headings to all but a few of the papers in Part II. These headings are designed to help you understand how the paper is organized—to help you follow the flow of the paper. Check with your instructor, who may or may not want you to use headings. (Also consult the appropriate style sheet for proper heading format, because we've deviated slightly from the MLA and APA requirements.)

How to Use Part II of This Book

This book was designed from the ground up to help you *learn by example*. In other words, rather than simply telling you how to write a term paper, we've shown you how—in Part II. Regardless of the academic course you're writing for, you should read all 50 papers in this book. Why? By doing so you'll pick up many, many ideas about

- ▶ Organizing your paper

- ▶ Introducing your topic

- ▶ Presenting your ideas in a logical, easy-to-follow, sequence

- ▶ Concluding your paper

- ▶ Writing effectively and with an appropriate style and voice

- ▶ Using correct grammar and sentence structure

You'll also see the MLA and APA citation forms "in action"—a great way to familiarize yourself with the basic citation requirements of the two style sheets.

How *Not* to Use Part II of This Book

The sample term papers in Part II are intended to illustrate the ideas, advice, and style-sheet requirements discussed in Part I; but they are not for copying! Copying any material from these papers or from any other source without crediting that source is not only unethical, it also constitutes plagiarism and violates federal copyright laws. And that's not all. Experienced college instructors will have access to this book, and in any event usually recognize plagiarized material when they see it. So by copying material you'll risk receiving a failing grade as well as academic suspension—perhaps even expulsion. Enough said?

To further discourage you from copying the material in Part II, along with the accurate sources cited in these papers we've intentionally injected our own original material and have cited fictitious sources for that material. Besides, *we do not vouch for either the accuracy or completeness of any citation appearing in Part II*. The lesson here is simple: Do your own research and do your own writing!

Using a Research Assistance Service

Numerous research assistance services are available to help jump-start your own research. (Two credible such companies, both of which contributed model term papers to this book, are listed below.) By providing model term papers, lists of research sources, and customized research, these firms can help you gain a better understanding of your assigned topic and can point you in the right direction as you conduct your own research:

Collegiate Care
www.papers-online.com
1-888-44-REPORT (toll-free 24 hours a day, 7 days a week)
Collegiate Care maintains a database of more than 2,500 research papers, and can perform customized research as well. At its Web site, you can perform a keyword search or browse among various categories for titles and descriptions.

The Paper Store, Inc.
www.papers24-7.com
1-800-90-WRITE (toll-free 24 hours a day, 7 days a week)
The Paper Store maintains a database of more than 4,000 research papers, and can perform customized research as well. At its Web site, you can perform a keyword search or browse among various categories for titles and descriptions.

Should you decide to seek help from a research service, keep in mind that their model papers are intended solely as research aids, and only with the mutual understanding that you will list their model papers in your own paper as bibliographic sources. In any event, as all these companies emphasize, copying material from any other source without crediting that source constitutes plagiarism and violates U.S. federal copyright laws.

PART I

RESEARCHING AND WRITING YOUR PAPER

1

CHOOSING A TOPIC AND DEVELOPING A THESIS

There are two basic types of term papers:

▶ In a *research* paper, you demonstrate your ability to locate appropriate source material on a topic and to demonstrate that you understand the material, by presenting it in an orderly and articulate manner.

▶ In a *thesis* paper, you take a position on a topic, and then defend that position through the use of other appropriate source material.

Any experienced college professor will tell you that you can't squeeze an A+ term paper out of a C- topic or thesis statement. Whether your assignment involves writing a research paper or a thesis paper, the advice in this chapter will help you start off in the right direction—with an appropriate subject and a good angle on that subject.

CHOOSING A TOPIC

Whether your assignment involves writing a research paper or term paper, chances are your instructor has allowed you at least some leeway in choosing the subject of your term paper. You'll probably need to do some initial research to settle on a topic *before* you begin serious research on that topic. Keep in mind the following DO's and DON'Ts as you dig for potential term paper topics:

▶ DO check the bibliography of your class textbook for ideas. The assigned course text will in all likelihood provide a gold mine of ideas for research papers. Surprisingly, most students never think to check this valuable resource.

▶ DO select a topic that has been the subject of *serious* research. If all you can find on the subject are some articles from popular magazines, you need to revise your topic.

▶ DO make sure you can find *enough sources* on the subject. If you can't find at least 10 sources, you probably need to revise your topic.

▶ DO make sure you can find sources of *different types* for the subject (books, periodicals, news reports, and so on). If all source material you use comes from one source type, you risk leaving the impression—deserved or not—that you're a lazy researcher.

▶ DON'T select a complex, graduate-level topic. By all means, try to demonstrate in your paper that you can grasp complex ideas, analyze them, and write thoughtfully about them. But in your zeal to impress your instructor, try not to be overly ambitious. If you get in over your head, you will have wasted a lot of time.

▶ DON'T restrict yourself to parochial topics (that is, those of only regional interest or significance). Otherwise, you might not have enough to write about, and you might not find enough source material. Besides, choosing a topic of strictly local interest or significance suggests that you lack awareness of the world beyond your immediate environment.

▶ DO obtain your instructor's feedback before settling on your topic. Otherwise, you'll run the risk of turning in a paper that the instructor deems hackneyed, inappropriate, or otherwise not worthwhile. If your instructor has provided a list of acceptable topics, you might want to talk with the instructor anyway about whether and how you might refine one of those topics. You might be surprised how often instructors award grades of B or C rather than A solely because the student appeared to adapt a passive, lazy approach toward topic selection.

▶ DO avoid your instructor's pet areas of research. If you write about your instructor's specialty, the instructor is bound to know whether you've overlooked important source material, misrepresented facts, or otherwise turned in a paper worthy of less than an A+.

ANGLES FOR APPROACHING A TERM PAPER TOPIC

Are you convinced that you have nothing new to say about the topic you've chosen for your term paper? If so, you're not alone; nearly all your classmates suffer from the same insecurity. To gain an advantage, you simply need to *ask the right questions* about the topic.

An average term paper simply describes the subject—by answering these questions:

Who? What? Where? When?

An A+ paper goes much further—by also exploring these questions:

How? Why? So what?

Exploring these three additional questions will set your paper apart from the rest by demonstrating a depth of analysis as well as a multidimensional way of thinking about the topic. By the way, the last question above ("So what?") might sound a bit cynical, but it's not. Exploring this question shows you've dug deeper than your classmates—to consider the relevance, importance, or significance of some aspect of your topic.

Now let's get specific. To help you develop an A+ thesis or other angle on your topic, we've listed below a variety of questions for you to ask and then answer about your topic. These brainstorming questions are divided into 12 categories, each of which represents a distinct approach to—or way of thinking about—a topic. Pick the categories that seem most fitting for your topic. (Not all the categories will apply to your topic, but at least a few should.) Fill in the blanks with your topic, and then try answering the questions based on what you know about the topic at this point.

 NOTE: Notice that for each category the initial questions are more obvious ones that most students would think of, whereas subsequent questions dig deeper by asking the more thoughtful and insightful questions that an A+ term paper would explore. (Notice how often the two questions "Why?" and "How?" show up among these lists!)

Classification

How can ___ be classified? Is ___ part of some larger phenomenon, group, movement, or trend? Is there disagreement as to how ___ should be classified? Is one particular view the best? Why?

What are some varieties of ___? How might these examples or varieties be classified further?

Are there different ways to classify types of ___? Is the current classification system adequate (is it adaptable to new discoveries, changing circumstances, and so on)? If not, have better classification systems been proposed or adopted? If not, why not?

Comparison and Contrast

What are the similarities and differences between ___ and ___? What is the significance of these similarities/differences? Which of these is most significant? Why?

How can ___, ___, and ___ be ranked or rated (in terms of quality, effectiveness, and significance)? Are there differing views about how they should be ranked or rated?

What is ___ similar to? In what ways? How do these similarities help one to understand ___?

What is ___ different from? In what ways?

Cause and Effect

How did ___ come about? What factors contributed to ___?

What are/were the causes of ___? Are all causes required? Is/was one cause the precipitating one? Why?

What was the effect, impact, result, or consequence of ___? How have scholars evaluated these effects? If scholars disagree, on what basis do they disagree? With whom do you agree, and why?

Do two (or more) phenomena generally occur in a certain sequence? Why or why not? What factors might alter the pattern in the future?

Process
What are the steps involved in producing ___ ?

What underlying principles or laws are at work in the process of going from ___ to ___?

What conditions or circumstances are required for ___ to occur? to not occur? to change? to cease?

How much can ___ change and still retain its essential identity or character?

Has ___ assimilated (or been assimilated by) something else? Why? What was the process?

What are the dynamics of ___ (flux, ebb-and-flow, increase-and-decrease, or other patterns of change over time)?

How often does ___ occur? Is there a pattern? If so, what might explain the pattern?

Purpose, Function, and Application
What is/was the purpose of ___? How has the purpose of ___ been served, undermined, or defeated in the past?

What is the function of ___ as part of a larger phenomenon?

What conditions facilitate or impede ___?

How can/should ___ be used? What happens if ___ is misused?

Does ___ have multiple functions, applications, or purposes? If so, which one is primary, and why?

Definition
How is ___ defined? How would you describe ___? What are some examples of ___?

Is ___ defined differently by different people? What accounts for this discrepancy? Is one definition more accurate than others?

Has the definition of ___ changed over time? If so, how and why? (For example, has the definition expanded or contracted? Has the definition changed due to cultural or technological change?)

Do any popular metaphors, analogies, or proverbs provide insight about ___? What are the short-comings of these metaphors, analogies, or proverbs? (For example, do they over-generalize?) Are they outmoded? What are the positive or negative consequences when people adhere to popular or conventional wisdom?

Description

What are the various components, parts, or aspects of ___?

How would you characterize ___? How have others characterized ___?

Is ___ described differently by different people? What accounts for this discrepancy? Is one view more accurate or enlightened than others?

Is the meaning of ___ misunderstood? By whom? Why? What are the consequences? What efforts have been or should be made to clarify the meaning of ___?

Reflection and Interpretation

What is your personal impression or recollection of ___? If it differs from the impressions or recollections of others, how and why?

What was your initial reaction to ___? Upon further reflection, what was your reaction to ___? How might your reactions by colored by your personal biases, experiences, or lack of knowledge, insight, or information?

What is your personal (emotional and intellectual) response to ___? Are these responses at odds with each other? If so, why?

What is your personal interpretation of ___? Are there other reasonable interpretations?

Journalism (Examining Evidence)

What do surveys or polls indicate about ___? Are these surveys reliable (that is, is the sample representative, sufficiently large, and unbiased)?

Does the common view about ___ differ from that of certain experts or authorities? How and why?

What are the most notable or impressive statistical facts about ___? In what ways might these statistics distort ___ (for example, by painting an unfairly positive or negative picture of ___)?

Evaluation

What is the value of ___ (to the individual or to society)?

What arguments can be made for or against ___?

What are the advantages and drawbacks of ___ compared to ___? On balance, which alternative is better? Why?

Prescription and Direction

What is the best solution to the problem of ____? Why is this solution better than other proposals?

Should ___ be encouraged or discouraged? On what grounds?

What is the best future direction of ___?

How would ___ best serve certain interests of the society? Why are these interests preferable to competing interests?

TECHNIQUES FOR EFFECTIVE BRAINSTORMING

If you're still having trouble coming up with just the right angle on your topic, try these brainstorming techniques:

▶ Carry around a notepad as a journal for free association about your term paper topic; collect as many ideas as you can. It doesn't matter whether the ideas are initially any good. Just jot down everything that comes to mind—even if you think you might discard it eventually.

▶ Pretend you're on a panel television show with other guests, each of whom has a distinct point of view (think of *Nightline*, *Meet the Press*, or *The News Hour with Jim Lehrer*). How would the discussion play out? What questions would the other guests ask? What kind of opinions would they have?

▶ Take one entire day and talk to your friends about nothing but your topic. Try to sum up your idea for them in a few sentences. What questions do they have? Record their questions in your journal.

DEVELOPING AND REVISING YOUR THESIS

If your assignment is to write a thesis paper, your initial research should help you formulate a thesis, which will probably evolve as you do further research. Your paper's thesis is its central idea—stated in a single sentence. The thesis defines your paper's scope as well as its approach toward the topic at hand. Your thesis should be specific, *not* vague:

VAGUE (INCORRECT): Beowolf and Hrothgar, two characters from two different medieval epic poems, are similar in many ways.

SPECIFIC (BETTER): Beowolf and Hrothgar, two characters from two different medieval epic poems, both illustrate that the medieval king–warrior relationship was much like the relationship between a father and son, in that a warrior-son was motivated primarily by a desire to please his king-father.

Also, your thesis should be a sentence, *not* a question:

> QUESTION (INCORRECT): What was the most significant long-term social consequence of the hippie movement of the 1960s?

> STATEMENT (BETTER): One of the most profound, and most surprising, long-term consequences of the 1960s hippie movement has been the baby-boomer generation's newfound penchant for accumulating material possessions.

Many college students carve their thesis statements in stone before they start their research. Big mistake! By all means, come up with a *tentative* thesis early in your research. Don't marry yourself to your initial thesis; until you actually sit down to write your paper, think of your thesis as a work in progress. As you do your research, continually test your thesis. Don't be reluctant to revise—or perhaps abandon—your thesis along the way.

2
FINDING AND ORGANIZING SOURCE MATERIAL

Now it's time to get down to the nitty-gritty: the research. If you don't know how to use a library for research, help is readily available from many different resources (your college librarian, for instance). Teaching you how to use a library is not what this book is about. Instead, we'll focus on how to do research as efficiently as possible, as well as on how to use the Internet for term paper research.

STARTING AT THE LIBRARY REFERENCE DESK

We'll begin with some basic tips for library research that should keep you from going astray once you've passed through the doors of your college library.

A great place to begin your research is in the general reference section of your college library. General references (encyclopedias, current events yearbooks, dictionaries, and so on) provide useful background information and overviews; they also point you in the right direction by listing *primary sources:* the books, articles, speeches, and so forth consulted for these overviews.

Your reference librarian can provide you with several reference-book guides (reference books about reference books). Check in one of these guides, under your term-paper topic's category, for a list of general reference sources to explore.

Your next stop in the library should be at the indexes to periodicals and newspapers. The following are the ones most frequently used for college term papers:

- ► *Reader's Guide to Periodical Literature:* Lists articles from several hundred American periodicals (by author and subject)

- ► *Social Science Index:* Lists articles in scholarly and technical journals about anthropology, archeology, economics, geography, history, political science, and sociology (by subject and author)

- ► *Humanities Index:* Lists scholarly and technical journals containing articles about art, literature, philosophy, and religion (by subject and author)

- ► *The New York Times Index:* Provides summaries of all world events as recorded day-by-day in the *New York Times;* you can locate the original articles by these summaries (classified alphabetically by subject, and then chronologically)

- ► *Biography Index:* Lists full-length biographies as well as biographical material appearing in other sources (by subject and author)

One of the following specialized periodical indexes might also come in handy:

- ▶ *Applied Science and Technology Index*
- ▶ *Art Index*
- ▶ *Business Periodicals Index*
- ▶ *Education Index*
- ▶ *Music Index*
- ▶ *Nineteenth Century Reader's Guide*
- ▶ *Public Affairs Information Index*

 NOTE: If your topic isn't covered by any of the specialized indexes listed above, don't despair; the ones listed here are the most widely used ones, but not the only ones. Ask the reference librarian for other suggestions.

Once you've exploited secondary source material (encyclopedias, dictionaries, and so forth), don't stop! Never rely solely on general reference sources for your term paper. Take heed: If the list of citations at the end of your paper contains only secondary sources, don't expect to receive an A for the paper; your instructor will suspect that you threw together your paper at the last minute and without due care. An A+ term paper does *not* rely on secondary source material, but rather demonstrates that the student has dug deeper—by going to primary sources: the actual books and articles written by the scholars and other experts. Let's go there now!

HITTING THE STACKS

Okay, you've checked a variety of secondary sources and periodical indexes, and you've compiled a long list of potential primary source materials for your paper. Now it's time to retrieve each source and scrutinize it to determine whether it might be useful to you. Don't hit the stacks yet, though . . . at least not without your backpack and the following items:

- ▶ A big loose-leaf binder
- ▶ A three-hole punch
- ▶ A stapler
- ▶ Some tabbed dividers for the notebook
- ▶ A role of dimes (or a photocopy card)
- ▶ A pen or pencil
- ▶ A highlighter

Why drag all these items to the library just to look up stuff? For maximum efficiency! As you locate each source, follow these steps (don't skip a step, or you'll probably regret it):

1. Peruse the source material to determine whether it has term paper potential. Reject a source if it is

   ▶ Obsolete (perhaps scholars writing more recently had access to information that renders the particular source material obsolete)

   ▶ Inflammatory (appealing to emotion rather than intellect)

   ▶ Too biased (there's nothing wrong with material that reflects a strong point of view, as long as the viewpoint is defensible and not based on prejudice or unfair bias)

   ▶ Too superficial (look for in-depth analysis, not hackneyed, self-evident tripe)

   ▶ Of dubious (that is, doubtful) credibility

2. If the source material has potential, photocopy all pertinent pages—immediately! Don't skimp on the dimes; when in doubt, photocopy!

3. Staple together all the pages from one source, and then jot down the source at the top of the first page. Be sure to include all the information you'd need for a proper citation. (In Chapter 3 you'll learn how to cite outside source material.)

4. Read your photocopy carefully, highlighting anything that might be useful.

5. Again read the highlighted material. Summarize important ideas (in your own words) in the margins near where those ideas are expressed. Circle or underline passages you think might be worthwhile to paraphrase or quote (rather than to summarize).

6. Insert the material in your binder, under the most appropriate tabbed heading. (Add page dividers with new headings as you go.)

 NOTE: If you think these steps amount to obvious advice that most college students would follow, think again! Wander around your college library on a weekend afternoon during term paper season. How many students appear to be using an efficient research system such as this one? The answer: only students who have read this book.

ORGANIZING YOUR SOURCE MATERIAL

Now it's time to organize your source material. The best way to do it is with a computer database program (such as Microsoft Access). Don't even think about organizing the material the old-fashioned way: by shuffling papers or 3 × 5 note cards. Your parents probably used the note-card system, but they didn't have a choice. You do! Head back to your dorm room or to the computer lab, hunker down at a PC or Mac, and transcribe what's in your loose-leaf binder onto your hard drive. Here's how to do it:

▶ Create a different database field for each photocopied source. If you know the correct citation form, you might as well enter the proper citation at this time.

▶ Create a different field for each tabbed subject in your loose-leaf binder.

▶ Go through each photocopied page in your binder, and create a distinct record (that is, entry) for each summary (those margin notes you jotted down at the library). Assign to the record its appropriate fields.

▶ Enter word-for-word each passage that you highlighted for paraphrasing or quoting. Assign at least one subject to each entry. (Try to be very selective about material for possible paraphrasing or quoting; otherwise, you'll type your fingertips to the bone.)

Think of your records as separate notes, which you'll put into piles and shuffle into just the right order for your paper. Keep in mind that each record (entry) should contain only one idea and should identify the page number of the work from which the material is taken. (You might want to create an additional field for this purpose.)

NOTE: If you don't already know how to use Microsoft's Access database program, you can get up-to-speed quickly with either of these two books, both published by Que: *Complete Idiot's Guide to Access* and *10-Minute Guide to Access*. Of course, you don't need to use Microsoft's program; many other database programs are available as well, including freeware or shareware programs that provide all the features you'll need for your term paper.

CREATING AN OUTLINE

Now it's time to rough out an outline, based on the subject headings (and subheadings) you've already created. You'll need an outline to reveal any gaps you need to fill by doing more research. How you should organize the ideas into outline form depends on the type of paper you're writing, your thesis, and your instructor's specific instructions and requirements. Nevertheless, certain rules of thumb apply to any outline:

1. As you construct your outline, ask yourself:

   ▶ Can you break down any of your main headings into subheadings?

   ▶ Are any of the main headings more appropriate as subheadings under another main heading?

   ▶ Are two or more main headings related closely enough that they can be merged?

2. Be sure all parts of your outline relate to your thesis statement. (You might need to refine your thesis at this point.)

3. Be sure the outline serves to convey your ideas in a logical, easy-to-follow sequence. There are several ways to accomplish this, such as the following:

   ▶ Through chronological development

   ▶ By arguing from your weakest point to your strongest one

   ▶ By starting with a "micro" view, and then moving to a "macro" one (or vice versa)

   ▶ By moving from simple ideas to complex ones

   ▶ By moving from fundamental laws or axioms to unknowns or uncertainty

   ▶ By moving from agreed-upon views to controversial issues

4. Be sure each heading contains at least two subheadings, if it has any (that is, don't use only a single subheading under a heading).

Once you've settled on an outline, you can arrange your electronic note cards sequentially and begin your first draft!

USING THE INTERNET FOR TERM PAPER RESEARCH

Unless you've recently crawled out from under a rock, you know how to surf the Web, and you've used an Internet search engine. But you might not yet have put the Internet to the test for term-paper research. Performing term-paper research on the Internet can be rewarding, but it can also be frustrating. You might strike a mother lode of information that is right on point for your paper; on the other hand, you might hit nothing but dead ends.

Today's Internet: Great Index, Lousy Library

The Internet is a godsend for college students and other scholars—no doubt about it. But while the Internet is a great tool for putting together a bibliography for a term paper, it's not a good place to retrieve source material itself. In other words, think of the Internet as the ultimate card catalog, but a lousy library. Face facts: You'll have to trek over to the real library and hit the stacks to retrieve the source material you need for an A+ term paper. (Eventually, of course, all printed books will be available in electronic form; but you'll be very late submitting your term paper if you wait for that day!)

The Ephemeral Nature of Internet Resources

Be forewarned that Internet information can be ephemeral—here today, gone tomorrow. Imagine relying heavily on Internet sources for you term paper, only to have your instructor discover that you've cited numerous electronic sources that no longer exist. Here are three lessons to take to heart:

▶ Unless your instructor specifies otherwise, don't rely solely on Internet sources for you term paper.

▶ Always store Internet documents you intend to use as source material on your personal computer, and always generate a printed copy of the source material. Be sure your printed copy includes the source's Internet location.

▶ Before you revise your first draft, go online and check your sources again to make sure your cited sources haven't disappeared or moved.

Printed Versus Online Sources—The Credibility Gap

Unlike traditional print publishing, Internet publishing is available to almost anyone. How can you ensure that the Internet source material you incorporate into your term paper is authoritative—or at least credible? Here's a checklist to help you assess online sources:

☐ Check authorship of the source material. If the document does not clearly identify the author, look for a link to a home page, or go up to the next directory level.

☐ Check the bottom of the page for copyright notices and other legal information for clues.

☐ Check whether the document indicates the date it was created.

☐ Check to see if the document (or site) is linked to, sponsored by, or otherwise associated with a credible, established organization or other authority. If the authority maintains a Web site, does that site acknowledge the author by providing a reciprocal link to the author's site?

☐ Use a search engine to search for the author's name by performing a name search as well as a subject search. Be sure to search not just the Web but also other Internet resources such as Usenet. Go to the Library of Congress search engine, and check for books by the author.

☐ Check the domain type for the site—for example, *com* (commercial), *org* (non-profit organization), *gov* (government), or *edu* (educational institution). Be wary of using source material from a commercial site, especially if the site includes advertisements, is selling a product or service, emphasizes graphics more than information, or otherwise appears to be motivated by profit rather than by a commitment to scholarship or intellectual inquiry.

☐ Examine the content of the site for its underlying goal, purpose, or intent. Is its purpose to advocate a position or to objectively examine various sides of an issue? Does the material employ inflammatory language or rhetoric that might indicate an extremist (and noncredible) author?

☐ Check for grammatical and typographical errors; such errors strongly suggest a lack of care in terms of content as well.

Using Search Engines and Indexes

Search engines simply store documents, and then retrieve information based on your queries. *Indexes* categorize Internet documents to help you perform a focused search for a topic. The major indexes now also incorporate search engines, and the major search engines are beginning to include indexes as well. The following are the most widely used search engines and indexes (you can find any of these search engines simply by clicking the Search button on your Web browser):

- ▶ Alta Vista (search engine)

- ▶ Excite (index with search engine)

- ▶ HotBot (search engine)

- ▶ Infoseek (index with search engine)

- ▶ Lycos (search engine)

- ▶ Open Text (search engine)

- ▶ WebCrawler (search engine)

- ▶ Yahoo (index with search engine)

You should exploit both types of research tools, of course! But keep in mind that each type holds inherent advantages and drawbacks, as described in the following sections.

Getting the Most from Web Indexes

Indexes function well to perform broad searches of prominent and well-established sites. But indexes can leave out lesser-known and highly specialized sources—sources that might be very useful to you. Also, an index can easily lead you down many dead ends before you find a path that bears fruit. Why? An index essentially tells you how a topic or key word should be categorized, thereby controlling and limiting your search. But although *you* know exactly what you're searching for, the index doesn't. So don't trust the index to lead you down the best path to source material that is most relevant and useful for you.

When you use an index, be sure to maintain a running log of categories and subcategories as you explore them. Make notes (yes . . . using paper and pencil!) about which paths bear fruit and which ones lead to dead ends. Keeping a written log will help you avoid performing the same research again and remind you which categories are worth returning to later to explore further.

Tips for Using Search Engines

If it's out there anywhere in cyberspace, a major search engine can find it for you. The advantage of using search engines is that they filter source material only according to user-defined queries. In other words, you control the search. The disadvantage is that they make no attempt to control the quality of the Web sites and other sources that they archive.

Here are some basic tips for using search engines effectively:

☐ Some search engines check only document titles and headers (descriptions) for matches to your query words. Others check entire documents. Use the latter type to be sure you don't overlook potential sources for your term paper.

☐ Learn how each search engine works. Each one is slightly different. Go to the engine's home page on the Web, and spend a few minutes reading the instructions and FAQs.

☐ Learn the particular advantages of each search engine. For example, HotBot permits you to specify date, location, media type, and so on. Infoseek permits you to pose a query in the form of a question. (In all likelihood, all major search engines will eventually offer essentially the same features.)

☐ Select your key words (queries) carefully. Designing a query is a bit of an art form. The trick is to choose words and phrases for your query that filter out irrelevant sources but not relevant ones.

☐ Avoid using generic keywords—such as *literature* or *environment*—in your queries. Otherwise, you'll generate a list of many thousands of sources, the vast majority of which are sure to be of no use to you.

☐ Most search engines allow you to use Boolean operators—key words such as AND, OR, NOT, and NEAR—to narrow your search. Knowing how to use these operators is critical to a successful search. (Each search engine employs its own Boolean operators in its own way; be sure to read the instructions at the engine's Web site.)

☐ After you submit a query, the search engine lists documents according to their *relevance*—that is, based on where and how many times your key words appear in the title, description, and text of a document. But a document that repeats the same key term many times might nevertheless not be useful at all for your paper. So never assume that documents high on the list will be more helpful to you than ones further down the list.

☐ Some search engines also list related keywords in response to your queries. You can then refine your search by including or excluding these additional key words.

When you're satisfied that you've collected enough useful source material from enough different (and credible) outside sources, you're ready to move ahead to your first draft. In the next chapter you'll learn how to do it.

3

WRITING YOUR FIRST DRAFT

Okay . . . you've scoured the stacks, surfed the Net, created and arranged your electronic note cards, settled on a thesis, and created an outline. Now it's time to open your favorite word processing application and start composing your first draft. If you think that this phase will entail little more than merging together your note cards and importing them sequentially into a word processing file, think again! The writing process requires judgment, effort, and skill. As you write, you'll need to determine

- ▶ How best to incorporate outside source material into your draft

- ▶ How to cite outside source material in the text itself

- ▶ How to construct paragraphs in a way that leads the reader not only logically but also in a fluid way from one idea to the next

- ▶ How to present your ideas in a style and voice that are appropriate as well as pleasing to the mind's ear.

INCORPORATING OUTSIDE MATERIAL INTO YOUR PAPER

There are three ways to include material from other sources in your term paper:

- ▶ *Quotations:* When you quote another source, you restate an excerpt from the source document verbatim (that is, word-for-word).

- ▶ *Paraphrases:* When you paraphrase, you restate in your own words an excerpt from another work. Paraphrased material is usually a bit briefer than the original source material.

- ▶ *Summaries:* When you summarize, you indicate in your own words the main ideas, along with major supporting points, of another source.

Quotations, paraphrases, and summaries serve many purposes. For example, you might use them to

- ▶ Provide support for claims or add credibility to your writing

- ▶ Provide examples

- ▶ Provide one viewpoint or perspective on the topic at hand

- ▶ Expand the breadth or depth of your writing

SOME DO'S AND DON'TS FOR USING SOURCE MATERIAL

Here's a handy list of DO's and DON'Ts for weaving material from other sources into your paper.

In General

DO use all three methods of citing other sources, and try to intersperse them for variety in order to add interest.

DO cite *all* other source material you use for your paper—whichever method you use (quotation, paraphrase, or summary). Otherwise, you'll be committing plagiarism.

Summaries

DO use summaries in general discussion that leads up to a specific point.

DO use a summary to express the thesis of another work.

DO use summaries more frequently than either paraphrases or quotations. Why? A summary demonstrates that you've assimilated a large amount of material and are able to recapitulate main points and major supporting points. This task involves greater effort and skill than either paraphrasing or quoting. In other words, you'll demonstrate to the reader (your instructor) that you've taken the assignment seriously and made an earnest effort to learn about the topic at hand during your research.

Paraphrases

DO use paraphrasing to restate material that the reader might not understand if quoted word-for-word—either because the material is technical or because the author's original style is difficult to understand.

DO use synonyms when paraphrasing, and rearrange sentence structure; otherwise, without quoting word-for-word you run the risk of plagiarism.

Quotations

DON'T overuse quotations. Quotations interrupt the flow of your sentences and allow you no room to interpret the source material as you cite it.

DO use quotations to restate phrases that are particularly provocative or eloquently stated, or that would otherwise lose their impact if paraphrased.

DO use quotations to make particularly important points; readers tend to pay closer attention to quoted material than to other material.

DO use quotations to cite a particularly authoritative source (for example, a dictionary, a famous orator, a prophet, or a sage).

DO use quotations to distinguish your ideas from those of the quoted material's author; in other words, to make clear that the ideas expressed in the quotation are not your own.

DO weave your quotation into your text; always introduce each quote, and make sure the transition to the material that follows is smooth.

DON'T juxtapose two or more quotations; always insert other material between quotations.

DO explain and interpret each quotation; make sure the reader understands what the quotation means and your purpose for including it.

DO include short quotations directly in the text. Set off longer quotations as blocks—according to the MLA or APA guidelines. (You'll learn about the MLA and APA citation forms in the next section.)

DO be consistent in how you punctuate quotations. Follow the prescribed format (MLA or APA) strictly. Keep in mind that the proper method for punctuation depends on

- ▶ The position of the mark in the sentence
- ▶ The purpose of the punctuation mark
- ▶ The purpose of the sentence

You'll learn more about punctuation in the section titled "Punctuation" in Chapter 4.

DOCUMENTING OUTSIDE SOURCE MATERIAL

Different academic fields have adopted different standards—or *style sheets*—for citing source material in undergraduate term papers. The most widely used style, and the preferred style of most college instructors in the humanities and in fine arts, is the Modern Language Association (MLA) style. However, many instructors in the social sciences and natural sciences prefer the American Psychological Association (APA) style. The following sections provide an overview of both styles, to give you a sense of what they involve and of their similarities and differences. But don't rely on this overview for your term paper; always consult the official MLA or APA style sheet.

NOTE: These aren't the only two style manuals. Most major scholarly fields have their own sets of guidelines or preferred styles. But most of these specialized styles are variations on the MLA or APA style, and they are generally used only for upper-divisional and graduate course work. In any event, always check with your instructor as to which style he or she prefers!

THE MLA FORM

The MLA documentation form is based on the *MLA Handbook for Writers of Research Papers* (4th edition). Copies of this book are available at your college library and in bookstores. The *MLA Handbook* provides hundreds of examples covering almost every possible type of source.

The standard MLA documentation system calls for parenthetical references throughout the text of your paper, along with a *Works Cited* list at the end of the paper. The in-text references, together with the *Works Cited* list, indicate to the reader what works you've used in your paper, what you derived from each source, and where in the source you found the material. The next few pages provide an overview of the MLA documentation rules and guidelines. Keep in mind that these are only highlights. Always consult the *MLA Handbook*.

 TIP: The MLA maintains a Web site (www.mla.org), which provides some of the documentation from the printed handbook, as well as up-to-date information about citing electronic sources.

MLA In-Text Documentation

A proper MLA in-text reference generally contains the last name (surname) of the author of the source material and the page number(s) from which the specific source material is taken. You may indicate the author's name either in the text itself or in parentheses following the appropriate passage; but you must always indicate page number(s) in parentheses. Here are two simple examples (notice the placement of punctuation marks following the cited material):

```
One noted scholar disagrees with Gatlin's view (Madrich 187-88).
```

```
Madrich disagrees with Gatlin on this point (187-88).
```

If you cite the same source sequentially in the same paragraph, page number(s) alone will suffice for all but the first reference. Also, if you cite more than one work by a particular author, include a shortened title for the particular work from which you have taken the source material. Here are two examples (the second example cites two different books by Madrich):

```
One noted scholar disagrees with Gatlin's view (Madrich
187-88). But at the same time Madrich acknowledges that Gatlin's
argument has merit (190).
```

```
Madrich disagrees with Gatlin on this point (Medieval 187-88). But
in another work Madrich acknowledges that Gatlin's argument has
merit (Customs 27).
```

Keep in mind that specific rules for in-text documentation apply for citing

- ▶ An entire work

- ▶ Part of an article or part of a book

- ▶ Volume and page numbers of multivolume works

- ▶ A work listed by title

- ▶ A work by a corporate author

- ▶ Works by different numbers of authors

- ▶ Two or more works

- ▶ Non-print sources (such as Web pages)

- ▶ Personal communications (such as letters, interviews, and email)

Refer to the *MLA Handbook* for examples of each type of in-text reference.

MLA rules for indicating quoted material depend on the quotation's length. Incorporate prose quotations of four or fewer typed lines, as well as verse quotations of three or fewer lines, directly in your text, enclosing the quotation within double quotation marks. For verse, indicate original line breaks with slash marks (/). For every quote, you must provide the author and specific page (or line number for verse) citation in the text. Here are some examples (notice the placement of punctuation marks following the quoted material):

```
Berger asserts that Emerson "had become the cynosure of American
Renaissance consciousness" (142).

Some scholars argue that Emerson "had become the cynosure of
American Renaissance consciousness" (Berger 142).

Berger asks, "Why had Emerson become the cynosure of American
Renaissance consciousness?" (142)

Berger asserts that Emerson "had become the cynosure of American
Renaissance consciousness" (142); but Berger fails to adequately
defend his claim.

Hrothgar's speech to Beowulf is more than an expression of
gratitude: "'Let me take you to my heart, make you my son
too / And love you'" (lines 947-48).
```

The MLA form requires that longer quotations (more than four lines of prose, or more than three lines of verse) be placed in a freestanding block of lines. Indent the entire block 1 inch, or 10 typewritten characters, from the left margin, and omit quotation marks (but use double quotation marks for quotations within the blocked material). When quoting verse, maintain original line breaks. You should generally use a colon to introduce a block quotation, although the specific context may call for a different punctuation mark or none at all. Your parenthetical citation should come *after* the closing punctuation mark. Maintain double-spacing throughout a block quotation, as well as preceding and following it. Here's an example that includes a quotation within a block of quoted material:

```
Yates points out Hazlitt's conception of the portraiture experience,
as expressed in Hazlitt's 1823 essay "On Sitting for One's Picture":
            For Hazlitt, the bond between painter and sitter is most
            like the relationship between two lovers: "they are
            always thinking and talking of the same thing, in which
            their self love finds an equal counterpart." Hazlitt
            seemed to view the relationship, then, as a collabora-
            tive one in which the artist is both host and
            contractual employee. (Yates 79)
Yates goes on, however, to contrast Hazlitt's perspective to
Cartier-Bresson's perception of the portraiture experience as one
of confrontation, not collaboration (81).
```

The MLA *Works Cited* List

As noted earlier, the standard MLA documentation system calls for a *Works Cited* list at the end of your paper—beginning on a separate page. Your *Works Cited* list must include *all* works cited in your paper. (Conversely, all entries on the list must appear in your paper.)

NOTE: The *MLA Handbook* also provides alternatives to the *Works Cited* list. Some of the papers in Part II of this book, for example, include an MLA *Works Consulted* list, which contains not only the works cited in the text of the paper but other works consulted as well. Check with your instructor as to which type of list he or she prefers.

Different Forms for Different Sources

Each citation in your *Works Cited* list must provide all the information a reader would need to retrieve the cited source material. The specific information you'll need for documenting a source, as well as how you indicate that information, depends on the source type. For example, the MLA calls for distinct forms for each of the following sources:

- ▶ Books
  - ▶ A book with one author
  - ▶ A book with more than one author
  - ▶ A book with no author named
  - ▶ Part of a book (such as an essay in a collection)
  - ▶ An anthology or a collection
- ▶ Essays and articles
  - ▶ An article from a scholarly journal, newspaper, or magazine
  - ▶ An article from a reference book
  - ▶ An essay from a collection
  - ▶ An essay in a journal with continuous pagination
  - ▶ An essay in a journal that pages each issue separately
- ▶ Government publications
- ▶ Electronic sources
  - ▶ A Web page
  - ▶ An online journal or magazine article
  - ▶ Information on CD-ROM
  - ▶ An article in a reference database
  - ▶ An email message
  - ▶ A listserv posting
  - ▶ An electronic database
- ▶ An interview that you conducted
- ▶ Other media sources
  - ▶ A television or radio program
  - ▶ An advertisement

The *MLA Handbook* and the MLA Web site (www.mla.org) provide examples covering these and other potential sources. Always consult the *MLA Handbook* or Web site to determine proper citation form!

NOTE: Most of the sample papers in Part II conform to the MLA style; take a peek at the end of this chapter or at the papers in Part II to see what a *Works Cited* list looks like. Keep in mind that the MLA style calls for the *Works Cited* list to begin on a new page, and that we've deviated from the MLA style in this respect.

MLA Rules for Ordering Your References

The MLA form specifies a particular sequence for the entries in your *Works Cited* list. The basic rule is to organize the list in alphabetical order, by the last name (surname) of the first author of each source. (Consult the *MLA Handbook* for more details.)

Capitalizing, Underlining, Indenting, and Spacing

The MLA form also specifies formatting requirements for the citations in your list. This section highlights these requirements (consult the *MLA Handbook* for complete information):

- ▶ Use a *hanging indent* for each entry. The first line of each entry should be flush with the left margin, with subsequent lines each indented ¹/₂ inch or 5 typewritten character spaces.

- ▶ Capitalize each significant word in the titles of articles, books, and so on. (Consult the *MLA Handbook*, which is very specific about which types of words should be capitalized.)

- ▶ Underline or italicize book titles as well as journal titles and their volume numbers; capitalize each significant word in the title.

- ▶ Just as in the text of your paper, maintain double-spacing throughout the *Works Cited* list (no single spacing or additional spacing between entries).

Examples of MLA *Works Cited* List Entries

Each of your MLA *Works Cited* list entries should contain three basic components in the order listed here: (1) author information, (2) title information, and (3) publishing information. The following are four hypothetical *Works Cited* entries. In the order listed, they are a magazine article by two authors, a book by one author, a newspaper article, and an edited multivolume work:

```
Bauer, Patricia, and Frank J. Sussman. "The Role of Mass Media in
    a New Millenium Democracy." New Society Mar. 1998: 64+.
```

Gabelli, J. S. <u>An Introduction to Presidential Politics</u>. New York:
  Macmillan, 1991.

Newhouse, David. "The Clinton Legacy: Can Our Presidency Be Saved?"
  <u>Atlanta Constitution</u> 4 Jun. 1998: C-3.

Tanner, Robert K., Paul Willott, and Karen Fromer, eds.
  <u>A History of Western Culture</u>. 4 vols. Boston: Barham & Sons,
  1994.

MLA Guidelines for Formatting Your Paper

The following checklist covers the basic MLA formatting guidelines. Always check with your instructor, though, who might prefer that you deviate from these guidelines:

- ☐ Use standard-sized paper ($8\frac{1}{2} \times 11$ inches), and double-space all lines.

- ☐ Use 1-inch margins on all sides.

- ☐ Unless your instructor requests it, a title page is unnecessary. Instead, provide a double-spaced header in the top-left corner of the first page. This page should include your name, your instructor's name, the course, and the date. Center your title (using mixed uppercase and lowercase letters) on the next line, and begin the body of your paper immediately below the title.

- ☐ Begin your *Works Cited* list on a new page. Include the heading "Works Cited" (without quotation marks, underlining, and so on); center this heading at the top of the first *Works Cited* page.

- ☐ On every page after the first page of the paper, provide a header in the top-right corner ($\frac{1}{2}$ inch from the top of the page); this running header should include your last name and the page number.

- ☐ Underlining and italics are interchangeable. Choose one or the other form, and use it consistently throughout your paper.

- ☐ Headings for different sections of the paper are not required. (Consider adding headings for longer papers, but check with your instructor first.)

 NOTE: As you review the sample MLA-style papers in Part II, keep in mind that we've used less than double-spacing, we've omitted running headers, and the *Works Cited* and *Works Consulted* lists do not necessarily begin on new pages. We've also indicated the paper's title in uppercase letters, to help you identify it. But you should follow the MLA style strictly, unless your instructor specifies otherwise.

The MLA Documentation Notes (Endnotes) System

As an alternative to the documentation system described in the preceding sections, the *MLA Handbook* also provides a "documentation notes" system, in which superscript numbers are used instead of parenthetical references throughout the text of the paper. These numbers refer to numbered entries in an *Endnotes* list at the end of the paper, which provides complete references in numerical (rather than alphabetical) order. The format of MLA endnotes is a bit different from the format of *Works Cited* entries. (Consult the *MLA Handbook* for details.)

 NOTE: Some of the sample papers in Part II use the MLA endnotes system. Check with your instructor, of course, about whether you can use this documentation system for your term paper.

THE APA FORM

The APA documentation form is generally used for the social sciences and natural sciences. The APA form is based on the *Publication Manual of the American Psychological Association* (4th edition). Copies of this reference book are available at your college library and in bookstores.

The APA documentation system is very similar to the MLA system: It calls for in-text parenthetical references and a list of sources at the end of the paper. (The APA list is called a *References* list.) But specific APA rules differ in many respects from MLA rules. The next few sections provide an overview of the APA documentation rules and guidelines. Keep in mind that these are only highlights. Always consult the APA *Manual*, which provides examples covering almost every possible source.

APA In-Text Documentation

The APA in-text documentation system is similar to the MLA system, except that the APA form requires that the year of publication be indicated as well. You may include this information either in the text itself or in parentheses following the cited source material. If the source material is either paraphrased or quoted directly, also include the appropriate page number(s) in the parenthetical reference. Here are four related examples:

```
Greenberg (1992) measured the effectiveness of cochlear implants...

In an earlier attention-span study among young school-children
(Greenberg, 1992), the effectiveness of cochlear implants...

In 1992, Greenberg measured the effectiveness of cochlear implants...
```

One researcher found that with cochlear implants attention span among preschool children improved more dramatically than among older children (Greenberg, 1992).

As with the MLA documentation style, special APA guidelines for in-text documentation apply for

- ▶ Works by different numbers of authors
- ▶ Works by authors with the same last name
- ▶ Works by corporate authors
- ▶ Different types of print sources (books, articles in periodicals, and so forth)
- ▶ Non-print sources (Web pages, speeches, media broadcasts, and so forth)
- ▶ Non-recoverable sources (that is, personal communications such as letters, interviews, and email)

Be sure to consult the *APA Manual*, which provides guidelines and examples for these and almost all other possible source types.

Incorporate quotations of 40 or fewer words directly in your text, enclosing them with double quotation marks. Provide the author, year, and specific page citation for each quote—except that if you cite the same source sequentially in the same paragraph, page number(s) alone suffice for all but the first reference. If you cite more than one work by a particular author, include a shortened title for the particular work from which you have taken the source material. Here are three related examples of APA in-text references (notice the placement of punctuation marks following the quoted material):

According to Krautz, "all of these conditions ensure a high degree of ground water purification" (Krautz, 1994, p. 83); but Krautz did not delineate...

According to Krautz (1994), "all of these conditions ensure a high degree of ground water purification" (p. 83); but Krautz did not delineate...

Krautz (1994) asserted that "all of these conditions ensure a high degree of ground water purification" (p. 83) but he did not delineate...

If the quoted material consists of more than 40 words, the APA style calls for a freestanding block of lines. Indent the entire block five typewritten spaces, and omit quotation marks (but use double quotation marks for quotations within the blocked material). You should generally use a colon to introduce a block quotation, although the context may call for a different punctuation mark or no mark at all. Your parenthetical citation should come *after* the closing punctuation mark. If the quotation contains more than one paragraph, indent each one five additional typewritten spaces. Maintain double-spacing throughout the block quotation, as well as preceding and following the quotation. The following example includes a quotation within a block of quoted material:

```
To support a different theory, Michael Brahn refers to Edwards'
experiment:
        Data compiled by Edwards et al. (1990) suggest that oxides
        of nitrogen play a smaller role in catalytic ozone destruc-
        tion than previously thought. Edwards warns, however, that
        "simultaneous observations on the scale of 0.1 kilometer
        in vertical extent are needed to properly diagnose the
        operative mechanisms." (Brahn, 1993, p. 25)
According to Brahn, earlier NASA-sponsored aircraft studies were
partially responsible for the misconception.
```

The APA References List

The APA style requires that you include a *References* list at the end of your paper—beginning on a separate page. This list must include *all* works cited in your paper. (Conversely, all entries on the list must appear in your paper.)

NOTE: As you review the sample APA-style papers in Part II, keep in mind that they deviate from the style in that the *References* lists in these papers do not necessarily begin on new pages. But you should strictly follow the APA style, of course.

Different Forms for Different Sources

Each item in your APA *References* list must provide all the information a reader would need to retrieve the cited source material. Like MLA citations, APA *References* list entries should each contain three basic components in the order listed here: (1) author information, (2) title information, and (3) publishing information. However, the specific information you'll need for documenting a source depends on the source type. (See page 25 for a list of common source types.) The *APA Manual* provides examples covering these and almost all other potential sources. Always consult the *Manual* to determine proper citation form!

NOTE: Many of the sample papers in Part II include APA-style *References* lists; take a peek at those papers (as well as at the sample at the end of this chapter) to see what an APA *References* list looks like.

APA Rules for Ordering Your References

The APA style specifies a particular sequence for the entries in your *References* list. The basic rule is to organize the list in alphabetical order, by the last name (surname) of the first author of each source. (Consult the APA *Manual* for more details.)

Punctuating APA Reference Entries

The APA style also specifies certain punctuation for the citations in your list. Here are the two basic rules (for more details, consult the APA *Manual*):

▶ Use periods to separate the three major divisions of the entry: author, title, and publication information.

▶ Use commas within these three subdivisions.

Capitalizing, Underlining, Indenting, and Spacing References

The APA style also specifies formatting requirements for the citations in your list. This section provides some highlights from those requirements (consult the *APA Manual* for complete information):

▶ Capitalize only the first word of the title and of the subtitle (if any) of books, and articles; also capitalize any proper nouns in the title. Do not use quotation marks.

▶ Underline or italicize book and journal titles as well as their volume numbers (extend underlining beneath the punctuation marks that follow).

▶ Underline or italicize journal titles and volume numbers, and capitalize each significant word in the journal title (extend underlining beneath punctuation marks that follow).

▶ Either indent (5 spaces) only the first line of each entry or use a *hanging indent* for each entry (the first line flush with the left margin, subsequent lines each indented 3 spaces). The former method is generally acceptable for term papers, although the hanging indent style is required for published papers. (The sample on page 46 at the end of this chapter uses the manuscript style, but the papers in Part II use hanging indents because we've published them in this book.)

▶ Just as in the text of your paper, maintain double-spacing throughout the *References* list (no single spacing or additional spacing between entries).

Examples of APA *References* List Entries

The following are four hypothetical *References* list entries. To underscore the differences between the MLA and APA styles, we've used the same entries here as on pages 26 and 27. In the order listed, they include a magazine article by two authors, a book by one author, a newspaper article, and an edited volume from a multivolume work:

> Bauer, P., & Sussman, F. J. (1998, March). The role of mass media in a new millennium democracy. <u>New Society,</u> pp. 64-67.
>
> Gabelli, J. S. (1991). <u>An introduction to presidential politics.</u> New York: Macmillan.
>
> Newhouse, D. (1998, June 4). "The Clinton legacy: Can our presidency be saved?" <u>Atlanta Constitution,</u> p. C-3.
>
> Tanner, R. K., Willott, P., & Fromer, K. (Eds.) (1994). <u>A history of Western culture</u> (Vol. 1). Boston: Barham & Sons.

APA Guidelines for Formatting Your Paper

Here's a checklist that covers the basic APA formatting guidelines. Always check with your instructor, though, who might prefer that you deviate from these guidelines:

- ▶ Use standard-sized paper (8 1/2 × 11 inches), and double-space all lines.
- ▶ Use 1-inch margins on all sides.
- ▶ Assemble the components of your paper in the following sequence. (*Note:* Items 1–4 are required.)

  1. Title page (includes title, author's name, institutional affiliation, and running head for publication)
  2. Abstract (place on a separate page)
  3. Text (start on a new page)
  4. References (start on a new page)
  5. Appendixes (start each on a separate page)
  6. Author identification notes (start on a new page)
  7. Footnotes (start on a new page)
  8. Tables (start each on a separate page)
  9. Figure captions (start on a new page)
  10. Figures (place each on a separate page)

▶ Number each page of your paper, consecutively, beginning with the title page. The page numbers should appear in the upper-right corner of each page.

▶ Your *References* list should begin with the heading "References" (without quotation marks, underlining, and so on); center this heading at the top of the first *References* page.

▶ Underlining and italics are interchangeable. Choose one or the other form, and use it throughout your paper.

▶ Headings for different sections of the paper are not required; but if you use headings, you should also include a table of contents. (Consider adding headings for longer papers, but check with your instructor first.)

NOTE: As you review the sample APA-style papers in Part II, keep in mind that we've used less than double-spacing; we've omitted title pages, abstract pages, and running headers; and each *References* list does not necessarily begin on a new page. But you should follow the APA style strictly, unless your instructor specifies otherwise.

CITING ELECTRONIC SOURCES—A NEW FRONTIER

As this book goes to print, standards for documenting electronic sources, particularly Internet sources—are not yet firmly established. If you cite electronic sources in your paper, be sure to check the *MLA Handbook* or Web site or the current APA manual for current information. Also, check out the following online resources about electronic citations (listed in no particular order):

▶ Xia Li and Nancy Crane's "Electronic Sources: MLA Style of Citation"

▶ Janice Walker's "MLA Style Citations of Electronic Sources" (endorsed by the Alliance for Computers & Writing)

▶ Andrew Harnack and Gene Kleppinger's "Beyond the MLA Handbook: Documenting Electronic Sources on the Internet"

▶ Mark Wainwright's "Citation Style for Internet Sources"

TIP: You can use an Internet search engine to find these sites. Better yet, link to them from the official Website of the The International Federation of Library Associations (www.ifla.org). At this site you'll find a link to an "Electronic Collections and Services" area, which will take you to "Citation Guides for Electronic Documents." This page provides up-to-date links to the sources listed above as well as others.

INCLUDING FOOTNOTES IN YOUR PAPER

Use footnotes to explain or amplify the text or to add information presented in a table. Number footnotes consecutively throughout paper, with superscript Arabic numerals.

Provide the footnotes themselves at the end of the paper in a separate section following the *Works Cited* (MLA) or *References* (APA) list. List footnotes in numerical order; they should be double-spaced.

 NOTE: Check with your instructor about whether he or she prefers that each footnote appear at the bottom of the page on which the footnote reference appears (instead of at the end of your paper).

TIPS FOR BUILDING EFFECTIVE PARAGRAPHS

As you compose your first draft, take great care in constructing your paragraphs. Here are some tips to keep you on the straight-and-narrow paragraphing path:

- ▶ Be sure that each paragraph focuses on only one central idea, and that the paragraph develops that idea.

- ▶ Try starting a paragraph with what the reader already knows, and then depart from there to new information.

- ▶ Use the following techniques to connect together the various sentences in a paragraph:

  - ▶ Use similar sentence construction for successive sentences.

  - ▶ Repeat key words in successive sentences.

  - ▶ Use pronouns to refer to nouns in previous sentences.

  - ▶ Use transition words to connect ideas.

- ▶ As a rule of thumb, each paragraph should contain three to seven sentences. In general, longer papers call for longer paragraphs (five to seven sentences), and shorter papers call for shorter ones (three to five sentences).

- ▶ If a paragraph is too short, try developing the paragraph with examples, illustrations, details, definitions, data, or descriptions. If a paragraph is long (approaching a full page in length), try splitting the paragraph, relocating certain details, or omitting tangential information.

SUGGESTIONS FOR STYLE AND VOICE

For many students, the most difficult aspect of writing a term paper is not formulating good ideas, but rather finding the best words and phrases to express those ideas. Although the following checklist won't necessarily result in a Pulitzer Prize–winning masterpiece, it should help you get that A+ grade you want.

Think PBS, Not MTV

Use a relatively formal style and voice for your paper. Don't try to be conversational, informal, or "cutesy." Drop your use of colloquialisms like a bad habit; otherwise, your instructor will give you a lousy grade. (Did you catch the colloquialisms in the preceding sentence?)

Also, the tone should be critical, but not inflammatory or emotional. Don't try to overstate your position by using extreme or harsh language. Don't attempt to elicit a visceral or emotional response from the reader. Appeal instead to the reader's intellect.

Don't Call Attention to Yourself

Unless the assignment calls for it, don't refer to yourself in your paper. Simply omit phrases such as "in my view" and "I agree that." Also, never apologize to the reader or make excuses. For example, don't point out that you found no sources to support your view on an issue.

Vary Sentence Length

For rhetorical emphasis, try using an abrupt, short sentence following a longer sentence (or a sequence of longer sentences).

Don't Try to Impress with Vocabulary

By all means, demonstrate to your instructor that you possess an educated vocabulary. But don't overuse SAT-style words just to make an impression. This strategy can easily backfire, by warning the instructor that you're trying to mask poor content with window dressing.

Be Concise

With enough words, anyone can make the point; but it requires skill and effort to make your point with brief, concise sentences. Compute the average number of words per sentence; it should be between 20 and 25. If your sentences seem too long, check for wordy phrases that can be replaced with 1 or 2 words. For example:

Wordy:	*Concise:*
the reason for	because
for the reason that	since
due to the fact that	
in light of the fact that	
considering the fact that	
on the grounds that	

Develop an Arsenal of Transition Words and Phrases

Transitional devices are like bridges between parts of your paper, which help give the paper cohesiveness and help communicate your line of reasoning. This section provides a list of transition words and phrases you'll find useful in piecing together the components of your paper. You'll find many more transition words and phrases in the sample papers in Part II. Add your favorites to your writing arsenal to add sophistication and style to your paper and to help your ideas to flow. (The italicized words in the following lists contribute to an especially sophisticated style; just make sure you know how to use them.)

Use these transition words to connect ideas together:

> furthermore, additionally, in addition, also [first, second, . . .], *moreover,* most important/significantly, consequently, simultaneously, *concurrently,* next, finally

Use these words to signal examples:

> for example, for instance, to demonstrate, to illustrate, as an illustration

Use these words to indicate a contrast:

> conversely, in contrast, on the other hand, whereas, but, except, by comparison, where, compared to, weighed against, *vis-à-vis*

Use these phrases to set up a subordinate idea:

> although it might appear that, at first glance it would seem/appear that, *admittedly*

Use these words to argue for a position, thesis, or viewpoint:

> *promotes, facilitates,* provides a strong impetus, serves to, directly, furthers, accomplishes, achieves, demonstrates, suggests, indicates

Use these words to argue for a solution or direction based on public policy or some other normative basis:

> ultimate goal/objective/purpose, overriding, primary concern, subordinate, *subsumed*

Use these words and phrases to retort, rebut, or counter a proposition, theory, or viewpoint:

> however, *closer scrutiny reveals,* upon closer inspection/examination, a more thorough analysis, in reality, actually, when viewed more closely, when viewed from another perspective, further observation shows

Use these words to point out problems with a proposition, theory, or viewpoint:

> however, nevertheless, yet, still, despite, of course, serious drawbacks, *problematic, countervailing* factors

Use these words to argue against a position or viewpoint:

> works against, *undermines, thwarts,* defeats, runs contrary to, fails to achieve/promote/accomplish, is inconsistent with, *impedes*

Use these words to signal a conclusion of an argument:

> therefore, thus, *hence, accordingly,* as a result, it follows that

Use these phrases for your concluding paragraph:

> in sum, in the final analysis, in brief, summing up, in conclusion

Use Rhetorical Questions (Sparingly)

Rhetorical questions are ones for which the speaker (or writer) already has a response. Why should you use rhetorical questions? Like short, abrupt sentences, they help you to persuade the reader—or at least to make your point. (*Rhetoric* is the art of using words to persuade.) They also add interest and variety. Just make sure you answer the question! (Did you notice the rhetorical question a few sentences back?)

Avoid Empty Rhetoric

Many students try to emphasize ideas by relying on hackneyed rhetorical phrases. Avoid words such as the following, which add no substance to your ideas:

> clearly, absolutely, definitely, without a doubt, nobody could dispute that, extremely, positively, emphatically, unquestionably, certainly, undeniably, without reservation

Use Gender-Neutral Language

Try to avoid the use of *man,* as in these examples:

Avoid:	*Use Instead:*
mankind	humanity, people, human beings
man-made	manufactured, machine-made
the common man	the average person, ordinary people
chairman	head, chair
congressman	congressional representative

Also use any of the following techniques to avoid the use of the male pronouns *he, him,* and *his:*

▶ Recast in the plural form

▶ Reword to eliminate any gender reference

▶ Replace the masculine pronoun with *one* or the phrase *he or she,* as appropriate

Avoid alternating male and female pronouns; otherwise, you'll confuse the reader.

TEN DO'S AND DON'TS TO KEEP YOU MOVING ON YOUR FIRST DRAFT

Everybody has a special way of getting "unstuck" when it comes to term papers or other writing projects. If you find yourself resisting, procrastinating, or blocking, try one or more of these strategies:

▶ DON'T refrain from writing down an idea until it's perfectly worded; otherwise, you might stifle your creativity and productivity.

▶ DON'T be too critical of yourself or your ideas or your writing—at least not during the first draft.

▶ DON'T worry about what your instructor will think of your paper or how harshly he or she will evaluate it. This mode might keep you from writing anything.

▶ DON'T follow the conventional advice to rehearse the task over and over in your head beforehand. This age-old technique actually increases anxiety for most people, because it amounts to little more than obsessing about the task. Instead, do just the opposite: Think about anything but the task unless you're actually doing something productive to complete it.

▶ DO break up the writing task into small steps. Each step should take no more than an hour to complete. (You can make use of time between classes.)

▶ DO begin writing at any point you want—but not with the introduction and conclusion. Save these bookends until the end. Why? You're bound to change course as you put together your paper. By postponing the introduction and conclusion until the end, you'll avoid rewriting these parts.

▶ DO find a location that you dedicate to nothing but working on your paper. If you choose a spot in the library, make sure it's a place where your friends and classmates won't find you! Find a remote spot you need to "hike" to, so you've invested some time and effort just to get to your spot.

▶ DO carve out the same time period each day for your term paper. Earlier in the day is generally better than later; by putting off the task until late in the day, you'll have the whole day to obsess and build up anxiety.

▶ DO establish a ritual for study breaks. Try setting an alarm to go off every 30 minutes. When your alarm sounds, get up and go through you break ritual, whether it be stretching, walking, or getting a drink of water.

▶ DO use a particular pencil, and perhaps a special notebook, for term papers only (etch "Term Paper" right into the pencil).

ANNOTATED SAMPLES (MLA AND APA STYLES)

The next several pages illustrate many of the MLA and APA formatting requirements discussed in this chapter. Included on these pages are

▶ A sample first page of an MLA-style paper (pages 40–41), followed by an accompanying *Works Cited* list (page 42)

▶ A sample title page and first page of text for an APA-style paper (pages 43–45), followed by an accompanying *References* list (page 46)

First Page of Term Paper (MLA Style)

Steele 1

Julie P. Steele

Professor Taylor

Political Science 210

12 May 1999

The Burgeoning Chinese Economy:
Internal Political Implications

Indent ½"

In recent decades, the People's Republic of China has been one of the fastest-growing economies of the world. Its gross national product has increased at an average annual rate of 12.8% over the past 10 years and is projected to increase at an average annual rate of 8% to 9% during the next decade (Annual Almanac 28-29). Foreign trade as a percentage of China's gross national product rose from 10% in 1978 to 42% just 10 years later (30).

Economists attribute this dynamic growth to a variety of factors: the resumption of trade in 1972 between the United States and China, the normalization of diplomatic relations in 1979 between these two countries, and the reformation of China's internal economic policies during the 1990s (e.g., Howle and Bullard; Samuels, Asian). However, although Chinese leadership continues to stress economic development as the country's primary objective, it pays little attention officially to political reform. The possible intranational political consequences of the government's current agenda may in the end serve to undermine its purposes.

One reason for concern over China's internal political instability involves the fact that some regions in China are experiencing a greater economic boom than others, as economist Noel Samuels points out:

7 ←1"→
>
Such anomalies in economic development are likely to create unrest in the less prosperous areas. Political instability might also result if current inflationary trends become uncontrollable. Further, the question of leadership succession remains unresolved, a situation that might generate political unrest. (Samuels, "The Future" 296)

6

According to Samuels, although Guangdong province, for example, has benefited from neighboring Hong Kong's free-wheeling capitalistic economy, the movement of Hong Kong's manufacturing sector into the province has occurred at the expense of . . . .

1   Running head (last name of student-author and page number)

2   Title of paper (mixed upper- and lowercase)

3   Parenthetical reference to a book with no named author or editor (reference includes shorthand title and page numbers)

4   Parenthetical reference to a specific page of the work cited immediately above in the same paragraph

5   Reference to two different sources as examples of preceding point (the reference is to each work as a whole, not to any specific passage); two authors are listed for the first source; the second source lists the author and a shorthand title because more than one work by the same author appears in the *Works Cited* list)

6   Parenthetical reference to an article in a periodical (abbreviated article title included because more than one work by the same author appears in the *Works Cited* list)

7   Block quotation more than four lines in length

First Page of MLA *Works Cited* List

Steele 16

Works Cited —2

3

<u>Annual Almanac of World Commerce</u>. 6th ed. New York: McGraw-Hill, 1998.

4—Howle, Arnold J., and Pamela Bullard. "What's Ahead for China?"

<u>Journal of International Economics</u> 109 (1996): 49+.

5

Samuels, Noel T. <u>The Asian Economy in the New Millennium</u>. London:

Howell and Co., 1998.

6— - - -. "The Future of China's Most Favored Nation Status." <u>Modern</u>

<u>Economist</u> 15 Feb. 1997: 12+.

½"

1   Running head (last name of student-author and page number)

2   Heading (mixed upper- and lowercase, no underlining or quotation marks)

3   Book with no named author or editor

4   Article from scholarly journal, identified by volume number ("49+" indicates that the article begins on page 49 and runs continuously on at least one additional page); only the first co-author is listed, by surname first

5   Book by one author

6   Periodical article by the same author (Samuels) listed immediately above

Title Page of APA Term Paper

1"

The Burgeoning Chinese Economy 1

Running Head: THE BURGEONING CHINESE ECONOMY: INTERNAL

POLITICAL IMPLICATIONS

The Burgeoning Chinese Economy:

Internal Political Implications

Julie P. Steele

Political Science 210

1   Running head (abbreviated title of paper and page number)

2   Full version of running head

3   Title of paper, subtitle of paper, student-author, class

First Page of Term Paper Text (APA Style)

The Burgeoning Chinese Economy 3   _1

The Burgeoning Chinese Economy:

Internal Political Implications   _2

½"

    In recent decades, the People's Republic of China has been one of the fastest-growing economies of the world. Its gross national product has increased at an average annual rate of 12.8% over the past 10 years and is projected to increase at an average annual rate of 8% to 9% during the   _3 next decade (Annual Almanac, 1998, p. 28-29). Foreign trade as a percentage of China's gross national product rose from _4 10% percent in 1978 to 42% just 10 years later (p. 30).

    Economists attribute this dynamic growth to a variety of factors: the resumption of trade in 1972 between the United States and China, the normalization of diplomatic relations in 1979 between these two countries, and the reformation of China's internal economic policies during the 1990s (Howle & Bullard, 1996; Samuels, Asian, 1995). However, although Chinese leadership continues to stress economic development as the country's primary objective, it pays little attention officially to political reform. The possible intranational political consequences of the government's current agenda may in the end serve to undermine its purposes.

    The Problem of Anomalous Economic Development———6

    One reason for concern over China's internal political

←1"→instability involves the fact that some regions in China   ←1"→

are experiencing a greater economic boom than others, as

economist Noel Samuels ("The Future" 1998) points out: ——————7

    Such anomalies in economic development are likely to

    create unrest in the less prosperous areas. Political

    instability might also result if current inflationary

8 ←½"→trends become uncontrollable. Further, the question of

    leadership succession remains unresolved, a situation ——9

    that might generate political unrest. (p. 296)

According to Samuels, although Guangdong province, for

example, has benefited from neighboring Hong Kong's free-

wheeling capitalistic economy, the movement of Hong Kong's

manufacturing sector into the province has occurred at the

expense of . . . .

1   Running head (abbreviated title of paper, page number, which is 3 because abstract appears on page 2)

2   Title of paper (mixed upper- and lowercase)

3   Parenthetical reference to a book with no named author or editor (reference includes shorthand title, publication date, and page numbers)

4   Parenthetical reference to a specific page of the work cited immediately above in the same paragraph

5   Reference to two different sources as examples of preceding point (the reference is to each work as a whole, not to any specific passage); two authors are listed for the first source; the second source lists the author and a shorthand title because more than one work by the same author appears in the *References* list; underlining continues beneath punctuation mark

6   Level 1 heading (centered, mixed upper- and lowercase)

7   Parenthetical reference to article (a shorthand title of the work is indicated because more than one work by the same author appears in the *References* list)

8   Block quotation more than 40 words in length

9   Reference to page number of work cited in sentence preceding block quote

First Page of APA References List

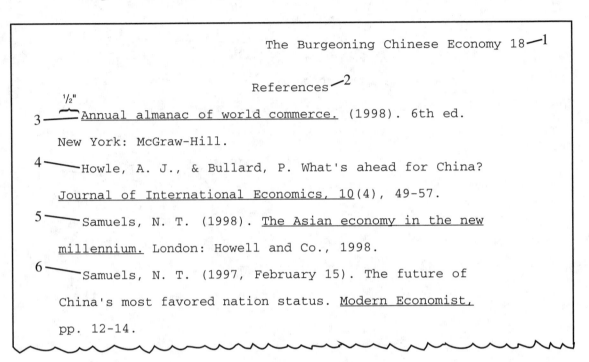

The Burgeoning Chinese Economy 18 ——1

References ——2

½"

3 —— Annual almanac of world commerce. (1998). 6th ed.

New York: McGraw-Hill.

4 —— Howle, A. J., & Bullard, P. What's ahead for China?

Journal of International Economics, 10(4), 49-57.

5 —— Samuels, N. T. (1998). The Asian economy in the new

millennium. London: Howell and Co., 1998.

6 —— Samuels, N. T. (1997, February 15). The future of

China's most favored nation status. Modern Economist,

pp. 12-14.

1   Running head (abbreviated title of paper and page number)

2   Heading (mixed upper- and lowercase, no underlining or quotation marks)

3   Book with no named author or editor

4   Article from scholarly journal, identified by issue number 4 bound in
     volume number 10 (note that underlining extends beneath volume number);
     all authors listed by surname first and by initials only (no first or middle
     names); ampersand (&) precedes final name; "p." or "pp." is omitted whenever
     a volume number is indicated.

5   Book by one author

6   Periodical article by the one author

4

EDITING, REVISING, AND "DETAILING" YOUR PAPER

Okay, you've produced your first draft. Perhaps it's a bit rough around the edges; but at least you've got something to work with. The remainder of Part I provides a variety of useful strategies, guidelines, and "to do" lists for editing, proofreading, and polishing your paper.

EDITING AND REVISING YOUR DRAFT: AN EIGHT-POINT PLAN

Once you've got your first draft under your belt, it's time to regroup. Back away from the details in your paper and take a fresh look at your assignment, your topic, and your thesis (if you've written a thesis paper). Follow the eight-point plan below to ensure that you've avoided all the major pitfalls and problems that might keep an A+ grade out of reach:

1. *Put your draft aside for at least a few days.* Try to put it out of mind as well. When you return to it, you'll be surprised how many ideas for improvement will occur to you.

2. *Teach your paper to a group of friends.* Try to talk through your paper over dinner or coffee. (You buy the coffee, of course!) Don't just read the paper to them. Instead, talk through the ideas in a less formal way. Invite your victims (excuse us, we mean "listeners") to interrupt you with questions—especially about any point that isn't clear or adequately explained. Take their advice as cues for revising and editing.

3. *If you've written a thesis paper, check your thesis.* Can you sum up your thesis in one sentence? If not, you might need to refine the scope of your paper a bit. Also, ask a friend to read the first paragraph of your draft and anticipate what the rest of the paper will discuss. If your friend has trouble anticipating the discussion, your thesis statement needs work!

4. *Check for appropriateness.* Does your paper fulfill your instructor's assignment? You'd be surprised how often a first draft "devolves" into something other than what the instructor asked for! Now's the time to catch this problem.

5. *Check for organization.* Does the paper progress in an organized, logical way? Read through the paper, jotting down a fresh outline of the major points and supporting evidence. Does your outline flow logically? Or are there gaping holes? Does it seem to ramble from one point to another, with no clear direction? Now's your chance to fix any of these problems.

6. *Check for cohesiveness (unity).* Have you connected all the major points? Are the relationships between them expressed clearly? Do they all relate directly to the research topic or thesis? If not, you've got some work to do.

7. *Check your introductory and concluding paragraphs.* Your opening paragraphs should provide a cue to the reader about how you've organized the body of your paper. Your final paragraphs should complement the opening ones by recapitulating (summarizing) the major points of your paper and perhaps by reiterating your thesis or opening remarks. (To see some good examples, read just the introductions and conclusions of some of the papers in Part II.)

8. *Check for adequate development.* Are there gaps in your paper where more details, examples, or other specifics are needed? Now's the time to add them. On the flip side, does your paper seem to express the same points over and over, just in different ways? If so, start trimming away the fat and take stock of what's left.

TOP PROOFREADING TIPS

Okay, you've revised your first draft, and it's well organized, appropriate, and cohesive. Now it's time to turn to the details. In the remainder of Part I, we'll examine grammatical errors, problems in expression, and word usage and diction errors that students make most often in college term papers. Refer to the strategies and tips that appear here with your revised draft in hand.

The following are strategies for proofreading your draft. Before you delve into the details, however, be sure to complete the preceding eight-point plan for fixing the "big" problems. Otherwise, you'll have to proofread again after you revise!

1. Get away from your paper (or computer screen) for at least a few minutes before you jump right into a proofreading session. Give your eyes a break.

2. If you've been staring at your draft on your computer screen, print out the draft, grab a red pencil, and go curl up in a comfy chair. You'll be amazed that errors and other problems you completely overlooked on your computer screen seem to jump off the paper at you.

3. Try *not* to read the paper as you proofread. Ignore the content; instead, focus on specific words, phrases, and punctuation.

4. Proofread aloud. The ear often catches what the eye overlooks.

5. Try proofreading for one type of error at a time. For example, go through your draft looking at sentence structure, and then check only for omitted words, and so forth.

6. Check punctuation and spelling last—after you've made all other revisions and corrections. Why? Chances are, as you correct other problems, you'll have created new spelling and punctuation errors.

7. Slide a blank sheet of paper down the page as you proofread; this technique helps you ignore content and focus instead on only a few words and phrases at a time.

8. Take inventory of the type of errors you typically make. (For clues, check your instructors' comments on old term papers and essays.) You'll proofread more effectively if you're on the lookout for these problems.

9. Check for grammatical, mechanical, and stylistic problems by referring to the sections that follow.

FINDING (AND FIXING) GRAMMATICAL ERRORS

Never rely on an electronic grammar checker built into word processing programs as a substitute for scrutinizing every sentence yourself! By all means, use one. But don't stop there. Automatic grammar checkers can only check for *possible* errors; they cannot make judgment calls, and they have little sense of what is and is not effective or appropriate expression.

 NOTE: We can't cover the entire areas of English grammar, usage, and diction here. To do so would take several volumes. Always consult a grammar book, dictionary, and usage reference book for the last word on the subject. For grammar and punctuation, most college professors recommend *The Chicago Manual of Style* and Strunk & White's *The Elements of Style*.

Improper Use of Reflexive Pronouns

Reflexive pronouns include such words as *oneself, itself,* and *themselves*. In general, use reflexive pronouns only when the subject of the sentence is acting upon itself (in other words, when the subject is also the object).

INCORRECT: Contrary to popular myth, war heroes rarely earn their status by acting *as if they themselves are invincible.*

CORRECT: Contrary to popular myth, war heroes rarely earn their status by acting *as if they invincible.*

CORRECT: Contrary to popular myth, war heroes rarely *honor themselves* but rather credit their subordinates for their victories.

Error in Choice of Relative Pronoun

Relative pronouns include *which, who, that, whose, whichever, whoever,* and *whomever.* Remember these four general rules about using relative pronouns:

1. Use *which* to refer to things.

2. Use either *who* or *that* to refer to people.

3. Whether you should use *which* or *that* depends on what the sentence is supposed to mean.

4. To determine whether to use *who* (*whoever*) or *whom* (*whomever*), turn the sentence into a simple question, and then answer the question with a pronoun. If you answer the question with a subject-case pronoun (*he, she, they*), then *who* is correct. If you answer the question with an object-case pronoun (*him, her, them*), then *whom* is correct.

INCORRECT: Economists disagree *who* the proposed Social Security reforms would harm more—the baby boomers or their children.

(Whom would the reforms hurt? *Them.* Replace *who* with *whom.*)

Error in Pronoun-Antecedent Agreement

An *antecedent* is the noun to which a pronoun refers. Be sure that pronouns agree in *number* (singular or plural) with their antecedents.

SINGULAR (CORRECT): Studying other artists actually helps a young *painter* develop *his* or *her* own style.

PLURAL (CORRECT): Studying other artists actually helps young *painters* develop *their* own style.

Singular pronouns are generally used in referring to antecedents such as *each, either, neither,* and *one.*

SINGULAR (CORRECT): The Republican and Democratic parties *each* seem to prefer criticizing *the other's* policies over making constructive proposals *itself.*

PLURAL (CORRECT): The Republican and Democratic parties *both* seem to prefer criticizing *each other's* policies over making constructive proposals *themselves.*

Error in Subject-Verb Agreement

A verb should always agree in number—either singular or plural—with its subject. An intervening clause set off by commas masks a subject-verb agreement error.

INCORRECT: Improved sonar *technology*, together with less-stringent quotas, *account* for the recent increase in the amount of fish caught by commercial vessels. (Replace *account* with *accounts*.)

INCORRECT: Grade school *instruction* in ethical and social values, particularly the values of respect and of tolerance, *are* required for any democracy to thrive. (Replace *are* with *is*.)

Keep in mind that the following pronouns are singular and therefore take singular verbs:

anyone, anything, anybody

each

either, neither

every, everyone, everything, everybody

nobody, no one, nothing

what, whatever

who, whoever

Improper Mixing of Gerunds, Nominatives, and Infinitives

A *gerund* is verb turned into a noun by tacking on *-ing* (by the way, *tacking* is a gerund). A *nominative* is a noun phrase that substitutes for a gerund (*the use of* is a substitute for *using*). An *infinitive* is the plural form of an action verb, preceded by *to* (as in *to go*).

A gerund takes a possessive noun in the manner illustrated by these two sentences:

CORRECT: Despite President Wilson's *supporting* (or *support of*, but not *supporting of*) the Treaty of Versailles, he was unable to rally enough support for it in the U.S. Senate, which defeated it in 1920.

CORRECT: Regardless of the historical, and decidedly adverse, consequences of its *constraining* (or *constraint of*, but not *constraining of*) market prices, the federal government seems compelled to do so anyway.

Avoid mixing gerunds with either infinitives or nominatives. In the next sentence, use either the italicized pair or the italicized parenthesized pair:

To assert (*Asserting*) that the nation's health care crisis can be remedied only by political means would essentially be *to ignore* (*ignoring*) the role of technological innovation.

Faulty Parallelism (in Lists)

Sentence elements that are grammatically equal—such as a list of items—should be constructed similarly. Check all lists for inconsistent or mixed use of

- ▶ prepositions (such as *in, with,* or *on*)

- ▶ gerunds (verbs with an *-ing* added to the end)

- ▶ infinitives (plural verb preceded by *to*)

- ▶ articles (such as *a* and *the*)

> CORRECT: Long before the abolition of slavery, many freed indentured servants were able *to* acquire property, *to* interact with people of other races, and *to* maintain their freedom.

> CORRECT: Long before the abolition of slavery, many freed indentured servants were able *to* acquire property, interact with people of other races, and maintain their freedom.

Faulty Parallelism (Correlatives)

Also check for faulty parallelism where you have used *correlatives*. Here are the most commonly used correlatives:

- ▶ either . . . or . . .

- ▶ neither . . . nor . . .

- ▶ both . . . and . . .

- ▶ not only . . . but also . . .

Make sure the element immediately following the first correlative term is parallel in construction to the element following the second term. Here's an example that contains the correlative pair *not only . . . but also:*

> FAULTY PARALLELISM: According to behavioral psychology, physiological responses to external stimuli *are not only* observable and measurable *but also can* explain why humans behave as they do.

> PARALLEL: According to behavioral psychology, physiological responses to external stimuli *not only are* observable and measurable *but also can* explain why humans behave as they do.

Error in Verb Tense

Tense refers to how a verb's form indicates the time frame (that is, past, present, or future) of the sentence's action. Do not *mix* tenses or *shift* tense from one time frame to another in a confusing manner.

CONFUSING: Due to the fact that fewer makers of personal computers *are* turning a profit *lately,* many such companies plan to hold prices at current levels. (The word *lately* establishes the present perfect tense, requiring the verb form *have been* instead of *are.*)

CONFUSING: Few writers *have mastered* the principle of the "objective correlative," by which words *are to be* arranged for emotional rather than logical effect. (This sentence shifts time frame inappropriately from the present [*have mastered*] to the future [*are to be*]. The phrase *to be* should be omitted.)

Error in Using the Subjunctive Mood

The *subjunctive mood* should be used to express a *wish* or a *contrary-to-fact* condition. These sentences should include words such as *if, had, were,* and *should.* In the following sentences, the italicized words in parentheses should replace italicized words:

If empty space *was* (*were*) nothing real, then any two atoms located in this "nothingness" would contact each other because nothing would be between them.

The Environmental Protection Agency would be overburdened by its detection and enforcement duties *if it fully implemented* (*were it to fully implement*) all of its own regulations.

Economist Adam Smith rejected mercantilism in favor of a free market, contending that the pursuit of individual self-interest *will better foster* (*would better foster*) economic progress.

SENTENCE CONSTRUCTION AND SENSE

This section lists the most common sentence construction pitfalls—and how to avoid them. You'll find few hard-and-fast rules here, because we're not dealing with rules of grammar but rather rules of thumb for the *art* of effective writing.

Part of a Sentence out of Balance with Another Part

An effective sentence gets its point across by placing appropriate emphasis on its different parts. Be sure that the main idea receives greater emphasis (as a main clause) than subordinate ideas.

> EQUAL EMPHASIS (CONFUSING): Treating bodily disorders by noninvasive methods is generally painless, and these methods are less likely than those of conventional Western medicine to result in permanent healing.

> EMPHASIS ON SECOND CLAUSE (BETTER): Although treating bodily disorders by noninvasive methods is generally painless, these methods are less likely than those of conventional Western medicine to result in permanent healing.

Unnecessary Use of the Passive Voice

In a sentence expressed using the *active voice,* the subject "acts upon" an object. Conversely, in a sentence expressed in the passive voice, the subject "is acted upon" by an object. The passive voice can sound a bit awkward, so the active voice is generally preferred. Mixing the two voices is even more awkward.

> MIXED (MOST AWKWARD): Although humans generally cannot perform repetitive tasks reliably for a prolonged time period, repetitive tasks can be performed endlessly by computers in a reliable manner.

> PASSIVE (AWKWARD): Although repetitive tasks are not generally performed reliably by humans for prolonged time periods, such tasks can be performed reliably by computers almost endlessly.

> ACTIVE (BEST): Although most humans cannot perform repetitive tasks reliably for a prolonged time period, computers can perform such tasks endlessly and reliably.

Confusing or Vague Pronoun Reference

Nouns to which pronouns refer are called *antecedents.* Make sure every pronoun in a sentence has a clear antecedent! One way to correct a pronoun reference problem is to reposition the noun and pronoun as near as possible to each other.

> CONFUSING: During *their* burgeoning independence from England, Madison and Hamilton, among others, recognized the need to foster allegiances among all the *states.*

> CLEAR: Madison and Hamilton, among others, recognized the need to foster allegiances among all the *states* during *their* burgeoning independence from England.

Another way to correct a pronoun reference problem is to replace the pronoun with its antecedent.

CONFUSING: Email accounts administered by employers belong to *them,* and *they* can be seized and used as evidence against the employee.

CLEAR: Email accounts administered by an employer belong to *the employer, who* can seize and use the accounts as evidence against the employee.

Improper Placement of Modifiers

A *modifier* is a word or phrase that describes, restricts, or qualifies another word or phrase. Try to place modifiers as close as possible to the word(s) they modify; otherwise, you might end up with an ambiguous and confusing sentence.

AMBIGUOUS: *Exercising frequently contributes* not only to a sense of well-being but also to longevity.

CLEAR: *Frequent exercise contributes* not only to a sense of well being but also to longevity.

AMBIGUOUS: Through careful examination, competent diagnosis, and successful treatment, *patients* grow to trust their physicians.

CLEAR: Through careful examination, competent diagnosis, and successful treatment, *physicians* help their patients grow to trust them.

Improper Splitting of a Grammatical Unit

Splitting clauses or phrases (by inserting a word or clause between them) often results in an awkward and confusing sentence.

SPLIT: The value of the dollar *is not,* relative to other currencies, *rising* universally.

BETTER: The value of the dollar *is not rising* universally relative to other currencies.

SPLIT: Typographer Lucian Bernhard was *influenced,* perhaps more so than any of his contemporaries, *by* Toulouse-Lautrec's emphasis on large, unharmonious lettering.

BETTER: Perhaps more so than any of his contemporaries, typographer Lucian Bernhard was *influenced by* Toulouse-Lautrec's emphasis on large, unharmonious lettering.

Dangling-Modifier Errors

A *dangling modifier* is a modifier that seems to refer to a noun that is not mentioned in the sentence. The best way to correct a dangling-modifier problem is to reconstruct the sentence.

> DANGLING: By imposing artificial restrictions in price on oil suppliers, these suppliers will be forced to lower production costs.

> (Who or what is imposing restrictions?)

> BETTER (NO REFERENCE): Imposing artificial price restrictions on oil suppliers will force these suppliers to lower production costs.

Stringing Together Too Many Adjectives

Avoid juxtaposing more than two adjectives, especially if the string includes a possessive (a noun with an apostrophe to indicate possession). The following sentence also uses the word *confusing* in a confusing manner.

> AWKWARD STRING: To avoid *confusing* oral medications, *different pills' coatings* should have different colors, and pills should be different in shape and size.

> CLEAR AND LESS AWKWARD: To avoid *confusion among different* oral medications, pills should differ in color as well as in shape and size.

Using Too Few (or Too Many) Commas

Comma placement is a bit of an art form. Use the minimum number of commas needed for a reader to understand the intended meaning of the sentence. Too few commas might confuse the reader, whereas too many can unduly interrupt the sentence's flow.

> TOO FEW COMMAS: Enzyme catalysis takes place in living systems and as it is not a laboratory procedure is therefore subject to cellular controls.

> TOO MANY COMMAS: Enzyme catalysis takes place in living systems, and, as it is not a laboratory procedure, is therefore subject to cellular controls.

> BEST VERSION: Enzyme catalysis takes place in living systems, and as it is not a laboratory procedure is therefore subject to cellular controls.

In long sentences, try using a semicolon instead of a comma to split the sentence into two clauses.

> Enzyme catalysis takes place in living systems; and as it is not a laboratory procedure it is therefore subject to cellular controls.

Redundant Words and Phrases

Check for words and phrases that express the same essential idea twice.

> The *reason* science is being blamed for threats to the natural environment is *because* scientists fail to see that technology is only as useful, or as harmful, as those who decide how to use it. (Replace *because* with *that*.)

> With laser technology, many forms of cancer can now be treated by *means of using* a quick and painless surgical procedure. (Omit *using*.)

Superfluous Words and Awkward Phrases

Just because a sentence is grammatically acceptable, don't assume there's no room for improvement. Check for superfluous words and phrases that can be omitted altogether. Also check for phrases that can be replaced with clearer, more concise ones.

Omission of Necessary Words

Check for the omission of key "little" words—prepositions, pronouns, conjunctions (*and*, *or*), and especially the word *that*—needed to make the meaning of the sentence clear and unambiguous. The italicized word *that* is needed in both of these sentences:

> The newscaster announced *that* the voting results were incorrect.

> Some evolutionary theorists believe *that* the main reason humans began to walk in an upright posture is *that* they needed to reach tree branches to obtain food.

Look out especially for an omission that results in an illogical comparison. The italicized words in the two sentences below are needed for the sentences to make sense.

> China's population is larger than that of any *other* country in the world.

> A recent study reports *that* lawyers' fees for class action law suits exceed *those for* all other types of legal services.

WORD USAGE

You commit a *usage* error when you use a word in the wrong way in a sentence. Covering all possible usage errors would fill volumes, of course. So here we'll limit the list to groups of words and phrases that college students misuse most often in term papers. Check your paper for any of the words appearing in the following groups. If you're in doubt about which word in the group you should use, consult an authoritative guide to modern English usage.

> more, greater, fewer, less, amount, number

> to be, as being, as

because, since, as a result of, so, being that (awkward)

if, whether, whether or not, that

as of, as for, as with, as in, as to, about

while, although

such as, like

which, under which, in which, by which, of which

based on, based upon, on the basis of

by, by means of, by way of

among, between

like, as, as if, as though

differ in, differ about, different than, different from

IDIOMATIC PREPOSITIONAL PHRASES

An *idiom* is a phrase that is either proper or improper simply based on whether it has become acceptable over time—through repeated and common use. The English language contains more idiomatic expressions than you can shake a thesaurus at. You'll recognize most idiom errors simply because they sound wrong to your ear. But certain prepositional idioms can easily fool you. Check your paper for any of the idioms in the following two lists.

In each of the following sentence groups, the proper preposition depends on the context.

> The minister was *compared to* a shepherd.

> Shakespeare's plays are often *compared with* those of Marlowe.

> It is not always easy to *distinguish* good art *from* (not *with* or *and*) bad art.

> The university *distinguished* the alumnus *with* an honorary doctoral degree.

> Fluffy the cat can be *distinguished by* her unique markings.

> The two analysts *agreed with* each other.

> The two analysts *agreed to* examine the numbers further.

> The two analysts *agreed on* (not *about*) only one conclusion.

> The contract *provides for* mandatory arbitration in the event of a dispute.

The contract *provides that* the parties must arbitrate any dispute.

The cave *provided* shelter for the bears.

The mother bear *provided for* her cubs.

Each of the following phrases illustrates the proper (and improper) use of particular prepositions.

acquiesce *in* (not *to*) illegal activity

alarmed *at* (not *about*) the news

apologize *for* (not *about*) a mistake

ignorant *of* (not *about*) the facts

independent *of* (not *from*) parental assistance

insist *on* (not *in*) a course of action

oblivious *of* (not *about* or *to*) the time

preferable *to* (not *than* or *over*) the other choice

required *of* (not *from*) all students

rich *in* (not *with*) resources

short *of* (not *on*) cash

succeed *in* (not *with*) an attempt

superior *to* (not *over*) the alternatives

aside from (not *outside of*) one particular instance

within (not *inside of*) a few minutes

price/cost *of* (not *for*) a shirt

could *have* (not *of*) won the game

contrasted *with* (not *to*) the darkness of the night

be sure to (not *be sure and*) brush your teeth

inferior to (not *inferior than*) the leading brand

could have (not *of*) been a contender

try to (not *try and*) finish your dinner

TWO-WORD PHRASES OFTEN CONFUSED WITH SINGLE WORDS

Here's a "hit list" of two-word phrases that are often confused with single words. In some cases, either one or the other is nonstandard (unacceptable).

all ready: everybody or everything ready

already: previously

all right: everything correct

alright: (unacceptable—no such word)

all together: everybody or everything together

altogether: completely

all ways: in every possible way

always: at all times

a lot: many

alot: (unacceptable—no such word)

any one: any specific person or thing in a group

anyone: any person at all

a while: a period of time (article and noun)

awhile: for a period of time (adverb)

every one: each person or item in a group (used to stress each one)

everyone: all people (used as a pronoun)

may be: might be; could be

maybe: possibly

some one: (unacceptable)

someone: one person

some time: a portion of time

sometime: at an indefinite time in the future

sometimes: occasionally

DICTION ERRORS—THE TERM PAPER HIT LIST

Diction refers chiefly to your choice of word as well as to the meaning and the manner in which a word is used. When you commit an error in diction, you might be confusing one word with another because the two words look or sound similar. Or you might be using a word that isn't the best one to convey the idea you have in mind. The following list includes diction errors appearing most frequently in college term papers.

accede: to consent to

concede: to yield (but not necessarily in agreement)

exceed: to be more than

access: availability

excess: too much

accept: to take when offered

except: excluding (preposition)

except: to leave out (verb)

adapt: to adjust or change

adopt: to take as one's own

adept: skillful

addition: the act or process of adding

edition: a printing of a publication

adverse: unfavorable

averse: disliking

affect: to influence (verb)

effect: a result, consequence, or influence (noun)

effect: to bring about; to achieve (verb)

allude: to make a reference to

elude: to escape from

allusion: a reference

illusion: a deception of the eye or mind

alternate: substitute (adjective)

alternative: another choice or option (noun)

ascent: the act of rising

assent: approval

beside: close to

besides: in addition to

cite: to quote

sight: seeing

site: a place (for a building)

complement: a completing part

compliment: admiration or praise

compose: to be an element of; to create or make

comprise: to include or contain

constitute: to consist of; to be made up of

consul: a government representative

council: an assembly that meets for deliberation

counsel: advice (noun)

counsel: to advise (verb)

decent: suitable; proper

descent: going down

dissent: disagreement

device: tool or instrument (noun)

devise: to invent (verb)

eminent: distinguished

imminent: about to happen

immanent: indwelling

formally: in a formal way

formerly: at an earlier time

lay: to place

lie: to recline

liable: responsible for

likely: probable

principal: chief or main

principle: a fundamental truth or belief

regardless: despite; notwithstanding

irregardless: (unacceptable—not a word)

respective: pertaining to each one of several

respectful: polite

rise: to get up

raise: to lift

historic: well-known or important in history

historical: pertaining to past events or to history

single: one only

singular: extraordinary; separate or individual

PUNCTUATION

Earlier in this chapter, you learned how to use commas effectively. Now learn some rules and tips for using other punctuation marks in your term paper. We'll save the quotation mark for last, because it's the peskiest of all the marks. You'll find more details about punctuation in the *MLA Handbook* and *APA Manual*.

Parentheses

Use parentheses sparingly, for extra material that isn't essential to communicate the sentence's idea. If your paper is running long, look first at your parenthetical material (except for in-text citations, of course) for possible cuts.

Semicolons

Use a semicolon, with or without connecting words such as *and*, *yet*, or *but*, to join clauses that can stand as independent sentences. You can also use semicolons instead of commas to separate long items in a list or series.

> Most people have heard the terms *solar eclipse* and *lunar eclipse;* yet most people could not explain how they differ from each other.

> From an external standpoint, Vere is the perfect captain: personable but not too friendly; direct but not overly verbose; concerned but not past the law.

Colons

Use a colon to introduce a lengthy (indented block) quotation. You can also use a colon to introduce a list or to define an idea (as in the second example above).

Em Dashes

An em dash is represented on a typewriter or in plain-text word processing files by a pair of hyphens with no spaces (--). In typography, an em dash is a single dash the width of a capital *M* (—). Use em dashes sparingly, to emphasize a point or to set off a disconnected expression, and as substitutes for commas to set off appositives.

> Victorian poetess Christina Rossetti is perhaps best known for her potent sensual imagery—the richest since Keats.

> Matthew Arnold certainly tried to define the arch—the legitimizing order of value—against the an-arch of existentialist democracy.

> However, the writings of the restorationists themselves—especially those of William Jordan and Frederick Turner—offer little evidence to support this indictment.

Italics (or Underlining)

Use italics or underlining interchangeably for titles of complete works such as magazines, books, newspapers, movies, long poems, and plays, as well as for foreign words that are not commonly used in English. Be consistent throughout your paper! Choose either italics or underlining, but don't use both.

Apostrophes

Check to be sure you've used apostrophes correctly (singular or plural) to indicate possession.

Quotation Marks

You can use quotation marks for a variety of distinct purposes: to quote outside source material; to indicate dialogue; to indicate titles; and to otherwise call special attention to the quoted word or phrase. Be sure you use these marks properly for each purpose. The following lists present basic rules for using quotation marks for these purposes and some additional guidelines for working with quotation marks.

Direct Quotations of Source Material

Here are the basic rules for using quotation marks to indicate direct quotations of source material:

► Use a set of quotation marks to enclose direct quotations, except for longer quotations, where indenting the entire quotation as a block serves as a substitute for quotation marks.

► If the quotation is a whole sentence, begin the sentence with an uppercase letter; otherwise, begin it with a lowercase letter.

► Use single quotation marks for a quotation enclosed inside another quotation.

► Use three ellipsis points (. . .) to indicate where you've omitted words within a sentence in the quotation. Use four ellipsis points (. . . .) to indicate an omission between two sentences. You don't need to use ellipsis points at the beginning or end of a quotation unless you wish to emphasize that the quotation begins or ends in midsentence. Both the MLA and APA style sheets call for one character space between points and before and after a set of ellipsis points.

► If you insert your own words (or the words of anyone else other than the author) within a quotation, enclose the inserted material in brackets ([ ]), *not* parentheses.

The following quotation illustrates the last two items above (notice that the first ellipsis point is actually a period at the end of the first quoted sentence):

> Yet, as the conversation progresses Wickham talks only too freely of Darcy: "His behavior to myself has been scandalous. . . . [He has] a dislike of me which I cannot attribute in some measure to jealousy" (XVI, p. 80).

Quotation Marks for Dialogue

Here are the basic rules for using quotation marks to indicate dialogue:

► Do not indicate the speech of more than one person in the same paragraph.

► It's okay to include narrative that is closely related to the speech in the same paragraph as the speech.

► If one person's speech continues for multiple paragraphs, use quotation marks at the beginning of each paragraph. Do not use quotation marks at the end of any of these paragraphs except the last.

Quotation Marks for Titles

Here are the basic rules for using quotation marks to indicate minor titles and parts of wholes:

- ▶ Use quotation marks for titles of parts of larger works (for example, book chapters and magazine articles).

- ▶ Use quotation marks for short or minor works such as songs, short stories, essays, or short poems.

- ▶ Do not use quotation marks for larger, complete works; use underlining or italics instead.

Other Uses for Quotation Marks

Use quotation marks for technical or unfamiliar terms used for the first time. Quotation marks are also appropriate for words used for irony.

Quotation Marks with Other Punctuation

Here are three rules for positioning quotation marks vis-à-vis other punctuation marks:

- ▶ Use a comma to set off expressions such as *he said* from a single sentence of dialogue. But use a *colon* to introduce direct quotations of outside source material as well as any quotations two or more sentences in length.

- ▶ Place commas and periods *before* the closing (second) quotation mark (except when a reference follows the quotation); place colons, semicolons, and question marks *after* a closing (second) quotation mark.

Unnecessary Quotation Marks

Do not use quotation marks for your term paper's title. Do not use quotation marks for common nicknames, technical terms that readers are likely to know, and trite or well-known expressions.

YOUR FINAL TASK: THE SPELL-CHECK!

Check your spelling *after* all other revisions and corrections. By all means, run the spell-checker built into your word processor. Keep in mind, however, that automatic spell-checking won't catch diction and usage errors—words that are spelled correctly but are the wrong words in context. Look out especiialy for typos involving these common words, which a spell-checker will overlook:

of, or, off	the, they, then
a, an, any	their, there
from, form	to, too
its, it's	you, your
on, one	*-ing* word endings versus *-ed* word endings

PART II
50 A+ TERM PAPERS

5

AMERICAN HISTORY

Jefferson's Society and the Slavery Question

The Iroquois League

The Great Awakening Movements

(A+) This student has taken on the popular issue of Jefferson and slavery from an uncommon perspective, and seems to have purposely avoided the current "hot topics" of Jefferson's sex life and slave ownership. The paper appears to be a defense of Jefferson's character, aimed not at the *facts* of recent popular scholarship, but at common *conclusions*. (APA style)

JEFFERSON'S SOCIETY AND THE SLAVERY QUESTION

In recent times, Thomas Jefferson has been under fire as a slave owner; for his sexual relationship with Sally Hemmings; and generally for putting great ideas and ideals on paper while failing to live up to them in his own life. This paper does not answer those issues. But it does seek to put Mr. Jefferson into the context of his society so that those issues may be discussed in that context. Please note that some older usages such as "negro" have been retained because those were the terms in use at that time.

The Descent

It is clear that the first black men to be brought to Virginia were not chattel slaves, but their descent to that condition was swift, if not precipitous. Laws and trial records are among the best kept and most useful sources for tracing the fall. In 1624 John Phillip was recorded as having acted as a witness in the trial of a white man, which would seem to indicate that he was considered a member of the community rather than property. By 1639, the onslaught had begun. In January of that year an act was passed arming "all persons except negroes." In July of the following year, three runaway servants, two whites and one black, were tried. The two whites were required to serve 4 extra years beyond their normal terms of service, and the one black was to serve for the rest of his life. A year later, a court case mentioned the sale of the child of a negro servant. Thus by 1641, only 22 years after the arrival of the first black men, true slavery--lifetime servitude for both black men and their descendents, was a fact in Virginia (Palmer, 1996).

Many blacks, of course, had not been reduced to slavery, but the trend had been set. Two acts of 1660 are indicative. The first held that servants brought to Virginia could not be kept in bondage longer than was customary for English servants. The catch was that the bill covered servants coming from a "Christian nation." The second bill reduced the export tariff on tobacco for foreigners from 10 shillings per hogshead to 2, provided that the tobacco was paid for with imported negroes (Boorstin, 1948).

In 1661 an act referred to runaway negroes who "are incapable of making satisfaction by addition of time" (Palmer, 1996, p. 360). The next year this law was amended to include for the first time the word slave. In 1662 an act was passed, stating that the children of female slaves would be slaves, regardless of who their fathers were (Boorstin, 1948).

Much emphasis was placed at first on the difference between pagan and Christian servants, and some blacks and Indians were freed from lifetime servitude after having been baptized (Boorstin, 1948, p. 320). To end this, the general assembly decreed in 1667 that "the conferring of baptism doth not alter the condition of a person as to his bondage or freedome" (Palmer, 1996, p. 360).

In 1669 slaves lost even their right to life, with the passing of "an act about the casuall killing of slaves" (Palmer, 1996, p. 361). It explicitly allowed the use of corporal punishment, and if "by the extremity of correction the slave should chance to die . . . his death would not be accompted felony, but the master . . . be acquit from estation, since it cannot be presumed that prepensed malice . . . . should induce any man to destroy his own estate" (p. 365). The black slave was now property that could be destroyed at will by his master.

By 1680 it was evident that the free negro was to suffer the consequences of his color, for an act of that year provided that "no Negro could carry weapons of any nature, offensive or defensive, or go from place to place without written permission" (Palmer, 1996, p. 361). Free blacks were by the end of the seventeenth century a "problem" whose very existence made slaveholders uncomfortable. They took action in 1691 by requiring that anyone who freed a slave must pay for transportation out of the country within six months. That same year it was decreed that the bastard child of a white woman by a black or mulatto would be bound to servitude for 30 years. This act effectively made slaves of the children of any black or mulatto for at least 30 years, and in some cases the servitude was extended to the descendents of these unfortunates, as we shall see later (Mayo, 1942). The year 1692 marked the end of the rights of both property and trial by jury for the slave. Slaves could no longer keep horses, cattle, and hogs, as they had in the past, and special courts in which an appointed individual would serve as both judge and jury were set up for cases involving negroes. These courts of oyer and terminer were to continue until abolition (Palmer, 1996).

The institution of chattel slavery was thus firmly entrenched by 1700; but the legislators of the early 18th century were not to be outdone by their predecessors. Two laws of 1705 were indicative of an assault on the black family structure throughout the slave states. The first excluded slaves from an act punishing fornicators and adulterers, and the second required that slaves have permission from their masters to marry. The black slave was thereby encouraged to breed rather than marry, and the very real possibility of the spouse and/or children of a slave being sold and never seen again likely discouraged close family ties (Boorstin, 1948).

After 1723 the punishment for "consulting, plotting, or conspiring" in groups of more than five, or running away, or even "going abroad in the night" included castration or death. The same act extended the length of service of mulattos born of white women by 1 year, and placed their children in bondage as well. In May 1732 the right of both free and slave blacks to bear witness in the courts was officially taken away, ending the ambiguity of previous laws which had essentially removed that right already (Palmer, 1996).

Refinement Rather Than Retreat

If we accept the position that the Virginia House of Burgesses and court system were generally representative of the public opinion and desires of the people of Virginia, we cannot escape the conclusion that colonial Virginia was avidly racist, and that any opposition was not effective enough to reflect itself in the courts. The years just prior to the revolution did see a slightly softer and less barbaric tone in the legislation (castration was restricted, although not eliminated). It seems, however, that the intent was refinement of the system rather than a retreat from it (Boorstin, 1948).

Enter Tom Jefferson

It was into this system that Thomas Jefferson was born. Prior to the Revolution, during the years when Jefferson was a practicing lawyer, there are only two existing legal arguments authored by him. The first, written in April 1770, is that in <u>Howell v. Netherland</u>. Howell was the grandson of a mulatto woman whose father was black and mother white. Under the previously mentioned law of 1691, as amended, the child (Howell's grandmother) was bound out to service by the churchwardens for 31 years. During this period Howell's mother was born, and she, too, was bound out for 31 years. Howell was born in 1742, and was bound out to his mother's master and served him for 28 years, finally bringing suit against his master to gain his freedom. Howell won the case on the grounds that succeeding generations were not legally bound by the law. But the argument prepared by Jefferson for the case went far beyond, with a clear statement that slavery itself violated the law of nature:

> Under the law of nature, all men are born free, everyone comes into the world with a right to his own person, which includes the liberty of moving and using it at his own free will. This is what is called personal liberty, and is given him by the author of nature, because necessary for his own sustenance. The reducing of the mother to servitude was a

violation of the law of nature: surely then the same law cannot prescribe a continuance of the violation of her issue, and that too without end, for if it extends to any, it must to every degree of descendants. (Boyd, 1950+, v. 1, p. 223)

Jefferson repeated the point near the end of the argument: "Under that law (of nature) we are all born free" (Boyd, 1950+, v. 1, p. 224). Six years later he was to say, "they are endowed by their Creator with certain unalienable rights: that among these are life, liberty, and the pursuit of happiness." He would also say, "All men are created equal." Words can be deceiving, and it must be asked just what Jefferson meant when he said that "all men are created equal," for he did not believe that blacks were of equal ability. The answer lies in the context of the document. The Declaration of Independence does not concern itself with the abilities of men, but rather with the rights of men. In that context, all men were born equal in the sight of God, and shared the unalienable rights granted by him.

The "Vehement Philippic"

Thomas Jefferson was a practical politician who weighed the consequences and possibilities of his political moves with great care. He knew that to espouse a truly unpopular cause was folly. If public opinion was set on an issue, there was little he could do to move the issue from the legislature. On the other hand, he might well damage his own reputation and lessen his ability to accomplish anything of import. This was the dilemma he faced on the slavery question. He attempted to include in the Declaration of Independence what John Adams called the "vehement philippic against negro slavery" (Becker, 1942, p. 220), but Congress omitted the passage altogether. The paragraph is misleading, for it gives the impression that George III forced slavery on the unwilling colonists, which we have seen to be untrue. Yet what is important is Jefferson's intent in including it. By linking the slave trade with George III and filling the paragraph with the strongest language he could muster, he hoped to stir emotions against the

crown; but Jefferson could not have failed to realize the implications of including such a strong antislavery statement in the
Declaration of Independence. Its inclusion would have linked the
independence of the colonies with an antislavery stand (Becker).
This certainly would not have caused the slaves to be freed, but
it would have lent a powerful hand to those who attempted to free
them. In 1784 Jefferson attempted to ban slavery in the new
western territories and came within one vote of success, but the
tide was turning against him.

A Last Success

Jefferson had made an effort in 1777 to prevent the importation of slaves in the Virginia legislature, and was successful in
1788. There are interesting differences, however, in the bill as
originally introduced and as passed by the legislature. The opening
of the draft read:

> To prevent more effectually the practice of holding persons
> in Slavery and importing them into the State. . . . Be it
> enacted by the General Assembly that all persons who shall be
> hereafter imported into this Commonwealth by Sea or by Land
> whether they were bond or free in their native Country upon
> their taking the Oath of Fidelity to this Commonwealth shall
> from thenceforth become free. (Ford, 1905, v. 2, p. 439)

It continued to set legal standards for manumitting slaves in the
will of the owner. After amendment by the legislature, the purpose
of the act became simply "preventing the further importation of
slaves into this commonwealth." It no longer freed slaves illegally
brought into the state, and it carried no provision for the manu-
mission of slaves. The Virginia legislature was clearly not ready
to follow Jefferson's lead on this question.

Five years later, Jefferson wanted to go even further in a
"Proposed Constitution for the State of Virginia," which forbade
the introduction of "any more slaves beyond the generation which
shall be living on the thirty-first day of December, one thousand
eight hundred; all persons born after that day being declared free"

(Ford, 1905, v. 3, p. 275). But by 1793 the defense of slavery in the South was solidifying, and the threat of a North/South split was growing so great that Jefferson wrote President Washington of the possibility.

Conclusion: "Like a Firebell in the Night!"

The time never came again when Jefferson could introduce legislation to end slavery with any result but political disaster and possible civil war. Jefferson's fears regarding slavery would haunt him for the rest of his life, and he said the news of the Missouri Compromise in 1820 "awakened me like a firebell in the night, and filled me with terror" (Boyd, 1950+, v. 14, p. 494). It would take a civil war to end slavery. Tom Jefferson knew it and dreaded it. His lack of grand gestures after 1788 may be lamentable in light of the course of history, and his relations with and opinions on blacks and their relative abilities are out of the scope of this paper. But any analysis of Jefferson must be undertaken with an understanding of the society in which he was born, educated, and grew to manhood. And it must be remembered that no major political figure of his society (or that of any other slaveholding state) made concrete attempts such as he did to end slavery.

Less than a year before his death, Jefferson responded to abolitionist Fanny Wright's request for assistance with words that state his position clearly:

> At the age of eighty-two, with one foot in the grave, and the other uplifted to follow it, I do not permit myself to take part in any new enterprises, even for bettering the condition of man, not even in the great one which is the subject of your letter, and which has been throughout life that of my greatest anxieties. The march of events has not been such as to render its completion practicable within the limits of time allotted to me; and I leave its accomplishment as the work of another generation. I am cheered when I see that on

which it is devolved, taking it up with so much good will,
and such minds engaged in its encouragement. The abolition of
the evil is not impossible; it ought never therefore to be
despaired of. Every plan should be adopted, every experiment
tried, which may do something towards the ultimate
object . . . these, however, I must leave to another
generation. (Mayo, 1941, p. 91)

References

Becker, C. (1942). <u>The Declaration of Independence.</u> New York:
    Harper.

Boorstin, D. (1948). <u>The lost world of Thomas Jefferson.</u> New York:
    Henry Holt.

Boyd, J. P., ed. (1950+). <u>The papers of Thomas Jefferson.</u>
    Princeton, NJ: Princeton University Press.

Ford, P. L., ed. (1905). <u>The works of Thomas Jefferson.</u> New York
    and London: Oxford University Press.

Mayo, B. (1942). <u>Jefferson himself.</u> Cambridge, MA: Harvard
    University Press.

Palmer, P. C. (1966, Fall). Servant into slave: The evolution of
    the legal status of the negro laborer in colonial Virginia,
    <u>South Atlantic Quarterly,</u> pp. 355-370.

This paper provides a brief history of the Iroquois League, the reasoning behind its structure, and the reasons it took place as a religious rather than a purely political innovation. It is not strictly a history paper. With only a slight change of emphasis, it could be appropriate for anthropology, political science, religious studies, Native American studies, or sociology. It includes the groundwork for a psychological study as well. (MLA style)

THE IROQUOIS LEAGUE

It would be a strange thing if six nations of ignorant savages should be capable of forming a scheme for such a union, and be able to execute it in such a manner as that it has subsisted ages and appears indissoluble and yet that a like union should be impracticable for ten or a dozen English colonies to whom it is more necessary and must be more advantageous, and who cannot be supposed want an equal understanding of their interests. (Wallace, P.A.W. 3)

The author of this quotation was Benjamin Franklin. The "six nations of savages" were the Iroquois. Prior to 1500 A.D. the Iroquois were not very different from their Indian neighbors, living off the land, warring among themselves and against the tribes around them, and having no unity. Within 100 years they were unified under an effective confederacy, able to settle their internal problems by council and speaking with a single voice when dealing with outsiders.

The Iroquois believed in a Master of Life, who had been the first being on Earth and had commanded men to love one another and live in peace. He was opposed by his evil brother, who led the Indians in wrongdoing, but the master had promised to send an ambassador to help them overcome the brother when the need became great. In the mid-16th century the ambassador seemed long overdue. The Iroquois had been warring among themselves for many years, and because each death of an Iroquois had to be avenged, there was no end to the wars in sight (Wallace, A.F.C. 43).

The Ambassador

One of the great men of the Mohicans (one of the five
Iroquois nations) at that time was a shaman who was known and
respected as a great orator as well. His name was Hiawatha.
According to a legend of the Onondaga (another Iroquois nation)
translated by J. N. B. Hewitt, "The men were ragged with sacrifice
and the women scarred with flints, so everywhere there was misery"
(97). Hiawatha was one of many men who sought an end to such
violence; but again, quoting from Hewitt's translation:

> In the times of our forefathers it came to pass that although
> the people unbanked many council fires they utterly failed to
> transact any business. Tha-do-da-ho, the notorious and
> unscrupulous wizard and tyrant, brought all their plans to
> naught. (113)

The Archvillain

Tha-do-da-ho, the chief of the Onondagas, had apparently
become a forest tyrant, and his heavy-handed "foreign policy" had
caused much of the trouble between the tribes. What he actually
did is not known; but he became the archvillain of Iroquois
mythology. He was described as having a body distorted by seven
crooks, his hair "was composed of writhing, hissing serpents, his
hands were like unto the claws of a turtle, and his feet like
unto bear claws in size and were awry those of a tortoise"
(Hewitt 115).

During this period of conflict, all three of Hiawatha's
daughters died. Legend attributes these deaths to witchcraft practiced by Tha-do-da-ho. Whatever the cause, Hiawatha, grief-stricken
from the death of his last daughter, left his people, blaming
Tha-do-da-ho for both the deaths of his daughters and the failure
of the chiefs to make a lasting peace.

The Man of Vision

The second important figure was Degandawida. Accounts differ
as to whether he or Hiawatha was considered more important by the
Iroquois. It appears, however, that the principles on which the

league was founded were for the most part formulated by Degandawida. Hiawatha served as his advocate because Degandawida had a serious speech defect. Unable to convince the Hurons of his special mission, Degandawida ventured into the land of the Iroquois, trying to spread the word of his vision (Wallace, P.A.W. 7).

Degandawida's vision was of a great tree, the roots of which were the Indian nations. Its upper branches stretched into "the everlasting light of the Elder Brothers" (Wallace, P.A.W. 27) above the sky and spread wide to protect the tribes that formed its roots. The Great Spirit had sent him to bring peace, not only to the Hurons and Iroquois, but to all men. To the Iroquois, peace means law, literally, for they use the same word for both. The same word is also used in their translation of the Christian words for noble and the Lord. To them, peace is not merely the absence of war; rather, it is a complex abstract ideal encompassing the whole of human cooperation. Indeed, the name they gave to their confederation was "The Great Peace" (28). The Mohawks showed some interest in what Degandawida had to say, but he had only minimal success with the other Iroquois, and had made little real progress by the time he met Hiawatha, who after leaving his people was living alone in the woods (28).

Iroquois Saint Paul

The importance of Hiawatha to the Iroquois can be compared to that of Saint Paul to the early Christians, for he was the prime mover in getting the teaching accepted by the five nations of the Iroquois. One of the first things Hiawatha did after accepting the teachings of Degandawida was to confront Tha-do-da-ho and convert him in one meeting--something Degandawida had been unable to do. The structure of the league indicates that the meeting was more of a political bargaining session than a true religious conversion, as I shall attempt to show later.

The Oneidas, neighbors of the powerful and warlike Mohawks, were persuaded without difficulty to join the league, as were the Cayugas, a mild-mannered tribe living between two powerful peoples, the Onondagas and Senecas. The two branches of the warlike and independent Seneca tribe ended their rivalries and joined the league as well, bringing the total number of tribes to five. According to legend, the bringing together of the five nations took five years; but the change from independent tribes to an effective confederacy probably took longer. The final consolidation is guessed to have taken place in about 1500.

Customs and Traditions of the Iroquois
Compared with Reforms of Degandawida and Hiawatha

Both Degandawida and Hiawatha had been adopted as Mohawks. Adoption was very common in all the Iroquois nations, and it served a useful function. The Iroquois spent a great deal of time fighting wars, and men are lost even in successful wars. To keep the male population from dwindling, certain prisoners were adopted into the tribe by the families of dead warriors. It was Indian custom that prisoners taken by an enemy were considered dead, and in the case of the Iroquois, this was usually true: Most of their prisoners were tortured to death. Only the bravest and most manly captives were singled out for adoption, and before one could be adopted, he had to swear an oath of allegiance to his new tribe and family. Once adopted, he truly became a member of the tribe and rarely fled after being released.

This custom set an important precedent, for it meant that it was reasonable to an Iroquois that an enemy of long standing could become a brother. When such a principle is extended to modern nations, it is easy to see how Degandawida's philosophy that warring nations could lay down their arms and become partners seems overly idealistic to most twentieth-century people; but it was perfectly reasonable and in keeping with age-old traditions among the Iroquois.

Men and Women

The five nations were made up of matriarchal totemic clans. The warriors were men, as were the chiefs; but the heads of the clans and families were women. Husband and wife were generally equal partners; but the children belonged to the wife and she had the final word in their upbringing. In matters of dealing with other tribes (such as in war), the men made the decisions, but at home, the women were the real power (Hewitt 282).

This tradition was put to good use when Degandawida set up his confederation, for the heads of the clans were to pick the representatives of their respective nations at the great council. One of the advantages was to preclude any possibility of a line of rulers passing power on to their sons and creating a dynasty, for the chief's children were in the clan of his wife and therefore could not be considered for the seat held by his clan. The system effectively kept the seats on the great council from staying in one family for more than a generation. It also meant that appointed rulers would be less likely to want war than those who might have been appointed by men. Degandawida made note of this fact, and further ensured it, saying that no man who took part in war parties could be a representative. War chiefs were created who took power only when the council declared war. Should any council representative take any active part in a war, he lost his seat and a new representative was appointed (Hewitt 175).

Peace . . . Or Else

To a twentieth-century mind, these reforms seem strictly political and not religious; but to Dagandawida peace--that is, peace among the members of the league--was the most holy goal that man could achieve. Other tribes were welcome to join the league, and several did, but those who opposed it were considered to be a threat to a divinely sanctified confederation. To oppose the league was, in effect, to oppose the will of God. Wars were to be avoided if at all possible; but if the issue was forced, war was carried out with a brutal efficiency never before seen in North America on so large a scale.

For example, in 1642, the Iroquois attempted to make a peace treaty to prevent hostilities from breaking out with the Hurons and their French allies. Peace was made, and it was agreed that it should be cemented by trade. The next year the Hurons, who were included in the treaty, continued to keep the fur trade to themselves, but the Iroquois made no move. In 1647, the Hurons made an aggressive alliance with the Susquehannocks, who promised to "lift the axe" whenever the Hurons called on them to do so.

This pushed the Iroquois to all-out war against the Hurons and their allies. The Iroquois attacked on March 16, 1649. The Hurons had not even considered the possibility of an attack when deep snow was still on the ground; but an Iroquois army numbering more than 1,000 warriors fell upon the stockaded walls of the Huron town of Taenhanteron and massacred its inhabitants. The next town, though prepared and defended, was slaughtered in an all-day battle the next day. Wholesale panic swept through the Hurons, who deserted their towns and villages and fled frantically through the forest. Hundreds froze to death in the snow. Within a week, the Huron nation had ceased to exist. French traders, trappers, and missionaries were barred from the territory formerly held by the Hurons. In December 1649 the Tobacco People, allies of the Hurons, were conquered in less than a week, when the Iroquois attacked unexpectedly during a blinding snowstorm (Morgan 302-310).

New Concepts, Old Symbols

The political structure of the league appears to have been a joint undertaking by Degandawida and Hiawatha, and reflects a very thorough understanding of both their people and the problems of government. The first problem they faced was how to get the various tribes to give up their independence and join the league. Years of constant warfare had made it clear to most of the chiefs that some sort of accord was necessary; but the league as proposed by Degandawida was a radical step in an unfamiliar direction that needed to be tied to more familiar conceptions before it could be fully accepted.

To achieve this, symbolism using unquestioned traditional institutions was employed. The league was compared to a clan, with several families sharing one extended house, or "longhouse," in the ancient tradition. This longhouse was one of the two great symbols of the league. The other was the council fire, which was an old tradition. It was stipulated that the council fire of the longhouse should always be kept burning, day and night, demonstrating the permanence of the longhouse and the fact that there would always be an honorable way to end disputes short of war.

The Balance of Power

To ease the fear of losing national identity, each of the five nations was given a specific title and duties. The powerful Mohawks were given the title "Keepers of the Eastern Door," and given a council veto. The Senecas, largest of the five nations and faced with vast numbers of people to the West, were known as "The Keepers of the Western Door," and given the right to supply the two war chiefs of the league.

The Onondagas were give the position of greatest honor, probably as a result of concessions made to Tha-do-da-ho by Hiawatha in the meeting mentioned earlier. With their geographically central position in the league, they were named the "Fire Keepers," or perpetual hosts. Their chiefs called the regular meetings (required once per year, but usually held more often), prepared the agenda, and provided the chair or moderator. The Onondagas did not normally vote; but like the Mohawks, they had veto power, and in addition, could vote to break a tie between the other four nations. The Iroquois believed in freedom of speech; yet precautions were taken to prevent its misuse. The constitution (made on wampum, which Hiawatha is said to have invented) prohibited council discussion after nightfall, so that overly long council meetings that might produce hot tempers were avoided. Public discussion of important proposals was not allowed on the same day they were received in council. This provided time to study and avoid rash decisions. If there were serious differences on a proposition, a committee was formed and an effort at compromise attempted before it was brought to the council for a vote (Wallace, P. A. W. 45-49).

The titles of the representatives are the names of the chiefs who met in the first great council at Hiawatha Point on Onondaga Lake, making the chiefs invested with these titles living reminders of the founders. The spokesman for the Mohawks is Hiawatha, the moderator, Tha-do-da-ho, and so on, but there would never again be a Degandawida (Hewitt 225).

According to legend, when the first meeting of the great council ended, Degandawida said farewell to the chiefs, got into a white canoe, and left, never to be seen again. After a time, the Tuscaroras, Nanticokes, Delawares, and Tuteloes were adopted into the league, and for the next 200 years they remained powerful and unified, facing the outside world as one nation, bringing the Great Peace to their neighbors with a fervor reminiscent of Islam. When the Eries asked by what power the five nations demanded their surrender, the reply was, "The Master of Life fights for us" (Morgan 252).

Conclusion

The Iroquois created a government that was not only unique among Native Americans, but that ranks among the most inventive and intelligent approaches to government ever established. And despite the slim record we have of its originators, they must be counted among the great leaders, for their creation met the ultimate test of outliving their own time by hundreds of years. And later, it strongly influenced the American Constitution, which governs the successor state over its territories.

Works Cited

Hewitt, J.N.B. "Legend of the Founding of the Iroquois League." American Anthropologist Apr. 1892.

Morgan, Lewis H. League of the Iroquois. Rochester, NY: Sage & Brother, 1851.

Wallace, Anthony F.C. The Death and Rebirth of the Seneca. New York: Knopf, 1970.

Wallace, Paul A.W. The White Roots of Peace. Philadelphia: University of Pennsylvania, 1946.

A+

This student presents a straightforward, traditional discussion of the two Great Awakening movements: that of colonial America and that of the United States of America. Although the most prominent individuals are discussed, the emphasis is on the issues of the movements rather than the personalities. The concluding paragraph effectively puts the movements in the context of their times. (MLA style)

THE GREAT AWAKENING MOVEMENTS

When we think of the United States and its historic birth, we tend to reflect on the ideas of liberty and freedom. Yet we often forget that so many of the social, political, and religious freedoms that are perceived to have been given life after the signing of the Declaration of Independence were actually quite functional during the 100 years preceding the American Revolution. The American colonies were, after all, an escape from the tightly traditional grip of England's religious beliefs, even before they were legally united. The new American frontier represented a place of new social freedoms and well-deserved justices that could previously have been only imagined. Freedom and liberty themselves had begun long before the first shots of the American Revolution were ever fired.

With these historical truths in mind, one cannot help but question where the disparity of perceived freedoms begins to exist between Colonial America and the United States of America. Of course, one must consider the political differences and the issue of taxation, but how does one definitively assess the difference between freedom of religious ideas before the Revolution and after the war ended? One sure way is through a comparative evaluation of the first and second Great Awakenings. The treatment of and issues concerning each of these were distinctly unique with regard to their respective degree of societal accept- ance. Whereas one Great Awakening occurred in colonial America, the second took place in the newly formed United States of America. Thus, the first was intrinsically a test of free thought overseas, and the second was a test of the American sociopolitical structure itself.

The First Great Awakening

Between 1720 and 1750 the first widespread and intense revival of interest in religion occurred in the American colonies. It was an attraction provoked largely by religious advocates who worked dutifully to stir up public interest in their cause. Their ability to arouse interest in religious subjects of yesteryear was the "awakening," and the subsequent fascination's ability to spread so contiguously is evidently what called for the addition of the word <u>Great</u> (Gaustad 4).

Probably the most famous contributor to this religious response was an English vagrant preacher named George Whitefield, who became the leader of Calvinistic Methodism. Some of the other important figures included Theodorus Frelinghuysen, a Dutch Reformed minister, and Gilbert Tennent, a Presbyterian minister. They were joined in their common preaching effort by Jonathan Edwards, who provided the best intellectual defense of the new emphasis on personal religious experience (Canton 44). Together with many other clergymen who shared a heritage of Calvinistic doctrine, these men stressed the importance of vital religious experience as the cornerstone of effective religious life. They were reportedly aggressive and commandeering (Bushman 33), but their work attracted an enormous number of followers who accepted religion into their lives. The Great Awakening caused a stirring from within New England society that was unmatched by any previously recorded religious movement (Gaustad 6).

Jonathan Edwards

Of those involved in the Awakening's leadership, Jonathan Edwards seems to provide the most interesting story for relevant study. Born into the first ranks of the New England clerical elite, Edwards had been raised in Connecticut, in the shadow of his father's church, and attended Yale College, then the most evangelically inclined school in the colonies (Rutman 43-47). Compared with his soon-to-be colleagues, Edwards's religious background seemed far superior, yet also much more traditional and ironically more conservative. For example, following a brief pastorate in New

York and an appointment as academic tutor at Yale, Edwards was ordained associate pastor of his 84-year-old grandfather's Northampton church in 1727. Two years later, on his grandfather's death, Edwards became pastor, agreeing to take one of the most prestigious pulpits in New England at the age of 24. It was this stability that Jonathan Edwards left to embark on his missionary involvement in the Great Awakening (Rutman 45-51).

Today, Edwards is sometimes known as the "postmillennialist's postmillennialist" (Haynes 259). It was, after all, through his preaching that revivalistic fervor spread throughout the colonies. Evangelistic zeal and millennial hopes went hand-in-hand. Edwards's preaching that the millennium would commence in America fueled reformation zeal within a nation not yet born. In his written work of the Great Awakening era, "History of Redemption," Edwards saw all of human history as a progressive march toward victory for the kingdom of God. Edwards believed that revivals in the colonies were a forerunner of what would commence in centuries to come--the ultimate glorious light of a "Golden Age." He taught that history moves through a pulsation of seasons of revival and spiritual awakening; that there are times of retreat and advance; and that the work of revival is carried out by remarkable outpourings of the Spirit (Cohn 60-61). It was this belief that the colonists lined up to follow.

Decline Is Preparation

According to Edwards, "Time after time, when religion seemed to be almost gone, and it was come to the last extremity, then God granted a revival, and sent some angel or prophet, or raised up some eminent person, to be an instrument of their reformation" (Cohn 61). Edwards himself was to be that angel or prophet of New England's reformation in the 1730s and 1740s. Reportedly, he always insisted that there would be times of conflict, remissions and lulls between the sovereign outpourings of the spirit (McNeill 108). A decline in the spiritual and moral character of our nation, according to Edwards, is to be interpreted as a preparation for an even greater outpouring.

Opposition

Unfortunately, most conservative ministers did not welcome the societal turmoil caused by the Great Awakening. Many resented traveling preachers who invaded their parishes and held competitive religious services. To them, Edwards, Whitefield, and their clan were just another set of "wandering" preachers--only louder and more compelling than any others that had come before them. Charles Chauncy of Boston argued that the new enthusiasm was a form of spiritual derangement where emotions destroyed man's rational control of his own destiny (Haynes 260). With an almost bitter irony, religious preachers began to do everything they could to combat this awe-inspiring religious excitement. Of course, their logic was sparse and their cries were ineffective against the back-drop of the enthusiastic awakening campaigns. And so despite the movement's opponents, thousands of individuals experienced a new sense of dependence on God's will. Many churches were revitalized, and new converts were added to the lists of faithful members (Bushman 47-48).

Driven by Enthusiasm

Apparently, the love for religion created by the Great Awakening was based primarily on enthusiasm. There was little schooling or intricate study of religion during the movement that would lend any worthwhile integrity to its followers. Instead, thousands of people were enthralled and enlightened by the spirit and fervor of the Great Awakening's leaders. They were similar to a marching parade--ripping through towns with loud, appealing music and dragging along as many followers as they could. Theoretically dancing, singing, and clapping their hands behind this religious band, members kept up their enthusiasm for at least 30 years. But by 1750, religious excitement waned and returned to the way things had been prior to the Awakening.

A movement as ferociously ignited as this does not completely die out. For years, devoted believers kept the faith alive within their own families and among members of their own cliques. During the Revolutionary period, many Methodist preachers even kept the

tradition going in their congregations (Rothenberg 182). The
smoking wood left from the original fire would soon be re-lit to
kindle a new blazing religious movement in America. This one would
begin barely 20 years after the birth of the United States itself
and last for nearly half a century. And so, commencing in 1795 and
growing tremendously through the 1840s, the new revival known as
the second Great Awakening appeared all over the country.
Evangelists such as Charles G. Finney emphasized free will, divine
forgiveness for all, and the need of each person to freely accept
or reject salvation (Rothenberg 194).

Similarities of the Two Awakenings

For the most part, a cursory examination of the two
Awakenings would suggest that they were very much alike indeed.
They both involved the work of preachers who traveled extensively
to stir up great religious excitement. In each case, the bearers
of "God's word" were largely successful--causing a renowned revitalization of America's interest in religion. The methods, tactics,
and approaches used by proponents of each movement were distinctly
similar, and the rallying effects of their efforts were measurably
equal in both cases.

It is, nevertheless, interesting to note that the second
movement lasted for about twice as long as the first. Arguably,
one reason for this was its facilitation by the structure of the
new U.S. government. For one thing, constitutional law and religious tolerance made it difficult for conservatives to fight the
movement with the same rough tactics as they had nearly half a
century earlier. For another, the American people were more open to
new ideas and religious experiences than ever before. It was a new
and struggling nation, easily accepting almost any sales pitch
whose bearers knocked on the door. They were trusting and
welcoming, they were new Americans, and they were free.

Differences Between the Two Awakenings

The primary difference between the two Great Awakenings is not
necessarily found in the American ideal or the new U.S. attitude.
In fact, intense disparities were to be found in the content of

each movement's respective religious emphasis. For example, the first movement drew on Calvinist theology, which was created barely a century before by those who opposed Arminianism, the philosophical genre on which the second Great Awakening was to be based. Calvin's doctrine was Catholic in its acceptance of the Trinity, human sinfulness, and the saving work of Jesus Christ. It was Protestant in its commitment to the final authority of the Bible, justification by grace through faith alone, and the bondage of the will for salvation (McNeill 88-97). It was distinctly reformed in its stress on the omnipotent sovereignty of God, the need for discipline in the church, and the ethical seriousness of life. Calvinism's well-known "five points" teach that (1) humankind is spiritually incapacitated by sin; (2) God chooses (elects) unconditionally those who will be saved; (3) the saving work of Christ is limited to those elected ones; (4) God's grace cannot be turned aside; and (5) those whom God elects in Christ are saved forever (McNeill 95-103).

A More Loving and Universally Accepting God

Arminianism, the theme of the second Great Awakening, differs from Calvinism primarily in that it allows human decisions in the salvation process. It removes the strictness and threatening tone of Calvinism, replacing it with a more loving and universally accepting God. Thus, for the most part, Arminianism is a moderate theological revision of Calvinism (although it is believed to predate Calvinism) that limits the significance of predestination (Olasky 311-312). Of course, this conflict was significant enough to change how followers led their lives, but actual tension between the two groups barely existed during either Awakening. (It should be noted, however, that conflict arose between them during the early decades of the twentieth century.)

Conclusion

Both Great Awakenings maintained a common emphasis on religion and its importance. Their successes made revivals a central feature of American religion throughout the years that would follow. It can be said that the acceptance of a more conservative religious movement during the nineteenth century was largely the result of a "freer" America--where people did not wish to be entrapped by anything--even religion. The first Great Awakening was, after all, based on a religious belief that commandeered the lives of its followers and that forced them to comply with strict rules. Thus, in theme, it is better associated with the attitude of colonial America than it is with the more liberated post-Revolutionary America.

The Second Great Awakening put religion into Americans' lives, but it supported the same idealistic freedoms and liberties on which the new nation was built. Its looseness and its ability to forgive are inevitably components that enabled the second Great Awakening to outlive its predecessor.

Works Cited

Bushman, R.L., ed. <u>The Great Awakening</u>. Little Rock, AR: Mission Press, 1989.

Canton, Edgardo. "A Greater Awareness of Truth." <u>UNESCO Courier</u> Jan. 1994: 44+.

Cohn, Robert. "The Humanities, in Memoriam." <u>Academic Questions</u> Jan. 1995: 60+.

Gaustad, Edwin S. <u>The Great Awakening in New England</u>. New York: Free Press, 1968.

Haynes, Charles. "How to Take Religion Seriously in American History." <u>Social Studies</u> Nov. 1993: 256+.

McNeill, John T. <u>The History and Character of Calvinism</u>. New York: Addams Press, 1976.

Olasky, Marvin. <u>It Seems We've Been Here Before Fighting for Liberty and Virtue: Political and Cultural Wars in Eighteenth-Century America</u>. New York: Crossway Books, 1995.

Rothenberg, Winifred Barr. <u>Transformation of Rural Massachusetts, 1750-1850</u>. Chicago: U of Chicago Press, 1992.

Pritchard, Robert. "The Great Awakening" [Chapter 3]. <u>A History of the Episcopal Church</u>. Harrisburg, PA: Morehouse Publishing, 1991.

Rutman, Darrett B. <u>Great Awakening: Event and Exegesis</u>.

    New Brunswick, NJ: Transaction Publishers, 1970.

Tolson, Jay. "The First Information Revolution." In <u>Civilization</u>,

    3: 52+ (New York: Time-Life, Jan. 1996).

6
ANCIENT HISTORY

Influences of Royal Patronage on Science in Ptolemaic Alexandria

The Role of Women in the Rise of Western Monasticism

The Stoics

(A+) This student demonstrates the two crucial elements for a successful *research* term paper in history: the ability to find the appropriate sources and the ability to demonstrate command of the material by presenting it in an orderly and articulate manner. (MLA style)

INFLUENCES OF ROYAL PATRONAGE ON SCIENCE IN PTOLEMAIC ALEXANDRIA

The Hellenistic kingdoms that arose in the last three centuries B.C. strongly influenced developments in the sciences through their patronage of intellectual pursuits. The patronage practiced by the Hellenistic monarchies was not new, for the Greek city-states had also given public funds for the support of some intellectual pursuits. The kings, though, had more extensive resources at their disposal than the city-states, so their patronage operated on a much larger scale. It also had a more "international" orientation and drew scholars and scientists from a larger geographical area.

Alexandria, that city which was by Egypt, but was not really a part of it, offers a prime example of this "internationalism" in scientific activity that was fostered by royal patronage. Much of the significant scholarly and scientific work in Alexandria was done by immigrant intellectuals rather than native Alexandrines (Fraser 307). That the Hellenistic kings also extended their support to scientists marks a new departure in patronage, for the earlier support in the city-states had been extended primarily to poets and dramatists. Under the stimulus of the new royal patronage, science ceased to be the private preserve of philosophy and while "philosophy remained at home in the city-state . . . science migrated to the new world of monarchies" (Walbank 184).

Immigrant Scholars

The scientists who were attracted by royal patronage to Alexandria were primarily immigrants from other parts of the Ptolemaic empire, especially from Cyrene, Cos, and Samos (Fraser II: 307). These immigrant Greeks seem to have enjoyed a great degree of

freedom in the city. This group may have been exempt from some
civic regulations, and there does not seem to have been much pressure on them to adopt Alexandrian citizenship. Thus they comprised
a significant community of Greeks in Alexandria who were untroubled
by restrictions of obligations, at least insofar as their civil
status was concerned (Fraser I: 52). Interference in the research
work of these scholars may have been minimal. We can see a
possible instance of this in the fact that the court physicians in
Alexandria, who were closely involved in the politics of the court,
were rarely known as medical specialists.

This distinction seems to suggest that the teachers of medicine were not drawn into court politics, and were instead left
largely undisturbed in the pursuit of their researches (Fraser II:
339). This could, however, also be interpreted to indicate that it
was advisable for scientists who wanted to pursue their researches
to remain aloof from social and political questions. There are some
instances of interference with intellectuals at the court, but it
seems that such problems became worse in the second century than
they had been in the third, and especially during the reign of
Ptolemy VII (Africa 55).

The early Ptolemies possibly created such an open intellectual atmosphere because of their own interest in intellectual
subjects. The first Ptolemy, Sotor, engaged in literary, especially
historical, pursuits; he composed an account of the campaigns of
Alexander, probably near the end of his life. His interest in this
area also stimulated other historical writing in Alexandria. His
son, Philadelphus, leaned more toward scientific interest and he
collected rare animals and studied their habits. These personal
intellectual interests of the monarchs undoubtedly contributed to
the success of their patronage (Fraser I: 311; Fraser II: 446).

The Museum and Library

The museum and library at Alexandria were two important
institutions established by the first Ptolemaic kings to support
intellectual activities. The museum was conceived in the tradition

of the Greek <u>mouseia</u>. These earlier institutions had been primarily religious cult centers where literary pursuits were also often followed (Fraser I: 333). The Alexandrian museum was more oriented toward intellectual and scientific pursuits than the traditional <u>mouseia</u>, but it still retained the same semi-religious administrative structure. The geographer Strabo offers a description of the museum at the end of the Ptolemaic dynasty, when the administration of the museum had come under Roman jurisdiction:

> The Museum also forms part of the royal palaces; it has a covered walk, an arcade with recesses and seats and a large house, in which is the dining-hall of the learned members of the Museum. This association of men shares common property and has a priest of the Muses, who used to be appointed by the kings but is now appointed by Caesar. (Austin 391)

The museum in Alexandria was also different from its predecessors in that it was a state-sponsored institution (Clagett 48). Alexandria, essentially the king's city, was dominated by the presence and influence of the monarchy. The royal palace occupied nearly one-third of the area of the city, and the museum and library were included within the royal precincts (Rostovtzeff I: 417).

Directly from Patronage

Some scientific work was probably carried out independently of royal patronage by those who had private incomes or earned livings as doctors, architects, or engineers (Walbank 185). But in general the presence and extent of royal patronage provided the basic material for scientific and scholarly work by offering the leisure time for certain men to pursue intellectual activities. This certainly made Alexandria a congenial location for scientific work and it is fair to say that most of the intellectual production of Alexandria derived directly from the patronage of the Ptolomies.

The quality of scientific work in Alexandria rose and fell under the influence of its kings. Scientific work in Alexandria reached its height during the third century, primarily under the patronage of the early Ptolomies, and it was markedly diminished when the scientific community of Alexandria was scattered by the persecutions of Euergetes II in the mid-second century.

Alexandria: Teacher of the Greek People

The persecutions of Euergetes II may have eclipsed the intellectual activity in Alexandria, but they also had the effect of supplying the rest of the Greek-speaking world with trained scientists and scholars. A close contemporary of these events, Menecles of Barcia, observed that "in this way Alexandria became the teacher of the Greek people" (Fraser I: 79, 461). And the later writer Athenaeus gives us the following account of the diaspora of scholars from Alexandria:

> The Alexandrines were the teachers of all Greeks and barbarians at a time when education had collapsed because of the endless disorders which occurred under Alexander's successors. In the reign of the seventh Ptolemy, another renaissance of culture took place . . . when the king sent many Alexandrines into exile, filling the islands and cities with men who had been close to his brother--philologists, philosophers, mathematicians, musicians, painters, athletic trainers, physicians, and other professional men. Reduced to poverty, the refugees [earned a living] teaching their skills to other men. (Africa 58)

The decline in scholarly activities in Alexandria in the mid-second century was due mainly to the expulsion of the intelligentsia from Alexandria by the measures enacted by Eugergetes II, beginning in 145, when he took power in Alexandria. There were other contributing factors, such as the rival cities of Pergamum or Antioch, and also the general decline in the creative power of the Greeks in the later Hellenistic period (Fraser I: 80).

After the persecutions of the second century, patronage came to a halt, and the only significant revival of royal patronage of intellectual pursuits occurred almost a century later at the end of the Ptolemaic dynasty, under Auletes and Cleopatra VII. This later patronage was also marked by the same personal interest in intellectual pursuits on the part of the monarchs and the gathering of immigrant Greeks at the court of Alexandria. Finally, after the Roman conquest, Alexandria ceased to be a major center of intellectual activity, as Rome became the new center of attraction for scholarly and scientific activity.

Conclusion

Royal patronage shaped several aspects of the scientific world of late antiquity. As it did in the political realm, so also in the scientific, the Hellenistic kings opened up the more provincial outlook of the Greek city-states. Cities such as Alexandria attracted scientists from throughout the Greek world, and this mingling of persons and ideas undoubtedly had a stimulating effect on scientific work. The achievements of Hellenistic science also raised the stature of scientists in the popular mind (Africa 64) and it would seem that the new support of science by the kings also contributed to this enhanced image of the scientist. Royal patronage created an environment that freed certain men to pursue scientific interests, although the personal interests of the kings always retained a strong influence on the scientific work undertaken.

Works Cited

Africa, Thomas W. _Science and the State in Greece and Rome_. New York: John Wiley & Sons, Inc., 1968.

Austin, M. M. _The Hellenistic World from Alexander to the Roman Conquest: A Selection of Ancient Sources in Translation_. Cambridge, Eng.: Cambridge UP, 1981.

Clagett, Marshall. _Greek Science in Antiquity_. New York: Collier Books, 1988.

Fraser, M. <u>Ptolemaic Alexandria</u>. 2 vols. Oxford: The Clarendon
    Press, 1972.

Rostovtzeff, M. <u>The Social and Economic History of the Hellenistic
    World</u>. Oxford: The Clarendon Press, 1941.

This paper traces the development and significance of Western monasticism, focusing particularly on the role of women not only as participants but also as catalysts. Notice how the student helps the reader to understand the topic at hand, by first establishing the historical and doctrinal context for the discussion that follows. (MLA style)

THE ROLE OF WOMEN IN THE RISE OF WESTERN MONASTICISM

Historical Overview

Monasticism is a religious way of life followed by those who choose to live in a community following a spiritual ideal or "order." Monasticism's deepest roots can be found in ancient India, but its emergence in Western countries and the Christian religion was probably influenced primarily by communities of Jewish ascetics in the Egyptian desert before and during the time of Christ. In these communities, described by Philo of Alexandria, a contemporary of Jesus and Paul, groups of men were called <u>therpeutae</u>, and women were called <u>therapeutrides</u> (Pelikan 2). Early writers assumed they were, in fact, Christians.

With the rise of the Roman Empire, alongside the spread of Christianity, more and more ascetics--men and women alike--fled the world to pursue lives dedicated to their religious principles (Pelikan 2). By the fourth century A.D. monastic communities were flourishing. With the founding of the first official monastery, Monte Cassino, around 529, Western monasticism had taken the basic institutional form we still see today. St. Benedict of Nursia established the Benedictine Rule, which formed the basis of life in most monastic communities until the twelfth century. At the same time, his sister, Scholastica, founded a nearby convent for women, Plombariola. Later, during the Middle Ages, monks and nuns brought both the Christian faith and Latin culture to the Franks and other "barbarians" and so were responsible for laying the foundations of Western medieval civilization.

The Monastic Ideal: Contemplation and Activism

Although monks and nuns chose a cloistered life primarily for the purpose of dedicating themselves to prayer, especially through the liturgy and chant, they did not see this activity as divorced from changing the world. To the contrary, monastics saw themselves as soldiers for Christ, attempting to transform and conquer the world for Christianity by rescuing souls (Nigg 1; Pelikan 1). An integral part of this effort was an emphasis on work--either manual, intellectual, or service oriented.

The monks and nuns of the Western world seemed to embody the classical Greek ideal of "everything in moderation," which they applied to food and drink, to clothing and speech, to self-denial, and also to work (Pelikan 5). At the same time, however, they blurred the Aristotelian distinction between the contemplative and the active life. Nuns embraced the reclusive, contemplative life of Mary of Bethany (from the tenth chapter of Luke), but also exercised the active role of Martha, with their ministry toward the poor and the sick (Pelikan 2). The monks also took on both active and contemplative roles, especially during the later medieval period, when the mendicant orders--Dominicans, Franciscans, and Carmelites--arose in the thirteenth century to encourage even more missionary work in the world beyond the cloister. In short, the life-style the monks and nuns pursued was at once contemplative and activist. After all, they were responsible for transforming Christianity into a worldwide religious and political force that drove the development of civilization itself.

The Role of Women in the Development of Western Monasticism

As the foregoing discussion suggests, women played a significant role in the development, proliferation, and influence of Western monasticism. Women played a key role even in the early developmental stages, during the time of Christ. In the New Testament women were given titles that indicate they had taken a special way of life; and in the second and third centuries, Tertullian and Cyprian in North Africa spoke of women taking vows of sexual continence (Pelikan 2). In her book <u>Sisters in Arms</u>, McNamara points out that never in the history of the church, and therefore in the history of Western civilization, has there been a Christianity that did not rely on the prayers of dedicated women (Pelikan 1). McNamara notes that "about a third of the monasteries that evangelized that frontier [between heaven and earth] were women's communities" (qtd. in Pelikan 1).

The broad participation of women in the monastic way of life can be explained at least partly as a reaction to the traditional role of women among the Roman aristocracy. In the early days of monasteries, nuns often came from aristocratic Roman families, where giving a daughter away in marriage was a way of cementing relations among the political and social elite. Entering a monastery became a way for women to avoid this sort of barter and to exercise some freedom of choice, if not of mate, at least of life-style. Thus, in addition to colonizing the barbarian world for Christ, monasteries established places where women could live a more autonomous life, including "an independence . . . sometimes far in advance of their secular contemporaries" (McNamara qtd. in Pelikan 1). McNamara writes, "Christianity opened the way for a positive ideal of womanhood as the repository of the virtues most prized in Christian teaching: meekness and humility oddly paired with the manly virtues of courage and perseverance when God's will ran contrary to that of man" (qtd. in Pelikan 5).

Interestingly, some scholars speculate that monasteries also afforded men a refuge--a place to develop friendships with other males in a way that was difficult in the outside world. For example, the great Cistercian Aelred is considered to have had homoerotic relationships before becoming a monk, and encouraged friendships in the monastery "where all the erotic intensity of men could be transformed into agapetic joy" (Cunningham qtd. in <u>Commonwealth</u> 29). Whether Aelred's vision was realized to any great extent is questionable, however, because the monastic literature speaks often of a "fear" of "particular friendships" which were becoming commonplace among monks (Commonwealth 29).

Monasteries as Models for an Egalitarian Community

Although the common notion about monasteries is that men and women were segregated, in fact both men and women had a choice in the matter. McNamara notes that "the most deeply radical social concept that Christianity produced" was the "ideal of syneisactism, women and men living together chastely without regard for gender differences" (qtd. in Pelikan 5). Although this syneisactistic ideal is mentioned in the New Testament and in other early Christian literature, it was in monasticism that it first took institutional form.

Syneisactism saw women and men as "equals in prayer" (Pelikan 5). In this way, monasteries provided an early model for egalitarian communities, essentially without rank among the brothers and sisters, except for the head of the abbey. Monasticism began as a community of lay people, not priests. The very first rule, that of the Benedictines of the sixth century, envisioned lay brothers and sisters all joined for work and worship, undistracted by either world duties or the duties of the outside church, which were taken on by the ordained priests (Pelikan 5).

The egalitarian ideal eroded with time, however, as the official church began to assume authority over the monasteries. Monks, who could read and write, were needed as parish priests and missionaries. The line between the contemplative life of spirit and the life of the outer church became further blurred in 1073, when Pope Gregory VII extended celibacy to the priesthood in an attempt to free them from "external claims" (Pelikan 5). At the same time, women were denied ordination, driving a wedge between monks and nuns, and the church increasingly seemed a male club (Pelikan 5).

Thereafter, only nuns and unordained monks were representative of the old type of monasticism. Priests could give sacraments, according to Augustine, regardless of whether they had committed sins. Because women could not become priests, "immoral priests could still deliver good sacraments, but nuns had to be personally holy to help their patrons" (McNamara qtd. in Pelikan 6). Thus, the initial model of an egalitarian community without gender bias had devolved into an example of a double standard for men and women (Pelikan 6).

Nuns as Catalysts for the Preservation of Knowledge and Art

Despite the erosion of the egalitarian ideal as monastic communities became more regulated by the church, unordained monks and nuns could still study, teach, and produce art (Leclercq 180). As Roman civilization declined, monasteries became centers of light, preserving much of the ancient world's knowledge in hand-written manuscripts as the Western world entered the Dark Ages (Leclercq 184).

Women were instrumental in the preservation of knowledge and art in two respects. First, and probably foremost, the women who entered monasteries brought with them substantial dowries, which greatly enriched the monasteries. Much of the wealth of the church resided in Benedictine abbeys, where art and architecture flourished under the patronage of a powerful aristocracy. Along with a concern for preserving texts and precious objects, monasteries also created beautiful metal and glasswork with stained-glass windows.

Second, typically both monks and nuns were the artists, writers, and musical composers. The English painter John Sifer and the Italian artist Fra Angelico were both Benedictine monks. Notable female contributors emerged as well. For example, the Holy Hildegard of Bingen of the twelfth century, who founded two convents for women, produced numerous books about her visions, and her sisters produced works of art that embodied these visions, as well as books on the lives of female saints, medicine, and natural history (Clinch 40). Recently, Hildegard's music has been revived as some of the most beautiful ever written for female voices (Clinch 41). Later, during the fourteenth century, when the mendicant orders began founding monasteries, many great churches, especially in Florence, Italy, were built and decorated by fully trained professional artists who had become monks and nuns (Leclercq 182).

Concluding Comments

By the late Middle Ages, the fact that the monasteries had become the centers of wealth brought them into conflict with the rising secular feudal class. With the Protestant Reformation, the secular class claimed this wealth by outlawing the monastic life and seizing the property of monasteries.

But history will not forget these men and women who were responsible for preserving and advancing Western knowledge and culture, most of which would otherwise have been lost with the fall of Roman civilization. Beyond this contribution, these men and women gave us an egalitarian model for communal life founded on principles of poverty, chastity, and obedience that continues to inspire many today. Moreover, the nuns who founded convents, who brought with them their dowries, and who wrote, painted, and composed, through their example serve to empower women of every profession and calling today.

Works Cited

Clinch, Dermot. "The Cult of the Weird Sister." New Statesman 16 May 1997: 40+.

Rev. of Great Christian Thinkers, by Lawrence S. Cunningham. Book Reviews. Commonwealth Apr. 1995: 29+.

Leclercq, Jean. The Love of Learning and the Desire for God: A Study of Monastic Culture. New York: Fordham UP, 1982.

Nigg, Walter. Warriors of God: The Great Religious Orders and Their Founders. London: Secker & Warburg, 1959.

Pelikan, Jaroslave. Rev. of Sisters in Arms: Catholic Nuns Through Two Millenia, by Jo Ann Kay McNamara. Cambridge, MA: Harvard UP, 1996.

A+

This student looks at the historical development of the Stoic philosophers, outlines some of the important beliefs of Stoicism, and then gives examples of how that philosophy still affects our world today. (MLA style)

THE STOICS

When the 22-year-old Zeno of Citium came to Athens from his native Cyprus as his Phoenician father's sales representative in about 310 B.C., he almost certainly had no intention of founding a philosophical movement. But the young man happened to read Xenophon's Memoirs, and was captivated by its description of Socrates as a moral teacher (Peters 129). Socrates had died less than 100 years before, and the spirit of the man himself (as opposed to the Platonic Socrates of the later dialogues) was still alive in the streets of Athens. Zeno found a teacher in Cratic of Thebes, a Cynic whom Zeno felt came closest to embodying the spirit of Socrates, and also admired Stilpon of Megara.

But Zeno didn't stop there. He also moved out of the streets and attended the more formally organized precursors to modern universities, the Lyceeum and Plato's Academy with Xenocrates of Chalcedon and Polemon of Athens. But although he "read in the traditional literature of he schools, the Socratic and Cynic note of a serious concern for the practice of virtue never deserted the school that he founded" (Peters 129). When he did found a school in about 300 B.C., he was very limited by being a metic, or non-citizen. He could preach in the streets as Socrates had 100 years earlier, but he could not use a building as the other schools did. Instead, he was allowed to use a painted colonnade (stoa poikele) in the agora at Athens, and from this stoa, the followers of Zeno became known as the Stoics. Although we may think of stoics as having, well, stoic personalities, the debate in the stoa was "free-wheeling and often acrimonious . . . the hallowed aura of reverence that surrounded Epicurus was totally absent" (Peters 130).

The Cynics had emphasized the simple life, which was unadorned and free of emotional involvement, and the popular Megarian philosophy studied dialectic, logical form, and paradoxes. Stoicism, on the other hand, stressed the material world. As R.J. Kilcullen of Macquarie University in Australia put it:

> According to the Stoics only bodies exist. Some of these are subtle like cloud, or more subtle still like air or fire, but everything is body in some way. The human souls and the gods are subtle bodies. The Stoics were not atheists: the whole world is, as in Plato, a living being, which is God. This world is eternal. It goes through phases: a central fire expands, and in doing so cools and turns into soldier bodies--air, water, earth, forming the world we live in now: then this all falls back to the center and becomes fire again, which again expands and cools, and so on forever.

Along with _fire_, which was clearly a broader term than our word _fire_, Zeno used the word _pneuma_, which was a medical term of the time perhaps better described as the vital spirit (Peters 133). "Pneuma, in turn, is the sustaining cause of all existing bodies and guides the growth and development of animate bodies" (Baltzly). The Stoics didn't think that there was any such thing as empty space or void. Pneuma passed through bodies, and as it moved outward gave them their qualities and as it moved inward made them unified. It was the connecting element of the kosmos, and the kosmos was the entire divine organism of the universe.

Zeno divided philosophy into three parts: logic, physics, and the ever-present ethics. Zeno established the central Stoic doctrines in each part. His followers would later expand on his views. He established the themes of logic as an instrument and not as an end in itself, human happiness as a product of life, a physical theory that provided the means by which right actions can be determined, perception as the basis of knowledge, and the wise man as a model of human excellence.

Zeno disagreed with Platonic thought that ideas are real, and believed that divine fire is the substance of all existing (just not living) things. He believed that the world began in a conflagration and renewed, and that all things are bound in a fated causality. He also believed that man is obliged to choose only those acts that are in accord with nature.

The Stoics wanted to know how to distinguish between real knowledge and opinion. They decided that the way to tell was sense perception, but only when perception was at its best. This, of course, was a controversial interpretation, and the Skeptics said that we cannot be sure, because what the senses perceive may be an illusion. Kilcullen said:

> In ethics, the Stoics built on Socrates' thesis that it is better to suffer wrong than to do wrong--that wrong-doing is the worst evil. In fact, the Stoics went further: wrongdoing is the only evil, virtuous action the only good. Other things are to be sought or avoided but don't count as goods and evils.

In the secondary schools that formed after Alexander's time, teachers attempting to influence morals used methods of allegorical interpretation developed by the stoics to "elicit from Homer or the dramatists any and all moral lessons necessary for the edification of [their] charges" (Peters 197).

After Zeno's death in 263 B.C., Cleanthese (331-330 to 232-231 B.C.) and Chrysippus of Soli (280-206 B.C.) led the discussions in the stoa. He taught that a person would be happy if that person conformed his or her will to the divine reason, which governs the universe. Chrysippus of Soli was the most productive of the early Stoics, credited with writing at least 750 works. He developed Zenonian themes in logic, physics, and ethics. In logic, he defended Stoic beliefs against Megarian logicians and the Skeptics.

In the following years, the neoplatonists took up the ethical theories of the Stoics, as did many of the church fathers. In the second half of the eleventh century, philosophers Cicero and Seneca became sources for discussions of social and political philosophies that ended up influencing Thomas Aquinas.

The Stoics' beliefs thus became part of the medieval Christian ethical tradition that forms the basis for our own. Thomas Jefferson's famous line in the Declaration of Independence that "all men are created equal" and its references to natural law are concepts that can be traced to the Stoics. And although the Stoics believed many things that have turned out to be in error, our knowledge that has supplanted theirs is often based on the evidence of physics that they helped develop.

Works Cited

Baltzly, Dirk. "Stoicism." <u>Stanford Encyclopedia of Philosophy</u>. Online. 3 Aug. 1997.

Kilcullen, R.J. "Tape 1: Greek Philosophical Background." Lecture in PHIL252 Medieval Philosophy. Macquarie University, Australia. Online. 3 Aug. 1997.

Peters, F.E. <u>The Harvest of Hellenism</u>. New York: Simon & Schuster, 1970.

7
COMMUNICATIONS

The Mass Media's Role in Politics

Cross-Cultural Communication

Upward Communications in Orgaizations

A+ This student describes the various views on the role of mass media and the effect these media have on shaping public opinion and voter stands on political candidates. The paper explores research and reviews several authors' arguments. The student is not awed by the sources, and presents some thought-provoking counterarguments that keep the viewpoints in perspective. (MLA style, with *Works Consulted* list)

THE MASS MEDIA'S ROLE IN POLITICS

The mass media is perceived as playing a larger and larger role in the public sector, especially over the past two to three decades. There are a plethora of studies and points of view, unfortunately many of them too superficial as to how much, or whether, the media influences or shapes individual viewpoints. This paper seeks to compare some of the leading voices in that debate to gain a better grasp of the issues. In any case, it is apparent that the pervasive presence of the media does affect public thought and action.

140 Million Newspaper Readers

In the United States, for example, more than 2,000 daily newspapers print a total of 70 million copies, and almost every copy is read by 2 people. Newspaper publishers estimate that almost 8 out of 10 adult Americans read a newspaper every day (Bogart).

In order to compete with "instant" television and radio news reports, newspapers from the 1960s until today have not been content to give the public just an account of news, but began to embellish, analyze, and comment on it (Smith, A.). Throughout the United States, newspapers are now a major force for informing people, and according to Julius Duscha, "helping mold public opinion."

Mass Media and Tradition--The Turning Point

Traditionally, media, especially journalists and newspapers, were seen as institutions that conveyed information. Integral to this was the ethic that they present news in an objective manner to the public at large. Despite the example of the Hearst papers' Spanish-American War, many political scientists and researchers in

the past refused to give much credence to the idea that the media
has the capacity to shape or change public opinion.

However, sociologists have long agreed that the media has a
marked impact not only on opinion, but on the way people dress,
act, and relate with one another (Swingewood). Sociologists use
surveys and public polling, as well as direct observation, for
scholarly and scientific purposes in nearly all subfields; surveys
were most often used in the study of voting behavior.

In the social or mass communications sociology, opinion
surveys of pre-election polling were first used in the 1930s; today
they are tools typically employed by politicians or those in the
political arena (Abramson). Over the past decade, a shift has
occurred: The consensus within most fields now appears to be that
mass media's impact was overlooked and has a major impact on
voting opinion. This is backed up by a great deal of research as
well. The move toward mass media's publishing of viewpoints or lack
of objectivity gained momentum in the 1970s, which contributed to
changing views on the matter.

In fact, Julius Duscha, author of <u>The Power of the Press</u>,
names the Watergate scandal---and the fact that the information was
gathered and published by investigative reporters in the <u>Washington
Post</u>--a landmark event for mass media and public political opinion.
The public saw the seamy, manipulative side of top politicians
firsthand, and response was overwhelming. Because the Watergate
information first came from the media, this led to increasing
public suspicion and doubt about political candidates, as well as
the fact that more and more people began relying on newspapers for
the "true" story on politicians.

Media's Growing Impact

The number of studies done in the 1960s and the early 1970s
concluding that the media does not have much of an effect on
influencing voters has changed today also because more people who
are not faithfully aligned to political parties, as Ken Dautrich
states. The result of this disalignment is that voters do not

trust the Democrats or Republicans to give them accurate information on presidential campaigns, so they turn to the media to give them the whole story, just as Duscha and Swingewood claimed.

Dennis Kilerich stresses the tremendous influence the press has on voters in U.S. presidential elections. He feels that with the press and television being primary sources of information for the modern voter, the media is free to present its own biased opinion on how candidates are likely to fare. In addition, Kilerich maintains that the media is largely responsible for the decisions made by voters because of news stories (positive or negative) and polling.

In Kilerich's scenario, democratic elections are controlled by the people; but today's elections in the United States are controlled by the media. Long before the first votes in primaries and caucuses are cast, the media present their stances on the elections (Kilerich 3); if a candidate loses media favor, he or she also loses coverage, and then the public no longer sees this candidate as valid, basically forgetting about the person. This argument might be rebutted by pointing out that the media is not monolithic, and that competition in the media leads to a wide range of opinions in print and on the air.

In the opinion of Duscha, Kilerich, Halberstram, and many others, the media in general, and specifically newspapers, can and do mold the voter's opinion by presenting stories certain ways. Ideally, media must present views objectively, but too much political reporting now shows bias.

The voters may go along with the majority as they perceive it through polls, articles, and news stories that do not necessarily present facts objectively. If the media bias is negative, claims Kilerich, the effect is "a reduction in the candidate's popularity, and subsequently . . . the candidate does badly in the upcoming primaries."

Destructive Media?

James Fallows claims that mass media's attitudes have played
a surprisingly important and destructive role in society. The press
is sometimes referred to as the "Fourth Branch of Government,"
which means that it should provide the information the public
requires to understand problems (Fallows 179).

But rather than make it easier for the public to deal with
political problems, the press often makes it more difficult. Fallows
argues that the press brings about public suspicion and the concept
of scheming and corrupt political candidates by presenting them as
such (Fallows 182-84). While creating new obstacles for American
politics, the media has also put itself in an impossible position.

Reporters as "Stars"

Fallows asserts that the media threatens the health of the
U.S. political system today. In his view, the change has torn
apart journalistic standards and values. He claims that the media
is increasingly controlled by individual reporters who become stars
through the stories they break. By giving power and latitude to
these individuals, the media institution as a whole is becoming
corrupt and poses a danger to the public (Fallows 182-86). (It
must be pointed out the phrase star reporter was common early in
the century, and Walter Winchell long predates the "recent" degradation purported by Mr. Fallows.)

Fallows posits that the individual journalist must maintain
integrity and be an asset to uphold media's traditional place in
society; because this has not been true in the past decade, journalism is losing its place as a reliable source of objective
reporting (162). The media system has fractured, feeding the public
whatever it wants, sensationalist or not.

Rather than argue that the media is entirely at fault,
Fallows significantly points out that if a particular newspaper
does not cover what the public wants in the way the public wants
it done, then that newspaper is faced with "possible extinction."

This large factor that shapes the media's choice of what is printed about politicians creates a paradox (Fallows 187). The contention is that the public shapes the media just as much as the media shapes public opinion (Fallows 182).

This, of course, is not a new phenomenon. History and movies are full of "courageous" editors. These are almost by definition editors who buck public opinion. So it is clear that both the problems and the solutions have existed for a long time.

Swinging the Vote--Expert Views

Some see certain temporary factors, such as media bias and the publishing of polls, as affecting the public's attitudes, whereas others dismiss them. However, research shows that the publishing of polls influences voters to favor politicians cast in a popular light by the media. Polling has gained acceptance as a method of research in the political arena only in the second half of the twentieth century, when statistical research, analysis, and proper sampling have been considered solid (Mueller).

William Schneider maintains that polls are a basically reliable source of where things are in a political campaign, and voters want and need to know this (Kalb). For example, disseminating "findings" that a candidate is far ahead in the polls may discourage people from voting at all, or encourage them to vote for that candidate, hence affecting election results. This is a major force in swinging undecided voters, as Kalb, Kilerich, Wheeler, and others assert.

Fallows decries polls as "meaningless" and would rather that they be forever abolished. But polls are not meaningless. Polls allow voters to choose the most electable candidate that fits their conceptions of good government instead of throwing their votes away on candidates with no chance. In a "winner take all" system, this is important knowledge. In any case, one cannot deny that the media wields tremendous power, particularly before and at campaign time, if one looks at the facts.

Swinging the Vote--Research

Jeffrey Mondak proved that people actively seek sources of information on candidates and that the formerly prevalent opinion that media did not influence votes is untrue. In 1992 Mondak produced a respected study, and then authored a book showing that newspapers are especially crucial to voters in gathering information and making political choices, rivaled only by television as a source. The majority of those involved in the study said newspapers were more important to them. As well, those studied made great efforts to gather information and even differentiated between various media sources; hence Mondak and several other authors have smashed prior claims that the public plays a mainly passive role in the political process.

The public itself holds contradictory views. A study published in 1995 showed that the majority of the American public was not happy with the "investigative" format media was taking, yet maintained that they approved of newspapers publishing information regarding politicians' private lives (PEW). And, it seems, mass media's largest impact is on undecided voters, or "swing voters." To determine the ways in which undecided voters were obtaining their information in the 1996 campaign, a study was conducted using 2,000 voters prior to the New Hampshire primary. The results? Sixty-seven percent of the people said that they get their political information from the media and took it into consideration when making voting decisions.

Ken Dautrich believes polling or survey results publicized by the media are more likely to be used as vote determining. He points out, just as Duscha and others asserted earlier, that people are not depending on "party labels as a voting cue" nearly as much as they were in the first half of the twentieth century.

Conclusion

Although views may differ slightly, the general consensus is apparent: The media is an important source and factor in the public's shaping of political standpoints. The past decade has shown the increasing influence the media has, and also that it is a two-way street: The public forms opinions, often based on media bias; however, the media caters to the voter's demand for information.

As studies have proven, the media is especially crucial in its ability to swing undecided voters over to the majority by providing polling information and giving attention to a political candidate. What some of the critics of the media do not seem to address is whether and how the voter's choices would be superior if there were no polls and the media undertook no investigative reporting and held no opinions.

Works Consulted

Abramson, Mark. <u>Sociological Theory: Concepts, Issues and Research</u>. Englewood Cliffs, NJ: Prentice Hall, 1981.

Boas, George. <u>Vox Populi: Essays in the History of an Idea</u>. Baltimore: Johns Hopkins, 1969.

Bogart, Leo. <u>Press and Public: Who Reads What, When, Where and Why in American Newspapers</u>. Mahwah, NJ: Erlbaum, 1989.

Dautrich, Ken. <u>Media and Voter Opinion in the 1990's</u>. New York: Roper Center, 25 Apr. 1996.

Duscha, Julius. <u>The Power of the Press</u>. New York: Funk and Wagnell, 1994.

Fallows, James. "Breaking the News: How the Media Undermines Democracy." N.p.: n.p., 1995, 160-162, 165, 182, 184-187.

Halberstam, David. <u>The Powers That Be</u>. New York: Dell, 1986.

Holloway, Harry and John, George. <u>Public Opinion</u>. New York: St. Martin's, 1986.

Kalb, Bruno. <u>Media Coverage Too Much</u>. Atlanta, GA: CNN Publishing, 1996.

Kilerich, Dennis. <u>The New Mediocracy: A Loss of Democracy in American Presidential Elections</u>. N.p.: n.p., 1996.

Mondak, Jeffrey. <u>Nothing to Read</u>. Pittsburgh, PA: U of Pittsburgh Press, 1992.

Mueller, John. <u>Public Opinion, Presidents and Campaigns</u>. N.p.:
    n.p., 1993.

PEW Research Center. <u>Public Attentiveness to Major News Stories</u>.
    New York: Times-Mirror Publishing, 1997.

Polsby, Nelson W. and Wildavsky, Aaron. <u>Presidential Elections:
    Contemporary Strategies of American Electoral Politics</u>.
    New York: Free Press, 1988.

Sabato, Larry. <u>Feeding Frenzy: How Attack Journalism Has
    Transformed American Politics</u>. New York: Free Press, 1991.

Schlesinger, Arthur M., Jr. and Israel, F. <u>History of American
    Presidential Elections</u>. 10 vols. White River Junction, VT:
    Chelsea, 1985.

Smith, Anthony. <u>The Newspaper: An International History</u>. New York:
    Thames & Hudson, 1979.

Smith, Evan. "Sarah McLendon: Critical Words for the Press."
    <u>Mother Jones</u> 1 Mar. 1996.

Stupak, Ronald J. <u>Understanding Political Science</u>. New York:
    Knopff, 1977.

Swingewood, Alan. <u>A Short History of Sociological Thought</u>.
    New York: St. Martin's, 1991.

Wheeler, Michael. <u>Lies, Damn Lies, and Statistics: The Manipulation
    of Public Opinion in America</u>. New York: Dell, 1977.

(A+) This student used a number of academic sources; but at the end he adds examples from his personal experience to demonstrate that he can apply what he has learned about the topic to a real-life situation. (APA style)

CROSS-CULTURAL COMMUNICATION

As the world grows increasingly smaller and communications become significantly simplified, dealing with people has actually become more problematic. The dramatic increase in the amount of cross-cultural communication due to improved means of communication has revealed disparate cultural patterns and a wealth of significant differences in both the nonverbal and verbal cultures of different groups around the world. What is a compliment to some may be an insult to others. If Americans are to participate in successful economic activities overseas, it is more necessary than ever before to understand and appreciate the communications, habits, and values of other lands.

The purpose of this report is to discuss and review various differences in cross-cultural communications as found in the relevant literature. Special attention is paid to workplace communications. Included are illustrative cultural cases from various countries. An understanding of cultural diversity, coupled with knowledge of different cultures, will lead not only to more successful business ventures, but also to the development of culturally appropriate strategies for overcoming difficulties in other areas of endeavor.

Even Within America

According to Leaper (1996), in today's world similar actions have different meanings for different people of disparate cultures. Even locally, communication differs in the United States from place to place. In New York City, for example, placing one's elbows on the dinner table while eating is not at all considered to be offensive, but the traditional culture of rural Alabama enables that state's citizens to find that anyone who puts his or her elbows on the table is downright rude. In California, gang culture dictates serious interpretive consequences for anyone who wears red on the streets of south-central Los Angeles, while the color means nothing more than stylish fashion in San Francisco.

Smiles Can Be Insults

Communicating between international cultures, especially in the world of work, is far more complex. This reality has presented obstacles for domestic businesses wishing to establish themselves overseas and for workers employed in foreign companies. For example, the corporate salesperson who does not realize that smiles are insults in some Asian countries and under certain circumstances will not likely succeed. Those using the American handshake will look quite foolish in Zimbabwe because the handshake is obsolete in much of Africa. The businessperson who becomes angry at the Peruvian who does not show up within an hour of the scheduled time for an appointment will not be likely to get another appointment (themes inferred from Bruzzese, 1995).

American workers employed in Japanese companies, for example, need to be aware of vastly different Japanese corporate culture values. March (1992) pointed out that many Americans working for Japanese companies claim that the top decision making is done only by Japanese executives, and that the ceiling for promotion for non-Japanese is relatively low. American managers who report to the top usually report to a Japanese "shadow manager" and are not allowed to make decisions on their own. This can lead to resentment and frustration and is usually taken as a sign of the low respect on the part of the Japanese for non-Japanese managers.

Training Is Important

Dillon (1990) emphasized the importance of human resource training programs to help employees of multicultural firms. In her study of seven multicultural firms, communication problems were related to "separateness" of the two cultural groups. The factors that caused problems included American withdrawal, the start-up effect, length of service, workload, and after-hours decision making. Several of the Japanese who were interviewed described a tendency on the part of Americans to give up and not even try to communicate with the Japanese.

As Leaper (1996) plainly pointed out, in order to understand how nonverbal communication differs from country to country, it is quite useful to first have some understanding of how verbal communication differs. Often, communicating information from country to country creates messages that can be confusing or even completely incomprehensible. Translations lose their meaning in waves of attempted colloquialisms, and the individual who is trying to tell someone that his or her shoes are untied might very well be telling them that the shoes are ripped in pieces.

Unintended Offense

Leaper (1996) cited a survey of 24 international communicators and discussed interesting illustrative stories. For example, one individual from Australia described an American executive attempting to make a point at a gathering of Aussies by exclaiming, "I'd be thrown out on my fanny." But as Leaper (1996) wrote, the word "fanny" to Australians denotes a different, female, part of the anatomy--causing the meaning of the man's statement to be interpreted either as comical or offensive.

Another of Leaper's examples (1996) is that of an employee from the United States who told about a circular created for the secretary of commerce in Mexico, in which the accent was dropped from the word <u>año</u> (year), resulting in <u>ano</u> (anus). He points out that Americans seem to simply not bother with the details, and that they have developed a worldwide reputation for it. When Americans are overseas, they often fail to appreciate the diversity of language and values of others. Interestingly, Eastern Europeans say the same about Russians. Perhaps, then, the denizens of very large countries, where it is possible to live without encountering other languages and cultures, simply don't perceive the need to develop cross-cultural communication skills.

Bad Translations

Bad translations are indeed often very bizarre from a cross-cultural perspective. In another case discussed by Leaper (1996), one individual was working in Asia for an Australian company that had just made its entrance into the container shipping industry. He was asked to assist in the commencement of operations in Singapore and Hong Kong, where containers were still fairly unknown. After registering the firm's name in Chinese, the Australian worker thought it would be wise to have the Chinese translated back into English. But because there was no Chinese word yet for "container," the translation from the "Australian Overseas Container Company" became "The Overseas Coffin Box Manufacturers."

Fichten and Tagalakis (1992), in their research, assumed that certain multicultural communication concepts were universal as, for example, the cliché that "love is a universal language." In actuality, this is not true. Actions and communication while dating and courting are completely different in different countries. Different cultures each have their own customs, many of which are communicated nonverbally.

Verbal and Nonverbal Communications

Verbal and nonverbal communications are especially difficult to master for those working temporarily in other countries. Black (1990) sampled 250 Japanese expatriate managers on temporary assignment to the United States. Of the 250 questionnaires sent, 85 were returned, for a response rate of 34 percent. All responders were male, and 97 percent were married. The results of this study provided support for a tree-faceted conceptualization of adjustment and for the validity of past empirical work that rates the five personal dimensions as important in cross-cultural communication and adjustment. The tree-faceted conceptualization of adjustment was measured in terms of adjustment to the general environment, to the work situation, or to communicating and interacting with host nationals. A practical implication of the study was that organizations, whether American or Japanese, could benefit from selecting for foreign assignments individuals who had high levels of cultural flexibility, social orientation, willingness to communicate, and collaborative conflict resolution orientations. Multinational corporations spend great amounts of money to send employees overseas, so it is important to determine the degree of ability to communicate on a multicultural level.

Nonverbal Communications: Cultural Examples

It is interesting to note that not every foreign country is completely different from others. Differences regarding formalities, such as different handshakes, and their relevance to nonverbal communication, exist among cultures. However, such differences regarding formalities are not regarded as being overly observable between natives of Ghana and Americans. Nevertheless, the careful examiner will always notice some subtle differences. For example, when conversing with colleagues, friends, and acquaintances, the people of Ghana seem to continuously evaluate the impact of what they are saying on the other person. The same is true in the United States. In Ghana, however, various facial expressions such as raised or squinted eyebrows are more commonly used by speakers to assess the listeners' reaction and level of comprehension.

Simultaneous Monitoring and Communicating

Natives of Ghana have a strong tendency to simultaneously monitor and communicate their own level of interest in others' utterances. According to my research, social interaction assumes the ability to convey one's own level of interest and to accurately measure the other's state. Clearly, there are obvious benefits in the ability to evaluate the other person's degree of interest; boring others can have a variety of adverse consequences. But in Ghana, people seem to carry out such evaluation while they are speaking, using overt and often exaggerated facial motions to assess their own progress and their own effect on others.

In both American and Ghanan cultures facial expression, gestures, and eye contact seem to help speakers make their meanings clear. For example, when an American child says "dat" (meaning "give me that"), he or she is likely to look at and point to the object in question. If the child's request is not answered, the expression on the child's face will indicate disappointment unless "dat" is provided. This inherent reality seems to be true in Ghana as well. Children point at what they want and scowl when they cannot obtain it. These elements of nonverbal communication among infants seem to be almost universal.

Through Gesture Alone

Although nonverbal symbols normally add to sound patterns, or language, they seem to also be used by themselves much more in the United States than in Ghana. When members of a U.S. football or basketball team hold their hands high in the air with the index fingers extended, the audience knows that the athletes are proud of their victory and consider themselves to be "number one"--the best team. Many other gestures have meaning when used by themselves. People with serious hearing problems who cannot communicate through sound patterns become skillful in signing (using hand signals to indicate their meaning).

A final distinctively unique nonverbal communication in Ghana involves the bobbing of heads. When two people are familiar with each other and see each other in passing, they quickly shake, or bob, their heads to the left and then to the right in a sort of acknowledgment. This is similar to a quick handshake or pat on the back when two fairly well-acquainted Americans hurry past each other on a busy street (Ray, 1986; Sharfstein, 1995).

Conclusions

Clearly, even the most subtle differences between cultures of the world can make an enormous difference in the level of effectiveness with which messages are communicated between people. As the world grows more interdependent, it will become increasingly important to maintain a committed focus on learning about the cultures, rules, and regulations of other countries. The growth of communication media will continue to produce universal communicators and make it easier for us to understand one another. In the meantime, the wide range of differences that exist in language and in gesture keep people apart. Things as simple as crossed legs and a pat on the head can ruin a friendship, whereas sampling every item from a large menu of food can help close a business deal. Every country is different, and every culture has its own distinct methods of nonverbal communication. Knowing and understanding these methods are keys to success in a rapidly shrinking world.

References

Abratt, R., Deon, N., & Higgs, N. (1992). An examination of the ethical beliefs of managers using selected scenarios in a cross-cultural environment. Journal of Business Ethics, 11, 29-35.

Black, J. (1990). The relationship of personal characteristics with the adjustment of Japanese expatriates. Management International Review, 30, 119-132.

Bruzzese, A. (1995, April 13). Non-verbal communication can affect your message. Gannett News Service.

Fichten, C., & Tagalakis, V. (1992, December). Verbal and nonverbal communication cues in daily conversations and dating. Journal of Social Psychology, p. 751.

Leaper, N. (1996, June). Ahh . . . the pitfalls of international communication. Communication World, p. 58.

March, R. (1992, January). Western manager, Japanese boss. Intersect, p. 11-16.

Ray, D. (1986). Ghana. Lynne Rienner Press.

Sharfstein, D. (1995, May). Radio free Ghana. Africa Report, p. 46.

A+ This paper discusses upward information flow in organizational communications. Note the liberal use of level 1 and level 2 headings, designed to render the paper easier to digest and review. Be sure your instructor permits the use of multiple heading levels before you use them in your term paper. (APA style)

UPWARD COMMUNICATIONS IN ORGANIZATIONS

The exchange of accurate and relevant information within an organization is essential. Upward communication is necessary in allowing feedback to reach the upper levels of the organization. This allows the organization to be changed so that desired organizational goals can be met.

Upward communication flow is critical to ensure informed decision making in an organization. Without the proper flow of information, decisions can be ineffective or simply wrong. An understanding of organizational communications is essential for anyone in a management position. If steps are not taken to promote upward communication, the organization will suffer.

This paper explores upward communication flow in organizations. Many factors exist that affect communication flows. By studying these factors, it is possible to form plans to modify communication flows and create a more dynamic organization.

Upward Communication

Upward communication generally pertains to information about (1) the subordinate himself/herself; (2) others and their problems; (3) organizational practices and policies; and (4) what needs to be done and how. When information flow is increased in these areas, it can play an important role in aiding upper organizational levels in making decisions.

A satisfactory flow of upward communication is often difficult to achieve in an organization. Upward communication requires a fair degree of openness between superiors and subordinates. For example, if subordinates fear retaliation when criticizing a superior, upward communication will be hindered.

Open Communications Equals Performance

Open communication between superiors and subordinates has
been shown to increase subordinate job satisfaction and performance
(Baird, 1974). However, simply maximizing upward communication flow
is not always desirable. Random and irrelevant information flow can
disrupt an organization. Superiors must learn how to restrict
upward communication flow so that they are not bombarded by irrelevant information, while still ensuring that they receive important
information.

Three main factors affect upward communication: (1) subordinate characteristics, (2) superior characteristics, and
(3) superior/subordinate relationships. These three factors, in
addition to message characteristics and structural characteristics
of the organization, combine to determine the frequency, accuracy,
and utility of upward communication.

Characteristics of Subordinates

Subordinate characteristics are those that relate to need,
personality, and situation of subordinates in an organization.

Gender

The different sexes engage in upward communication in
different ways. Women tend to transmit a greater quantity of information when engaged in upward communications (Young, 1978).
However, women also tend to distort information more than men do
(Athanassiades, 1974). One theory explaining this phenomenon is
that women, in order to compete in a male-dominated workplace,
must engage in more information transfer than do men. Moreover,
in order to receive a favorable evaluation from their superiors,
women may feel it necessary to distort information before they
transmit it upward.

Job Satisfaction

Another characteristic is job satisfaction. Generally, the
lower a subordinate's satisfaction with a job, the more distorted
upward communication becomes. Dissatisfied subordinates minimize

communications with employers or intentionally mislead employers. (O'Reilly, 1978).

Mobility

Mobile individuals who have a great need or willingness to move up in the organization tend to be more involved in upward communications than others. They also tend to be less critical of superiors and understand more clearly the importance of upward communication. However, mobile individuals tend to distort information about personal problems that they believe might hinder their potential for advancement.

Job Performance

Not surprisingly, the better a subordinate's job performance, the less likely he will be to distort upward communication (O'Reilly, 1978).

Characteristics of Superiors

Superiors, like subordinates, have certain characteristics. One such characteristic that may affect organizational communication is employee orientation, a term used to describe the support, trust, and back-and-forth communication that superiors maintain with their subordinates. When superiors show consideration and a willingness to listen to their subordinates, they facilitate upward communication. Furthermore, such consideration on the part of the superior also reduces the chance that information from the subordinate will be inaccurate or distorted (Baird, 1974).

Job Performance

Job performance is a characteristic of superiors that has a bearing on upward communication. Subordinates tend to distort information to a lesser degree and relay more information when dealing with superiors who have a high job performance rating (O'Reilly, 1978). One reason for this might be that a superior with high performance is more likely to be powerful and upwardly mobile within an organization. Subordinates desire to interact and associate themselves with a superior of this type.

Attitude

Another characteristic of superiors that is relevant when looking at upward communication is their attitude toward inter-action with subordinates. Many superiors do not value input from subordinates, thereby blocking upward communication.

Willingness to Listen

A superior who promotes upward communication is one who is willing to listen to subordinates, has a high job performance rating, and values interaction with subordinates.

The Relationship Between Superior and Subordinate

There are many factors in a relationship between a superior and a subordinate; but the three listed below are the ones to which most other factors are related.

Trust

One of the most important factors is trust. Generally, the more trust a subordinate has in a superior, the more frequent and accurate the upward communication (Roberts, 1974).

Power

A superior's power over a subordinate is also important in influencing upward communication. If a superior has power over the advancement of a subordinate, the subordinate will often distort information to that superior (Roberts, 1974).

Role Relationships

Leadership is the first type of role relationship. This occurs when a superior exerts influence on a subordinate without resorting to authority. The second type of role relationship is supervision; that is, when a superior uses influence that is mainly based on authority. Leadership is more effective than supervision in promoting upward communication (Dansereau, 1976).

Messages Without Information

Relevant information is not always included in communica-tions, and often the characteristics of a message play a part in determining whether it is transmitted. Even if a message is trans-mitted, it might be distorted.

Three characteristics play a part in determining frequency of transmission and distortion. The first and most important of these characteristics is favorability to the subordinate (Roberts, 1974). In most organizations, superiors have the power to reward subordinates who excel at their duties. This means that most subordinates, although willing to transmit information that portrays them in a favorable light, are unwilling to transmit information that may reflect negatively on their abilities. Subordinates also tend to limit the transmission of unfavorable information to a superior. This usually occurs because subordinates do not want to be associated with "bad news," especially when a superior has a great deal of power over their advancement and organizational rewards.

Conclusion

An organization is an information processing system. If we follow the information through the organizational cycle, we see that managerial decisions flow downward through the system. However, the information necessary to reach such decisions flows upward from lower organizational levels (Galbraith, 1977).

Traditional hierarchical organizations relied almost entirely on downward communication. The only upward communication that took place was subordinates reporting to their immediate superiors. Today, due partly to organizational communications research, the importance of upward communication is being realized. Downward communication is no more important than upward communication. In fact, they both contribute equally to the well-being of the organization; each relies on the other. Without upward communication, informed decisions cannot be made. Ultimately, this is detrimental to any organization.

Technology such as email provides new channels by which communications can flow; but although it is clear that email has been of great benefit to many organizations, it is not yet clear exactly what its overall effects are. I see no reason that the prevalence of email changes any of the factors discussed above. Its effect is more quantitative than qualitative in this instance.

References

Athanassiades, J. (1974). An investigation of some communication patterns of female subordinates in hierarchical organizations. <u>Human Relations,</u> pp. 195-209.

Baird, J. (1974). An analytical field study of "open communication" as perceived by supervisors, subordinates, and peers. <u>Dissertation Abstracts International,</u> p. 34.

Dansereau, F., Cashman, J., Graen, G., & Haga, W. J. (1976). Organizational understructure and leadership. <u>Organizational Behavior and Human Performance,</u> pp. 278-296.

Galbraith, J. (1977). <u>Organizational design.</u> Reading, MA: Addison-Wesley.

O'Reilly, C. (1978). The intentional distortion of information in organizational communication: A laboratory and field investigation. <u>Human Relations,</u> pp. 173-193.

Roberts, K., & O'Reilly, C. (1974). Failure in upward communication. <u>Academy of Management Journal,</u> pp. 205-215.

Young, J. (1978). The subordinate's exposure of organizational vulnerability to the superior. <u>Academy of Management Journal,</u> pp. 113-122.

8

COMPUTERS AND TECHNOLOGY

Artificial Intelligence: The Chess Board and Beyond

The Y2K Problem—Implications and Solutions

Computer Technology: Burgeoning Medical Applications

This paper discusses the field of artificial intelligence (AI), focusing on how scientists have used the game of chess to develop what some think constitutes artificial intelligence. Notice the chronological approach and the student's ingenious way of adding interest by telling a suspenseful story about IBM's chess experiment. The reader is kept in suspense as to whether the experiment will indeed provide a breakthrough in AI. (APA style)

ARTIFICIAL INTELLIGENCE: THE CHESS BOARD AND BEYOND

Artificial intelligence is the branch of computer science dedicated to increasing a computer's reasoning ability to the level of the human mind (McCarthy, 1996). Since the 1950s, scientists have been working to construct machines, which we call robots, that can perform human functions. Robots are now used extensively in the automobile and other manufacturing industries, and more recently by surgeons in the operating room. Yet robots such as these aren't really examples of AI because they aren't designed to think for themselves.

Until recently, the concept of true artificial intelligence has been relegated to the world of science fiction. Perhaps the most notable example is the 1968 film 2001: A Space Odyssey, which chronicles the emotional development of a computer aboard a space-ship; as the story unfolds, the computer, named HAL 9000, develops an immature and ultimately malevolent personality, murders one astronaut, and locks down portions of the ship to the remaining astronaut to avoid being killed itself (Magill, 1995). Whereas HAL showed the darker side of artificial intelligence, other science fiction depictions of artificial intelligence, such as those in the popular television series Star Trek, have generally been more benign.

Have advances in computer technology since Star Trek and 2001 enabled scientists to transform science fiction into reality? The best place to begin searching for the answer to this question is on the chess board.

Artificial Intelligence and the Chess Board

Computer scientists have been working for more than 40 years to design computers that simulate human thought. In 1954 the first full-time research group was formed at Carnegie-Mellon University to research and develop a computer program to simulate human intelligence. Some of the first programs displaying artificial intelligence involved language translation and the game of chess (McCarthy, 1996).

Chess has long stood as a benchmark for artificial intelligence as it has been regarded as a game that involves strategy and intuition--both of which are uniquely characteristic of human thought. Early versions of chess programs involved the computer analyzing thousands of positions and their possible outcomes, but they were no match for proficient human chess players (McCarthy, 1996). The AI community was dealt a serious blow in 1988, when IBM's state-of-the-art chess computer named Deep Thought was easily defeated at the hands of Garry Kasparov, world chess champion at the time (Guteri, 1996).

After Deep Thought's loss, grand chess master Joel Benjamin and a team of IBM scientists went back to the drawing board and developed Deep Blue, a computer with 32 microprocessors that enable it to look at 200 million chess positions per second through calculation and computational power. Although lacking the intuition and knowledge from prior experience that a human player utilizes in the game, Deep Blue develops a move-by-move analysis that can predict what the human opponent will do, and through sheer computer power can play chess with the best human opponents.

In a match held in 1996 against Kasparov, Deep Blue decisively won the first game of a six-game match, surprising and amazing onlookers (Guteri, 1996). As the match progressed through the fifth game, with Kasparov and Deep Blue deadlocked, Kasparov commented that Deep Blue appeared to be thinking (Guteri, 1996). Kasparov managed to win the fifth and sixth games, and observers commented that the computer appeared to be confused (Guteri, 1996).

But was Deep Blue actually thinking? No. It was merely programmed with an extensive knowledge of chess positions, games, and their outcomes, which allowed it to appear to play human-like chess (Guteri, 1996). All the knowledge and power of Deep Blue could not overcome human strategy, because Deep Blue has no strategy in and of itself. It simply reacts to the moves and countermoves of its opponent. Kasparov capitalized on his ability to exploit his opponent's weaknesses by making Deep Blue "think" that he had made some bad moves, causing the computer to misjudge and ultimately be checkmated (Guteri, 1996). Kasparov was simply able to think further ahead than Deep Blue, and as a result of Deep Blue's misjudgments, was able to win the game (Guteri, 1996). In an article written about the match in Time magazine shortly after the match, Kasparov stated that as soon as he realized that if the computer could not compare his moves to anything in its database, it would drift "planlessly and get [itself] into trouble . . . that may have been my biggest advantage. I could figure out its priorities and adjust my play. It couldn't do the same to me" (Kasparov, p. 55).

After the 1996 match, Benjamin and the IBM team programmed Deep Blue with more chess knowledge and worked to increase its computational power so that it could get at least one more move ahead (Guteri, 1996). The result was that in 1997, Deep Blue defeated Kasparov by 3 1/2 to 2 1/2 in a six-game match (PC Magazine, 1997). Computer scientists Herbert Simon of Carnegie-Mellon University and Toshinori Munakata of Cleveland University attributed Deep Blue's win to more than increased knowledge and faster computations. They theorized that a large opening book, containing possibly tens of thousands of game trees from actual games and Deep Blue's own analyses gave it information comparable to that possessed by Kasparov and other chess masters, enabling the computer to focus on the character of a given position through selective searching (Simon & Munakata, 1997).

Given a limited task--to play a game of chess--through its enhanced search capabilities, knowledge, and processing speed, the computer could mimic human intuition, but it still falls behind in pattern recognition to perform problem solving on a wider basis (Simon & Munakata, 1997). The true key to Deep Blue's prowess in chess, then, is the amount of knowledge contained in the system as well as the ability to perform computations at the rate of 200 billion per second, coupled with the ability to adjust its search functions to make a decision (Simon & Munakata, 1997).

After Deep Blue: The Quest for Simulated Human Thought Continues

As the preceding discussion suggests, Deep Blue and other AI applications are really a result of combining large knowledge bases with lightning-fast processors--impressive, but not thought per se. Even after nearly half a century, researchers are still having considerable trouble simulating human thought. Dr. Rodney Cotterill, a physicist at the Danish Technical University, theorizes that one of the crucial elements that is missing in current AI is the element that permits coordination of the human brain with the muscles (Economist, 1996).

Philosophers and scientists during the first half of the twentieth century theorized that muscular movement is the key to a person's main source of information, such as the minute scanning motions of the eye that keep the light-sensitive cells of the retina refreshed with new information (Economist, 1996). Dr. Cotterill's theory goes one step further by including another type of signal to the brain, called an efference copy, which alerts other parts of the brain as to what the muscles are about to do, activating certain nerve cells in the brain and allowing the brain to distinguish between what is self and what is not, which is a central aspect of consciousness. If a robot is programmed with efference copy, Dr. Cotterill believes it will make the difference between a robot that is controlled by a human at a computer console and a robot that will be able to act independently by tracking the relationship of its movements and the reactions of the environment, enabling it to change its mind under certain circumstances (Economist, 1996).

So the search for a way to make the computer emulate human thought continues, with some encouraging recent developments. In Texas Doug Lenat and his staff are teaching their computer, Cyc, common-sense statements such as "water is wet" and "birds have feathers" in an attempt to give Cyc tools so that it can reason on its own (Smith, 1997). Lenat compares Cyc to a preschool child by theorizing that, "You don't teach a small child everything it's going to know in life. You teach it enough so that it can go to school" (Smith, p. 38).

Meanwhile, at MIT, Lenat's former student Rodney Brooks has been working for more than 3 years to bring his creation, Cog, to the level of a 1-month-old. Cog's eyes are cameras, its ears are microphones, and its electronic arm or hand constantly reaches out to "touch" someone (Smith, p. 30). Brooks is hopeful that Cog will eventually use the accumulated information it gathers from its senses to make discoveries on its own and reach a state of self-awareness (Smith, 1997).

Conclusion

Neither Lenat nor Brooks can predict the outcome of their work. Until AI becomes self-aware, it is really no more than a vast collection of data with the electronic technology to sort through it rapidly--as Deep Blue so aptly demonstrated. Until scientists are able to emulate into AI human awareness and such things as common sense, intuition, and self-generated thought, we are safe from computers such as HAL 9000.

References

In the machine: Artificial consciousness. (1996, April 6). The Economist, pp. 88-89.

Guteri, F. (1996, June). Silicon gambit: Computer chess and human thinking. Discover, pp. 48-53.

Kasparov, G. (1996, March 25). The day I sensed a new kind of
    intelligence: Playing chess against the IBM Deep Blue computer.
    Time, p. 55.

McCarthy, J. (1996, February 28). Artificial intelligence (AI).
    Collier's Encyclopedia, 2. CD-ROM.

Deep Blue wins. (1997, June 24). PC Magazine, p. 10.

Simon, H. A., & Munakata, T. (1997, August). AI lessons (Artificial
    intelligence: IBM's Deep Blue chess computer). Communications of
    the Association for Computing Machinery, pp. 23-26.

Smith, G. (1997, April). Of minds and machines: Artificial intelli-
    gence. Popular Science, p. 38.

2001: A Space Odyssey. (1995, June 15). Magill's survey of cinema,
    p. 221.

This paper provides a substantive overview of the Year 2000—or Y2K—problem with computer systems, and considers alternative approaches to mitigating the potential economic implications if the problem is not solved. Because this paper involves a rapidly evolving area, keep in mind that some of the information may already be dated. (MLA style)

THE Y2K PROBLEM--IMPLICATIONS AND SOLUTIONS

The Year 2000--or Y2K--problem, also known as the "millennium bug," refers to the computer problems that might occur when we enter the year 2000. At the moment that we enter the new millennium, the simple change from the year 1999 to the year 2000 could create a computer catastrophe because many computer systems are designed only to recognize years beginning with 19. The problem can be traced back to developments in the 1960s and 1970s, when data storage space was far more limited than it is today. One simple way to save storage space for database records was to use two digits (instead of four) to denote years. In addition, many computer programs were designed not to accept dates with the digits 00. The result is that almost all mainframe computer programs written more than a decade ago when storage capacity was scarce, are likely to either read 2000 as 1900 or, more commonly, "simply to gag on the date, potentially stopping businesses in their tracks" (Anonymous 53).

Any business using older programs for accounting, payroll, banking, telephone, inventory or pensions--in short, almost every type of business--might be hampered by the problem. In retrospect, of course, the method of handling dates adopted decades ago was shortsighted. Yet recognizing this fact does little to solve the problem.

Speculation about the range of economic problems that will occur and their impact has resulted in considerable concern, and even panic (Safire 28). In fact, the most troublesome Y2K problem might be the panic rather than the Y2K problem itself.

Some theorists point out that panic oftentimes leads either to wrong-headed attempts to deal with the problem, to paralysis, or to inaction. Any of these results can be very costly. Accordingly, any viable solution to the Y2K problem must also serve to mitigate irrational fear among big business, small business, and the general public.

The Alarmists' Nightmare Scenario

The increasing concern, even mild panic, over the Y2K problem can be traced to the perceptions and actions of a number of Y2K alarmists. These alarmists warn that neither the government nor private industry is taking appropriate actions to deal with the programming problems in time to avoid what the alarmists predict will amount to worldwide economic, social, and political chaos (O'Driscoll B1). Specifically, the Y2K alarmists warn that failure to solve the Y2K problem before January 1, 2000, will result in a domino effect: Computer problems will cause power plant failures, disable planes and trains, cripple communications systems, shut down industry, cause the stock market to crash, and result in bank closures, food riots, general chaos, and long-lasting social woes (O'Driscoll B1).

In response to the alarmists, the U.S. federal government has taken steps to assure the citizenry that its computer transformation is well under way and that preventive measures have been implemented in a number of government agencies and computer systems. In further response to the alarmists, both government and industry argue that although they have not yet fully integrated the necessary programming changes into their systems, the current level of hysteria over this issue is not called for because the alarmists have overstated the problem's potential consequences (O'Driscoll B1). Nevertheless, both the public and private sectors concur that the problem will be both costly and difficult to completely evaluate and solve, that the costs of fixing the problem will increase with each passing day, and therefore that it is critical to take steps now to correct the problem.

Why the Panic?

A number of factors contribute to a growing hysteria about the Y2K bug. First, recent cost estimates for preventing the Y2K problem, or for fixing it after the fact, have been staggering, resulting in a kind of sticker shock for governments and businesses alike. In 1997 the Gartner Group, a Connecticut-based computer consultancy firm, calculated that removing Y2K bugs from the world's computers and software would cost up to $600 billion over the next four years, more than $10 million per average medium-sized firm (Weinberger 37). Worse, the longer companies delay, the more the solution will cost. J.P. Morgan, an investment bank, estimates that the cost of rewriting a line of code will rise from $1 today to nearly $7 by the year 2000, as panicky companies fight over an insufficient number of competent mainframe programmers (Anonymous 53).

Another factor exacerbating the panic is the extent of our use of and dependence on computers. Were the problem limited to corporate information systems, for example, the problem would appear manageable. But the Y2K problem also affects virtually all machines with embedded chips, communications and navigation systems, national security (defense) systems, systems that deliver electricity and other forms of power, and so forth. In short, the scale of the problem is enormous. Moreover, the systems affected are vital to a country's national security and to the safety and well-being of its citizens. In short, the pandemic and grave aspects of the problem serve to heighten panic (Peterson C2).

A third factor contributing to panic is the sheer enormity of the task of changing billions of lines of code manually in a rela-tively short amount of time. This time crunch affects the federal government--especially the Department of Defense and the Department of Social Security (Weinberger 37)--most severely.

Abating the Panic--Action Versus Inaction

Given these gloomy forecasts, it is not surprising that industry and governments are growing increasingly concerned

(Anonymous 53). Many countries, corporations, and even state governments have begun to evaluate the possible implications of the problem and have made initial attempts to determine how they can respond to the economic crisis that might accompany this problem. Some theorists speculate, however, that despite good intentions, panic will continue unabated until the problem is completely solved or until individuals become so weary of hearing about the issue that they begin to ignore the problem. (Anonymous 53). This speculation suggests three basic approaches to address the problem of panic: (1) a comprehensive, perhaps even multinational plan of action led by the government, (2) inaction (denial), and (3) simulation.

Abating Panic by Government Intervention and Planning

As for the first approach, Tony Blair, Prime Minister of the United Kingdom, recently unveiled a program designed to combat the problem that not only takes into consideration the need to change computer technology in large and small businesses, but also to assist in this change, provide grant money to help with the transformation, and provide economic support for the problem (Hoge C4). Blair stated that the government of Great Britain would contribute more than $16.5 million to a proposed World Bank fund in order to raise Y2K problem awareness in developing countries and to address the issue throughout Europe. Thus, Blair's proposal is for not only an internal focus on the problem, but a global perspective as well (Hoge C4).

To reduce the panic, the Clinton administration has also submitted to congress planning and programming legislation, aimed at dispelling fear among private businesses that they will have to face significant lawsuits if they provide information about their computers' Y2K compliance and whether this compliance proves ineffective (Broder B2). Recognizing that this kind of fear can reduce the free sharing of data across industries for fear of liability, the government has added it to its package of measures designed to reduce the overall economic impact and address the immediate and perceivable problems and subsequent solutions from the process of reprogramming (Broder B2).

The efforts of Blair and the Clinton administration are well intentioned. However, few of the efforts currently under way have made a significant impact on the problem of economic panic.

Abating Panic by Ignoring the Problem

Many small businesses appear to be following a second possible route toward dispelling fear and abating panic: simply ignoring the problem. Of the more than 5 million small businesses nationwide that are exposed to the possibility of computer glitches associated with Y2K, most have heard of the problem, but few have been quick to work toward a solution, according to recent small business surveys (Mukherjee 8). Even though U.S. businesses are expected to spend approximately $300 billion to reprogram their computers, 75% of surveyed small businesses had no plans to act before the year 2000 (Mukherjee 8).

Because small businesses are less dependent on technology than many large businesses, their approach to abating panic is to simply ignore the problem until it shows itself in the form of verifiable problems. By ignoring the problem, businesses seems to assume that the alarmists are wrong and that there is little need for the widespread response in the business community (Diamond PG). But some business specialists claim that small business will be caught off guard on January 1, 2000; as many as 370,000 small businesses will be temporarily crippled by the Y2K computer glitches and will be forced to close their doors until they fix the problem (Mukherjee 8).

Abating the Panic Through Simulation

A third approach, simulation, is beginning to gain wide recognition as perhaps the only effective means of abating Y2K panic. This approach calls for a computer-based simulation of the problem, evaluating the outcomes and possible impacts, and then providing this information to the public as a means of reducing fear about the impact of the problem. The most significant simulation to date is the recent one on Wall Street, a simulation that many think has indeed served to reduce the level of panic.

The Wall Street computer simulation in July 1998 provided valuable information about possible outcomes of the Y2K problem (Feder B6). After many months of preparation, the leading brokers, major exchanges, clearinghouses, and depository companies in the United States participated in a mock trading session based on the Y2K transition, and then evaluated how the industry and computers would respond to the problem (Feder B6). The simulation designers anticipated that computers might reject the year 2000, and that the reaction of the computers might be unpredictable. For instance, some might spew inaccurate data, create faulty calculations, or simply crash immediately, whereas others might appear to function normally but would not be able to be restarted once shut down (Feder PG). Although the data collected from this simulation is still being analyzed, the general perception is that Wall Street stood up against the Y2K problem with few large-scale problems, and that the system will be capable of maintaining the integrity of securities exchanges during the transition (Anonymous A4).

One of the primary concerns about the Y2K problem expressed by both corporations and the government is that economic panic might lead to a stock market crash. This concern makes sense because the stock market is driven by mass psychology, at least in the short term. The recent Wall Street simulation provided a valuable start at dispelling some of the major fears about the Y2K problem (Feder B6).

Conclusion

Some theorists claim that people will get tired of reading about the Y2K problem and that the panic that has now hit worldwide levels will dissipate over time (Raasch ARC). Even if this is true, however, inaction is not a proactive approach; given the projected magnitude of the problem, outcomes should not be left for fate to decide, nor should they be left for governments to decide.

The Wall Street simulation informs us that by implementing simulations as soon as possible and in as many different industries as possible, and then evaluating their outcomes as a diagnostic tool, prudent preventive measures can be taken, thereby minimizing economic panic (Abrahms B10).

Works Cited

Abrahms, Doug. "Traders Can Share Year 2000 Solutions." The Washington Times 3 Jul. 1998: B10.

Anonymous. "Wall St.'s Mock Trading Aimed at Millennium Bug." The New York Times 3 Jul. 1998: A4.

Anonymous. "The Y2K Watch." Newsweek 22 Jun. 1998: 12.

Anonymous. "Millennium-Bug Triage: 93 Weeks and Counting." Time 30 Mar. 1998: 16.

Anonymous. "Oh What a Lovely Millennium Bug." The Economist 3 Aug. 1996: 53+.

Broder, John. "Clinton Sees Computer Bug as Major Test." The New York Times 15 Jul. 1998: B2.

Diamond, Michael. "The Nation's Homepage: Small Firms Ignore Y2K Bug." USA Today 3 May 1998: B8.

Feder, Barnaby. "Wall Street to Turn Clock Ahead to See if Year 2000 Computes." The New York Times 12 Jul. 1998: B6.

Hoge, Warren. "Britain Moves to Combat 'Millennium Bug': Government Is Planning to Spend $160 Million in a Global Effort." The New York Times 31 Mar. 1998: C4.

Mukherjee, Sougata. "Small Business Putting Off Dealing with Y2K Problem." San Francisco Business Times 5 Jun. 1998: 8.

O'Driscoll, Patrick. "The Nation's Homepage: Y2K Bug Could Be a Plague, Many Warn." USA Today 2 Jul. 1998: B1.

Peterson, Melody. "Computer Consulting by Accountants Stirs Concern." The New York Times 8 Jul. 1998: C2.

Raasch, Chuch. "Don't Laugh about 2000 Computer Scare; Congress, White House Aren't." Gannett News Service 4 Jul. 1998: ARC.

Safire, William. "With a Euro in Her Pouch . . . : As Y2K
    Approaches, Two New Terms Gain Currency." <u>The New York Times
    Magazine</u> 7 Jun. 1998: 28.

Weinberger, Casper. "The Y2K Crisis." <u>Forbes</u> 20 Apr. 1998: 37+.

This brief paper provides a good survey of how computer technology has been applied to the medical field. By identifying past and current trends, as well as future directions, the student demonstrates that she has gained a good perspective on the topic as a whole. (MLA style)

COMPUTER TECHNOLOGY: BURGEONING MEDICAL APPLICATIONS

Computers and Medicine: A Brief Historical Overview

For as long as electronic computers have existed, medical engineers have pioneered ways by which to utilize their technology to solve technical problems. As concepts and ideas evolved into practical application, what Kaplan (5) refers to as "subcommunities" began to form in both the field of computer science and the field of medicine. Individually, computer engineers worked to develop systems that could be useful in the field of medicine and medical scientists explored how such machines could enhance and preserve human life. From their initiation into the world of medical science, computers were hailed optimistically as the "wave of the future." Citing a primary source from the mid-1960s, Kaplan says that computers were described as "absolute prerequisites to further progress in the biomedical sciences" (5). Today, these dreams of electronic productivity in medicine have indeed become contemporary realities.

Prior to the 1960s, computers were primarily regarded as tools for research that would improve practice (Kaplan 5). But by the early 1970s, their role in patient care and hospital communications became apparent. Becoming even more evident was the important role computers could play in patient care and patient monitoring. Those who were at the forefront of the new technologies also expressed a profound interest in using computers as indirect aids in patient care by advancing better communication of medical record information within an institution. Experts now considered computers a means of communicating medical information about individual patients through an institutionwide medical information system, rather than only as a way of handling information to promote understanding of disease and diagnosis (Kaplan 6-7).

Throughout the 1970s and 1980s, the role of computer technology in medicine expanded to include the controlling of costs in health and medial care (Kaplan 7). In fact, the focus began to shift in this direction, so that by the 1990s it was clear that there had been an "overwhelming trend away from their [automated hospital information systems'] original medical goals in favor of administrative priorities" (Kaplan 7).

The 1990s have witnessed some dramatic advances in the application of computing technology to the medical field. Now termed "medical informatics" (Kaplan 9), the latest "version" of this rapidly growing field is concerned chiefly with the cognitive, information processing, and communication tasks of medical practice, education, and research, including the information science and technology to support those tasks. For the most part, medical informatics has maintained a technological focus and continues to augment the level of participation that computer science plays in saving human lives while simultaneously decreasing health care costs and expediting administrative functions.

Tele-Medicine

Perhaps the most exciting developments in the joint field of computers and medicine during the 1990s has been the implementation of telecommunications and multimedia technology in the medical field. In this burgeoning area, surgery has been the primary beneficiary. Special software and hardware produced by companies such as Medical Media Systems Incorporated enable surgeons to get a better view inside the patient's body (Mangelsdorf and Bianchi 33). Surgeons can now insert surgical instruments accompanied by minute video cameras into small incisions, thereby minimizing the invasiveness of surgery. The technologies offered by companies such as MMS combine radiologic data from CAT scans and X-rays with mathematic models to create 3-D images of a patient's anatomy. The

3-D image is then blended with the live video coming from the scope to provide a virtual road map for the surgeon (Mangelsdorf and Bianchi 33).

Another company, BioControl Systems, is developing technology that computerizes the signals of the human nervous system. A bioelectric signal controller called the BioMuse uses electric activities in the body like muscle movements or eye motions in order to control and operate computers. A patient wears a specially designed band around his or her head, arm, or leg to capture electrical signals. With the band, the patient can guide objects on a screen with an eye-controlled mouse or create digital-synthesizer music by flexing a muscle. This product will make it possible to map the movement of a surgeon's forearms onto remote computer-controlled instruments (Mangelsdorf and Bianchi 34).

Another company, Exus, has created the prototype for a surgical simulator that allows doctors to actually experience the hand motions and sensations of operating on a patient. The simulator is currently being marketed both to medical educators to train students and to practicing surgeons who wish to practice certain procedures from their own home before performing them on actual patients. The potential of this technology to improve the quality of health care is palpable (Mangelsdorf and Bianchi 33-4).

More primitive, but nevertheless useful, simulators have been widely used for several years. For example, doctors have been able to simulate surgical procedures on a computer to determine by trial and error how best to cut without harming the patient. Radiologists have been able to generate a computer-stored geometry of a patient's brain in order to better concentrate destructive radiation on brain tumors, thereby sparing nearby organs (Manning 66). These presurgical technologies are quickly becoming integral parts of the modern surgeon's work.

Computer-Aided Surgery in the Future

As medical systems technology has already done a commendable job of facilitating administrative operations and cutting costs, the main focus of this technology now seems to be on improving surgical quality and saving more human lives. Although surgical simulation seems to be emerging now as a useful tool, robotics are still largely in development but will probably be far more significant in the future.

As computers grow increasingly powerful, doctors will soon be able to view more accurate video-like images simulating the motions of joints and limbs both before and after surgery. In the very near future, expert systems will even help guide physicians through their decision-making process by giving the physician preferred options and advice based on what has already proven effective in earlier simulations (Manning 66).

By the year 2000, computers should be capable of sending information from their databases to operating rooms, where robotic units will pinpoint precise locations for incisions and guide cuts and the placement of body parts (Manning 66-67).

According to F. King, the advantage that robots offer as virtual surgeons is twofold. For one thing, they are faster than their human counterparts and potentially more accurate (King 100). Speed reduces trauma and hurries recovery; accuracy implies that robots moving quickly will do a minimum of damage along the way. King also writes that robots do some jobs better or even faster than most humans do them (100).

Before robots can play a major role in medical surgery, several problems must be solved. In order to maximize safety, robots have to be designed so that they do not slip while working. They must be made easily interruptible, so that if one fails to execute a procedure properly, a live surgeon can immediately take over the task without endangering the patient. Finally, although robots do indeed have steady "hands," they also have no way of knowing whether those hands are in the right place; so reliable monitoring systems and procedures need to be developed (King 100-1).

Conclusion

In sum, the medical field has indeed been a primary bene-ficiary of computer technology, and medical applications seem to be growing in number, variety, and significance with each passing decade. Although the field of informedics may have matured, computer technologies for surgery are clearly in their infancy. It is probably safe to predict that the next century will bring more accurate diagnoses, better-trained physicians, and more precise surgical procedures. In the end, life will be healthier and more productive and life spans will grow; in short, society will be better off for having computerized the practice of medicine.

Works Cited

Kaplan, Bonnie. "The Computer Prescription: Medical Computing, Public Policy, and Views of History." Science, Technology & Human Values 1 Jan. 1995: 5.

King, F. "Robodoc." Economist 14 Mar. 1992: 100.

Mangelsdorf, Martha and Alessandra, Bianchi. "Long-Distance Medicine." Inc. 1 Aug. 1994: 33.

Manning, R. "Scalpel! Clamp! Floppy Disk!" Technology Review 1 Oct. 1991: 66.

9

ECONOMICS

The Origins of the Euro

Ricardo's Solution to England's Monetary Crisis

U.S.–Japan Trade Disputes: Causes, Consequences, and Cures

The Economics of *Oz:* How Communist Inefficiency Was Not Just a Cause, but Also a Consequence of Shortages

This paper traces the origins and development of the European Currency Unit (Euro), identifying the many organizations and treaties that culminated in full monetary union. The paper closes by raising provocative and forward-looking questions about whether the Euro will work and whether it is good for Europe. Notice that the student presents the subject in strict chronological fashion, leading the reader logically from one paragraph to the next. (MLA style)

THE ORIGINS OF THE EURO

The Origins of the Euro--The 1960s and 1970s

The roots of the Eurodollar--or simply Euro--extend all the way back to the early 1960s--specifically, to proposals before the already existing European Council (EC), which at that time included six member states. In 1962, the Marjolin Memorandum pointed out that, whereas the Treaty of Rome, upon which the EC was formed, had foreseen a common <u>trade</u> policy, it had not envisioned a common <u>monetary</u> policy, and that this void should be filled. The memorandum suggested that after a period of transition, it would be necessary to fix the exchange rates of the currencies of the EC's member states, subject to narrow fluctuation margins. Although the EC did not immediately adopt the memorandum's proposals, in May 1964 the EC did indeed adopt the memorandum's call for the creation of a committee of governors for the purpose of promoting cooperation between the central banks of the member states.

The call for monetary union rose again in 1970, when the Werner Report, prepared at the request of the EC, presented a plan for the attainment, in stages, of an economic and monetary union among member states. The plan's final objective was to "realize an area in which goods and services, people and capital will circulate freely and without competitive distortions, without giving rise to structural or regional disequilibrium" (Eichengreen 86). In March 1971, the government heads of the member states expressed their political will to establish an economic and monetary union, by unanimously approving the plan and by recommending a move toward a single currency by 1980 (87).

Initial plans to reach a complete economic and monetary union by 1980 proved overly optimistic; currencies of member states fluctuated against one another, and the currency devaluation in some countries led to high inflation in those countries and limited overall economic growth. By the end of the decade, it was clear that further measures were needed for Europe to achieve true economic and monetary union as envisioned by the Werner Report. Accordingly, in March 1979 the European Monetary System (EMS) emerged as a concrete step toward this end (El-Agraa, 1990). The EMS was designed to stabilize exchange rates and curb inflation-- the two chief impediments to monetary union in the 1970s--by limiting the margin of fluctuation for each member currency to a small deviation from a central rate; in other words, it linked currencies in a semi-fixed way. The hope was that all along its exchange-rate mechanism would result in full monetary union.

First, the system created a common European Currency Unit (ECU), by which the central exchange rates could be set. The ECU was composed of all the European Union (EU) currencies, weighted according to the economic importance of each country. When any currency reached the limit of the margin of fluctuation, which was set at 2.25%, the central banks of the respective countries were required to intervene by selling off the stronger currency and buying the weaker one. The EMS also required member governments to take appropriate economic policy steps to prevent continued deviation from the central rate.

As the EMS and its ECU were set into motion at decade's end, the 1980 Werner deadline came and went (Economist). The next decade would prove to be discouraging for proponents of ECU.

The 1980s--Problems with the EMS and ECU

To its credit, the EMS and its ECU helped to lower inflation rates in the EC and ease the economic shock of global currency fluctuations during the 1980s. However, several problems frustrated its broader objective of full economic and monetary union.

One obstacle to full economic integration involved the Common Agricultural Policy (CAP). The CAP encouraged the production of large surpluses of certain commodities by committing the EC to buy them; the CAP was essentially a government farm subsidy program. During the 1980s the CAP accounted for about two-thirds of annual EC expenditures. However, the CAP resulted in windfalls to those countries that produced the subsidized commodities, at the expense of other countries. So the CAP did nothing to stabilize the overall economy of the European community.

A second problem was that some countries, particularly Great Britain, voiced continual opposition to the EMS and ECU, expressing concern that a shared European currency would threaten national identity and sovereignty. Third, many of the EU's member countries struggled to meet the economic requirements for participating in a shared currency. The EMS required that each country have a budget deficit no greater than 3% of its gross domestic product. Some countries imposed budget cuts and new taxes, but such measures failed to bring these countries into compliance; moreover, budget cuts and higher taxes were generally met with considerable resistance from within each country.

By 1988, as at the close of the previous decade, it had become clear that the EC's plan for achieving economic and monetary union was inadequate. Immediate steps were taken to alleviate current problems. Most notably, at an emergency summit meeting in 1988, EC leaders agreed on mechanisms to limit commodity subsidies, and under the 1989 EC budget, agricultural subsidies comprised less than 60% of total EC spending for the first time since the 1960s. But it was clear that such measures were merely bandages and that the plan needed to be overhauled.

Fixing the Problems--The Delors Plan of 1988

After two decades of failed attempts to achieve full economic union came a growing consensus that a single market (or currency) was impossible as long as restrictions on money transfers and exchange premiums limited the free flow of capital. The result of this consensus was the Delors Plan, which called for a sweeping three-stage plan for achieving true economic union (Hackett).

In June 1988, the EC created a committee to study the problem and propose concrete stages leading to full union (Eichengreen 101). The committee was chaired by Jacques Delors, a former French finance minister, current president of the European Commission, and one of the leading proponents of monetary union. The committee also included the governors of the EC central banks, the manager of the Bank for International Settlements, a professor of economics from Copenhagen, and the president of the Banco Exterior de España. The resulting report, which the EC immediately approved, was two pronged: (1) It proposed a 7-year timetable for removing nearly all the remaining trade barriers between member states (Gelb 10), and (2) it called for economic and monetary union through three discrete but evolutionary stages (Paxton).

During the first stage, the process of creating economic and monetary union would begin by strengthening central economic and monetary policy, yet coordinating these policies with the existing institutional framework of individual countries. Stage 2 would be a period of transition to the third and final stage, during which the basic organs and structure of the economic and monetary union would be set up. Stage 3 would commence with the move to irrevo- cably locked exchange rates and the introduction of a single currency to replace national currencies. The European System of Central Banks (ESCB) would be responsible for determining the exchange rate and reserve, formulating and implementing monetary policy, and maintaining a properly functioning payment system.

The Masticht Treaty of 1992

In July 1990 the first stage of the Delors Plan was set into motion. The committee of governors of the EC Central Banks took the additional responsibility of promoting and coordinating the monetary policies of member states, with the aim of achieving the price and monetary stability needed for the EMS to function prop- erly. Before the second stage could begin, however, it was necessary to revise the Treaty of Rome in order to establish the institutional structure called for by the Delors Plan.

To this end, in 1991 the government heads of the 12 EC member states--Belgium, Denmark, France, Germany, Great Britain, Greece, Ireland, Italy, Luxembourg, the Netherlands, Portugal, and Spain-- convened in Masticht in the Netherlands. The conference resulted in the Treaty on European Union, also known as the Masticht Treaty of February 1992.

The Masticht Treaty created the ECU, the EU, and a central bank to help member banks transition to the new common currency. The treaty also called for member states to seriously consider joint policies on defense, citizenship, and the environment (Devinney 12). For example, under the treaty European citizenship was granted to citizens of each member state, customs and immigra- tion agreements were enhanced to allow European citizens greater freedom to live, work, or study in any of the member states, and border controls were relaxed.

The Masticht Treaty was scheduled to take effect beginning January 1993--one year before the planned start of Stage 2 of the Delors Plan. However, problems in the ratification process delayed effectiveness until November 1993. The European Monetary Institute (EMI) came into being early in 1994, marking the beginning of second stage of the Delors Plan.

With the provisions of the Masticht Treaty in place, Europe has progressed slowly but inexorably during the 1990s through the second and third stages of the Delors Plan, and is now antici- pating the introduction of the common currency--the Euro--in early 1999. The question remains, however, whether full monetary union will work.

Is the Euro Good for Europe?

Defenders of the Euro claim that full economic union and a common currency will work for two chief reasons--one economic and the other political. First, the economies of Euro members will be less vulnerable externally than they are now, simply because the share of trade in the Euro zone's collective GDP will be far smaller than those of the individual EU members. Second, Euro defenders claim that it will be impossible for Europe to go back once the Euro arrives; no member country will in practice be able to leave the Euro or the EU.

Critics of the Euro warn that with state political sovereignty still intact, nothing can prevent the government of Spain or France, for example, from withdrawing from the Euro zone if it calculates such a move to be in the national interest. Between 1999 and 2002, national currencies will remain in circulation with irrevocably fixed parities. During this time, the markets will be watching for signs of faint-heartedness, to see whether, for instance, the German authorities are willing to see Italian lire converted to German marks without limit on demand. Whether to stay with the regime through difficult economic times will in all likelihood be a political decision, based ultimately on whether citizens of individual countries believe this bold innovation is worth the sacrifice.

Concluding Remarks

The Euro represents the culmination of four decades of reports, conferences, summits, treaties, and disputes among the EC's member nations. Given the economic and political implications of the Euro, Europe's leaders should think seriously about whether Europe really needs the Euro. It is interesting to note that throughout history almost every attempt at monetary union across national borders has failed. But is the past necessarily a prologue for Europe's future? Or should Europe's current leaders honor the efforts of all those who have worked toward the union, and do all they can to see through to a successful completion their great adventure, which began with the Marjolin Memorandum in 1962?

Works Cited

Devinney, Timothy M. _European Markets After 1992. Forecast of Economic Conditions When All Barriers to Free Trade in the EEC Are Removed_. Columbus, OH: Lexington, 1991.

Eichengreen, Barry, and Jeffrey Frieden. "The Political Economy of
European Monetary Unification: An Analytical Introduction."
<u>Economics and Politics</u> Jul. 1993: 85-104.

El-Agraa, Ali M. <u>The Economics of the European Community</u>. 2nd ed.
New York: St. Martin's, 1990.

Gelb, Norman, "The Looming Euro: Threat or Promise? (planned
European monetary unit)." <u>The New Leader</u> 4 Nov. 1996: 10+.

Hackett, Clifford P. <u>Cautious Revolution: The European Community
Arrives</u>. Westport, CT: Greenwood, 1990.

Paxton, John. "A Dictionary of the European Economic Community."
<u>Facts on File</u>. 2nd ed., 1990.

"Ready or Not, Here Comes EMU." <u>The Economist</u> 11 Oct._1997: 67.

This paper focuses on one particular contribution of nineteenth-century economist David Ricardo. The student identifies a problem with England's monetary policy during that era, and then explains how Ricardo solved the problem. The paper closes by providing a broader perspective on Ricardo's contributions to the field of economics. (MLA style)

RICARDO'S SOLUTION TO ENGLAND'S MONETARY CRISIS

David Ricardo was probably the most important and influential economist in Europe during the early nineteenth century. His lasting contributions included those in the theoretical areas of marginal analysis and diminishing returns as they relate to agricultural production. His primary contribution, and legacy, involves his monetary theories and his successful call for the Bank of England to return to the gold standard in order to revitalize the ailing British economy.

England's Monetary Dilemma

Although the debate over England's Corn Laws during the early nineteenth century was arguably that country's greatest economic debate of the century, another debate was brewing as well during this era. Concern over Britain's ability to finance the war while at the same time maintain economic stability mounted into a controversy over Britain's monetary policies--particularly as they involved the gold standard. The gold standard provided the basis of the international payments mechanism prevailing in the European countries at the time. Under the gold standard, large foreign expenditures are settled by way of gold flows from the debtor country (buyer) to the creditor country (seller). At the same time, however, the country experiencing gold outflows should maintain a sufficient supply of gold to satisfy any domestic demand for converting paper into gold--in other words, for redemptions of domestic currency (Ricardo, Essays 57).

Near the end of the eighteenth century, the Bank of England could no longer accommodate both foreign and domestic demands for gold. In 1797 parliament was forced to adopt the Bank Restriction Act, which prohibited the bank from redeeming its notes in gold. The act moved England from its long-standing gold standard to an inconvertible paper standard. This shift in England's monetary standard resulted not only in a sharp rise in prices of goods and services from 1797 to 1814 but also in the depreciation of England's paper monetary unit, the pound, in relation to other foreign currencies. At the same time, England's negative balance of payments vis-à-vis other European countries continued unabated (Ricardo, Essays 58).

Ricardo's Criticism of England's Monetary Intervention

David Ricardo's concern with government intervention in economic matters was evident long before his major publications such as his "Essay on Profits" and The Principles of Political Economy and Taxation. Some of his first economic writings were for an English newspaper, the Morning Chronicle. Ricardo wrote three letters to the newspaper in 1809, discussing the problems he thought were undermining England's monetary system. He believed that there were many negative effects of removing the gold standard. Ricardo attempted to demonstrate that the return to gold payments by the bank would lead to a smoothly expanding national economy (St. Clair 95). He argued that continued use of a paper standard, which did not allow convertibility, could only lead to the decline of England's status as a financial power and more importantly reduce the likelihood of economic expansion. Ricardo also argued that the Bank of England was taking unfair advantage of the 1797 legislation by overissuing paper currency in order to profit from excessive loans to the government and private sectors of the economy. For these beliefs, Ricardo was labeled a "bullionist" (St. Clair 96).

Here's how Ricardo's argument proceeded. He began by exploring the determinants of the value of currency and how banks use monetary policy. Ricardo rejected the new system of paper currency, claiming that the Bank of England's notes were not money.

Rather, he felt that gold was the only true form of tangible money. The key for Ricardo was the close relationship between the supply of money and price levels. In his pamphlet <u>The High Price of Bullion</u>, which was simply a more formal proposal of the letters published in the <u>Morning Chronicle</u>, Ricardo explained that given a volume of goods, prices were dependent on the quantity of money employed in the distribution of these goods. Therefore, prices rose if the quantity of money increased, and fell if the quantity of money diminished (Blaug 110). This theory, known as Ricardo's Quantity Theory of Money, applied to both paper and gold currencies.

Ricardo then contended that when gold is used as money, and there are no hindrances to its exportation and importation, its value remains constant, unlike the value of paper money (Blaug 111). The reason is that the value of gold as a medium of exchange is determined by the metal itself. In other words, both coined and uncoined gold had the same value, thereby alleviating any discrepancy in what the gold money (coins) represents. Paper currency is a different issue, however. It cannot be melted down, nor can it be exported. Therefore, its supply can continually increase, ultimately leading to a downward spiraling in the paper currency's purchasing power, a problem known as inflation.

Because the Bank of England was unable to convert its paper money into gold following the Bank Restriction Act of 1797, it could not reduce the amount of paper money held by the public, and the quantity of paper money in circulation increased. As Ricardo's Quantity Theory of Money had predicted, prices rose commensurate with an increase in the supply of money. Accordingly, the value of the pound depreciated compared to the gold it was supposed to represent (Ricardo 55).

Ricardo's Solution: The Ingot Plan

As Oswald Sinclair wrote regarding Ricardo's attempt to find a plausible solution to the decreasing value of the new currency, "'To discover the cause was to discover the remedy'" (Gootzeit 28). Ricardo had certainly found the reason for the current devaluation problem, at least in his own mind. He attributed this loss in value of paper money, which can also be stated as an increase in the price of gold, to the excessive quantity of notes issued by the Bank of England. His solution to this monetary catastrophe was simple: Diminish the quantity of currency. Ricardo concluded that doing so would add value to the paper currency. Accordingly, in his pamphlet he wrote:

> "The remedy which I propose for all the evils in our currency, is that the Bank should gradually decrease the amount of their notes in circulation until they shall have rendered the remainder of equal value with the coins which they represent, or in other words, till the prices of gold and silver bullion shall be brought down to their mint price." (Blaug 112)

With this diminishing quantity of paper currency, the value or purchasing power of each unit would rise. This conformed to Ricardo's aforementioned assertion that the purchasing power of one unit of money depended on the quantity in circulation. With Ricardo's broad solution, eliminating economic instability seemed attainable. However, the question remained how best to implement a plan to return England's monetary system to a gold standard capable of convertibility.

Always employing a practical approach to economics, Ricardo developed a plan for reinstating a convertible currency. The Ingot Plan, which was named after the 60-ounce solid gold bar, was extremely popular and was approved by a legislative act of Parliament in 1819. The plan's central idea was to keep paper currency as a medium of exchange for most domestic purchases. Gold coins, on the other hand, were to be used in settling inter-national debts. Ricardo advocated using paper instead of gold for domestic purchases for two reasons. First, if a persistently negative balance of payments caused the pound to decrease on the foreign exchange market, coins could be illegally melted and

shipped away, causing a shortage for legal transactions. Second,
Ricardo was concerned about gold coins being clipped (used for
individual domestic exchanges), thereby deteriorating in value over
time. The Ingot Plan also called for the Bank of England to begin
exchanging gold for notes, with a minimum transaction of 20 ounces.
However, gold from the bank would only be in the form of bullion,
and not coin. This provided a means to restrict gold from being
used for individual domestic exchanges.

Ricardo hoped this plan would bring about several desirable
outcomes. He wanted his plan to counteract the rapid inflation that
Great Britain was experiencing. His efforts were also directed at
gaining control of the money supply in order to reduce the amount
of paper money in circulation. Overall, falling prices were to
occur and economic stability was to be restored. However, Ricardo's
plan relied too heavily on decreasing the paper money supply, an
idea that was incomprehensible in England at the time. Even though
the war had ended, the bank still played an important role in the
commercial loan market. Removing paper credit funds would have
created serious consequences for both private and public borrowers
(Milgate 88). Ricardo's Ingot Plan, however, was only intended to
be a temporary measure until a fully operational gold standard
could be implemented, which finally occurred in 1823.

Ricardo as an Advocate for Free Trade

By demonstrating the negative effects that a paper standard
has on the purchasing power of a country's currency, Ricardo had
successfully advocated England's return to a gold standard. But he
was also concerned with larger economic issues, particularly with
free trade among nations and its significance not only to one
country's economic health but to the well-being of the international community. Ricardo developed a larger theory on
international trade of currency; at the theory's core was Ricardo's
notion that unfettered exportation of gold was essential and his
assumption that an increase in a country's currency supply caused

prices to rise, whereas a decrease causes prices to fall (Ricardo, Notes 3).

According to Ricardo, rising and falling currency values is actually healthy and desirable. Ricardo noted that "such a difference of prices is the natural order of things, and the exchange can only be at par, when a sufficient quantity of money is introduced into the country" (Ricardo, Notes 47). By money, of course, Ricardo meant gold. Once the movement of gold from one country to another other has ceased, goods continue to be exchanged for goods. However, this state of equilibrium can only be achieved when free trade, or free flow of bullion, is allowed to continue unfettered by artificial government restriction. In other words, no matter what the difference in currency values, Ricardo asserted, the exchange would always be at par (equilibrium) if an unimpeded flow of gold bullion is allowed.

Concluding Remarks

As demonstrated here, Ricardo was indeed the critical figure in early nineteenth-century European economics. His Quantitative Theory of Money and resulting Ingot Plan, fueled by his heart-felt desire to help improve the English economy for the working class, established Ricardo as one of the most important and influential economists in modern history. For his contributions, he will always be remembered by economic historians as an economist with a compassionate agenda: a concern for the economic well-being of the underrepresented English working class. And his broader theories on monetary policy continue to this day to influence the thinking of economic scholars and the policies of central banks.

Works Cited

Blaug, Mark. Ricardian Economics; a Historical Study. New Haven, CT: Yale UP, 1958.

Gootzeit, Michael J. David Ricardo. New York: Columbia UP, 1975.

Milgate, Murray. Ricardian Politics. Princeton, NJ: Princeton UP, 1991.

Ricardo, David. <u>Economic Essays</u>. London: G. Bell and Sons, 1923.

Ricardo, David. <u>Notes on Malthus' "Principles of Political Economy and Taxation"</u>. Oxford, Eng.: Oxford UP, 1928.

St. Clair, Oswald. <u>A Key to Ricardo</u>. New York: A. M. Kelley Bookseller, 1965.

(A+) This paper analyzes U.S.–Japan trade dispute issues both from a cause-and-effect angle and from a prescriptive angle. The discussion moves both logically and chronologically from the cause of these trade conflicts, to their possible consequences, to proposed solutions. (APA style)

U.S.-JAPAN TRADE DISPUTES: CAUSES, CONSEQUENCES, AND CURES

In recent years, news about trade conflicts between the United States and other countries have focused mainly on Japan. The reason for this lies in the extent of imbalance of trade between these two countries, and in the U.S. response to this growing imbalance. Two important international initiatives, Asia Pacific Economic Cooperation (APEC) and the World Trade Organi-zation (WTO), might appear to be prepared to thwart any threat to global marketplace or world peace that these trade conflicts might pose. Upon closer inspection, however, one notices that private business is leading the way to build and maintain bridges of cooperation and free trade between the United States and Japan.

The Current Trade Imbalance Between
the United States and Japan

From 1945 to 1965 the balance of trade between the United States and Japan was tipped in favor of the United States, by an average of $315 million per year. In 1965 the balance shifted in favor of Japan. However, nobody foresaw that the imbalance in Japan's favor would grow as large as it has in recent decades. The imbalance of trade in Japan's favor since 1965 has averaged in excess of $27 billion per year, is now running above $50 billion per year, and is rising rapidly each successive year.

What has caused the trade imbalance between these two coun-tries to become so large? Helmut Schmidt, the former German Chancellor, points out that since the early 1980s, United States citizens have simply consumed and invested more than they have produced. As a direct result, the United States can no longer finance the towering annual deficits that plague it. The end result is that annual U.S. imports exceed its exports, making the United States the largest debtor country vis-à-vis the world economy (Schmidt, 1995). At the same time, Japan's production has greatly exceeded its domestic consumption and investments. The extraordinary savings of the Japanese have turned Japan into the world's largest creditor (Schmidt, 1995). Given, then, that the United States is the largest debtor country and Japan is the largest creditor country, the logical consequence is a tremendous trade imbalance between the two countries.

Is the trade imbalance as extreme as the raw numbers offered above suggest? Perhaps not. The trade imbalance is likely to obscure the fact that Japan imports 11.2% of all United States exports, making it the second largest United States export market, after Canada. Without argument, Japan is a main export market for U.S. manufactured products and the largest export market for agricultural products. Japan is the primary source of tourism income for the United States. The United States is Japan's largest technology trading partner. It is not widely acknowledged that Japan has a large deficit in service trade with the United States. Finally, approximately 80% of Japanese affiliates in the United States undertake philanthropic activities, adding to the economy and social services (Tyler, 1995).

Nevertheless, a large trade deficit is a symptom of an ailing economy. Decreased foreign demand for U.S. goods and services results in production cutbacks, loss of jobs, a lower standard of living, and so forth. Accordingly, it is in the best interests of the United States to reduce its deficit--particularly with Japan.

The Problem with Government Intervention

The most immediately effective solution to a trade deficit would be to simply stop the inflow of goods from the other country, through quotas, or at least to make those goods so expensive, through tariffs, that domestic consumers will buy cheaper domestic goods instead. Until now, these have been Washington's favorite ideas for reducing its trade deficit with Japan. One example is Washington's pressure on Japan to agree to import quotas on Japanese automobiles. Pressuring Japan to agree to various artificial trade arrangements, the U.S. government has tried to use its role as guarantor of world peace as leverage, at least tacitly.

But there are several critical problems with such tactics, problems which suggest that other approaches to the problem might be more appropriate. First, quotas violate a treaty established by the WTO. Second, as Schmidt points out, even in the event that Japan were to yield to such pressure, the structural illnesses of the U.S. economy would still remain untreated (Schmidt 1995). Third, the U.S. threat to withdraw its military peacekeeping force from Japan (born of a postwar treaty in 1945) may simply not have teeth. U.S. citizens and Japanese alike tend to agree that Japan has outgrown the need for U.S. defense and that the treaty is anachronistic. In other words, it makes sense that as the world's second biggest economy, Japan should now do its own soldiering. Moreover, many Japanese feel that reliance on U.S. troops is a slur on the nation's pride (Medina, 1996).

To put the U.S. position in perspective, a half century after the end of World War II, at a time when the United States is running a $50 billion trade deficit with Japan, the United States maintains 46,000 troops in Japan in order to provide a <u>unilateral</u> security guarantee for the Japanese state. So the world's largest debtor nation is providing the security for the world's largest creditor nation at a time when many in the United States regard Japan's economic power as a greater threat than any other country's, including that of the United States (Pyle, 1996).

The Problem with APEC and the WTO as Arbiters of Trade Disputes

Political leaders and economists worry that the U.S. government's tactics, such as import quotas, might ultimately result in trade disputes with Japan and other nations that threaten not only the world's economic health but also world peace. Singapore's Lee

Kuan Yew worries, for example, that noisy U.S.-Japan trade disputes might lead to conflicts about other issues as well, and that ill will about automobiles, film, and airline treaties will begin to affect support for regional security pacts (APEC, 1996).

To prevent disputes that might link trade and economic issues with security, APEC began six years ago. One way to view APEC is as a way to avoid conflict between the United States and Asia Pacific countries, including Japan. APEC's potential for assisting commerce and for facilitating new trade and investment is immense. However, specific problems for each country involved have slowed the process of cooperation that seems so vital for peaceful trade and economic activity. The size of APEC's 18 members differs dramatically, prompting the smaller economies, particularly those of Southeast Asia, to voice frequent objections to possible domination by the United States, Japan, and China. The cost of failure is measurable in economic loss, and is in essence still closely tied to the overall security and stability of Asia (APEC, 1996).

A second multinational initiative designed to ensure peaceful and free trade among nations is the WTO, whose potential power is ostensibly similar to that of the United Nations (Fallows, 1995). Enforceability problems similar to those that face the United Nations prevent the WTO from acting effectively to enforce trade agreements among nations.

A recent article in the Economist points out that during the 1970s and 1980s, Japan repeatedly yielded to foreign-trade demands, whether for access to its domestic market or for "voluntary" restraints on its exports, explaining the miraculous profits of Japanese firms during these years of catch-up growth. But now that they are less flush, these firms are far less receptive to those demands. Instead, the Japanese are now counting on the protection of the WTO (Medina, 1996). However, this reliance may not be as secure as it seems on the surface. The theory is that this expert, neutral body can resolve economic disputes and make them go away. The reality, as opponents of the WTO have long pointed out, is that major countries, on major issues, will disregard the rulings of the WTO.

The Virtues of Maintaining Free Trade

Despite the worry about potential trade disputes and their potentially dangerous fallout, many are optimistic that the United States will maintain a free-trade policy with Japan simply because doing so would on the whole be in its best interests. The United States would lose important economic advantages if trade were impaired or reduced, and it stands to gain if trade with Japan can be brought closer to a balanced, reciprocal status. For instance, Japanese manufacturing facilities in the United States have created approximately 728,000 jobs for American workers. In recent years the U.S. share of Japan's foreign direct investment has been about 40% (Tyler, 1995).

The automobile industry provides the best single argument for maintaining a free-trade policy. Because export-oriented industries such as the automobile industry employ more people and pay higher wages than the declining industries that would be protected by tariffs, a policy of raising tariffs to restrict automobile imports would result in an overall net loss of jobs as well as a net loss in worker wages. Ironically, this has happened in Japan, where domestic regulation and agricultural protection have driven home prices so high that the Japanese have a standard of living half that of Americans. This is one reason most economists advocate free trade, even if our trading partners keep their markets closed (APEC, 1996).

Private Business Takes Charge
in Preventing Trade Conflict

Japan's emergence as the leading economic power in East Asia makes essential the restructuring of bilateral trade relations involving that country. But this issue has not been systematically and forcefully addressed yet by either Washington or Tokyo. Instead, private business leaders, especially those in the semiconductor industry, have been leading the way, by working cooperatively to establish fair-trade practices.

For example, the Semiconductor Arrangement was established as a temporary measure in the late 1980s to address specific complaints of the U.S. semiconductor industry with respect to alleged market access barriers and alleged injurious dumping. The Users' Committee of Foreign Semiconductors (UCOM), a group comprising companies that are consumers of semiconductor products, has dispatched 9 trade missions to date to seek foreign semiconductors, has received 7 missions from overseas, and has sponsored 25 symposiums and seminars. Because of such efforts, some groups believe that government intervention is no longer needed or desirable in the formerly volatile semiconductor area (Whitepaper, 1996).

Conclusion

As an effort toward bettering trade relations with Japan, President Clinton's lavish and deft homage to the Japanese during an April 1996 visit appear to have soothed animosities in Tokyo. So did a deliberate decision by Washington to downplay all trade conflict during the 1996 presidential election season (Hoagland, 1996). Nevertheless, summit meetings by the world leaders will no doubt remain largely photo-op sessions. However, when combined with multinational initiatives such as APEC and the WTO, but especially with cooperative efforts of the world's private business leaders, the potential exists to bring together the economies of Japan and the United States with liberalized trade and increasingly harmonized regulations on investment, production, and even distribution.

References

Anderson, S. "From crisis to information society in Japan." America Online reference (11-15-96). Available at ifrm.glocom.ac.doc/ a01.001/txt1.html.

Asia Pacific Economic Corporation summit: Avoiding trade wars in the pacific, leaders of pacific countries dread trade conflicts. America Online reference (11-15-96). Available at www.geocities.com/TimesSquare/1848/apec.html.

Balance of Trade with Japan (1996, September 30). America Online
reference (11-15-96). Available at nationaldebt.com/
balance_of_trade_with_japan_2.html.

Fallows, J. (1995, May 23). NPS commentary: "The truth about the
trade war." <u>Atlantic Monthly.</u> America Online reference (11-15-
96).

Hoagland, J. (1996, July 1). Foreigners for Clinton '96.
<u>Indianapolis Business Journal,</u> p. 7B.

Medina, J. (1996, April 13). "Friends in need." <u>Economist,</u> p. 17.

News and analysis on environmental issues and markets in the Asia
Pacific region. (1995, May). <u>Asia Environmental Review,</u> America
Online reference Available at www.asianenviro.com/aser595.txt.

Pyle, K. (1996, April 1). Uncertain future. <u>Harvard International
Review,</u> p. 36.

Schmidt, H. (1995, June 1). America is dead wrong. <u>New Perspectives
Quarterly,</u> p. 46.

Tyler, G. (1995, July 21). Clashing cultures . . . and doctoring
the economy. <u>Forward,</u> p. PG.

<u>Whitepaper.</u> (1996, November 15). Mission accomplished: Why there is
no need for a semiconductor arrangement with Japan." America
Online reference. Available at www.liaj.org/semiconductor/
whitepap.htm.

(A⁺) In this paper the student begins with a simple premise about a complex subject, communist economies, and then demonstrates a good understanding of the topic as he explains the premise. This device allows him to engage the reader in a complex topic and use a somewhat literary "twist" at the end that both reveals the meaning of the title and provides a memorable example of how skewed the system was. (MLA style)

THE ECONOMICS OF <u>Oz</u>: HOW COMMUNIST INEFFICIENCY WAS NOT JUST A CAUSE,
BUT ALSO A CONSEQUENCE OF SHORTAGES

Soon after the introduction of Soviet communism, everyone from students and professors to workers and housewives knew that the economic system was constructed of smoke and mirrors. But the Soviet political leaders could not admit error because economic theory was the justification for their power. If the economics were wrong, then the entire system was built on sand. As it turned out, it was built on quicksand, and the more the government struggled to force the economic system into its predetermined model, the worse things became. One illustration involves the effects of shortage.

The Fogged Looking Glass
of Heavy Capital Accumulation

Newsreel images of communist states in their early years showed Russian dams, East German smokestacks, Czech locomotives, and Polish shipyards; in other words, heavy industry with a capital "H." And these images were fairly accurate. But command economies misallocated resources because they lacked relative prices, which would reflect both scarcities of resources and consumer prefer- ences. Planners simply could not know, without market prices, what was efficient and what was not. Because of this, Ludwig von Mises (12) predicted a slide of socialist economies toward inefficiency, limping behind more efficient market economies. He was right, but it took decades until the truth of his prediction became obvious. The main reason was heavy capital accumulation, undertaken in every socialist country immediately after the revolution.

Communist leaders and planners did not care much about consumer satisfaction. They intuitively felt that industrialization, especially expansion of capital-intensive industries, was the way out of backwardness (Mises 17). They were able to carry out rapid industrialization by transferring resources from agriculture and consumer goods industries to capital goods industries. Command economies could do this more rapidly than markets. Rapid industrialization of agricultural countries excited admiration and gave rise to the illusion that socialism is capable of more rapid and stable economic growth than market economies. It took decades to see that this "growth" meant only the construction of monstrous and inefficient industrial plants that devoured industrial capital.

The second consequence of command economy was the decline of individual motivation. Hard work, entrepreneurship, and thriftiness are the ultimate source of the wealth of a nation (Mises 75). A society where everything belonged to everybody in fact meant that everything belonged to nobody. And nobody took care of buildings, plants, soil, forests, and so on. Capital stock and natural resources were continuously being eaten up without being replaced (Sik 192).

Robin Hood Redistributions

Command economy gave rise to redistribution processes called "Robin Hood redistributions." Whereas capital markets in market economies transfer funds from the hands of those who failed to those who are profitable, socialist bureaucrats made it quite the other way around. Money was "stolen from the rich" (profitable businesses) to support those that were failing, because failure could not be admitted and loss of jobs was not allowed.

Socialist bureaucrats <u>never</u> left enterprises alone with their profits to invest them how they wished. Somebody who has unlimited power wants to rule. Free-market economy is based on individual freedom, on free consumer choice of what to consume and free producers' choice of what to produce, with only prices accommodating their decisions. So much freedom cannot be tolerated by a totalitarian system. Communist party chiefs wanted to control enterprises--they wanted them to be dependent--which was probably more important than their efficiency. That's why central planning had to replace free markets, and that's why a new class--the economic bureaucracy--came into existence (Kornai 125).

Economic bureaucrats in the ministries decided who would get funds and how these funds would be used. These decisions were extremely important because they justified the existence of the central planners. The state simply could not let inefficient enterprises go bankrupt because it would show that socialism does not flourish as claimed in communist propaganda. Robin Hood redistributions occurred because communist leaders feared unemployment; unemployed workers are totally unacceptable in "a state of workers and farmers" (Pfska 50-51).

Under this system managers didn't bother very much about the working discipline of their employees or the efficiency of their enterprises. Everyone knew there was no danger of losing their jobs. Although, enterprises had to fulfill plans to be allowed to pay extra money as premiums to employees, this could be achieved more easily by lowering product quality of output than by economizing. No premium system ever induced efforts so much as market competition and threat of losing one's job.

Soft Planning and Suppressed Inflation

It was not the Central Planning Bureau that initially developed plans, but enterprise mangers. But it was in the manager's interest to set plans that they could fulfill easily. "Soft planning" (Sik 70-122) was a result. Enterprises also kept considerable hidden reserves that nobody else knew about. This was part of the "soft budgeting" of enterprises (Kornai 20-33). The combination caused one of the most striking phenomena of socialist economies: <u>suppressed inflation</u>, which created serious shortages in socialist countries. These were shortages of a special kind, created by a system where production has little if any relation to demand or purchasing power. People had money, but there was nothing in the shops anybody wanted. With nothing to buy and no fear of layoff, the workers had no incentive to work. A common description of the situation was, "We pretend to work, and you pretend to pay us" (Pfska 60).

The soft budgeting of state enterprises meant that they had easy access to funds either from the state budget or from the state credit system. This contrasts with the situation of a privately owned firm that can spend only what it earns. Of course a privately owned firm can borrow, too, but potential lenders (private banks, firms, or households) are under hard budget restraints as well. That's why private firms spend and invest much more carefully. They must be sure that their investment projects will pay themselves and bring at least the profit needed to cover interest payments (Robinson and Latwell 187).

State enterprises were in a different position. A paternalistic relationship developed, with enterprises like children under the safe wings of their father, the state. They knew the state wouldn't let them go bankrupt, reduce production, and dismiss their workers. Although the state didn't give them materials and workers directly (though some strategic raw materials were centrally rationed), it could give them money. And state enterprises were insatiable in asking for money. Each enterprise knew that if it didn't ask for (and receive) funds, other enterprises would. They were all very inventive in justifying their requirements, much more inventive than in saving materials and resisting wage increases (Kornai 105). State authorities were seldom successful in resisting requests from enterprises because they were afraid that if they lacked funds, they might not be able to fulfill their plans or would even have to do the unthinkable--reduce production and dismiss their workers. And nothing is more unsettling to communist rulers than unemployed workers. That's why the state was so generous to enterprises and provided funds for them. Why not? After all, the state printed the money.

The Proportion of Inefficient Enterprises Increases

At the beginning, when the economy was still functioning efficiently, the state began redistributing resources and funds to inefficient enterprises from efficient ones. But the proportion of inefficient enterprises increased and the state suddenly saw that there were not enough funds to save inefficient enterprises. So they printed additional money. "Cheap investment money" for enterprises encouraged them to invest, which soon led to overinvestment of the economy (Kornai 167). Their investment activity was enormous, but investment projects were only started, not finished. This was because investors soon found out that it was very difficult to find the necessary raw materials, spare parts, or skilled labor on the market for the project because all were in short supply. The state could print money, but not real resources. With prices fixed, strong sellers' markets soon prevailed. The consequences were alarming: Buyers spent huge amounts of time looking for suppliers and waiting for their orders to be executed. Time costs were enormous. Sellers stopped bothering about the quality of their products and services, and buyers lost the courage to complain of poor quality and long delivery times.

Corruption was visible everywhere, and a strange kind of "underground economy" appeared, with even enterprise buyers offering their outputs in exchange for required inputs instead of money. Inputs, not money, were scarce and valuable. Barter economy spread over money economy. Monetary managers were more involved in searching for necessary inputs than in innovations and quality of output. Strong sellers' markets produce little, if any, incentive for producers to improve and innovate. Why bother when they are sure to sell anything and sales revenue isn't the most important source of funds? (Robinson and Latwell 292) Therefore, an economy of shortage becomes inefficient; in communist economies, inefficiency is not just a cause, but also a <u>consequence</u> of shortage.

Conclusion

The problem of shortages, examined in this paper, is just one of many examples of an insane system that is difficult to grasp if one has not lived through it; but this brief introduction should provide a sense of the situation. Try to imagine generations of people whose only economic examples came from this system. No matter how much one reads or studies, much of one's understanding remains based on experience, even if one knows that the experience was based on lies. Kansas is a strange and exotic place when one has grown up and been educated in Oz. It will take some time for the citizens of the former Soviet block to adjust entirely to the ways of the West.

Works Cited

Kornai, J. <u>Economics of Shortage</u>. Amsterdam: North Holland Publishing Company, 1980.

Mises, L. <u>Human Action</u>. New Haven, CT: Yale UP, 1963.

Pfska, D. T. "Consumer Under Supply Constraint." <u>Ekonomicko-matematick Journal</u> 24.3: 40+.

Robinson, J., and Latwell, J. <u>An Introduction to Modern Economics</u>. London: MacGraw-Hill Book Co., UK, 1974.

Sik, O. <u>Humane Wirtschafts-Demokratie</u>. Hamburg: Albrecht Knaus Verlag, 1979.

10
FINE ARTS

It's All Kitsch Today

The Steadicam Revolution

The Architecture of Leon Baptista Alberti and of Philip Johnson

A+ This paper was written for an art history class. The assigment specified that the thesis should be a provocative one that might cause vigorous debate. Notice the student's use of definition, chronology, and evaluation in her approach to the topic, as well as her provocative concluding remarks. (MLA endnote style)

IT'S ALL KITSCH TODAY

The adage "art reflects culture" has perhaps never been truer than it is today. Our present culture revolves around electronic media, rapid communication, mass production, glitzy advertising and, yes, kitsch art. Visit any art gallery, open any fine art magazine, or read any newspaper, and one thing becomes clear: All art made today is kitsch.

What Is Kitsch?

The dictionary defines kitsch as art or artwork characterized by sentimental, often pretentious, bad taste; the aesthetic or mentality in which such art is conceived or appreciated; and culture or civilization in a degraded state of sentimentality and vulgarity.[1] Going back in time to 1860 Germany, we find that kitsch was a derivative of the German word kitschen, meaning "to cheapen," or "to make do," believed to have been used in Munich by dealers trading sentimental trinkets.

The artistic definition of kitsch comes from another source: Renowned art critic Clement Greenberg's far-reaching, ground-breaking 1939 essay "Avant-Garde and Kitsch." Greenberg described kitsch as follows:

> A new cultural phenomenon [that has] appeared in the industrial West: that thing to which the Germans give the wonderful name of Kitsch: popular, commercial art and literature with their chromeotypes, magazine covers, illustrations, ads, slick and pulp fiction, comics, Tin Pan Alley music, tap dancing, Hollywood movies, etc.[2]

Discussing the masses who migrated into the city as a result of the industrial revolution, and who had neither the formal education nor the inclination to appreciate and interpret avant-garde art, Greenberg denounced their demand for entertainment:

> Kitsch, using for raw material the debased and academicized simulacra of genuine culture, welcomes and cultivates this insensibility. It is the source of its profits. Kitsch is mechanical and operates by formulas. Kitsch is vicarious experience and faked sensations. Kitsch changes according to style, but remains always the same. Kitsch is the epitome of all that is spurious in the life of our times. Kitsch pretends to demand nothing of its customers except their money--not even their time.[3]

Greenberg alerted us to kitsch in 1939, at a time when it was only a small part of art and culture. Since then, however, its presence has completely infused the art world and our culture.

Kitsch Is Everywhere Today

Kitsch is everywhere today. As American art critic Harold Rosenberg put it:

> Kitsch is the daily art of our time, as the vase or the hymn was for earlier generations. . . . It has that arbitrariness and importance which works take on when they are no longer noticeable elements of the environment.[4]

Rosenberg was right; we are surrounded by kitsch. In fact, our culture has assimilated kitsch so thoroughly that we would truly miss it if it weren't there. Why? Media is at the center of our culture today, and kitsch pervades all forms of media: magazines, billboads, television, movies, radio, and now CD-ROMs. Even PBS, which boasts its arts programming, airs programs known for their appeal to the masses. Kitsch's newest and perhaps largest playground is, of course, the Internet. At the click of a mouse, we are instantly connected to an enormous volume of glossy, mechanical, and cleverly packaged information. What better example to illustrate Greenberg's commentary about kitsch's spurious nature?

Artists use mechanical means to accomplish their work; designers of expensive clothing use their names on garments to promote themselves; even the "native of China, . . . the American Indian, the Hindu, . . . have come to prefer . . . magazine covers, rotogravure sections and calendar girls."[5] Kitsch has even reached the highest office in America, according to <u>Los Angeles Times</u> syndicated columnist Suzanne Fields, who commented in a recent article that Bill Clinton is our first kitsch president.[6] We all see movies, watch television, read glossy magazines, and surf the Net. Kitsch is an integral part of our lives.

In sum, kitsch is no longer exclusive to Greenberg's peasants; it belongs to all of us. Today it seems that kitsch is everywhere, and that everything is kitsch. The natural question, then, is "How did this happen?"

How All Art Became Kitsch

Art is irrevocably tied to culture, and our culture has changed dramatically during the twentieth century. The kitsch of Greenberg's era was limited to slick advertising, magazine covers, and small sentimental trinkets. But kitsch as we know it today is born of mass consumption, rapid communication, immediacy, and vulgarity that characterizes our culture. Art has merely kept pace with the times.

Greenberg's essay suggested that kitsch was the opposite of avant-garde and high art and that generally the two were easily distinguishable.[7] As the years have passed, however, kitsch has become more insidious and prevalent, and altogether less distinguishable from high art. Objects that were once dismissed as kitschy, trashy, or sentimental are no longer so easily branded.

Several movements in art in the early and mid-twentieth century contributed to the structure and acceptance of kitsch. Particularly noteworthy is the Dadaist movement, followed by Surrealism. Artist Marcel Duchamp contributed by using household objects in his work, especially in his Ready-made series. Pop art, which originated in the 1950s, mastered the use of mass-produced consumer goods and advanced the proposition that mass culture was the culture shared by all, regardless of one's skills or training.

By the mid-1970s this pnenomenon had become extremely apparent. During the 1970s, art was made of anything, particularly those everyday, ready-made things that are ingredients of kitsch. Even the medium with which an artist worked was kitsch. Instead of fine and pure materials such as marble and bronze, sculptors were using manufactured materials such as plastic and styrofoam. As Brandon Taylor, author of <u>Avant-Garde and After: Rethinking Art Now</u>, noted about sculpture being created during that time:

> It was increasingly argued that no entity . . . could automatically be disqualified from, or fail to actually be, art: lines worn in the ground, empty boxes, filing cabinets, ordinary tables and chairs, even documentary photographs of physical activity elsewhere.[8]

Perhaps the archetypal examples of kitsch as art during the 1970s were the works of New York artist Jeff Koons, who used cheap, ready-made plastic ornaments in his work. Despite the controversy and contempt surrounding Koons's works, they have been displayed in a number of prestigious museums in the northeast, including the Museum of Contemporary Art in New York, the Boston Institute of Contemporary Arts, and the Museum of Modern Art in New York. Koons's work is outrageously kitschy. For example, the 1978 piece <u>Inflatable Flower and Bunny (Tall Yellow and Pink Bunny)</u> clearly illustrates Koons's use of ready-made consumer products--in this case a cheap plastic bunny and flower--to make art.

Since the 1970s, kitsch has continued to infiltrate the legitimate art world. One blatant example of kitsch as art involves the incorporation of visual advertisements into art. We're all familiar with Andy Worhol's repeated use of the Campbell's soup can in one of his most well-known works. But also consider, for example, a more recent work, <u>Le Art</u>, created by Ashley Bickerton in 1987. Bickerton used a multitude of corporate logos in a large, bright arrangement, setting off the composition with his own name in bold yellow lettering. This combination of logos, symbols of mass production, and mass consumer consumption is the epitome of kitsch. Its irony and cynicism are part of its appeal and are derived from its kitschy content. Perhaps the ultimate kitsch, however, was a particular work advertised in the October 1997 edition of <u>ARTnews</u>. On page 59 the reader sees <u>Looking for Mr. Goodbars, III</u>, a large panel in acrylic depicting a pile of Hershey miniature chocolate bars.[9]

Evaluating the Pervasiveness of Kitsch Today

The art we have described as kitsch may not necessarily be <u>bad</u> art just because it is kitsch. Art was originally a way of communicating by using methods that appealed to popular taste. The fact that all art today is kitsch suggests merely that it is made to appeal to the mainstream. Has art's purpose changed so much that it can no longer be for everyone? Probably not. If the majority like the work and think it good, then perhaps it is good.

Greenberg's observations lend support to the notion that kitsch can be good. Greenberg noted that the luxury trade has its own kitsch. He describes <u>The New Yorker</u> magazine as being "high-class kitsch," noting that "not every single item of kitsch is . . . worthless."[10] He went even further by admitting that there were "borderline cases," particularly in literature, that were hard to define as either avant-garde or kitsch.[11] In his interview "Fifty Years Later" he even admitted that "kitsch is better than it used to be. Movies have become much, much better over the last thirty years."[12]

The idea that art merely reflects culture and, therefore, kitsch is not bad per se finds further support in George Kubler's <u>The Shape of Time</u>:

The discoveries and inventions of the past three
centuries outnumber those of the entire previous history
of mankind. . . How does artistic invention differ from
useful invention? . . . Artistic inventions alter the
sensibility of mankind. They all emerge from and return
to human perception, unlike useful inventions, which are
keyed to the physical and biological environment. Useful
inventions alter mankind only indirectly by altering his
environment; aesthetic inventions enlarge human awareness
directly with new ways of experiencing the universe,
rather than with new objective interpretations.[13]

Kubler's observations give credence to the assertion that today's
art, while it may indeed be kitsch, serves to enlarge human awareness, and therefore can be positive. For example, Bickerton's
Le Art, if viewed as artistic invention, has helped alter our
sense of what art is, and to accept Le Art despite its kitschy
nature. At the same time, as an aesthetic invention Le Art
provides perspective on the world that is very different from the
perspective we would have had 50 years ago.

But other commentators disagree, claiming that the increasing
pervasiveness of kitsch portends a culture in decline. In an
article titled "The End of Aesthetic Experience," Richard
Shusterman, using critic Walter Benjamin's work as his standard,
addresses the idea that we are declining culturally:

The decline of aesthetic experience . . . also reflects
a growing preoccupation with the aesthetic thrust of
this century's artistic avant-garde, itself symptomatic
of much larger transformations in our basic sensibility
as we move increasingly from an experiential to an
informational culture.[14]

According to Shusterman, Benjamin sees that it is nearly
impossible to coherently experience culture and the aesthetic while
we are exposed to "the fragmentation and shocks of modern life,

the mechanical repetition of assembly-line labor, and the haphaz-ardly juxtaposed information and raw sensationalism of the mass media."[15] Schusterman adds:

> Modernization and technology . . . have eroded aesthetic experience's identification with the distinctive, tran-scendent autonomy of art. Such experience once had what Benjamin called aura, a cultic quality resulting from the artwork's uniqueness and distance from the ordinary world. But with the advent of mechanical modes of repro-duction like photography, art's distinctive aura has been lost, and aesthetic experience comes to pervade the everyday world of popular culture and even politics.[16]

Conclusion

What Greenberg defined as kitsch is clearly the art of our time. Just look around. But perhaps this begs the question. If it's all kitsch, is it still kitsch? Or does it become something more . . . something refined, higher, perhaps avant-garde? The answer depends on how narrowly, or narrow-<u>mindedly</u>, one defines art. Yes, it's kitsch, and no, it cannot be elevated to a higher, more refined plane. It is what it is.

Endnotes

[1] <u>The American Heritage Dictionary of the English Language</u>, 3rd ed. (Boston: Houghton Mifflin Company, 1992).

[2] Clement Greenberg, "Avant-Garde and Kitsch," <u>Art and Culture, Critical Essays</u> (Boston: Beacon Press, 1961) 9.

[3] Greenberg 9.

[4] Harold Rosenberg, <u>The Tradition of the New</u> (Chicago: University of Chicago Press, 1960) 268.

[5] Rosenberg 268.

[6] Suzanne Fields, "Bill Clinton: The First Kitsch President," <u>Los Angeles Times</u> (Oct. 3, 1996) B2

[7] Greenberg 10.

[8] Brandon Taylor, _Avant-Garde and After: Rethinking Art Now_ (New York: Harry N. Abrams, Inc. 1995) 83.

[9] _ARTnews_ (Oct. 1997) 59.

[10] Greenberg 11.

[11] Greenberg 12.

[12] Saul Ostrow, "Avant-Garde and Kitsch, Fifty Years Later: A Conversation with Clement Greenberg." _Arts Magazine_ (Dec. 1989) 57.

[13] George Kubler, _The Shape of Time: Remarks on the History of Things_ (New Haven, CT: Yale UP, 1962) 65.

[14] Richard Shusterman, "The End of Aesthetic Experience," _The Journal of Aesthetics and Art Criticism_ (Winter 1997) 29.

[15] Shusterman 29.

[16] Shusterman 29.

(A+) This paper discusses the development, implementation, and applications of the Steadicam—a revolutionary camera system used extensively today for movies and television. Notice that the paper proceeds logically from one topic to the next, beginning with a chronological approach, and then moving to a pro-and-con analysis. (MLA style)

THE STEADICAM REVOLUTION

Although it has been possible to hold a camera in hand since 1908, not until the invention of the Steadicam could operators in the film industry move around freely with the camera, following the action from one setup to another (Samuelson). The advent of the Steadicam brought a quiet revolution to the moviemaking industry. In fact, the Steadicam has radically changed not only the way scenes are shot but also how movies and television shows are conceived.

Development and Introduction of the Steadicam

Garrett Brown invented the Steadicam in a roundabout way. After working as an advertising copywriter and self-taught spot commercial filmmaker, he started his own production company with purchases from a bankrupt production house. One of those purchases was an 800-pound cast iron dolly. "It was a wonderfully smooth dolly, but it was a pain in the neck. It absolutely astounded me that you couldn't isolate the camera so you could walk 20 feet with it and not have it shake," he later told <u>American Cinematographer</u> (Samuelson). Brown conceived the Steadicam as a stunt camera for running shots over rough ground; he came up with several variations, based on drawings of older cameras and on his low-tech experiments, such as balancing brooms on his fingers. Jack Hauser, a retired Navy machinist, helped Brown fabricate parts, based on Brown's drawings. The prototype, complete with the fiber-optic viewfinder, came together in 1973 (Comer 73).

Brown first debuted his Steadicam in the 1975 film <u>Bound for Glory</u>, less than two years after he had developed his prototype.

By the time of the Steadicam's debut, every cinematographer and camera operator in the industry already knew of it and recognized its potential to drastically alter the way movies were made. Initially the Steadicam was used only occasionally, and primarily as Brown had conceived--for those shots up stairs and across rough ground. Within a short time, however, it had become an indispensable tool for cinematographers, proving itself a reliable shot-making tool for a variety of different shots.

Uses, Advantages, and Limitations
of the Steadicam

To fully understand the Steadicam's uses and limitations, it is necessary to first understand how the system operates. According to Steadicam operator Eric Swanson, an articulated arm stabilizes the camera so that one gets the steadiness of a camera on a dolly and the freedom of movement of a hand-held shot. To accomplish this, writes Swanson, the articulated arm isolates the camera from all but the operator's largest movements--specifically, by spreading the camera's mass, increasing resistance to rotation, and bringing the center of gravity outside of the camera to where the operator can manipulate it directly. Swanson notes, however, that although less effort is needed to tilt, pan, or roll the camera than to displace the entire camera, a small change in camera angle generally affects the image more than even a large change in camera position (Swanson).

The Steadicam is not limited to the jib and rails of a dolly and track, so it is particularly useful for shots in tight quarters where a dolly cannot fit, for shots over rough ground, and where a shot continues across a threshold or up steps. Experts advise using a Steadicam instead of a dolly setup in a variety of situations; for example, where the floor cannot bear the load of a dolly, or where the camera needs to be isolated from the movement of a car or other vehicle. The Steadicam provides other logistical advantages as well. Putting on the hardware takes little time, so scheduling emergencies can be accommodated. A director can adjust between takes without major restructuring, and the equipment can be mounted on a vehicle for fast-action car chases. Finally, because it requires only a single operator, it is far more cost-effective than a dolly setup.

Despite its versatility, the Steadicam is not without limitations and problems. Brown points out that effective use of the Steadicam requires more practice and more familiarity with the equipment than is required for a simple dolly shot. Also, as the Model 3A operation and maintenance manual points out, despite its versatility, the Steadicam should not be used while running or for quick pans, and it should not be mounted on a platform or carried on items that regularly crash (The Steadicam Stop). In addition, the Steadicam's unique ability to continually change path direction and angle can make arrangement of lighting for such shots extremely challenging. Finally, the Steadicam's considerable weight poses a physical risk to operators vulnerable to lower lumbar disc damage (Comer 74). Cinematographers and camera operators agree, however, that the Steadicam's advantages far outweigh its limitations and drawbacks.

Practical and Artistic Applications of the Steadicam

Bob Ulland, who was a Steadicam operator for the films <u>Days of Thunder</u>, <u>Parenthood</u>, and <u>No Way Out</u>, found the device most useful in the film <u>Fried Green Tomatoes</u>. A particular bee scene could not have been shot without the Steadicam. In the movie, Mary Stuart Masterson's character lets bees swarm over her beside a hive. Ulland recounts, "By using Steadicam, we were able to stay with her wherever she went and get out quickly if we had to" (Comer 74). A large portion of the film <u>A Time to Kill</u> was shot with the Steadicam. According to cinematographer Peter Menzies, Jr., for outdoor shots the Steadicam allowed him to take advantage of brief windows of good natural light by allowing him to set up and shoot a scene very quickly; this advantage also helped the actors, who didn't have to wait around long enough to forget their lines (Pfefferman 72).

The Steadicam is usful not just to solve logistical problems, but also for artistic impact. Cinematographers prefer the Steadicam, for example, where the quality of the move affects the emotional qualities of the scene, as well as where human, animal, or alien points of view are required. Jean-Pierre Guens asserted in Film Quarterly that the Steadicam has "significantly altered the visual look of films." How a movie camera moves during a scene has a marked impact on the emotion one feels when viewing the scene; and whether the camera rolls along a track or goes where only people can go is what mainly accounts for this impact.

The Steadicam also lets the audience feel what the actor is feeling, because the camera can bounce off the performer and then become his point of view in the one-shot. It makes viewers feel as if they're part of the story, not as if they're watching a fast-cutting, MTV type of film. "It's as if the camera almost becomes a third person, an observer of the many emotions in the movie" (Guens 8). Jeff Mart (Bugsy, Bonfire of the Vanities, and The Doors) adds that the Steadicam's slightly less-than-perfect motion simulates very closely what one experiences as a human being. Humans don't glide along smoothly like dollies; we bob and rock just a bit. The Steadicam mimics this imperfect motion, a motion that in many cases is exactly what the film's director is after (Comer 78).

The Steadicam is also becoming a staple in the television industry, not just for its logistical advantages, but also for its artistic impact. An article about its use in ER underscores how it is changing the face of television:

> The Steadicam is more than just a locomotive system; it is a storytelling tool. Up until ER, medical dramas traditionally relied on set pieces: pan somebody in, sit them in a chair, then cut to an over-the-shoulder shot. The Steadicam pulls the audience into the action--and the storyline--in a way that more conventional camera-work and editing doesn't. It calls for a whole new

approach to conceptualizing and staging scenes, a challenge which falls not only on the cameraman and director
but also the writer. (Oppenheimer 50)

Michael Wiese, video producer, looks upon the use of
Steadicam as an almost spiritual experience. In an article titled
"Zen and the Art of Steadicam JR" in <u>Videography</u> (Wiese), he
wrote:

> One technique I experimented with to capture impressions
> of Bali and Java was writing down daily incidents and
> moments <u>as if they were a dream</u>. The important thing was
> to take this attitude when recording these experiences.
> Often we may not understand the meaning and value until
> we've turned these gems over in our minds and let every
> facet reflect. . . . What if we let the Steadicam JR
> float into the experience guided by the unconscious and
> we just followed? Don't think, don't pre-edit, just be.
> A Zen approach to Steadicam taping. To shoot success-
> fully you have to "be." You have to let go into the
> experience. (43)

Concluding Comments

Not everyone in the film industry believes that the Steadicam
has contributed positively to the art of making films. For example,
Guens characterizes the Steadicam as a "bloodthirsty vampire . . .
The Steadicam sucks all life, all force, all guts out of the
image, leaving it but a pale ghost, a safe, sanitized version of
its former self--in short, the perfect tool for an oh-ever-so-cool
Hollywood" (Guens 16). Its detractors might very well resent that
the Steadicam has made filmmaking easier, quicker, and cheaper. In
any event, all cinematographers would agree that not since the
advent of 35-millimeter film has any film technology transformed
the industry to as great an extent as the Steadicam. Garrett's
invention, born of broomsticks atop fingertips, has made both the
moviemaking and moviegoing experiences more Zen-like.

Works Cited

Comer, Brooke. "Steadicam Hits Its Stride (Part 1)."
American Cinematographer Jun. 1992: 85+.

Comer, Brooke. "Steadicam Hits Its Stride (Part 4)."
American Cinematographer Feb. 1993: 73+.

Guens, Jean-Pierre. "Visuality and Power: The Work of the
Steadicam." Film Quarterly Winter 1993: 8+.

"Main Page." The Steadicam Stop on the Web. Available online at
home.sprynet.com/sprynet/joebrod, 7 May 1997.

Oppenheimer, Jean. "Diagnosing ER's Practical Approach."
American Cinematographer Oct. 1995: 46+.

Pfefferman, Naomi. "Taking the Stand." American Cinematographer
Aug. 1996: 72+.

Samuelson, D. "Equipment Inventions That Have Changed the Way Films
Are Made." American Cinematographer Aug. 1994: 76.

Swanson, Eric. "Steadicam Frequently Asked Questions." Available
online at www.kiwifilm.com/steadfaq.html, 7 May 1997.

Wiese, Michael. "Zen and the Art of Steadicam JR." Videography Dec.
1991: 41+.

This paper examines the ideas and buildings of two architects who lived four centuries apart. The student shows architectural styles that appear to be radically different to be grounded in similar aesthetic, if not philisophical, ideals. Notice that instead of jumping back and forth in time, which might confuse the reader, the student leads the reader from Alberti to Johnson, and then bridges the gap between them at the end of the paper. (APA style)

THE ARCHITECTURE OF LEON BAPTISTA ALBERTI AND OF PHILIP JOHNSON

Architects Leon Baptista Alberti (1403-1472) and Philip Johnson (1906-), although they lived more than four centuries apart, both designed buildings with the same basic principle in mind: harmony through unity and proportion. Alberti achieved a remarkable harmony in his works by combining Classical, Gothic, Romanesque, and Renaissance elements. Johnson created a kind of harmony with the simplistic application of geometric unity that defined the entirely new style of Modernism.

Alberti's Architectural Principles

During his lifetime, Alberti produced a large body of writings, one of which was a treatise on architecture titled <u>De architectura</u>. A collection of ten books completed in 1452, it marked the culmination of an attempt to relate art to politics and morality. Central to Alberti's philosophy is the concept of "natural beauty," the beauty in architecture defined by the proportion to be found in the organic nature of an edifice (Borsi, 1977). In the spirit of the Renaissance, Alberti's theories on architecture centered on the idea of art as an imitation of nature. For Alberti, this imitation involves three distinct aspects: <u>numerus</u> (number: nothing can be taken away), <u>collocation</u> (arrangement: nothing can be differently placed), and <u>finitio</u> (measure: nothing can be decreased or enlarged). According to Alberti, agreement among the parts of the building in each of these aspects would lead the way to the <u>telos</u> of architectural work: harmony. (Gadol, 1969).

In terms of the <u>numerus,</u> Alberti adhered to medieval conceptions of symbolization (Gadol, 1969). He drew analogies between architectural attributes and those of living things in nature. The supports in ancient buildings were even in number, just as were the legs of humans and animals. Apertures, in contrast, were generally odd in number, just as the mouth is a singular orifice. Remarkably, however, Alberti's writings provide no directions for applying his numerical symbolism; nor did he relate <u>numerus</u> to any of his own works of architecture. As Joan Gadol (1969) points out:

> It is almost as if he did not really expect his remarks
> on number to be carried out. He set down everything he
> had learned about the evaluation of the various numbers in
> antiquity, but in a way that would baffle anyone looking
> for specific directives.

Alberti developed his idea of <u>finitio</u> (measure) even more fully than <u>numerus</u> and <u>collation</u>. According to Alberti, a building's measure has to do with "the correspondence of those several lines whereby proportions are measured, namely the length, the breadth, and the width" (Gadol, 1969). In Alberti's words, the proportions of the architectural work were to be determined "'not confusedly and indistinctly, but in a manner as to be constantly and in every way conformable to Harmony'" (Gadol, 1969). Hence, the proportional aspects of a building were to be analogous to nature.

Alberti's ideas about proportion ultimately led him to the Pythagorean musical ratios. Pythagorus asserted that nature will act in constant proportion to all her operations. Thus, whether it be sight, hearing, or any of the other senses, the same beauty is conveyed to the mind. Alberti surmised that the same ratios that produce musical harmony could also create visual harmony. Just as the interval between harmonic tones can be measured spatially, in terms of the length of the strings that produce them, harmonic ratios should be inherent in the dimensions of architectural design (Gadol, 1969). The result of Alberti's applying Pythagorean ratios to architectural design was a confusing and complex mathematical system of sequences and progressions. Under this system, ratios are used to bring about proportional harmony so that the different parts of the building have "that proportion among themselves so that they may appear to be an entire and perfect body, and not disjointed and unfinished members" (Gadol, 1969).

Alberti's Principles as Embodied in His Santa Maria Novella Facade

One of the best examples of Alberti's attempt to apply his system of ratios is his second church facade, Santa Maria Novella in Florence. Designed in the late 1450s, it completed the exterior of a medieval church and has been described as a "great Renaissance exponent of classical eurhythmia" (Gadol, 1969). Alberti's Pythagorus is evident in its dimensions, which are bound together by the 1:2 ratio of the musical octave. In addition, the marble panels, which create a mosaic-like effect of discrete color patches, contribute to a sense of rhythmic and geometric unity (Gadol).

Interestingly, Alberti's facade of Maria Novella includes characteristics of three different architectural styles: Romanesque, Gothic, and Classical. Prominent Gothic elements include six pointed arches over the marble coffins placed just above the base of the facade, two small fourteenth-century doors under their pointed arches, and a great circular window. At the same time, Alberti used Romanesque marble encrustation, but used the entrance to the Pantheon as his model for the fine classical doorway. He set off the areas of the main story with giant Corinthian columns.

Hence, if we attempt to identify an architectural "meaning" in Maria Novella, we are led to Alberti's principle of harmony and the arrangement of parts. The seemingly jarring elements of three different styles--Romanesque, Gothic, and Classical--are combined to produce a kind of unity and, ultimately, harmony. The proportional rhythm of the entire facade comes to life, mainly through his ingenious segmenting of the facade into different sections and then their rhythmic relations to each other. As such, it becomes an architectural expression of the Renaissance notion of nature's congruity.

Johnson and the Modernists

Architect Philip Johnson is credited with bringing a new International Style, developed by Europe's Modernist school of architecture, to America in 1932 by serving as co-curator for the ground-breaking International Style show at New York's Museum of Modern Art. During the show's opening ceremonies, one of Johnson's close colleagues, Alfred Barr, described on Johnson's behalf two main principles of the emerging Modernist style. One principle involved the concept of volume: The modern architect thinks in terms of a space enclosed by planes or surfaces, not in terms of mass and solidity (Shulze, 1994). A second principle involved the notions of positive and negative:

> Positive quality of beauty in the International Style depends
> upon technically perfect use of materials . . . upon the
> fineness of proportions in units . . . and in the relation-
> ships between these units and the whole design. The negative
> or obverse aspect of this principle is the elimination of any
> kind of ornament or artificial pattern. (Shulze, 1994)

These characteristics, especially the absence of any external ornamentation, are evident in Johnson's famous Glass House (1949) in New Canaan. The simplicity is abundantly apparent in the four walls of floor-to-ceiling glass surrounding a single room. Johnson was taken by the sensation of existing in an environment separated from nature by a transparent membrane. Thus not only did he find beauty in the simplistic geometry of the Glass House, but also in the close relationship with nature that the occupant could experience. At the center of his vision was the idea first espoused by the French neoclassicist Claude Ledoux and promulgated by the architect Le Corbusier. Franz Shulze (1994) described this idea:

"Clarity was all, volume was all, independence was all, anything less pure was a fudge."

Modernism was criticized by many architects, including Frank Lloyd Wright, as well as by influential architectural critics such as Robert Venturi, for its cold and seemingly inhuman aspects; its rectangular glass structures looked no different from city to city (Norberg-Shulz, 1988). Venturi's book <u>Complexity and Contradiction in Architecture</u> very nearly sounded the death knell for Modernism. Venturi pointed out that he liked "complexity and contradiction in architecture," and he criticized the Modernists for the "easy unity of exclusion" that they employed. He felt that the orthodox Modernists had recognized "complexity insufficiently or inconsistently" (Norberg-Shulz, 1988). It seemed, then, that Johnson and the Modernists did not tackle what Alberti had and what Venturi advocated: the difficulty of inclusion. In the Maria Novella, Alberti united three distinct styles in a harmonious facade. Perhaps Johnson had avoided the challenge, and had taken the easy road to unity--via the Modernist style.

Johnson's Postmodernism: Recalling Alberti

Johnson rose up against his detractors by developing a new Modernist genre, referred to as Postmodernism. The AT&T Corporate Headquarters in New York, perhaps Johnson's greatest work, was a landmark of the Postmodern style. At ground level and the top of the building, Johnson imposed design elements that gave the building a unique image. The elements were in the historical forms that the Postmodernists claimed communicated more to an urban audience than the abstracted lineaments of the International Style. The entrance has a 116-foot-high round arch surrounded on each side by three shorter rectangular openings that create the effect of an arcade. Some critics associated the design with Alberti's Church of Santa Andrea in Mantua (Shulze, 1994). The pediment crowning the building was conceived because, in Johnson's words, "a pediment, by raising the middle higher, was the only way to unify the verticality and the symmetry of the facade . . . we were classicizing" (Shulze, 1994).

The emphasis on proportion, and the geometric relationship of the parts to the whole, trademarks of Johnson's Postmodernism, were also Alberti's main concerns four centuries earlier. Alberti, although certainly employing ornamental design, felt that the inherent beauty of a building was found in the base structure, in the absence of ornamental design (Borsi, 1977). Four centuries later, Johnson brought the idea of beauty in geometric harmony down to its simplest form.

Conclusion

Any attempt to define the essence of architecture for Alberti and for Johnson is bound to be easier for the former. Alberti left a whole body of literature on architecture and what he hoped to achieve in the design of his buildings. In contrast, the Modernist movement lacks meaning as a whole; Johnson was never clear in what he wanted to achieve. Indeed, the meaning of Modernist art in architecture is seemingly lost in the sheer monotony of the cityscape, which seems to concern itself with nothing beyond the demands of practical, social, and economical conditions. (Norberg-Shulz, 1988)

Yet Johnson's Postmodern style did demonstrate that he could achieve unity through the use of both modern and classical elements. Unity, then, was the essence of architecture for both Alberti and Johnson. The idea of achieving perfect proportion and symmetry was important to both of them. Alberti found harmony through the expression of perfection of the natural world, and Johnson found architectural harmony through simple geometric form.

References

Borsi, F. (1977). <u>Leon Batista Alberti.</u> New York: Rizzoli
    International.

Gadol, J. (1969). <u>Leon Battista Alberti: Universal man of the early
    Rennaisance.</u> Chicago: University of Chicago Press.

Norberg-Shulze, C. (1988). <u>Architecture: Meaning and place.</u>
    New York: Rizzoli International.

Shulze, F. (1994). <u>Philip Johnson.</u> New York: Knopf.

11

LAW AND SOCIETY

Should the Death Penalty Be Abolished?

Alternative Dispute Resolution (ADR): Its Past, Present, and Future as a Mechanism for Resolving Employment Disputes

Euthanasia and the Case of *Rodriguez v. British Columbia*

This paper examines several arguments for and against capital punishment (the death penalty). Notice that the student takes a firm position against the death penalty, but argues for her position appropriately—by appealing to the reader's intellect. Also notice the use of questions as section headings, a perfectly appropriate technique used effectively here to stimulate interest and spur on the reader. (MLA style, with *Works Consulted* list)

SHOULD THE DEATH PENALTY BE ABOLISHED?

In 1976 the U.S. Supreme Court ruled that the death penalty, or <u>capital punishment</u>, does not violate the U.S. Constitution. The court held that although certain state laws relating to the administration and regulation of capital punishment might be in violation of the constitutional prohibition against "cruel and unusual punishment" or other provisions of the Bill of Rights, the death penalty per se is not unconstitutional. Six months later, in January 1977, the first execution under the new death penalty law took place in the United States (Bedam 7), ending the moratorium on capital punishment that began in 1967. Since that first execution, 220 death sentences have been carried out in a dozen states ("Justice . . . " 24).

By no means is there consensus today about capital punishment. According to a recent Gallup poll, just over 60% of U.S. citizens favor capital punishment. The justification cited most often among advocates was the notion of retribution; that is, the death penalty amounts to payment by the wrongdoer of his or her crime against society (Radelet 12). Among other reasons cited in support of the death penalty are that it serves as an effective deterrent against crime, it is more economical than life imprisonment, and it satisfies a moral obligation to the victim's families (Bedam 9). In response to the same poll, those opposed to capital punishment cited a variety of reasons: It is morally wrong--humans should not play God by taking the life of other humans; it can result in the execution of wrongly convicted, innocent people; it does not deter crime; it is unfairly applied; and rehabilitation is a better alternative (Bedam 9).

Scholars, philosophers, politicians, and criminologists disagree among themselves as well, and for the same reasons as the ones cited in the Gallup poll. Among academicians, death penalty supporters are referred to as <u>retentionists</u>, and their opponents are referred to as <u>abolitionists</u>. The following discussion examines various points of dispute between the two camps, and argues that the abolitionists have the stronger argument on all points. The two groups also disagree on the constitutionality of capital punishment: a threshold issue that must be addressed first.

Is Capital Punishment Constitutional?

The Eighth Amendment of the U.S. Constitution prohibits "cruel and unusual punishments." Retentionists interpret <u>cruel</u> as disproportionate and irrational, and <u>unusual</u> as rare or infrequent. The retentionists' position is that capital punishment is neither disproportionate nor irrational, and that whether such punishment is infrequent is irrelevent. They also remind us that after a moratorium of 10 years, the Supreme Court ruled again in 1976 that capital punishment was not in violation of the Eighth Amendment.

Abolitionists disagree, claiming that capital punishment violates the Eight Amendment. Their argument is twofold. First, they assert that the Supreme Court should and does continually reinterpret the Constitution in light of an ever-changing social climate (Death Row 52). This argument is convincing in light of the fact that the court has indeed changed its position (capital punishment was unconstitutional between 1967 and 1976). Second, given that the right to life and the right not to be subjected to cruel, inhuman, or degrading treatment or punishment are now enshrined in the Universal Declaration of Human Rights and other international human rights declarations ("Critics . . ." 25), the current social climate demands that the Supreme Court return to the

position it held between 1967 and 1976: that the death penalty is
unconstitutional.

Is Capital Punishment an Effective Deterrent?

Supporters of the death penalty claim that punishment,
including capital punishment, helps deter crime by intimidating
potential offenders. In theory, this argument seems plausible. But
its empirical support is meager, at best. In one and only one
study, conducted in the 1940s by criminologist Isaac Enrich, the
death penalty was shown to save innocent lives--7 to 10 per year,
according to Enrich's study (Goldberg 76). Virtually all criminologists and social scientists agree that Enrich's study is
meaningless, and that a sound methodology for isolating the death
penalty's deterrent effect has yet to be developed (Radelet 6).

Bolstering the abolitionists' position are statistics
suggesting that the rate of homicide actually increases after
executions. For example, during the summer of 1987, eight convicted
felons were executed in Louisiana; during that summer the murder
rate in New Orleans rose by nearly 17%, to the highest level in
years (Masour 23). Even more convincing is the fact that the
overall crime rate in states that do not impose the death penalty
is lower than in those that do.

Is Capital Punishment Inherently Immoral?

Retentionists and abolitionists also attempt to support their
respective positions on moral, ethical, and religious grounds. Some
retentionists argue that punishment, including capital punishment,
is a "categorical imperative and need not be justified in any
moral, ethic or religious code" (Goldberg 149). In fact, retentionists remind their opponents that among Western democracies, capital
punishment has traditionally been considered an axiomatic, even if
tacit, moral obligation of the judicial system to the society
(Goldberg 121). Many retentionists also claim support in the many
religious traditions that ostensibly sanction the death penalty
(Masour 57).

Abolitionists respond that however heinous the crime, deliberately executing a defenseless convict is just as bad, and perhaps even worse. Their position is that "legal executions violate an inalienable human right, even of murderers, to live, and is therefore inhumane" ("Critics . . ." 25). For abolitionists, capital punishment is judicial murder, which by mirroring the brutality of the crime degrades and cheapens human life ("Critics . . ." 25). Abolitionists recognize the logical yet patently absurd extension of the retentionists' argument: "If we kill murderers, [then] rapists should be raped and burglars should be burglarized" (Goldberg 27). Abolitionists further point out that "the state is a teacher and when it kills, it teaches vengeance and hatred" (Wright 17); thus, constitutional murder carries dreadful consequences for all civilizations and for the human race.

Abolitionists also have a response to the retentionists' argument from religious tradition. They point out that all doctrines of religion, ethics, and morality are clear that "human beings must not harm one another, nor should they do to others what they would not have others do to them" ("Give mercy . . ." 18). In this light, the eye-for-an-eye argument truly loses its teeth.

What About the Families of the Victim and the Executed Felon?

What about the impact of the death penalty on the families of both the victim and the convicted felon? Retentionists claim that execution gives comfort and support to the families of the homicide victims (Goldberg 91), helping them to cope with their shock and grief. In his book Rites of Execution, Louis Masour provides an illustration, describing the case of a daughter whose parents were brutally killed: "She cries every day. She doesn't sleep through a single night and thinks a part of her died too. She reports she doesn't find much joy in anything" (Masour 144).

But what about the pain and grief that the families of the condemned prisoner experience? The abolitionists' view is that when we punish the convicted felon, we are not really punishing him because he is now dead and does not feel the brunt; instead, we are punishing the people who loved him. Moreover, the pain that the prisoner's family experiences should not be underestimated, especially as they anticipate the impending execution. "They feel as helpless bystanders in a slow dying process that they know cannot be stopped" (Masour 142).

The prisoner's family must also endure the loneliness that results from knowing that their loved one's death is being celebrated almost universally (Masour 142), as justice well served. As philosopher H.L. Hart wrote, "to take any life is to impose suffering not only on the criminal but also on many others. That is an evil to be justified only if some good end is achieved thereby that could not be achieved by any other means" (Bedam 3).

Is Capital Punishment Sensible from an Economic Standpoint?

Yet another retentionist argument is that the costs of imprisoning an inmate for life outweigh those of executing the inmate. But this claim is not borne out by the evidence. In fact, each execution costs from $2 million to $3 million, several times more than life imprisonment (Goldberg 12). Retentionists retort that costs could be reduced by the proper application of the law and that the appeals of "lifers" are in some cases just as costly in the end as the appeals of felons awaiting execution (Goldberg 73).

But the abolitionists' position here is far more compelling. First, they point out that the additional money the government spends to execute prisoners could more effectively be used to provide assistance for the victim's family or for inner-city anticrime programs. Abolitionists further point out that the United States and South Africa are the only nations that not only lawfully permit death sentences but also insist on long, painful, profitless delays associated with the legal process; in both countries, the end result is a distortion of the entire criminal justice system (Goldberg 73). The high cost of a death sentence is not inherent in the penalty itself, say the abolitionists, but rather is imposed by judges who tend to sabotage capital punishment (Bedam 31).

Does a Death Sentence Affect a
Prisoner's Access to the Legal System?

The Fourteenth Amendment of the Constitution guarantees due process to all citizens, which includes equal access to the legal system. Retentionists claim that all death row inmates are afforded equal access, regardless of their economic status; they have the same right to the appointment of a public defender on their behalf, free of charge.

But abolitionists strongly disagree. As the number of condemned prisoners in the United States grows, so does the problem of finding competent attorneys to handle death penalty cases as the execution date draws near; very few lawyers are willing to handle capital cases at this late stage (Dicks 27). As a result, a decent defense is available to only a small, financially privileged minority of death row inmates. Economic disadvantage at the trial stage also nullifies any Constitutional guarantee of equal access, claim the abolitionists. Criminal defendants are sentenced to death not because they have been found uncontrollably violent but because they are poor; according to one abolitionist, "you won't find a wealthy person on death row" (27).

Does Capital Punishment Undermine
Our Presumption of Innocence?

A final point of contention involves the presumption of innocence afforded by the U.S. criminal justice system, to help ensure that innocent people are not wrongly punished. Retentionists admit that the occasional execution of an innocent inmate is inevitable (Goldberg 63), but that the benefits of the death penalty outweigh this drawback. Abolitionists disagree, asserting that the risk of killing an innocent person is intolerable. According to one report, at least 350 people have been wrongfully sentenced to death in the United States (Radelet 17). This number is intolerably large for the abolitionists, who point out that England abolished capital punishment indefinitely after <u>one</u> executed convict was proven innocent (Goldberg 46). The English understand better than we in the United States that a pardon is of no value to a dead person (Goldberg 46).

Conclusion

In the final analysis, the abolitionists seem to make a stronger case. There is virtually no evidence that capital punishment deters crime; it violates the morals and tenets of all religions; it breeds violence; it results in suffering for the inmate's innocent family; it is expensive for taxpayers; and it discriminates against those without money or power. Moreover, its constitutionality is dubious. But even though the case against capital punishment seems convincing, the issue is so controversial on so many fronts that it is unlikely to be settled soon, if ever.

Works Consulted

Bedam, Hugo Adam. <u>Death Is Different</u> Boston: Northeastern UP, 1987.

"Critics Charge Death Penalty Unfair." <u>Human Rights</u> Spring 1993: 25.

"Dead Man Walking." <u>The New York Times</u> 26 May 1993: A:21.

<u>Death Row</u>. North Carolina: McFarland and Co., Inc., 1990.

Dicks, Shirley. <u>Congregation of the Condemned</u> Buffalo, NY: Prometheus Books, 1991.

"Give Mercy a Day in Court." <u>The New York Times</u> 4 May 1993: A:18,24.

Goldberg, Arthur. <u>The Death Penalty: A Pro-Con Debate</u> New York: Plenum Press, 1983.

Hulpern, Sue. "Sister Sympathy." <u>The New York Times</u> 9 May 1993: D:82.

"Justice Revised." <u>Time</u> 15 Mar. 1993: 16+.

Masour, Louis P. <u>Rites of Execution</u> New York: Oxford UP, 1989.

Radelet, Michael. <u>Facing the Death Penalty</u> Philadelphia: Temple UP, 1989.

Wright Jr., Ellis B. "Opposed." <u>The Christian Century</u> 16 Jun. 1993: 17.

This ambitious paper examines mediation and arbitration as alternatives to civil litigation. The paper's primary focus is on how alternative dispute resolution (ADR) is being used to resolve employer–employee disputes. Notice the use of MLA-style endnotes, an acceptable alternative to the parenthetical (in-text) citation form discussed in Chapter 3. (MLA endnote style)

ALTERNATIVE DISPUTE RESOLUTION (ADR): ITS PAST, PRESENT, AND FUTURE AS A MECHANISM FOR RESOLVING EMPLOYMENT DISPUTES

It is obvious to anyone who has been to civil court lately that there are far more cases than the system can handle. The dockets for civil cases are overflowing. According to the Committee on Long Range Planning of the Judicial Conference of the United States, there are currently about a quarter million civil cases on the docket across the country, and those figures are expected to quadruple in the next 25 years.[1] Further, these numbers refer only to civil cases. Employers have fared particularly badly with the American judicial system over the past 20 years. Studies have shown that litigation against employers has increased 400% in the past two decades, with an average jury verdict in a wrongful-termination case running between $250,000 and $500,000.[2] The time is ripe for some means of settling disputes other than a jury trial.

Increasingly, that means is ADR, or alternative dispute reso-lution, originally formulated for use in the insurance industry and in union negotiations. In ADR, an impartial mediator meets with all parties in a conflict to work out a mutually agreeable solution. Several techniques may be used, all of which stress the advantages of using informal problem solving and negotiation strategies to arrive at amicable solutions in cases where the disputing parties have an ongoing relationship that may be worth saving.

Arbitration Versus Mediation

The two most important ADR forms are arbitration and media-tion. In arbitration, the two parties involved in the dispute pick a neutral third party, who listens to both sides and then makes a final and binding decision. Witnesses are generally called, and a stenographer may transcribe the proceedings. Arbitration is technically an adjudicatory process, but it typically takes place outside the courtroom and is not necessarily subject to courtroom procedures. Agreements forged through arbitration are legally binding and enforceable.

Mediation may look similar, but its differences are important. In arbitration, the neutral third party listens to both sides and then makes a binding determination he or she feels is in the best interests of both. In this respect, the arbitrator is more like a judge. In mediation, however, the neutral third party--the mediator--is more like a peacemaker or diplomat; he or she works with both parties to hammer out an agreement acceptable to everyone.[3] Should one party later break the agreement, a court order can easily be obtained to enforce it.[4]

The Growing Popularity of ADR

Although it has its critics, ADR has increasingly been hailed by court judges and attorneys around the country as an important alternative to litigation. In fact, according to Harris Bock, an ADR advocate and practitioner with the Philadelphia firm Bock and Finkleman, both Florida and Texas have now passed laws making pretrial ADR mandatory in all cases.[5]

How popular is ADR at present? A study released by the General Accounting Office focusing on employment discrimination claims reports that almost all employers with 100 or more employees have used one or more ADR approaches. Admittedly, some of these approaches may amount to no more than informal problem-solving sessions, but it is significant that three-quarters or more of the companies surveyed reported using these techniques. Ten percent of the surveyed employers had a formal arbitration policy in place, and 40% used trained internal mediators to help resolve employer-employee differences. Interest in ADR is clearly growing.[6]

Howard Venzie, partner with Venzie Phillips and Warshawer of Philadelphia and chair of the ADR Committee for the Pennsylvania Bar Association, is committed to the propagation of ADR:

> I believe ADR has grown as dramatically as it has
> because of the failure of our court system to adequately
> handle the cases presented before it. In the early '80s,
> [it] was relatively new, but now it's in vogue. . . .
> It's added to a lawyer's arsenal of techniques used to
> resolve disputes.[7]

The Center for Public Resources, a New York nonprofit organization that promotes ADR, has persuaded more than 1,000 law firms
and more than 600 corporations across the country to sign a policy
statement ensuring that their staff knows about ADR techniques and
will discuss their application in appropriate cases.[8]

Advantages of ADR over Litigation

ADR has a number of advantages over litigation. Because the
case is not waiting for a slot on the court docket, it is apt to
be scheduled more quickly. In addition, because mediated cases
don't become bogged down with depositions, fewer billable hours
result. Further, ADR cases are typically resolved more quickly--
usually in a matter of days. Because no jury is involved, ADR
cases are not usually appealed. (In some cases, they cannot be.)
The results of cases settled using ADR techniques are confidential,
and not a matter of public record; therefore, they preserve the
parties' privacy. ADR is cost-effective, too; fees, based on the
dollar amount of claims and disputes, range from $500 to $7,000.[9]

Finally, the unpredictable, and sometimes bizarre, rulings
that can result from the whims of a jury are less likely to occur
with an arbitrator, who has been trained in dispute mediation.
"With litigation, you're injecting risk into the process by asking
a jury with no expertise in a subject to offer a judgment over
what are often highly technical issues," Bock said, adding:

> You go into [ADR] with a much different mind-set. You're
> much more open. The sides are trying to strike a deal
> rather than play hide the ball with each other. . . .
> That's what industries like about ADR. It gives them a

chance to talk, think, and focus on the issues, not each other. The whole idea is to make a deal, whether you slug it out now or $300,000 later.[10]

ADR Providers

As ADR becomes more popular, ADR providers, such as the New York-based American Arbitration Association (AAA), have become more high profile. Although it has been in existence for 70 years, the AAA has seen its influence soar during the past decade, and the AAA now maintains 37 offices nationwide and cooperative agreements in 51 other countries. Kenneth Egget, vice president of the AAA's Philadelphia office, explains:

> We don't decide cases. Rather, we provide a forum for the hearing of disputes, using tested rules and procedures that have broad acceptance, and a roster of nearly 15,000 impartial experts . . . recognized for their expertise in their fields, their integrity, and their dispute resolution skills, to hear and resolve cases. Anyone who has a dispute can make use of our services.[11]

In 1991 the AAA handled a mere 7,161 cases.[12] At the end of 1995, Egget projected that AAA arbitrators and mediators would handle 66,000 cases in 1996 (whether they did so has not yet been published)--with only two more offices than they had had five years previously.

There is no formal accreditation program for arbitrators and mediators, but most are retired judges, attorneys, and business professionals with experience in the industry in which they are resolving the dispute. Still, Venzie says, there not enough qualified mediators with substantive knowledge and interpersonal skills to fill the demand.[13]

ADR Clients

The demand for, and use of, ADR cuts across a wide range of industries. Insurance industries have used arbitration techniques for years, for matters such as product and professional liability, reinsurance, and no-fault and uninsured motorist claims. ADR is now becoming more common in the securities industry, where customer-broker disputes over investments are commonly resolved by using these techniques. The construction industry, which is heavily unionized, also uses ADR techniques to resolve labor conflicts. Arbitration clauses are often incorporated into contracts with foreign industries to avoid the confusion and delay of litigation in foreign courts. And across the board, conflicts involving breach of contract, discrimination, sexual harassment, and wrongful termination are increasingly being resolved by using ADR.

ADR as a Means of Resolving Employment Disputes

Alternative forms of dispute resolution are particularly important in the corporate world, and in fact ADR programs have been written into company policy, often in a stepped pattern, to catch and prevent incipient problems early in the process--before the employee becomes really angry.[14] A common pattern involves at least one, often facilitated, interaction between the aggrieved employee and a supervisor, and then a second review with a manager further up the hierarchy. The last step is generally some form of binding arbitration.

The presence of such a program gives employees the feeling that the firm is willing to listen to their problems and is concerned about their feelings, thereby improving company morale. In many cases, just having a supervisor able and willing to listen to the employee's complaint, and make a serious attempt to resolve it, is sufficient to prevent the need for any further meetings or arbitration processes. In the rare cases in which such cases end up in litigation, the documented ADR proceedings provide the employer with a record of the entire situation that would not have been available without such a background.

In addition, the use of such a multistepped process screens out claimants with frivolous or minor complaints; they become bored, disinterested, or intimidated by the process, and drop the claim along the way. Occasionally, lawyers may decline to represent less-than-solid cases they know will end up in arbitration instead of litigation, particularly when the success of those cases would prevail largely on a jury's sympathy. There is, of course, no jury in an arbitrated case.[15]

In many cases, this multistepped process works to an employer's advantage rather than the employee's. Many employers are seeing the advantages of writing an official, mandatory-arbitration clause into their employee handbooks and employment contracts. The reason for doing so right away rather than waiting for a dispute to arise is obvious. A newly hired employee, or a prospective employee close to clinching the deal, is in a psychologically vulnerable position and is willing to accept clauses in his contract that could potentially bargain away rights he or she might never use in exchange for the offer of employment. Later, however, after a dispute with the employer has arisen, the employee is less likely to agree to procedures (such as mandatory arbitration) that the employee might perceive as taking away his or her leverage created by the costs and publicity of litigation and access to a trial by jury. From the employer's point of view, then, an ADR program has the best chance of success if implemented before there is any argument about it.

The U.S. Supreme Court's 1991 ruling in <u>Gilmer v. Interstate Johnson Lane Corporation</u> accelerated the practice of requiring employees to sign away litigation rights by agreeing to arbitrate all claims. This particular case involved an employee, Gilmer, who had signed such a waiver, and then was dismissed at the age of 62. Gilmer attempted to sue his former employer under the Age Discrimination in Employment Act, but the court upheld the company's arbitration ruling.[16]

Does this imply that ADR in a corporate setting inherently favors the employer rather than the employee? Some critics feel that it does. For instance, James Wallihan, a professor of political science at Indiana University-Purdue University Indianapolis, feels that although ADR techniques work extremely well in a unionized setting--where many of these approaches evolved in the first place, from the practices of collective bargaining--they do not translate well to the non-union setting. He studied the use of "stand-alone" arbitration--arbitration severed from any system of collective bargaining and/or early grievance representation--in cases involving discharged workers. His findings bear closer inspection.

ADR and Collective Bargaining (Labor Unions)

The past 20 years have seen a continual decline in union membership. This parallels a corresponding decrease in legislative and judicial attention paid to <u>labor</u> (union) law, and an increasing amount to <u>employment</u> law, which is primarily concerned with indi-vidual workers.[17] The movement toward ADR can be seen as reflecting a "translation" from the techniques of labor negotiation to employ-ment law--from the union shop to the corporate roundtable. Proponents of this movement argue that broad and easy access to these negotiation techniques offer to the non-union employee the security and benefits formerly offered only within a unionized setting.[18]

Wallihan, however, argues that this is not true. The "security" extolled by Steiber and Blackburn derived from the union culture, which was founded on the principle of collective bargaining and employee solidarity. The non-union culture, on the other hand, emphasizes competition versus collectivity. Whereas the union-management dichotomy frequently translates to "us versus them," the non-unionized employee is placed not only against the company brass, but also against every other employee in the office, all of whom are placed at risk by siding with, or even identifying with, the dissenting, "blacklisted" employee.[19] This is not simply a cultural perception; it is a fact. Richard Edwards of the Brookings Institute notes that collective bargaining no longer serves "as the central institution of workplace rights."[20]

The possibility that another employee's job might be threatened by backing up his co-worker's claims is real. What is more, the possibility that one employee's dismissal could lead to another's promotion leads to a conflict of interest in office politics. Prospective employees considering signing contracts with arbitration clauses in them might do well to consider exactly what rights they are signing away.

The prevalence of corporate arbitration clauses in employment contracts continues to grow, however, along with increased reliance on ADR in a variety of organizational settings. This has been fortified by the 1991 drafting of the Model Employment Termination Act (META) by the National Conference of Commissioners on Uniform State Laws. META would have extinguished common law claims and access to the courts for discharged non-union employees, in exchange for easy access to arbitration. Arbitrators would have remained unable to award punitive damages, which therefore would have rendered non-union employees ineligible to receive such damages, regardless of how heinous the offense that had been committed against them. In addition, employers would have remained free to dismiss non-union employees "at will," without any need to prove "just cause."[21] It would seem that we have not progressed too far from the 1884 Tennessee court decision proclaiming the right of employers to discharge employees "for good cause, for no cause, or even for a cause morally wrong."[22]

Had the National Conference of Commissioners approved META by a majority vote, META's provisions would have been introduced to the legislature of all 50 states in recommendation that they become state law. The fact that the vote was reasonably close indicates how close we have come to accepting ADR as a substitute for the court system--which it is not. The use of litigation in civil cases has clearly reached epidemic and ridiculous proportions, and in most cases ADR techniques solve the problem more cheaply, more efficiently, and more kindly. But it is equally clear that there are instances in which litigation is the appropriate resource, and to mandate it out of existence is a disservice to those who need it.

The Future of ADR

What is the future of ADR? Overall, it is very bright, say most experts. Few people want to be tied up in legal disputes that drag on for years, eat away at their savings, and produce peculiar verdicts that are not what either party wanted. In addition, mediation and arbitration are boons in situations in which both parties will need to maintain some form of ongoing relationship, but just need help getting past a particular hurdle. But one area in which ADR is most enthusiastically hailed--employee-employer disputes-- may be one area in which reformers should proceed with caution, due to the inherently unbalanced nature of the relationship.

In short, the techniques of alternative dispute resolution pose both real benefits and real challenges to the future of the judicial system in the United States. The most important factor is making sure that everyone's interests are served equally well.

Endnotes

[1] Bob Brooke, "Companies Turn to ADR to Avoid Court," Philadelphia Business Journal 29 Nov. 1996: 21.

[2] Robert V. Kuenzel, "Alternative Dispute Resolution: Why All The Fuss?" Compensation and Benefits Review 17 Jul. 1996: 43.

[3] Brooke 21.

[4] Steve Kaufman, "See You out of Court," Nation's Business 1 Jun. 1992: 58.

[5] Brooke 22.

[6] Kuenzel 45.

[7] Brooke 22.

[8] Kaufman 58.

[9] Brooke 23.

[10] Brooke 24.

[11] Brooke 23.

[12] Kaufman 58.

[13] Brooke 24.

[14] Kuenzel 43.

[15] Kuenzel 43.

[16] Gilmer v. Interstate Johnson Lane Corp, 111 S. Ct. 1647, 500 U.S. 20, 1991.

[17] Steven L. Willborn, "Individual Employment Rights and the Standard Economic Objection: Theory and Empiricism." Nebraska Law Review 67 (1988): 101-2.

[18] Jack Steiber and John Blackburn. Protecting Unorganized Employees Against Unjust Discharge (East Lansing, MI: Michigan State U, School of Labor and Industrial Relations, 1983) 1.

[19] James Wallihan, "Too Little, Too Late: The Limits of Stand-Alone Arbitration," Labor Studies Journal 1 Apr. 1996: 39.

[20] Richard Edwards, Rights at Work: Employment Relations in the Post-Union Era (Washington, DC: Brookings, 1993) 82.

[21] National Conference of Commissioners on Uniform State Laws, "Model Uniform Employment Termination Act (META)," In Labor Relations Reporter, Individual Employee Rights Manual Washington, DC: Bureau of National Affairs (Dec. 1991) 540.

[22] Payne v. Western & A.R.R., 81 Tenn. 507, 519-20, 1884.

This paper analyzes a Canadian Supreme Court decision about physician-assisted suicide, and concludes with a brief commentary about the problems inherent in legalizing euthanasia. Notice that the student avoids taking a side on the issue, instead looking at the arguments for and against euthanasia in a critical but objective manner. Also notice that the student does not merely summarize the arguments, but goes further, to evaluate them, thereby demonstrating that the student truly understands the issues at hand and deserves an A+ grade. (MLA style, with *Works Consulted* list)

EUTHANASIA AND THE CASE OF <u>RODRIGUEZ V. BRITISH COLUMBIA</u>

Although the debate over euthanasia has only recently reached the United States Supreme Court, it has already reached and been decided by the Supreme Court of Canada--in the 1992 case <u>Rodriguez v. British Columbia</u>. At issue in <u>Rodriguez</u> was the constitutionality of a particular provision in Canada's Criminal Code which prohibits the assistance of any suicide. The Supreme Court of Canada upheld the provision of the criminal code in a tightly contested 5-to-4 vote.

Close examination of the <u>Rodriguez</u> case, especially the majority and dissenting opinions, is worthwhile for two reasons. For U.S. citizens, <u>Rodriguez</u> provides a primer on the constitutional issues and arguments likely to surface in pending U.S. appellate cases; and more generally, the case provides insight into the various social and legal forces that surround the euthanasia debate.

The Facts of the <u>Rodriguez</u> Case

Sue Rodriguez age 42, had suffered for many years from amyotrophic lateral sclerosis, a degenerative disease. In 1992 the prognosis was that she would die within 2 to 14 months. Although Ms. Rodriguez wished to stay alive, she foresaw a day when her condition would become so debilitating that she might change her mind. Anticipating that she would be too weak to commit suicide by herself, she brought a constitutional challenge against Canada's ban on assisted suicide. Rodriguez argued that the ban, provided for in Criminal Code section 241(b), violated the following three sections of the Canadian Charter of Rights and Freedoms:

> 7. Everyone has the right to life, liberty and security of the person and the right not to be deprived thereof except in accordance with the principles of fundamental justice.
>
> . . .
>
> 12. Everyone has the right not to be subjected to any cruel and unusual treatment or punishment.
>
> . . .
>
> 15(1). Every individual is equal before and under the law and has the right to the equal protection and equal benefit of the law without discrimination and, in particular, without discrimination based on race, national or ethnic origin, colour, religion, sex, age or mental or physical disability.

The scope of the guarantee of these rights is determined by section 1 of the Charter, which stipulates:

> The Canadian Charter of Rights and Freedoms guarantees the rights and freedoms set out in it subject only to such reasonable limits prescribed by law as can be demonstrably justified in a free and democratic society.

The trial court dismissed Rodriguez's application, and the British Columbia Court of Appeals upheld the trial court's decision. Ms. Rodriguez committed suicide with the assistance of an unnamed physician in February 1994. Under Canadian law, enforcement of criminal law is within federal jurisdiction, in contrast to U.S. law. Nevertheless, the government of British Columbia did not prosecute the physician.

The Majority and Dissenting Opinions in <u>Rodriguez</u>

By a vote of 5 to 4, the Supreme Court of Canada affirmed the Court of Appeals decision. Justice Sopinka wrote the Supreme Court's majority opinion. He began with the premise that the Canadian Constitution recognizes a right to life, and then went

further, to assert that respect for the sanctity of life is fundamental to Canadian society. Justice Sopinka acknowledges, however,
that the right to life coexists with the right to liberty, and
that on occasion it is subject to exceptions based on personal
autonomy. Justice Sopinka thus recognized a right to corporeal
autonomy--the right of control over one's own body.

Having determined that the ban infringed on this right,
Sopinka nevertheless held that the ban did not violate the principles of fundamental justice. In contrast to corresponding provisions
in the United States Bill of Rights, section 7 of the Canadian
Charter expressly limits the scope of the rights to life, liberty,
and the security of the person. If restrictions accord with the
principles of fundamental justice, reasoned the majority, then they
are permissible. In what amounts to the crux of its holding, the
majority found that the restriction was fundamentally just.

Justice McLachlin's dissent, like the majority opinion, began
with the premise that section 7 protects a right to corporeal
autonomy. But on the issue of whether the infringement was in
accord with the principles of fundamental justice, she departed
from the majority. According to Justice McLachlin, the ban violated
the principles of fundamental justice because its impact was arbitrary. Specifically, the ban was arbitrary because it had the
effect of preventing people "like Sue Rodriguez [those physically
unable to commit suicide] from exercising the autonomy over their
bodies available to other people." Justice McLachlin added:

> Under the scheme Parliament has set up, the physically
> able person is legally allowed to end his or her life;
> he or she cannot be criminally penalized for attempting
> or committing suicide. But the person who is physically
> unable to accomplish the act is not similarly allowed to
> end her life. Assuming without deciding that Parliament
> could criminalize all suicides, whether assisted or not,
> does the fact that suicide is not criminal make the
> criminalization of all assistance in suicide arbitrary?

Two other justices issued their own dissenting opinions, both using a death-with-dignity analysis. Justice Cory, for example, forcefully asserted that death with dignity should be part and parcel of the right to life:

> The life of an individual must include dying. Dying is the final act in the drama of life. If, as I believe, dying is an integral part of living, then as a part of life it is entitled to the constitutional protection provided by s. 7. It follows that the right to die with dignity should be as well protected as is any other aspect of the right to life. State prohibitions that would force a dreadful, painful death on a rational but incapacitated terminally ill patients are an affront to human dignity.

In sum, the crux of the debate between the majority and the various dissenting justices seems to be about which is the state's more important duty: protecting the lives of its citizens or protecting the individual rights of its citizens.

Problems with Legalizing Euthanasia

Admittedly, the Rodriguez dissenting opinions have merit. However, the dissent's position, and the legalization of euthanasia in general, are problematic in two significant respects. First, any person who claims a right to assisted suicide in fact asserts that some other individual has a duty to assist. Given this corollary, upon whom does this duty to assist fall? If it becomes the duty of physicians, what should be the limits and boundaries of their duty? For example, should the law carve out exceptions in which the physician has the right to decline the terminally ill patient's request?

The second major problem with legalizing euthanasia is that doing so would open the floodgates to abuse, especially if euthanasia legislation is not crafted carefully to limit its scope. For example, imprisoned felons, particularly those serving long sentences, might claim a right to assisted suicide because of the inhumane conditions they must endure in prisons.

Judges on both the Court of Appeals and the Canadian Supreme Court were troubled by these potential problems, and in their dissents offered specific guidelines for euthanasia legislation--guidelines that could very well serve as models for Canadian or U.S. legislation authorizing physician-assisted suicide. For example, the following legislative guidelines are based on the dissent of Chief Justice McEachern of the Court of Appeals:

1. A psychiatrist must certify that the individual is mentally competent to make a decision to end his or her own life, that the individual truly desires to end his/her own life, and that the individual has reached this decision free of coercion or undue influence.

2. Physicians must certify that (a) the individual is terminally ill and near death, and (b) but for medication the individual would suffer unbearable physical pain or severe psychological distress.

3. Not less than three days before the examination leading to the preparation of these certificates, notice must be given to the Coroner who would be entitled to send a nominee to the examination.

4. The individual must be re-examined on a daily basis to see if she had changed her mind, and in any event the certificates would expire after 30 days.

Summary

With *Rodriguez*, the Supreme Court of Canada finally addressed the issue of physician-assisted suicide. Yet the Court did not quiet the debate over this controversial and emotional issue. The various opinions in the *Rodriguez* case demonstrate that the euthanasia issue boils down to a tug-of-war between two competing interests: the interest of each individual person in maintaining his or her corporeal autonomy, and the broader societal interest in protecting the lives of citizens.

Having acknowledged legitimate arguments on both sides of this debate, one conclusion seems clear: Should the Supreme Court ever reverse the <u>Rodriguez</u> decision and sanction physician-assisted suicide, the legislature must take great care to draft euthanasia law that is clear and unambiguous, and that discourages abuse of the law.

Works Consulted

"Assisted Death Ruled Legal; 9th Circuit Lifts Ban on Doctor-Aided Suicide." <u>Los Angeles Times</u> 7 Mar. 1996, home ed.: A-1.

James-Coleson, Richard. "The Constitutional Case Against Permitting . . . " <u>Issues in Law and Medicine</u> 1 Jan. 1995.

Milton, Neil. "Lessons from Rodriguez v. British Columbia." <u>Issues in Law and Medicine</u> 1 Sep. 1995.

Snyder, Allen. "Competency to Refuse Lifesaving Treatment: Valuing the Nonlogical Aspects of a Person's Decisions." <u>Issues in Law and Medicine</u> 1 Dec. 1994.

Wood, Chris-Caragata. "The Legacy of Sue Rodriguez." <u>Maclean's</u> 28 Feb. 1994.

12
LITERATURE

William Faulkner's "Wash": The Title Character's Emerging Consciousness

Wickham's Role in Jane Austen's *Pride and Prejudice*

Captain Vere of Melville's "Billy Budd": A Man Conflicted?

The King-Father and Warrior-Son in *Beowolf* and *Sir Gawain and the Green Knight*

(A+) This paper explores the evolving consciousness of the title character of William Faulkner's short story "Wash," and how Faulkner used this character as an indictment of the social structure of the South during the Civil War era. Notice that the student describes the story's action in the present tense, and refers to the reader as *we*. Both devices are perfectly appropriate in papers about literary works. (MLA style)

WILLIAM FAULKNER'S "WASH":

THE TITLE CHARACTER'S EMERGING CONSCIOUSNESS

Compared to his full-length novels, William Faulkner's short story "Wash" is relatively simple in its thematic development--yet no less poignant. The story concerns the events of a single day on which Wash Jones kills Thomas Sutpen, Sutpen's granddaughter Milly, and the infant daughter of Milly and Sutpen. He then commits virtual suicide by charging the armed men who have come to take him into custody. At the onset of the story Wash is content with the servile nature of his relationship with Sutpen. During the same morning, however, out of the frustration of Sutpen's insensitive behavior toward Milly and her newborn child, Wash kills Sutpen. From this drastic change in consciousness and the fatal results of it stem the central theme of "Wash": Through his realization of Sutpen's true nature, Wash comes to see the viciousness and corruption of the whole South--as embodied in Sutpen.

Wash's Initial Consciousness

The story's theme finds its expression in the relationship between Wash and Sutpen, and ultimately, in Wash's realization about Sutpen's true character. Initially, we see Wash's foolish trust and admiration of Sutpen, particularly in one passage in which Sutpen is riding his horse up to see the newly born child. Admiration is evident enough in the words "fine proud figure" and "beyond all fouling of human touch":

> There broke suddenly free in mid-gallop the fine proud
> figure of the man on the fine proud stallion, galloping,
> and then at which thinking fumbled, broke free too and
> quite clear, not in justification nor even explanation,

but as the apotheosis, lonely, explicable, beyond all fouling of human touch: "He is bigger then Yankees that kilt his son and his wife and taken his niggers and ruined his land, bigger than hyer durn country that he fit for and that has denied him into keeping a little country store; bigger than the denial which hit helt to his lips like the bitter cup in the Book."

As a result of his reverence for and larger-than-life image of Supten, Wash fails initially to see the grotesque dimension of Sutpen's sexual relationship with 15-year-old Milly; though we do not know Sutpen's age, we know that he is nearly 60 years old. Wash's blind devotion is perhaps most clearly evident in a particular conversation between Sutpen and him, in which Wash avoids confronting Sutpen about his inappropriate relationship with Milly, changing the subject instead and uttering these devotional remarks:

"I ain't afraid. Because you air brave. It ain't that you were a brave man at one minute or day of your life and got a paper to show hit from General Lee. But you air brave, the same as you air alive and breathing. That's where hit's different. Hit don't need no ticket from nobody to tell me that. And I know that whatever you handle or tech, whether hit's a regiment of men or ignorant gal, that you will make hit right."

As telling as Wash's dialogue is, Sutpen's reaction is just as revealing in its own way: "Now it was Sutpen who looked away, turning suddenly, brusquely. 'Get the jug,' he said sharply." Sutpen's avoidance of the subject and his curt dismissal of any further conversation on the matter reveal the true nature of his feelings toward Milly. Their relationship merely serves his selfish needs and feeds his arrogance. Sutpen views Milly in the same vein that he views the slaves of his plantation--as objects no more worthy than animals. In the social hierarchy of the southern aristocracy, lower-class whites were only slightly higher on the social scale than the black slaves.

Wash's Realization

Wash finally realizes the great extent of his disillusionment just after the birth of Milly's child, in the few seconds it takes for Sutpen to utter the seemingly unspeakable: "Well, Milly, too bad you're not a mare. Then I could give you a decent stall in the stable." The metaphor is clear enough, but it is made even more clear when Sutpen, still at the bedside of Milly and the newborn child, casually mentions to the midwife that one of his horses foaled that morning. There is simply no difference in Sutpen's mind between the birth of his child and the birth of a colt; in fact, he praises the newborn colt as being "damned fine," while offering no such praise about his baby girl. The old symbols of his prestige--his plantation, his horses, and his slaves--are more important to Sutpen than the birth of a human being who is his own daughter.

Wash becomes enraged over Sutpen's arrogant remarks, and rage leads quickly to murder. Not until Wash unleashes his rage does he come to fully understand himself, Sutpen, and their relationship; and in the process he comes to understand the evil that pervades the South, which is the only land he knows. He realizes that he cannot escape the wickedness of the South, so he decides to stand his ground in the face of the throng coming to seize him:

> If he ran, he would merely be fleeing one set of bragging
> and evil shadows for another just like them, since they
> were all of a kind throughout all the earth which he
> knew, and he was old to flee far even if he were to flee.

The most poignant words of the story follow shortly there-after, when Wash recognizes not only Sutpen's cruel nature but also his own shortcomings:

> "Better if his kind and mine too had never drawn the
> breath of life on this earth. Better that all who remain
> of us be blasted from the face of the earth than that
> another Wash Jones should see his whole life shredded
> from him and shrivel away like a dried shuck thrown into
> the fire."

This self-condemnation helps establish the story's theme. Not only does Sutpen embody what is wrong with the South, but so does Wash; after all, it is men such as Wash who, through their admiration of the Sutpens of the South, perpetuated the evil arrogance that pervaded the land. As such, the killing of Milly and her daughter are logical conclusions of this new knowledge. Wash finally realizes that the aristocratic men of the South, whom he had greatly admired, were in truth "instruments too of despair and grief." Wash even suggests that the despair, grief, and "rule of living" that these men imposed on the South had a part in the outcome of the war.

Conclusion

"Wash" is one of Faulkner's clearest portrayals of the social and cultural malady that plagued the South during the Civil War era. Through the dramatic change in Wash's consciousness, Faulkner is able to reveal the wicked nature of Sutpen, and, most importantly, relate that nature to the whole of the South.

(A+) This paper discusses the role of George Wickham, a minor character in Jane Austen's novel <u>Pride and Prejudice</u>, in the story's plot development. The assignment for this paper called for the student to analyze the work without resorting to outside source material. Accordingly, this paper's *Works Cited* list contains only one citation: for Austen's novel. (MLA style)

WICKHAM'S ROLE IN JANE AUSTEN'S <u>PRIDE AND PREJUDICE</u>

Few novels are so aptly titled as Jane Austen's 1813 work <u>Pride and Prejudice</u>. Indeed, a central theme of the story is the misguided combinations of both pride and prejudice on the part of the two main characters, Darcy and Elizabeth. Admittedly, the inner conflict that the two main figures undergo in overcoming their own pride and prejudice provides the impetus for much of the novel's plot. However, the other, minor characters in the novel play an essential role in this respect. In particular, George Wickham, the charismatic but unprincipled officer, serves an important part in the plot's development. It is his actions that help fuel Elizabeth's initial prejudice toward Darcy, and that delay the coming together of these two main characters. Moreover, it is Wickham's behavior, particularly during one important episode, that compels Darcy to a course of action that convinces Elizabeth of his fine character and virtue.

Wickham's Contribution to Elizabeth's

Antagonism Toward Darcy

Wickham's role in plot development is evident in his very first conversation with Elizabeth, which highlights--and heightens--Elizabeth's prejudiced attitude toward Darcy. This prejudice is manifested in her inability to notice certain inconsistencies in Wickham's statements. When Wickham broaches the subject of Darcy, he professes to be too humble to offer an assessment of a man he has known for a long time: "I have no right to give my opinion as to his being agreeable or otherwise. I am not qualified to form one" (XVI 77). Yet, as the conversation progresses Wickham talks only too freely of Darcy: "His behavior to myself has been scandalous . . . [he has] a dislike of me which

I cannot attribute in some measure to jealousy" (XVI 80). Wickham extends his slanderous remarks to include Darcy's sister, whom he calls "too much like her brother--very, very, proud" (XVI 82).

Wickham's role in exposing and heightening Elizabeth's prejudice continues at the Netherfield ball. One notable incident occurs during her dance with Darcy. Elizabeth is unable to resist mentioning that she has made Wickham's acquaintance. Though it is surely her attempt to vex Darcy when she declares that "[Wickham] has been so unlucky as to lose your friendship, and in a manner which he is likely to suffer from all his life" (SVII 92), Elizabeth finds his response constrained. Darcy will only say that "Mr. Wickham is blessed with such happy manners as may ensure his making friends--whether he may be equally capable of retaining them, is less certain" (XVIII 92).

Another revealing incident occurs at the beginning of the ball, when Elizabeth learns that Wickham refused the invitation to attend in order to avoid Darcy. Elizabeth's resentment of Darcy grows even greater upon learning this. Yet, in the earlier conversation between Wickham and Elizabeth, it was Wickham who declared that he would not avoid Darcy: "It is not for me to be driven away by Mr. Darcy. If he wishes to avoid seeing me, he must go. . . . I have no reason for avoiding him" (XVI 78). Elizabeth is so blinded by her prejudice that she fails to notice this obvious inconsistency.

A third episode, in Chapter XI, also highlights Wickham's role in fueling the antagonism between Elizabeth and Darcy. When Darcy declares his love for Elizabeth and proposes to her, in addition to accusing Darcy of arrogance and conceit, she accused him of ruining Wickham by denying advantages promised to him by Darcy's father:

> "You have reduced him to his present state of poverty, comparative poverty. You have withheld the advantages, which you must know to have been designed for him.
> You have deprived the best years of his life, of that independence which was no less his due than his desert.
> You have done all this!" (XI 192)

Darcy is so struck by the accusation that he cannot muster a defense at the moment. It is interesting to note the irony in this scene: Elizabeth accuses Darcy of prejudice against Wickham, when in fact it is she who is holding a strong prejudice against Darcy.

Wickham's Contribution to Elizabeth's Change of Heart

In addition to playing an important role in bringing to light Elizabeth's antagonism toward Darcy, Wickham also serves a critical function in Elizabeth's change of heart toward the end; specifically, at the turning point of the novel after Darcy's failed proposal and the ensuing, heated conversation. In response to the accusations bestowed upon him, Darcy writes a letter to Elizabeth in which he reveals Wickham to be a dishonest and unprincipled man. Among other things, Darcy reveals that Wickham tried to elope with Darcy's teenage sister. Upon reflection, Elizabeth begins to realize the inconsistencies in Wickham's behavior, both his forceful demeanor during their first conversation and his subsequent actions:

> She was now struck by the impropriety of such communications to a stranger, and wondered it had escaped her before. She saw the indelicacy of putting himself forward as he had done, and the inconsistency of his professions with his conduct. She remembered that he had boasted of having no fear of seeing Mr. Darcy . . . yet he had avoided the Netherfield ball the very next week. (XIII 207)

Elizabeth's realization of her own misjudgment concerning the Wickham affair is part of her overall realization that she has been blinded by prejudice in her evaluation of Darcy: "She grew absolutely ashamed of herself. Of neither Darcy nor Wickham could she think, without feeling that she had been blind, partial, prejudiced, absurd" (XIII 208). And in dramatic fashion, she spills forth in self-realization:

"How despicably I have acted! I, who have prided myself
on my discernment! . . . Had I been in love, I could
not have been more wretchedly blind. But vanity, not
love, has been my folly. . . . Till this moment I never
knew myself." (XIII 208)

Then, when Wickham elopes with Lydia, and the potential for
extreme disgrace is brought to bear on the Bennett family, it is
Darcy who secretly arranges the marriage in order to preserve some
respect for the Bennetts. Almost by accident, Elizabeth learns of
his role through her aunt, Mrs. Gardiner, who tells her in a
letter that Darcy persuaded Wickham--who had no intention of ever
marrying Lydia--to marry Lydia with a substantial marriage settle-
ment. Upon learning of Darcy's role in the restoration of honor
upon her family, Elizabeth finds final confirmation of the honor
and character of Darcy. At the same time, her regard for him
swells:

Oh! how heartily did she grieve over every ungracious
sensation she had ever encouraged, every saucy speech
she had ever directed towards him. For herself she was
humbled; but she was proud of him. Proud that in a
cause of compassion and honour, he had been able to get
the better of himself. She had read over her aunt's
commendation of him again and again. It was hardly
enough; but it pleased her. (X 326)

Wickham has created an urgent dilemma that Darcy humbly and
unassumingly resolves, to the delight of Elizabeth, who rejoices in
this show of character and virtue by Darcy. It is at that point
that Elizabeth's feelings become truly confirmed in her mind, and
her admiration and respect for Darcy fully developed.

Concluding Remarks

In sum, although some might consider the character, Wickham,
in Pride and Prejudice a minor one, closer examination reveals
him to be one of the work's major antagonists. His role in the

development of the plot is essential. It is Wickham, through his dishonest and wily tactics, who creates the large rift between Elizabeth and Darcy that much of the story works to close. Moreover, in the final episodes, it is Wickham who creates the urgent dilemma that results in Darcy's demonstration of character and virtue and, in turn, the full development of Elizabeth's admiration and respect toward him.

Works Cited

Austen, Jane. <u>Pride and Prejudice</u>. Oxford, Eng.: Oxford UP, 1988.

(A+) This paper provides a psychoanalytical perspective on the character of Captain Vere in Melville's "Billy Budd." The discussion proceeds by pointing out a commonly held view about Vere's character, and then argues for a distinct, more insightful view, based on the student's reading of the novel as well as on the views of certain literary scholars. (MLA style)

CAPTAIN VERE OF MELVILLE'S "BILLY BUDD": A MAN CONFLICTED?

Captain Vere, the pivotal character who determines the fate of the title character in Melville's "Billy Budd," appears from the start to be a man conflicted. Vere's personality seems defined by his strong sense of duty as captain--a duty that creates inner conflict when it requires that he apply the law to the actions of the innocent Budd. But one can also view Vere from a psycho-analytical perspective: as a man driven by narcissistic motives that underlie his decision to call for Budd's execution. These conflicting visions of Vere's personality provide a starting point for gaining insight into Vere's sense of self, his behavior, and the story as a whole.

Vere as a Man Conflicted

In order to gain insight into Vere's essential character, and thereby fully appreciate an argument <u>against</u> a man conflicted, it is useful to first examine Billy's character through the words of both the author and Captain Vere. Billy is not a character who initially challenged authority or who could be perceived at the onset of the novel as Vere's antagonist. Instead, Billy is a popular crew member, compliant and content, and embodying the best personal characteristics. Melville does not bring Billy's virtue into question in the early part of the story; indeed, the author leaves an impression of a virtual nexus between Billy's nature and the very notion of virtue. Billy's virtuous nature is further underscored by way of direct contrast to the patently evil John Claggart, the deceitful master-at-arms.

Vere himself acknowledges Billy's virtue; he considers Billy's virtue a fundamental component of his personality, and even goes so far as to compare Billy to the Biblical character Adam. Thus, when faced with the decision about Billy's punishment for Claggart's death, Vere appears to be a man conflicted by his circumstances and his admiration of and emotional attachment to Budd. But is Vere the compassionate leader Melville initially introduces? Melville's description of Vere might suggest to some readers that he is a man of genuine compassion and concerned for the crew, and for Billy in particular. However, a closer look at the author's narrative and at Vere's own words and actions belie this characterization, as discussed below.

The Argument Against the "Man Conflicted" View of Vere

Some theorists have argued that Vere's personal characteristics appear so conflicting and so unnatural that it is impossible to understand him as a man merely wrestling his conscience; nor is this view supported by the text itself (Shaw 591). Shaw argues not that Captain Vere is a good man who is forced by his sense of duty to apply the law and allow the execution of Billy Budd, but instead that certain underlying psychopathological motives drive Vere to order Budd's execution for the murder of the evil Claggart (Shaw 591).

Here's how Shaw's argument proceeds. Melville portrays Vere as a kindhearted and brave leader defined by his sense of duty. Yet this portrayal seems ironic in light of the work as a whole. Throughout the story Vere appears almost pragmatic in the way he pursues his career. He is careful that his behavior not undermine his position, and it is clear that he has allied himself with others in a manner that has served him well in defining his role as captain. Nevertheless, he is not so careful as to prevent varying perspectives on his character. His actions reveal a dual personality; he is a different man than the captain perceived by his crew (Shaw 591). This perspective on Vere finds support in Melville's own description of Vere:

Though allied to the higher nobility his advancement had
not been altogether owing to influences connected with
that circumstance. He had seen much service, been in
various engagements, always acquitting himself as an
officer mindful of the welfare of his men, but never
tolerating an infraction of discipline; thoroughly
versed in the science of his profession and intrepid to
the verge of temerity, though never injudiciously so.
(Melville 79)

This dual-personality view provides a starting point for
analyzing Vere. It also foreshadows events to occur, and establishes
a premise from which Vere and Budd are delineated by Vere's actions.
One can argue that this early information about Vere that Melville
offers almost drives the reader to consider the possibility of an
ironic twist to Vere's character. Melville seems to tell the reader
too much: Why was it necessary to know at the onset that Vere would
seek justice?

Hints of Vere's Dual Personality

Underscoring Shaw's argument for a self-directed Vere are
specific aspects of Melville's narrative that hint not of a man
experiencing a conflict of conscience but rather an ironic character with a narcissistic streak. First, from an external
standpoint Vere is described as the perfect captain: personable but
not too friendly; direct but not overly verbose; concerned but not
past the law. Vere appears both empathetic and separate, two
conflicting elements that underscore the irony of his character
(Shattuck 430). Second, Vere himself was at times extremely
"undemonstrative," even when the circumstances might suggest that
demonstrative behavior would be appropriate (Melville 79).

How does one evaluate such self-contradictions? One can
argue that through his introspection Vere hides his true self
from those around him, and that a part of this hidden personality
is difficult to evaluate as a result. Rather than display his
personal feelings or express them (if he naturally has them),

Vere separates himself both from his choice and from the consequences of his behaviors, by pointing out that his actions were in
compliance with the law. Individuals generally take such a stance
without thought as to the consequences for others because they
believe they can benefit personally from doing so. Vere is both
attracted to Billy Budd's natural charisma and repelled by it, and
so one can argue that Vere's motives were based not on the law but
rather on his disdain for Billy's beauty, innocence, and perception
of what is right.

In sum, the development of his personality and the ironic
plot that unfolds as a result suggest that Vere is not a man
conflicted or a man struggling with his decision about Budd.
Instead, they suggest a calculating, intense man, able to justify
his actions on the premise that they are legal and in compliance
with regulations.

Vere's Decision Belies His Inner Conflict

Although Vere appears sympathetic to Billy as an accused
killer, he does not appear to put his personal feelings above his
sense of duty. Instead, he argues that Billy must be treated as
any other crew member would; and though other officers suggest that
Billy be pardoned from his crime, Vere will not allow it:

> "To steady us a bit, let us recur to the facts--In
> wartime at sea a man-of-war's-man strikes his superior
> in grade, and the blow kills. Apart from its effect the
> blow itself is, according the Articles of War, a capital
> crime." (Melville 132)

A truly conflicted man who feels disdain for a process he is
required to apply would surely take far less comfort in the
process than Vere appears to take. Although Vere does show emotion
when he informs Billy of his decision, this emotion seems a mani-
festation of an internal division between Vere and his actions, not
a truly compassionate response.

In the language of psychoanalysis, the externalization of Vere's true personality--his narcissistic tendencies and his pathological personality--define his inability to accurately determine his own perspectives on Billy and are directly correlated to his behavior (Winter et al. 230). Theorists have long posited that introversion deflects social motives and moves individuals away from their characteristic goals, and this appears to be what occurs as a result of Vere's inherent introspection (Winter et al. 230).

Conclusion

In the final analysis, Vere is conflicted not by ordering the execution of a virtuous man, but by the fact that his choice undermines his long-standing concerns for self and career. Some suggest that the level at which Vere is challenged in his decision to execute Billy amounts to self-destructive behavior, insofar as Vere's actions appear to undermine his own personal success (Elliot and Sheldon 171). In this facet of Melville's story of Billy Budd--that Vere's actions appear to conflict with the reader's perception of what drives him--lies the most conflicting element, and the nub, of Vere's character.

Works Cited

Elliot, A., and K. Sheldon. "Avoidance Achievement Motivation: "A Personal Goals Analysis." _Journal of Personality and Social Psychology_ Jul. 1997: 171+.

Melville, Herman. "Billy Budd." In _Six Great Modern Short Novels_ New York: Dell Publishing, 1954.

Shattuck, Roger. "Guilt, Justice, and Empathy in Melville and Camus." _Partisan Review_ Summer 1996: 430+.

Shaw, Peter. "The Fate of a Story." _American Scholar_ Autumn 1993: 591+.

Winter, D., O. John, A. Steward, E. Klohnen, and L. Duncan. "Traits and Motives: Toward an Integration of Two Traditions in Personality Research." _Psychological Review_ Apr. 1998: 230+.

This paper explores how the king-warrior relationship in two epic poems is similar to a father–son relationship. Through a careful reading of each poem and through insight gained by perusing some secondary source material, the student sets up the comparison as a metaphor, and presents it this way throughout her four-pronged analysis. (MLA style)

THE KING-FATHER AND WARRIOR-SON IN <u>BEOWOLF</u>
AND <u>SIR GAWAIN AND THE GREEN KNIGHT</u>

While heroism would appear to be the most persistent theme throughout medieval epic poetry, in both <u>Beowulf</u> and <u>Sir Gawain and the Green Knight</u>, it was not primarily for the heroic ideal that monsters were slain and dragons were beheaded; instead, the king's praise and gratitude were of primary importance. Each of these medieval warriors sought to prove himself to his king, his bonds of kinship and loyalty driving him to perform. Indeed, the relationship between Beowulf and Hrothgar, and between Sir Gawain and King Arthur, can best be viewed as familial: the warrior-son wanting to please and honor his king-father by doing great deeds, by conforming to familial customs and codes of conduct, and by acting in the father's stead.

Heroism Versus Acceptance and Honor

A hero is judged by the things he does and the way he reacts and relates to other people. His deeds are marked by nobility of purpose, and he must be willing to risk his life for his ideals. Gawain and Beowulf both seem to meet these requirements. Yet even in their heroic deeds, they seem driven primarily by their desire to prove themselves worthy of the king's approval.

In medieval society, when a person performed a great favor for another, as Beowulf had done for Hrothgar and the Danes, the immediate response was to take that person into one's family. It was a world dominated by kings and their warriors; a successful king was one who was generous to his warriors, rewarding them with rings and gold in exchange for their loyalty ("Wealth is shaped with a sword." Beowulf, line 25), but it was just as important for the warriors to feel that they had pleased their king, as a son seeks to please his father. The praise and acknowledgment that the warrior had completed a job well done, and thus secured himself a place in the king's favor, was equal to corporeal rewards (Cunningham 8).

When Beowulf first hears of Hrothgar's trouble with the monster, Grendel, he sets sail from his home in Sweden to rescue the Danes from their terror. He boasts to Hrothgar of his previous successes as a warrior, particularly in fighting sea monsters, and assures Hrothgar that he can defeat Grendel. Why should Beowulf leave his homeland to show his warrior prowess in another country? Although the treasures he'd be guaranteed as a reward were certainly an incentive, Beowulf's driving need is to prove himself, to be accepted by his king. When Beowulf tears off the monster's arm (ultimately killing him and ending the years of terror), Hrothgar's speech to Beowulf is more than an expression of grati-tude: "Let me take you to my heart, make you my son too / And love you" (947-48).

The actions demanded of Gawain in facing the monstrous Green Knight are very much the same as those demanded of Beowulf in facing his monsters. The very worst thing that can happen to him is beheading, an honorable fate, and one worth risking to gain his king's acceptance (Spearing 184). Gawain takes up the challenge for the honor of Camelot, and to ensure himself a place of favor with Arthur, and not primarily to prove himself a hero to the inhabi-tants of Camelot or to protect them from physical harm at the hands of the Green Knight. In fact, the dangers and challenges Gawain meets as he travels to the Green Chapel and subsequently returns to Camelot are all part of his personal journey to increase his worth in the eyes of the king.

Gawain's honor of his king-father finds further support as Gawain is called upon to exercise his most courteous behavior during his meetings with Morgan le Fay. In these moments of temptation, he must maintain his courtesy so as not to dishonor the king, even though his manners and his moral virtue are thoroughly tested. The lady (whom he does not yet know to be Morgan le Fay) tempts him unrelentingly, yet he maintains his honor, and therefore Arthur's, by not succumbing to Morgan's temptations.

Familial Codes of Conduct--Chivalry and Humility

In <u>Beowolf</u>, as any good father would do Hrothgar points out to Beowulf the importance of never feeling too self-important as a result of one's accomplishments. King Arthur demonstrates this same paternal concern for Sir Gawain, emphasizing the importance of chivarly, manners, and humility. Gawain and the other knights of the Round Table were expected to meet strict standards of behavior and speech, much as any family member would be expected to conform to certain family codes.

In <u>Gawain</u>, one instance in which the knight's manners are put to the test is at the banquet table, when he first asks to take Arthur's place in the Green Knight's challenge. As any dutiful and respectful son would do, Gawain first asks respectfully if he may leave Guinevere's side to approach the king. Gawain acknowledges with the proper and expected humility that he is the least worthy of the knights and would be the least missed if he should be killed (Monarch Notes 01-01-1963).

The Son Acting in His Father's Stead

In a father-son relationship, as the son matures he slowly assumes the responsibilities of his father, eventually assuming the role of father himself. Medieval kings were dependent upon the so-called residual principle, by which if a king no longer possesses the ability to take advantage of an enemy, the king was dethroned and power to do so was given elsewhere. Accordingly, for an aging medieval king it was all the more crucial to prepare a warrior-son to do the bidding on the king's behalf (Cunningham 10).

Both Gawain and Beowolf exemplify this aspect of the father-son relationship and epitomize the residual principle. When Gawain receives the Green Knight's ax from Arthur, he becomes the king's personal substitute, Arthur agreeing that Gawain act in his stead. At this point the king and warrior take on the roles of father and son, the father passing on responsibility to his son. In deed, Gawain's doing battle with the Green Knight was an act performed in a kingly fashion. Although fond of the idea of a confrontation, Arthur fully expected that one of his knights would step forward to do battle in his stead. Indeed, Arthur's reaction to Gawain's stepping forward was one of expectancy--as a father would expect a son to assume the family business one day. Arthur could now turn his attention to the upcoming holiday banquet, knowing that Gawain would act in his stead.

Although Hrothgar wasn't preoccupied with festivities as Beowulf challenged Grendel, Hrothgar too allowed his "son" to act in his stead. In fact, Beowulf goes on to become king of the Geats, thereby assuming the role of father--to Wiglaf. He performs this role in much the same way that Hrothgar performed the role of Beowulf's father. Admittedly, Beowulf differs from his own father-king; he does battle along with Wiglaf, rather than send his warrior-son to do battle for him. Yet, the father-son relationship is undeniable.

Other Father-Son Role-Playing in Beowolf and Gawain

The father-son relationship in these two epic poems can be seen in other ways as well. For example, one reason Beowulf comes to help Hrothgar is to pay his own father's debt. He has no desire to become king of the Geats. In fact, when first offered the throne, Beowulf refuses, preferring to play the role of warrior-son. Also, when Beowulf leaves Hrothgar for the last time, telling him if he ever needs assistance again he will gladly come to his aid, they exchange an emotional embrace, like father and son.

In Gawain, just as a father might overlook a son's faults, Arthur chooses to ignore any possible wrongdoing by his warrior-son Gawain as he returns home after vanquishing the Green Knight. Even though Gawain tries to explain to Arthur the significance of the green sash he wears around his neck, Arthur prefers to know only that Camelot has been saved from the evil Green Knight and that his knight has dutifully maintained the splendor of Camelot and the virtues of the Round Table. In this respect, Arthur plays the father figure to his recalcitrant but victorious son, closing his eyes to any minor slip of morality that Gawain might have committed along the way.

Conclusion

The heroics of Beowolf and of Gawain can be interpreted, of course, as heroic adventures and as quests for something beyond ordinary existence. But another interpretation of their heroics sees these two warriors as sons whose primary motivation is to honor and please their fathers. Whether one focuses on the warrior's words and deeds, on the king's, or on the social customs and codes of conduct, the metaphor is undeniable.

Works Cited

"Beowulf: Early History of England." <u>Monarch Notes</u> 01-01-63.
    New York: Simon & Schuster, 1990.

Cunningham, Bruno. "Medieval Customs and the Epic Hero." <u>Literary
    Journal</u> IX (1992): 1-14.

"English Epic Poems: Sir Gawain and the Green Knight." <u>Monarch
    Notes</u> 01-01-63. Simon & Schuster, 1990.

Spearing, A. C. <u>The Gawain-Poet</u>. Cambridge, Eng.: Cambridge UP,
    1970.

13

MODERN WORLD AFFAIRS

Russia's Change to a Free-Market Economy

Japan and Korea: Neighbors and Rivals

Why Vaclav Havel? Why Czechoslovakia?

This student discusses some of the complex history behind Russia's transition to a free-market economy. This is a very broad topic for a term paper, so the student focused on one particular aspect of the transition. (APA style)

RUSSIA'S CHANGE TO A FREE-MARKET ECONOMY

The unexpected collapse of the Soviet block transformed the "Evil Empire" into a partner and an ally overnight. That is a beautiful idea; but it is no more based on reality than was the cold war vision that preceded it. The Soviet empire covered 12 time zones and dozens of languages. It was a huge, sprawling, complex society built on fundamental lies. Its transformation cannot be smooth, even, and uneventful. But in the minds of many Russians (especially the elderly), <u>anything</u> would be an improvement over the sociopolitical chaos that exists today.

This fact provides a solid measure of support for today's Communists, who control many seats in the Duma still reserved for their party as part of a compromise some years ago. The same political chaos also provides support for ultra-nationalist right wingers. Although the roles of the left and right wings are reversed, there is some comparison to be made with Germany in the 1920s, when the end of the monarchy left society without a moral compass and poor economics gave weapons to extremists of both the left and right. We are even seeing members of the Duma blaming Jews for all of Russia's problems and the collapse of the Soviet Union.

Recent U.S. Policy and Its Results

The U.S. government's view has been that so long as the Communists are not victorious, Russia and the other Newly Independent States (NIS) will be among the fastest growing markets of the twenty first century. This was based on the supposition that they would succeed with their political and economic reforms (Clinton, 1994). The U.S. government has pursued the twofold purpose of opening these new markets for U.S. goods and services and promoting the growth of market democracies. These goals are viewed as complementary. In this scenario, the Western business community, not governments, would supply the capital and technology that the NIS needed to reform and restructure their economies. U.S. manufactured exports to Russia doubled in 1993, to $1.6 billion. U.S. companies also increased their investment in Russia, currently estimated at about $1 billion, and maintained their position as the leading Western investors (Nelson, 1994).

The emerging market democracies of Central and Eastern Europe became an important growth market for U.S. exports and a major target for U.S. investment. U.S. exports grew to over $2.3 billion in 1993, building on surging export growth over the previous six years. U.S. companies invested nearly $8 billion in the region over four years; U.S. companies were the leading investors in Hungary, Poland, and Romania (Nelson, 1994). It seemed that as the region fully emerged from economic recession and as the major state-owned industries were privatized, U.S. commercial links with the region would expand.

A number of issues were not addressed in this process. Because Russian enterprises were just in the process of privatization or still under government control, the West preferred to deal with banks, many of which were run by young men with decidedly Western outlooks. Billions of investment dollars and billions more from the International Monetary Fund poured into these banks, many of which had also picked up major enterprises, such as gas and oil companies at fire-sale prices in rigged auctions. It soon became clear that a half dozen banking groups were supporting a half dozen political figures who had also created matching media empires. This gave them the media and the money to maintain their political bases. Russia became an oligarchy (Cunningham, 1998).

Primitive Financial Tactics

The new financial empires had very different politics, but they all had one thing in common: They didn't pay taxes, and they didn't pay their bills, including salaries for workers in some of the industries under their control. The IMF and others had poured in billions, but much of it seems to have vaporized into personal fortunes and Swiss bank accounts. In any case, the money was not in circulation. Even huge industries and government ministries were reduced to barter in order to keep afloat. Workers went months without pay. As the situation got worse and worse, even the government got involved in covering up for the banks for fear that investors would leave if they understood the situation. Another $15 billion IMF loan was approved on the basis of figures doctored by the finance ministry. When the bubble finally burst, many foreign investors closed their Russian operations and left the country with huge losses, and a few hunkered down to ride out the storm (Cunningham, 1998).

The IMF had just been forced to bail out Korea and other Pacific Rim countries. Now it turned out that the money it had sent to Russia had evaporated, and the country was again on the brink of chaos. No matter how distasteful it was to the bankers of the IMF, something had to be done because Russia is still a military superpower and a huge economy. Collapse could lead to dictatorship or civil war in a country with thousands of nuclear weapons and delivery systems. The IMF had little choice but to come to the rescue again, and attempt to do so with better controls (Cunningham, 1998).

Causes and Solutions

Yet even if Russia remains democratic, other barriers exist to successful and continued trade with the West. For example, there has been much bluster in the Russian parliament about crime prevention; but since casting aside Communist rule in 1991, Russia's new leaders have failed to adopt any significant measures to curb organized crime. What's more, the reformers' most substantial achievements (demolishing the last vestiges of the police state and lifting most restrictions on private ownership) have had the perverse effect of creating the perfect environment for mafia growth (Cunningham, 1998).

Russian policymakers committed a fundamental mistake: They tried to develop a free market at the highest level without constructing a civil society in which such a market could safely operate. As a result, businesspeople, politicians, and law enforcement agencies suffer at the mercy of the lingering ideological prejudices of Soviet jurisprudence. Many activities that are required for a market economy to function remain illegal or unprotected by legislation; other activities that are considered unlawful according to Western norms, such as organized crime, are not specifically prohibited (Kurth, 1995; McFaul, 1995).

Westerners underestimated the extent to which organized crime and corruption hampered Russian political and economic reforms. Early assumptions that the introduction of free enterprise would smooth the way for democracy failed to take into account the lingering power of the former Soviet establishment. According to Michael McFaul (1995), organized crime has reinforced the old structures in their battle to retain control over key sectors of the economy and strengthened popular hostility toward the free-market democratic policies pursued by pro-Western reformers.

The West should to take Russian organized crime far more seriously than it has until now. The current situation poses a double dilemma to policymakers in Western capitals. While internal Russian developments have moved once again to the top of the international agenda, the West has increasingly less influence over Russia's domestic affairs. Western advice and financial assistance, albeit limited, have reportedly been discredited by Russia's bruising encounter with the chaos of the marketplace. Nationalist and authoritarian remedies are now ascendant. But important areas of influence remain unexplored (Kurth, 1995).

The first area requires a conceptual change in economic aid policies and in strategies for developing the Russian market. Until recently, the West concentrated on helping Russia meet its international debt load while encouraging it to carry on with austerity policies. Since the December 1993 elections, opinion has shifted toward providing more overt support for social safety net programs as a way of easing economic discontent (Nelson, 1994). But among the many issues these policies still have not addressed is the legal vacuum at the heart of the Russian economy. Western advice and assistance in creating a commercial infrastructure, including a viable banking system and regulatory agencies, and in developing a legal framework for business activities, would go far toward meeting the security concerns of Russian and foreign investors (McFaul, 1995).

Finally, the primary U.S. interest in Russia and the NIS is to prevent their re-emergence as a security threat to the West. This can be best achieved if (1) these states make a transition to market economies and democratic systems of government; (2) they behave responsibly in foreign affairs, recognizing the sovereignty and territorial integrity of their neighbors; and (3) security agreements reached with the Soviet Union are implemented by these successor states, particularly with respect to nuclear weapons.

History shows two alternate paths. The West isolated Germany after World War I, which caused World War II. After World War II the West integrated Germany and Japan into a peaceful and prosperous international order. It is in our own national interest that the United States, the victors in the cold war, not treat Russia and its neighbors as the vanquished.

Developing partnerships with these successor states is, and should be, the focus of our relations. Russia, the most powerful successor state, also has the most profound sense of loss. It is a fertile field for hostile nationalist revisionism. Only a successful transition to democracy and free enterprise will be able to steer Russia in the same positive, peaceful direction that Germany and Japan followed after World War II. If Russia succeeds in building a free society and a market economy, the benefits for the United States are considerable. They include a reduced threat of nuclear war, lower U.S. defense budgets, new markets for U.S. exports, and cooperation with Russia on global and regional issues (McFaul, 1995).

Conclusion

If Russia fails, the risks for the United States are also great. Russia still has thousands of nuclear weapons. Instability could result in the use of these weapons against Russia's neighbors, or in the weapons and technologies' falling into the wrong hands. The rise of an authoritarian, ultra-nationalist government could lead to the reversal of reform and a return to hard-line policies. This could also force a return to cold war defense budgets. Other consequences of instability and failure include a severe strain on the new democracies of central and eastern Europe. It will be difficult to maintain stability and prosperity in the western half of Europe if there is chaos to the east.

References

Clinton, W. (1994, January). Strengthening Russia's economic and political future. Dispatch [Speeches], 5, 26.

Cunningham, P. (1998). The Russian dilemma. Unpublished doctoral disseration, University of California, Santa Barbara.

Gibbons, G. (1996, May 29). Whitewater: just one of Clinton's election hurdles. Reuters.

Kurth, J. (1995, January). The clash in Western society. Current, p. 19.

McFaul, M. (1995, January). Why Russia's politics matter. Foreign Affairs, 74, 87.

Nelson, L. D., & Kuzes, I. V. (1994). Property to the people: The struggle for radical economic reform in Russia. Armonk, NY: Sharpe.

Specter, M. (1996, March 24). Soviet echoes: Russia and Belarus form "union state." The Atlanta Journal and Constitution, p. A18.

(A+) This student has wisely narrowed the focus of the paper and included enough history to put the current issues and relations in context, while at the same time demonstrating a broad understanding of the underlying issues between these rival Asian countries. (MLA style)

JAPAN AND KOREA: NEIGHBORS AND RIVALS

Since World War II Japan has been the strategic ally of the United States in the northern Pacific. With communism crumbling around the world in the late 1980s, Japan has been summoned by the United States to play a greater role in that region's security. Factors not limited to economics, defense, and diplomacy have made Japan and the United States logical, if at times dysfunctional, bedfellows. Trade is at the heart of the issue.

Communists in North Korea remain unpredictable and at large, remindful to democracies that it's still not safe to sleep at night. What began as a totally dependent relationship where the United States was supporting and protecting South Korea has now become more of a partnership. Korea is still dependent on U.S. military might, but has become an economic powerhouse in its own right, second only to Japan in Asia. Once again, trade and security are intertwined (MacMurtie 4-5).

The fact that Japan and Korea have been arch-enemies for 1,000 years complicates the issue more than a little for everyone involved. So does the U.S. role as the former conqueror of one and savior of the other. The level of complication might be compared to a divorced couple who have married into the same family and share children all around; for Russia and China are involved, as are the Philippines, Thailand, Vietnam, and the rest of Asia (MacMurtie 1-3). The whole mix of relationships is far too complex for the limits of this paper, which focuses on the relationship between Japan and Korea.

Background

Japan had ruled Korea from the end of the Russo-Japanese War (which was fought largely in Korea) until the end of World War II. The Japanese takeover had been a long time in coming. The seafaring Koreans had been in conflict with the Japanese and concerned about the potential threat of invasion for hundreds of years when the Japanese launched their first all-out attempt in the 1500s. A powerful Samurai army embarked for Korea, confident of success against the far less organized Korean defenses. The Korean "army" stood little chance against trained and disciplined Samurai (MacMurtie 22-50).

But the Japanese underestimated the Koreans, as they always seem to have done. The Koreans chose to meet the Japanese at sea; they built a fleet of armored ships with cannons, against which the Japanese had no protection. The resulting battle was no contest. The pride of Japan went down with the ships, and Japan was left defenseless. At this point, the Koreans decided to eliminate the Japanese threat once and for all. Having no substantial army of their own to invade the larger country, they offered the Mongol army a ride to Japan on their fleet (MacMurtie 22-50).

The Japanese were facing doom, and knew it. Their fleet and army were both on the bottom of the Japan Sea. Only the gods could save them. And the gods saved them in the form of a "divine wind": A typhoon sank the Korean ships and the Mongol army. Thus the populations of both countries were saved from devastation. But neither side forgot. The Japanese word for the divine wind that saves from utter destruction is Kamikaze. The wind failed them in World War II, and the Koreans were freed from nearly 50 years of brutal subjugation that compares with the treatment of blacks in the Jim Crow South of the early twentieth-century United States (MacMurtie 50-75).

Japan has few natural resources of its own. Japan's early postwar relations with the rest of Asia were concerned mainly with the promotion of its far-flung economic interest in the region through trade, technical assistance, and aid programs (Toshio 6D). Although the military threat was removed by the U.S. victory, there remained (and remains) widespread apprehension about Japan's continued economic power. Mistrust and resentment don't fade overnight.

Postwar Relations Between Japan and Korea

Japan had begun to normalize relations with its neighbors during the 1950s, which led to the payment of war reparations to Burma, Indonesia, the Philippines, South Vietnam, and Thailand. These payments were rigidly bound to self-interest projects that promoted plant and equipment purchases from Japan (Toshio 6D).

In the early and mid-1960s the Japanese government adopted a more forward posture in seeking to establish contacts in Asia. As trade expanded, leaders began to question the propriety and wisdom of what they variously described as "mere economics," an "export-first policy," and the "commercial motives of aid" (Toshio 6D).

Meanwhile Japan's relations with its age-old foe South Korea remained difficult. Japan's stake in keeping close ties was still very important following the end of World War II. South Korea had historically served as a vital security barrier. But it was political suicide in Korea to build strong relations with Japan without an apology and reparations. An apology from the Japanese and admission of guilt was equally unthinkable to the Japanese. Resolution of the political differences of the early postwar period didn't really develop until a normalization treaty, signed in mid-1965, improved relations between the two countries considerably. South Korea became Japan's largest trading partner after the United States. Close political ties between members of the Japanese establishment and key South Korean government and business leaders were instrumental in keeping the relationship friendly despite the lack of mutual respect at the popular level (Toshio 6D).

Renewed Friction and Korea's
Rise as an Economic Power

After 1973-1974, however, official relations between Japan and Korea became very cool. One source of friction was the Japanese delay in ratifying an agreement on joint Korean-Japanese development of the continental shelf adjacent to their coasts (Tosio 6D). This came on the heels of the assassination of the South Korean president's wife, who was the inadvertent victim of bullets intended for the president. President Park Chung Hee had essentially been an elected dictator since shortly after the over-throw of the former president in the early 1960s. His popular wife was perceived as a moderating influence, and Park remained popular outside the major urban centers of Seoul and Pusan, where his opponents were in the majority. After his wife's death, however, Park became more reclusive, and some said paranoid. Finally, the head of his own CIA pulled out an automatic and shot him dead at a cabinet meeting. Turmoil and military presidents followed, delaying progress with Japan. Economically, however, Korea roared ahead in a frenzied attempt to "catch up" with Japan and level the playing field with its arch-enemy (MacMurtie 115-132).

In September 1981 Japan-South Korea ministerial-level meetings were revived after a three-year lapse. This eleventh ministerial conference ended in a stalemate, with no agreement on major issues. South Korea had taken the position that Japan owed part of its peace and security to South Korea's large defense responsibility and should therefore be willing to give it $6 billion (U.S.) in development assistance over a five-year period, beginning in 1982. Japan refused to link its aid to security and turned down the South Korean request, pointing out that the amount involved would be equal to almost two-thirds of Japan's projected bilateral official development assistance (ODA) for all countries for the 1972-1987 period. However, indications were that Japan would increase its aid to South Korea, but not to the level demanded by Seoul (Toshio 6D).

Economic growth in South Korea remained high, and the Seoul Olympics boosted both the national pride and the visibility as a new player on the world economic stage. Korea's average economic growth rate of 7.26% between 1991 and 1995 was higher than that of any member country of the Organization for Economic Cooperation and Development (OECD). Although 1994's gross domestic product of $379.5 billion would have been ranked ninth among OECD nations, the per-capita gross national product of $7,513 would rank 23rd (Coleman 37).

The great Korean success brought grudging respect from Japan. Some progress was made in getting the Japanese to admit to, and even pay for, such atrocities as the use of Korean women as "comfort ladies" for the Japanese troops in World War II. There remained battles over depictions of the war in Japanese textbooks and other issues, but there was progress, and the huge level of trade helped to bring Japanese and Koreans together for mutual benefit. But trouble was coming that was only partially connected to their rivalry.

For many years to come, 1997 will remain a black year on both Korean and Japanese calendars. The Japanese productivity that had driven the economic miracle was matched by the United States, which finally responded to the threat and could still use its superior resources and cheaper land to great effect. Meanwhile, the Koreans (and Taiwanese) were producing high-quality goods with labor rates the Japanese could not match. Encouraged, the Koreans massively expanded their capacity in a bid to match the Japanese. But when Indonesia and then Thailand collapsed in a morass of red ink and could not afford to buy from the Koreans, it became clear what some had been forecasting earlier: that Korea had massive over-capacity and overinvestment. The bubble burst, and the Korean economy took a huge dive. This, in turn, made Korean goods even less expensive on the world market, putting even greater pressure on the Japanese, whose products were now perceived as being expen-sive (MacMurtie 134).

Epilogue

The Japanese and Koreans are still wary of each other, and will probably remain so for years. Competition in the world market will almost certainly lead to mixed results, bringing these peoples closer in some ways and setting them against each other in others. But the trend of recent years has been generally positive. Relations between these Asian powerhouses are better and more equal than they have been for 1,000 years. And the fact that the United States is a strong ally of both serves to reduce tensions and fears between them. In the short term, both economies are struggling; but this will pass. And in the long term (especially after Korea unifies), the sheer volume of economic interchange should continue to make Japan and Korea build closer ties.

Works Cited

Coleman, C.S. "Economic Growth and Inflation in South Korea Remains High." <u>Korea Times</u> 7 Jun. 1995: 37+.

MacMurtie, Robert L. "Japan and Korea: Co-Dependent Rivals." Diss. Boston U, 1998.

Toshio. G. "Japan and Other Countries in Asia." <u>Countries of the World</u>. 1 Jan 1991: 6D.

When this paper was written (1993), Czechoslovakia had not yet split into the Czech Republic and Slovakia; but despite being slightly dated, it tells us much not only about *what* happened there, but also *why* events transpired as they did. Notice how the student relates historical events and issues to modern ones. An A+ term paper would not normally include as many lengthy quotations as this paper does. However, this student uses quotations in a manner that conveys mastery of the topic, not an attempt to pad the paper. The one very long quotation is a beautifully written firsthand account that substantially aids in the understanding of the topic. (MLA style)

WHY VACLAV HAVEL? WHY CZECHOSLOVAKIA?

The success or failure of politics and economics in any country under any system has as much to do with the people themselves and their culture as it does with economic systems. Vaclav Havel as an individual and Czechoslovakia as a country have attained unprecedented level of respect in the West only two years after the "Velvet Revolution" brought them out from the yoke and obscurity of the Soviet block. This paper seeks to clarify some of the reasons this has happened.

Why Is This Small Country Leading the Way?

With the fall of the Soviet empire, Czechoslovakia emerged with influence not only in central Europe, but in the world. This degree of both political and moral leadership is remarkable for a "small" country; for as Czechoslovakia's great novelist Milan Kundera has said, "A small country is one whose existence is in doubt from year to year" (Kundera 163). Much of the credit for renewed interest in Czechoslovakia must go to Vaclav Havel; but he is not operating in a vacuum. We really shouldn't be too surprised that this small country is leading the way.

Vaclav Havel has emerged as not only a leader of his country, but as a leader with influence far beyond his country's military or economic significance. As remarkable as his story is, it is perhaps even more remarkable that this is the third time in 50 years that Czechoslovakia has staked out its moral position and caused the world to have to deal with that stand. First, in 1938 Czechoslovakia stood as the representative of democracy against

Hitler; 30 years later came Alexander Dubcek and the "Prague Spring" of 1968; and today we have Havel speaking to a joint session of Congress not of petty politics or even grand politics, but of the essence of Democracy in a way that has seldom been heard there in recent years (Friedman A1).

The Voice of Czech Experience

Only 20 years after the 300-year-old Hapsburg yoke was thrown off in 1918, the English and French sold out the Czechs to the Germans in 1938. Then the Poles and Hungarians pounced like vultures to take what pieces they could. In 1948 the Russians engineered a Communist coup. In 1968 the Russians, Germans, Hungarians, and Poles invaded again.

The Czechs have not forgotten, and that memory has served as a reminder that in the end, they must provide their own leadership and create their own security. In this light Havel's surprising suggestion to congress in 1990 that the United States could best help Czechoslovakia by helping the Soviet Union is the voice of Czechoslovak experience, saying, in essence: "We can take care of ourselves if you big boys don't mess with us" (Friedman A1).

Dubcek, the Honest Slovak

Havel's support of Russian reform at that time is also understandable since the concepts of "Perestroika" and "Glasnost" were not created by Mikhail Gorbachev. They are only the names he gave his version of what Alexander Dubcek brought to Czechoslovakia in 1968 and called "Socialism with a Human Face." Dubcek and Gorbachev were classmates at Moscow State University, and Gorbechev's Czech roommate was Zdenek Mlynar, who played a key role in Dubcek's Prague Spring (Dubcek 143). Mlynar's wife taught The History of Economic Thought and The Economics of The Anglo-Saxon Countries at Charles University in Prague. She had spent the war years going to public schools in New York and became a champion cookie seller in the Girl Scouts. Her name was Rita Klimova, and by 1990 she was the Czech Ambassador to the United States, but that is getting ahead of our story (Unger 36).

We Want Light!

Around Christmas 1967 a group of engineering students in Prague were fed up with the periodic lack of heat and light in their dorms. They took to the streets and marched to the castle to complain directly to the president. In the United States that would hardly raise an eyebrow, but this was Prague in the heart of the cold war, and the president was the hard-line neo-Stalinist Antonin Novotny. The sight of students marching through the night chanting "We want light!" in that subtext was like a lightning bolt. The demonstration was quickly and forcefully broken up, but for the first time in the history of the regime, it was felt necessary that the president personally meet and negotiate with a group of student leaders (Goldflam). Novotny's long-overdue end came soon after.

The Soviets supported a change because it seemed that Novotny had lost control. They had no objection when Alexander Dubcek was made party leader because all they knew about him was that he was a second-generation communist who had grown up and been educated in the Soviet Union. The Russians were appalled when censorship ended and a fresh wave of new ideas and confidence spread through the land. Dubcek asked a simple question: "Where there once was light, why should there be darkness?" (Dubcek 122) The Soviets were terrified of that question and crushed the Prague Spring, but it was too late. Dubcek, the honest Slovak and dedicated Communist, had forced the Soviet's hand with his restructuring of the party (now called Perestroika) and with his openness (now called Glasnost). By failing to follow through the door of reform Dubcek had opened and suppressing Socialism with a Human Face the Soviets set down the road that would lead them in 20 years to "Communism with Its Face Kicked In."

A Tradition of Leadership

Havel is continuing the tradition of leadership by pushing to create an "Adriatic Trade Group," including Czechoslovakia, Austria, Italy, and Yugoslavia, to replace his country's ties with the nearly defunct COMECON. He is also proposing a European Security Commission to coordinate security discussions now that the Warsaw Pact is breaking up. The headquarters of this organization may be in Prague. His proposal for a neutral, unaligned Germany has both the United States and the Soviet Union squirming, but Havel's prestige is too great at the moment for anyone involved in the issues to ignore (Friedman A1).

Vaclav Havel is making us all look a little closer at the issues, and that is good for us all. The poet is proving to be a very effective president, and making his country the focus of attempts to solve the region's problems.

Why Vaclav Havel?

The Western world seems amazed at the prospect of a poet/playwright becoming president. In some segments of U.S. society, intellectual is almost a dirty word. In Czechoslovakia, on the other hand, there have been only three elected presidents (outside of the Communists) since 1919: Two were professors and now a poet/playwright. To the Czechoslovak way of thinking, that is one of their greatest strengths. In fact, one of the earliest calls for independence came in April 1917, when virtually all prominent Czechoslovak writers and poets, in a stirring manifesto, demanded a free and democratic Czechoslovak state. In 1938 journalist/historian Maurice Hindus described the phenomenon of the "Intellectual State" perfectly in a single (if long) paragraph of his remarkable book We Shall Live Again:

> Czechoslovakia had the good fortune of being headed by a group of remarkable men, the so-called "professors"; Thomas Masaryk, a half Czech, half Slovak professor of philosophy and political science, Benes, a Czech professor of sociology, and Stefanik, a Slovak general and astronomer. These professors were the guiding spirit of Czechoslovak emancipation, the mid-wives and the nurses of the Republic. Slavs all of them, they were unlike any Slav or any other intelligentsia on the

European continent. In other lands the intelligentsia, though noble enough of tongue, had collapsed under the burden of the political responsibilities which the war and the peace had thrust on them. In Russia they were crushed by the Bolsheviks. In Germany they were trampled to destruction by Hitler. In Czechoslovakia they remained triumphant. Czechoslovakia was the one country in Europe in which the college professor and the intellectual had vindicated not only his dream but his class. His ideas prevailed, and his chief concern was to fit them into a democratic framework. He abhorred the thought of violence and totalitarianism, whether of the right or the left. He would override hate, trouble, conflict by the peaceful authority of democratic usage. There was nothing that preoccupied and excited him so much as democracy, not only as an ideal but as a way of life. He would inoculate the whole population, especially the youth of the land, with a faith in it, and all-pervasive, indomitable faith which could withstand the blandishments and the threats of the nearby dictatorships. (Hindus 232-234)

"By violence?" asked Masaryk. "Or by moderation, with a plow or with a sword?" And he answered: "By compromise, with the plow, by work--that is the answer of the Czech spirit and of Czech history" (Masaryk 12). Certainly the Czech people were ready for such an answer. The battle of the White Mountain against the Hapsburgs in 1620 had not only ended their independence but had left them leaderless. Their aristocracy and intelligentsia had been annihilated. They became a nation of peasants (Masaryk 6). "There is scarcely one of us Czechs," said Masaryk, "who wasn't born in a peasant hut, and if he wasn't his father was" (Masaryk 182).

Egalitarians

Masaryk's comments are probably more accurate for his native Moravia and Slovakia than for Prague, whose residents were hardly peasants living in huts. But it is quite true that under Hapsburg rule the Czech aristocracy never recovered from White Mountain (Masaryk 28). Partly because of this, the Czechs became a much more egalitarian people than, say, the Hungarians, where 10% of the population were nobles, and the noble class was dominated the country (Hindus 256):

> They had no ruling class and never developed it. Nor had they ever acquired the swank, the haughtiness, the grace, the lavishness of a ruling class. They were common people and chose to remain so. In all my contacts with Czechs, the wealthy, the poor, the intelligentsia, I never sensed any effort to ape the manners, the habits, the extravagances of a ruling class. (Hindus 257-58).

These uncommonly well-educated "common" people were led by democratic intellectuals in their finest hours, and their literacy, literature, culture, and history helped them maintain their identity even while under the political domination of others. As Prime Minister Jiri Dienstbier noted, "Essential ties of history and thought that bind Czechoslovakia to the European tradition go back centuries, as does the activism of its leaders" (Dienstbier).

Education as a Core Value

The Czechoslovaks are a mature people with a 1,400-year history behind them. We in the United States tend to forget (if we ever knew) that Jan Hus, a professor at Charles University, led a successful revolution against the power and corruption of Rome that called upon every man to read the Bible and come to terms individually with God. This same focus on self-interpretation in their religion was the reason our own forefathers put such value on education. That was an old tradition in Czechoslovakia: Jan Hus lived 100 years before Martin Luther. To put it in perspective, when Harvard was founded in 1636, Charles University was 300 years old. Harvard even offered the presidency of the college to a professor from Charles (Heymann 146).

As Masaryk pointed out in a speech in 1910 on Jan Hus and the Czech Reformation, the Czechs may have been the most literate people in the world at that time, with or without their aristocracy:

> The Czech people were predisposed toward the reformation by their relatively high education level. We know that a certain Roman prelate who visited our country during the Hussite days stated that our peasant women knew the bible better than most Roman prelates. . . . Only educated, thinking people could make use of the Bible as their sole religious authority. (Masaryk 82-83)

Havel's Place; The Czechs' Place

It was into this society that Vaclav Havel was born. Havel's plays reflect a profound understanding of his people and their situation. From Masaryk the philosopher, to Benes the sociologist, to Havel the playwright is really a natural transition interrupted by 40 years of Communism. Havel's own words are the best description of the role he sees for his country:

> We have the chance to transform a wreath of European states which were until recently colonized by the Soviets . . . into a special body which will approach the richer Western Europe not as a poor apostate or a helpless amnestied prisoner, but as somebody who also brings something. That is, spiritual and moral impulses, daring peace initiatives, unexploited creative potential, the ethos of freshly won freedom and inspiration for courageous and speedy solutions. (Havel 19)

Czechoslovakia, for all its potential, still faces serious problems. Many of these are such that correction will take years. One is a lack of recent democratic experience. This is a problem faced by all of the newly free Eastern European countries. Although Czechoslovakia's leadership has proved excellent so far, that leadership is shallow; there just aren't that many people with democratic political experience.

The underground movement Charter 77 (named after a charter signed in 1977 by 242 dissidents, including not only Havel but 140 former Communists) was small. Civic Forum, the political party that grew out of Charter 77, was a larger, "mass movement," but still small. When the new government was formed, the leadership of Civic Forum became the leaders of the government, and Civic Forum, as a proto-political party, was left very short of experienced leaders and organizers (Ash 118). Grassroots development of a participatory political system to provide that leadership should be a major priority. New leaders will come along and gain experience; but that takes time, and much needs to be done right away.

The Future

Many see an excellent first step in the election of Vaclav Klaus as the chairman of Civic Forum, and then as prime minister. The former finance minister is a popular, pragmatic economist who advocates a rapid transformation of Czechoslovakia's economy from communism into a market system. Klaus was not Havel's choice for the post, but many people on the streets of Prague see him as the kind of nuts-and-bolts leader needed to make the transition from revolutionary movement to functional political process. His pragmatism clashes with the idealism of many of Havel's associates, who privately call him a "Thatcherite." But Havel's reaction to Klaus's election set a hopeful, and decidedly Czech, tone for the difficult discussions that are sure to come: He invited Klaus to the castle for a beer the next day.

Works Cited

Ash, Timothy Garton. Inside the Magic Lantern. New York: Vintage
    Books, 1993.

Dienstbier, Jiri. Address at Harvard University, Boston. 14 Oct.
    1990.

Dubcek, Alexander. Hope Dies Last. New York: Kodanshna
    International, 1993.

Friedman, T.L. "Havel's 'Paradoxial' Plea: Help Soviets."
    New York Times 22 Feb. 1990: A1.

Goldflam, Rudolf. Personal interview. 22 Mar. 1993.

Havel, Vaclav. "The Future of Central Europe."
    New York Review of Books 29 Mar. 1990: 18+.

Heymann, Frederick G. Poland and Czechoslovakia. Englewood Cliffs,
    NJ: Prentice Hall, 1966.

Hindus, Maurice. We Shall Live Again. New York: Doubleday,
    Doran & Co., 1939.

Kundera, Milan. The Unbearable Lightness of Being. New York:
    Harper & Row, 1984.

Masaryk, Tomas G. The Meaning of Czech History. Chapel Hill:
    U of North Carolina Press, 1974.

Unger, Stanford. "Havel's Choice." New York Times Magazine 1 Mar.
    1990: 36.

14
PHILOSOPHY

Three Philosophers on Individual Freedom, Authority, and the Interests of Society

The Republic: What Were Plato's Primary Motive and Intent?

Free Will Versus Determinism, and the New Scientific Determinism

This paper discusses the views of three political philosophers regarding individual freedom and authority. The instructor's assignment required that the student summarize the philosophies in a brief space, and use only the philosophers' writings—not other source material. (Normally, however, you should avoid taking on such a broad subject for your term paper.) The paper's conclusion, which demonstrates the student's original thought, distinguishes this as an A+ paper. (MLA endnote style)

THREE PHILOSOPHERS ON INDIVIDUAL FREEDOM,

AUTHORITY, AND THE INTERESTS OF SOCIETY

The political philosophies of John Stuart Mill, Edmund Burke, and Thomas Paine as they relate to the notions of authority and individual freedom, might seem strikingly different. Yet they have at heart a common concern for the welfare of the citizenry and of the society. This paper examines how each one reconciles and balances individual interests and those of society, and, in concluding, how Darwin's evolutionary theories might provide some insight into their differences.

John Stuart Mill's "Tyranny of the Majority"

Nineteenth-century spokesman for liberalism John Stuart Mill advocated that we should each act so as to promote the greatest happiness for the greatest number of people--a notion that became known generally as <u>utilitarianism</u>. Yet paradoxically Mill also championed the cause of individual rights. For Mill, this paradox was essential, and in fact was at the heart of his political philosophy.

Liberty and authority, claimed Mill, are always at odds with each another, and in fact must coexist in order to achieve social and political order. On the one hand, authority is inherent in the system to protect the society from the corrupt among them; as Mill put it:

> "To prevent the weaker members of the community from being preyed upon by innumerable vultures, it was needful that there be an animal of prey stronger than the rest, commissioned to keep them down."[1]

On the other hand, liberty is established to protect the governed from the abuses and excesses of the governors.

In his treatise <u>On Liberty</u>, Mill argued that in the past the danger had been that monarchs held power at the expense of the common people, and that the real struggle was to gain liberty by limiting such governmental power. But now power was largely passed into the hands of the people at large through democratic forms of government. The danger with this shift in power, as Mill saw it, was that the majority denied liberty to individuals, whether explicitly through laws, which he called "acts of public authority," or more subtly through social pressure, which he called "collective opinion."[2] Fearing that the will of the majority might be imposed on the rights of the minority, a problem that he labeled "tyranny of the majority,"[3] Mill proposed setting limits on the powers of the rulers who represent the majority.[4]

Even so, continued Mill, the majority rule meant having the will of the majority imposed on the dissenting minority.[5] As Mill explained, "Like other tyrannies, the tyranny of the majority was at first, and is still vulgarly, held in dread, chiefly as operating through the acts of the public authorities."[6] In fact, Mill went so far as to assert that when society imposes "mandates," it imposes a kind of social tyranny worse than that of absolute despotism:

> There needs [to be] protection also against the tyranny of the prevailing opinion and feeling; against the tendency of society to impose, by other means than civil penalties, its own ideas and practices as rules of conduct on those who dissent from them; to fetter the development, and, if possible, prevent the formation, of any individuality not in harmony with its ways, and compel all characters to fashion themselves upon the model of its own.[7]

In short, although the exercise of political power over the community together with the limitation of such power were what Mill meant by liberty, Mill seemed to be more fearful of a diffuse social power, which left unfettered might undermine, and perhaps overwhelm, this liberty.

Edmund Burke: Experience as the Method of Nature

A political thinker whom conservatives still enjoy quoting, Burke's view is in essence that the notion of individual liberty cannot be severed from the interests of society as a whole. Burke's philosophy is tied up in his concept of nature. According to Burke, human nature is both the present reality--of habits, needs, and wants--and the aspiration to virtue and excellence.[8] For Burke, perfection of the latter nature can be achieved only by the state (political government); in fact, for Burke the state is part of the created order. Burke boldly asserts that "[God] who gave our nature to be perfected by our virtue, willed also the necessary means of its perfection--He willed therefore the state."[9]

Burke expanded this notion that the state is part and parcel of nature by drawing an analogy between the human spirit, or heart, and the spirit of the state. Just as abstract thought is only one component of any person's life, asserted Burke, an underlying political philosophy is only one component of any civil order. To shape a government completely according to metaphysical calculation is to try to swallow the whole into a part. In essence, Burke complained that it is not reasonable to treat humans as only rational. Political life--as all human life--is a matter of the heart. Every state comprises people with reflexes, habits, prejudices, and affections. Every person participates in a proper civil order only through experience, and any state must look to this past experience for its future vitality.

Thus, continued Burke, in order to create and maintain a natural state, the conduct of the state should be guided by philosophic analogy to past experience, not by ground-up philosophizing. Burke chided the French because they "chose to act as if [they] had every thing to begin anew."[10] Instead, he contends, they might have revisited their own distant past in order to "build on those old foundations."[11] In politics, asserted Burke, it is more important that we look to past experience than that we abstract from past experience. Thus Burke looked to human experience as a guide for the form and conduct of the natural state. Each generation should see itself as part of the true continuum of humanity, as part of an old and noble family, rather than as standing new-sprung in an imagined and unreal state of nature.

This underlying philosophy led Burke to an argument for hierarchical lineage, colloquially known as a pecking order. He insisted that excellence is often inherited and virtue is usually inculcated, and because family is the most natural vehicle of both inheritance and education, a wise state will cultivate some form of hereditary aristocracy. The aristocracy should be open, admitting those who possess a "rare merit" that has "passed through some sort of probation."[12] He continues,

> "Every thing ought to be open, but not indifferently to every man. . . . Some decent regulated pre-eminence, some preference (not exclusive appropriation) given to birth, is neither unnatural, nor unjust, nor impolitic. . . . In the state, as in families, the idea of inheritance furnishes a sure principle of conservation, and a sure principle of trans-mission; without at all excluding a principle of improvement."[13]

In the same way, asserts Burke, the rights and benefits of government are best seen as a hereditary legacy rather than as self-existent abstractions. "The rights of men in governments are their advantages,"[14] and those real-world advantages flow from institutions and allegiances that precede any single generation. When we see those benefits both as a inheritance we have received and as a legacy that we will leave to our children, we are imbued with the gratitude of a fortunate child and the care of a nurturing parent. Instead of presuming to reform solely according to our own speculations, we attend to the business of state with a practical seriousness and humility.[15]

The Natural Rights Model of Thomas Paine

Also called the father of libertarianism, Thomas Paine left his mark with <u>Rights of Man</u>, which was a poignant rebuttal to Edmund Burke's <u>Reflections on the French Revolution</u>. Paine answered Burke's pro-monarchy stance, explaining the advantages of a republic over a monarchy. <u>Rights of Man</u> reflected Paine's belief in natural reason and natural rights, political equality, tolerance, civil liberties, and the dignity of man:

> Natural rights are those which appertain to man in right of his existence. Of this kind are all the intellectual rights, or rights of the mind, and also all those rights of acting as an individual for his own comfort and happiness, which are not injurious to the natural rights of others.[16]

Paine claimed that he and other ordinary men had been endowed by nature with the same reasonable faculties as their privileged betters. Indeed, he continued, had the productive artisans and farmers of America and Britain not contributed far more to the public good than the well-born ladies and gentlemen who had never produced a thing in their lives?[17]

Paine called for sweeping away the entire aristocratic structure and beginning anew, with a wholly republican government, freed from any traces of those "two ancient tyrannies," monarchy and aristocracy. "Lay then the ax to the root," he declared, "and teach government humanity."[18] In the wake of the Jacobin Terror in France, Paine repeatedly remarked on how, without setting up self-limiting constitutions, democracy would degenerate into tyranny.

In <u>Rights of Man</u>, Paine stated his belief that mankind was harmonious. Individuals entered into relations with each other in order to fulfill individual desires; the sum of those relations was what he meant by society, a wholly natural and reasonable entity ever attentive to the common good. It was government, established by a parasitic hereditary caste--a caste that stood outside society--that was the cause of human misery. Society is produced by our wants and government by our wickedness; the former promotes our happiness positively by uniting our affections, the latter negatively by restraining our vices. The one encourages exchanges, the other creates distinctions. Society is in every state a blessing, but government, even in its best state, is but a necessary evil.[19]

Conclusion

Thus witness three strikingly different political philosophies about individual freedom and authority. Burke's position reminds us, interestingly, of Charles Darwin's evolutionary theory and his ideas about survival of the fittest, which in turn might help us to understand how these three philosophers differed.

For Burke, giving power to a privileged few was not just acceptable, it was part of the natural order of things--survival of the fittest. Paine seemed to want to protect the little fish from being swallowed by the bigger, more "fit" fish. Yet Paine saw this measure of protection as natural in the sense that the common good can be achieved only through unfettered individual freedom. Meanwhile, Mill seemed to side with Burke, at least insofar as he acknowledged that a powerful state is desirable. Yet for Mill a powerful state is not a natural result of our pursuit of virtue. Instead, it is needed to prevent the greater potential evil of social tyranny by the majority--a large school of fish ganging up on one lone fish, or at least pressuring it to join the gang.

Endnotes

[1] John Stuart Mill, <u>On Liberty</u>, ed. Currin V. Shields (Englewood Cliffs, NJ: Prentice Hall, 1956) 4.

[2] Mill 19-22.

[3] Mill 7.

[4] Mill 93.

[5] Mill 95.

[6] Mill 95.

[7] Mill 95.

[8] Edmund Burke, <u>Reflections on the French Revolution</u>, ed. Conor Cruise O'Brien (London: Pelican Books) 120.

[9] Burke 120.

[10] Burke 118.

[11] Burke 118.

[12] Burke 118.

[13] Burke 340.

[14] Burke 370.

[15] Burke 370.

[16] Thomas Paine, <u>Rights of Man</u> (New York: Penguin Books, 1985).

[17] Paine 174.

[18] Paine 175.

[19] Paine 175.

This paper explores Plato's possible motives, intent, and thesis in his work *The Republic*. The student relied heavily on Internet resources to survey the views of different scholars. The student's insightful analysis and provocative introductory and concluding remarks earned her an A+. (MLA style)

The Republic: WHAT WERE PLATO'S PRIMARY MOTIVE AND INTENT?

Plato's The Republic, written more than 300 years before the birth of Christ, continues to be a subject of academic debate. Is it a treatise advocating democracy, or is it the inspiration for The Communist Manifesto? Is The Republic an exercise in political ideology, or is it a study in dialectic philosophy? Is there a correct viewpoint, or are various viewpoints valid in there own ways?

Socrates, who was Plato's teacher, would vigorously question all points of view, and if he could find a flaw in one of them, he would immediately discount it. This paper provides varying scholarly perspectives on Plato's intent and his motives in writing The Republic. It is up to the reader to draw his or her own conclusions as to the validity of each argument.

The Republic as an Exercise in the Art of Rhetoric

Plato wrote The Republic in active first-person narrative style. However, the narrator is not Plato himself, but his philosophical mentor, Socrates. Why? Because the narrator is the ultimate judge in the philosophical arguments presented in The Republic, perhaps Plato felt that Socrates, the most famous teacher of philosophy in Greece, would be perceived by readers as a more authoritative figure on the subjects of justice and of right versus wrong than one of his students.

According to one scholar, The Republic is in fact primarily an examination of the role of rhetoric within the political arena. Anckaert claims that Plato indeed aimed to demonstrate the persuasive power of rhetoric, and used subtle rhetorical devices, including the grammatical first person and the narrator Socrates, to entice the reader into accepting his conclusions. Anckaert does not go so far as to say that this was Plato's primary motive in writing The Republic. But given the disagreement among scholars as to Plato's central substantive theme, some of which are examined in this paper, perhaps what Plato was up to primarily in writing The Republic was to demonstrate the power of rhetoric.

Equal Opportunity and Plato's Concept of Justice

When scholars examine The Republic, more often than not the discussion turns to Book I--specifically, to the conversation among Socrates and his friends as to the meaning of justice. In the conversation, after all arguments are presented, Socrates concluded that justice is inherently good, but that it takes different forms for an individual than for the city-state as a whole. Here Plato's concept of the ideal city, where all citizens are assigned to specific roles, emerges. Children are relinquished by their parents after birth to become wards of the state, so that equal opportunities can be accorded to all. In Plato's republic, women are theoretically entitled to the same rights as men. Plato (as the narrator Socrates) wrote:

If women are to have the same duties as men, they must have the same nurture and education.

Yes.

The education which was assigned to the men was music and gymnastics.

Yes.

Then, women must be taught music and gymnastics and also the art of war, which they must practice like the men?

That is the inference, I suppose. (Plato [online] 140)

Military historian Leon Harold Craig questioned Plato's contention that women of The Republic were regarded as equal to men. How could this be possible, Craig asks, if the warrior was still vital to ensuring the survival of the republic? As Plato wrote, "The males are stronger and the women are weaker" (Plato 140). Therefore, if Craig's assertion is correct, this "seems to place severe practical limits on the full participation of most women even in the most just regime" (Christian).

Some scholars have sharply criticized Book I of The Republic as containing Plato's weakest arguments on the subject of justice. Why, then, is there even a need for Book I? One scholar maintains that the purpose of Book I "is to attack the view that justice is external to the soul--external to the power humans have to render things good" (Lycos). Lycos concludes that Book I is necessary to establish the concept that justice is an internal condition that is dependent not on written external laws, but rather on the moral virtues of the philosopher-kings that exist within.

The Allegory of the Cave and Dream Interpretation

For most readers, the most memorable part of The Republic, aside from Book I, is Plato's Allegory of the Cave, which begins Book VII. This allegory is the metaphorical journey a person undertakes from ignorance to wisdom. The origin of Plato's cave metaphor has been the subject of much academic speculation. The prevailing view is that Plato borrowed the idea from ancient religious cults that sent potential members into caves for ritualistic purposes.

Pierre Grimes contends that through the Allegory of the Cave, Plato intended to demonstrate the importance of dream interpretation in the acquisition of individual knowledge and wisdom. As Grimes notes, "The truth [Plato] refers to is not a general kind of knowledge as with those other studies but a knowledge personal and particular to the individual." According to Grimes, Plato continued to develop this theory in Book IX, where the narrator Socrates encouraged the philosopher to

> "search out his own inner most thoughts," and to ponder and reach out to that which 'he did not know, past or present or future,' and if one proceeds in this endeavor properly then it is in the dreams that "the state of the soul touches truth."

Grimes theorizes that although dreams may initially appear to be merely a hodgepodge of symbolic occurrences, these symbols are firmly rooted in an individual's reality. It is only through closer examination that these dreams become more than a collection of images, and through understanding, they can guide an individual to his own personal truth. According to Grimes, only by understanding dreams do "we learn how the dream communicates meaning and how it uses analogy, allegory and symbol." In Grimes's opinion, this is the most lasting lesson of The Republic because "it alone brings us to see that there is the personal side of philosophy that needs cultivating for our enrichment."

Plato as Political Advocate for a Philosopher-King

So what was Plato's central thesis in The Republic? Author and history professor Stebelton H. Nulle believes Plato's chief concern was with answering the question, "How can society be reconstituted so that men may know happiness and justice?" (114). Nulle reasons that Plato's intentions were political rather than philosophical. Government may be theoretically for the people, but should not necessarily be by the people in terms of the masses. Government should be entrusted to the few dispassionate philosophers who are first and foremost guardians of the truth. Nulle determines that Plato's conclusion in The Republic was, "The philosopher alone is qualified to govern; and that until philosophy and political power meet in one authority there will be no end of human misery" (115).

Is The Republic a Call for Philosophical Inquiry?

Finally, musical scholar and author Dennis Monk has his own unique view of Plato's message in The Republic. Throughout the book Plato emphasized the need for a strong mind and body, and frequently mentioned the importance of gymnastics and music in the lives of the republic's citizens. Yet Monk maintains that Plato was leery of the emotional responses that music tends to conjure in its listeners, making it "dangerous on purely moral grounds" as well as "dangerous on political grounds." In Monk's opinion, Plato, like his mentor Socrates, believed that the only true path to wisdom was through philosophic inquiry. Philosophy enabled the rulers of the republic to prudently rule, using pragmatism rather than passion. Music was regarded by philosophers such as Plato as threatening because of its tendency to overpower human emotions.

Conclusion

Perhaps determining Plato's intent and motives in writing <u>The Republic</u> amounts to little more than Monday-morning quarter-backing. Whether he truly advocated the creation of a political utopia ruled by philosophers or was just using the concept as a metaphor to demonstrate the importance of reason in defining justice and knowledge will never be known. However, it is precisely this ambiguity which allows the reader to take something uniquely individual from <u>The Republic</u> and apply it to his own personal quest for reason. Perhaps ambiguity was Plato's point in the first place.

Works Cited

Anckaert, L. "Language, Ethics, and the Other Between Athens and Jerusalem." <u>Philosophy East and West</u> 1 Oct. 1995. Online at www3.elibrary.com/search/getdoc, 4 Oct. 1997.

Christian, William. "Feature Review." <u>Perspectives on Political Science</u> 1 Sep. 1995. Online at www3.elibrary.com/search/getdoc, 4 Oct. 1997.

Grimes, Pierre. "Dreams and the Philosopher." 6 Jan. 1997. Online at www.gwc.cccd.edu/FAC_STF/GrimP/Philo3.html, 4 Oct. 1997.

Lycos, Kimon. "Plato on Justice and Power." 1 May 1997. Online at www.sunypress.edu/sunyp/backads/html/lycosplato.html, 4 Oct. 1997.

Monk, Dennis C. "Dionysius Redux: Rethinking the Teaching of Music." <u>Arts Education Policy Review</u> 17 Jul. 1996. Online at www3.elibrary.com/search/getdoc, 4 Oct. 1997.

Nulle, Stebelton H., ed. <u>Classics of Western Thought</u>. New York: Harcourt Brace Jovanovich, 1968.

Plato. <u>The Republic</u> Trans. Benjamin Jowett. 20 Jul. 1996. Online at www.utm.edu/research/iep/text/plato/rep/rep.txt, 4 Oct. 1997.

This paper briefly explains the concepts of free will and determinism, and then examines the implications of each vis-à-vis modern genetic engineering. Keep in mind that this paper is not really a term paper per se, because its length is less than 1,000 words, per the instructor's requirements. The student does a good job highlighting a very complex topic within this specified word limit. (MLA style)

FREE WILL VERSUS DETERMINISM, AND THE NEW SCIENTIFIC DETERMINISM

Many are apt to believe that no one should be held morally responsible for an act not freely done; that is, freedom is a necessary condition for moral responsibility. The idea of freedom renders us morally responsibility for our actions because we choose them. In marked contrast, the idea of determinism excuses us from the choices we make because we are all simply acquiescing to some sort of predestiny. These two opposing ideas are both deeply rooted in philosophical tradition. However, determinism has been given new teeth lately, with the advent of genetic research. At the same time, those who advocate free will have risen up against this new scientific determinism.

What Is Determinism?

Determinism is a philosophical school of thought which holds essentially that the past and the laws of nature together determine a unique future. More specifically, its thesis is that every event that occurs, including human actions and choices, is physically necessary given the laws of nature and events that preceded that event or choice (Wolf). The determinist argument is not based on fanciful notions or wishful thinking; rather, it is grounded in deductive logic:

> If determinism is true, we cannot avoid the choices we make.

> If we cannot avoid the choices we make, then we are not responsible for what we do.

> If indeterminism is true, then some of our choices are not under our control.

If our choices are not under our control, then we are not responsible for what we do.

Either determinism or indeterminism is true.

Therefore, we are never responsible for what we do. (Honderich 27-43)

According to strict determinism, then, the "choices" that seem to be part of the essence of our being are actually beyond our control. As a result, we are not accountable for our actions. Determinism lends itself to the belief that everything that happens, including everything one does, is preordained by God. We are mere puppets and God is the puppeteer (Wolf). In this mode of thinking, our life decisions become trivial, unimportant. Throughout history those who have advocated autocratic forms of government, such as monarchies and dictatorships, have embraced determinism, at least ostensibly, to bolster their claim that certain individuals are preordained to assume positions of authority or to rise to the top levels of the socioeconomic infra-structure.

What Is Free Will?

Free will is the capacity to fully control one's behavior. Those who maintain that human beings have free will claim that we control our actions and choices, and therefore we are responsible for the outcomes of those actions and choices (Wolf). In other words, with freedom comes responsibility. The notion of free will, then, would seem to lie at the heart of democratic forms of government, in which choices dictate outcomes.

In order to fully understand free will, it is useful to determine what constitutes an action. According to the volition theory of John Stuart Mill, an action is two things: a state of mind--called a volition--followed by an effect. The intent is one thing, and the effect that is produced is another (Honderich 95). Assuming that an individual has the power to will an action or to stop an action, the individual has free will. This distinction is important; for if intent is lacking, it might be wrong to hold a person responsible for the outcome of his or her actions.

Free will allows one to make decisions throughout life that can change its course, for better or worse. Under the concept of free will, failure is acceptable because one can always choose to redeem oneself. The notion of free will, then, would seem to be essential for the Christian religion, which affords every person the opportunity for redemption.

Scientific Determinism

Determinism suggests that human beings are intrinsically physical beings whose actions are governed by physical forces (Perebroom 27). In other words, people's actions are controlled by and are at the mercy of others' actions. Advances in molecular biology and genetics are lending new credence to determinism by providing evidence that these physical forces include our own individual genetic make-up. Technology is rapidly changing our ideas of human freedom and responsibility. As one commentator put it: "The hurricane speed of genetic discoveries and the driving winds of ethical turbulence seem to be blowing our once secure notions of human freedom off their foundations" (Peters 3).

Genetics has given rise to newfound notions about what human beings are and what we should be. Together these ideas are commonly referred to as scientific determinism, or what critics call the "gene myth." One such notion sees genes as "the ultimate explanation of human being" (Peters 3). "It's all in the genes!" many people now say, believing that our genes determine both who we are--in terms not just of physical make-up but also personality and character--and what we do (Wolf). Another popular yet dubious notion is that when we understand our genes, we will be able to control our future. This kind of thinking has helped to fuel, financially speaking, much of current genetic research. A third level at which the gene myth operates is known as "germ-line intervention," which involves engineering germ cells to influence heredity and possibly reduce the prevalence of disease and improve the quality of life for future generations (Peters 14).

Concluding Remarks

Without question, advances in genetic research and technology present opportunities to improve the human condition on a variety of levels. Many warn, however, that under the pretense of alleviating human suffering, practitioners of genetic engineering will end up playing God (Peters 4). The gene myth also holds serious theological, legal, and social implications: Are we accountable to God? to the courts? to our fellow humans? These are questions that the religious, philosophical, legal, and scientific communities will no doubt continue to grapple with well into the twenty first century, as well they should.

Works Cited

Honderich, Ted. How Free Are You?: The Determinism Problem. Cambridge, Eng.: Oxford UP, 1993.

Peters, Ted. Playing God? Genetic Determinism and Human Freedom. New York: Routledge Press, 1996.

Perebroom, Derk. "Self-Understanding in Kant's Transcendental Deduction." Synthese, Apr. 1995: 1-42.

Rose, Steven. Lifelines: Biology, Freedom, Determinism. London: Allen Lane/Penguin Press, 1997.

Wolf, Susan. "Free Will." Colliers Encyclopedia, 10. CD-ROM, 1995.

15
PHYSICAL SCIENCES

The thesis of this paper, which is fully fleshed out in the final section, is that the distinct morphology of captive-bred alligators impedes their ability to survive in the wild, thereby threatening the species' survival. The paper leads up to this thesis by first discussing the physiology and evolutionary adaptation of the American alligator, and then analyzing the differences in morphology between captive-reared and wild alligators. Notice that the student's introduction provides a clear road map for the reader. (MLA style)

THE ENVIRONMENTAL ADAPTATION OF THE ALLIGATOR

The ability of animals to adapt to their environments is essential for survival. One of the most interesting examples of adaptation is the alligator, in particular the American alligator, which has adapted over millions of years to survive in its natural marine habitat. Its anatomy and other physiological features have allowed the alligator to remain one of the most fierce predators in the swamp.

This report first describes the physiological adaptations that most directly enhance the alligator's predatory abilities. Next, the report examines certain morphological and physiological differences between captive-reared and wild alligators, and how these differences bear negatively on a captive-reared alligator's predatory ability. The paper concludes with a brief exploration of the plight of captive-bred alligators and what is being and can be done to ensure the species' survival.

The Physiology of a Fierce Predator

The American alligator lives in lowland rivers, lakes, and marshes and can be found in coastal plains from North Carolina to Texas. Like all other alligators, the American alligator is classified in the order <u>Crocodilia</u>, family <u>Alligatoridae</u>, genus <u>Alligator</u> (Clark). Although the American alligator closely resembles the American crocodile, they are classified in different families within the <u>Crocodilia</u> order because of differences in their snouts and teeth. The alligator has a broad snout, and its upper teeth clearly overlap the teeth of the lower jaw. In contrast, the snout of the crocodile is tapered, and there is little overlap between its teeth and jaw. Other families within the Crocodilia order that are now extinct exhibited yet other snout and teeth characteristics. Variations included the deep-snouted semi-terrestrial taxa with serrated teeth and hoof-like claws, and several strange duck-billed forms with broad, flat snouts and small (or no) teeth on the lower jaw; some extinct forms were even horned (Clark).

The extraordinarily complex and sophisticated anatomy of the alligator is necessary for it to survive in the wild. The most obvious characteristic of the alligator is the large, ossified, horny plates that cover the entire body, thereby providing the animal with incredibly strong and durable skin. Relating more directly to the alligator's predatory ability, though, are its jaws and mouth. The alligator has exceedingly strong jaws, and up to 80 teeth, which it uses to capture, crush, and dismember its prey. The alligator cannot chew its food; instead, it must swallow it either in whole or in chunks. Oddly, the alligator's tongue is fused to the floor of the mouth, which can make swallowing difficult; further, the alligator cannot swallow while underwater in any event.

Perhaps the most impressive adaptive physiological feature of the alligator is its teeth. When alligators hunt, they use violent attacks, which often result in their losing teeth. But the alligator's physiology has adapted to this problem. Each tooth contains a small replacement tooth within its pulp cavity, and sometimes a further tiny tooth ready to erupt within the replacement tooth (Coulson).

Other Adaptations That Enhance Predatory Ability

Adaptations that have served to enhance the alligator's predatory prowess are not limited to those involving its jaws and mouth. Just as impressive are the alligator's aquatic adaptations-- involving its eyes, ears, nostrils, and feet--which afford the alligator its notoriously stealthy hunting ability.

We're all familiar with the image of the alligator gliding along the water's surface with only the top of the head exposed above water. This behavior provides enough camouflage for the predator as it hunts, while allowing it to look around for prey at the same time. Certain adaptations allow the alligator to hunt in this manner. It has developed highly acute binocular vision, and its eyes, ears, and nostrils are all located near the top of the head. But the alligator is not limited to surface navigation. The ears and nostrils contain valves, which close when the alligator is submerged, allowing it to navigate underwater for long distances; in fact, the alligator can stay underwater for 45 to 60 minutes at a time (Rootes 489). These adaptations allow the alligator to disappear completely from sight, and lie in wait for unsuspecting prey to approach the shore.

Another aquatic adaptation involves locomotion through water. Although it can walk or even run for short distances, the alligator prefers to slide on its belly across land; it has not evolved to chase its prey across land, except for very short distances. Instead, it has developed webbed feet to enhance its locomotive ability through water, so that it can lunge from the water at its prey. Like many aquatic creatures, the alligator has toes joined at the base by webbing, allowing it to move swiftly and efficiently through water. Alligators are excellent swimmers; they swim with a serpentine movement of the body and stroke of their tail, using their hind feet as rudders to change direction. These locomotive abilities in water are astonishing for such a large creature. Again, the animal has developed these abilities for survival--to enhance its predatory prowess.

It should be noted that not all of the alligator's survival adaptations are linked directly to its ability to hunt. The alligator exhibits other survival adaptations as well. One notable such adaptation involves the regulation of body temperature. The alligator has developed an ectothermic system of heat regulation, which means that the primary source of its body heat is external

(Elsey 667). As a result, the animal is forced to self-regulate its body temperature by finding the most suitable immediate external environment. For example, an alligator might lie on the banks of its aquatic habitat in order to bask in the sun for warmth; or to cool its body, it might submerge itself under water during the hottest time of the day. The physiological adaptations for underwater locomotion, discussed earlier, serve a temperature-regulation function as well. Curiously, the alligator can also adapt to external temperature simply by opening its mouth.

Morphological Differences Between Captive-Reared and Wild Alligators

For hundreds of years, the alligator has been widely hunted for its tough and attractive hide. Moreover, much of its marshy habitat has been drained and many thousands of young have been sold as pets. These factors have led to a diminishing American alligator population. Through protective measures, particularly captive breeding programs, the American alligator has made a strong come-back. But breeding alligators in captivity has resulted in certain physiologic changes among captive-bred specimens--changes that impede their ability to survive in the wild after being released.

Like many animals in captivity, the American alligator has undergone physiological and morphological changes from being captive reared. A study by Mason B. Meers at the Johns Hopkins University School of Medicine revealed that the captive-reared American alligator is different from its wild counterpart in both cranial and postcranial morphology. In his study, Meers examined skulls of 16 wild alligators and 4 captive alligators. Meers found that the primary ecophenotype in captive-bred alligators involved the morphology cranium and postcranium--development of the skull's shape. (For the purpose of further classifying a species as either wild or captive, scientists refer to captive-bred characteristics as ecophenotypes, meaning that the animal's distinct morpho-logical characteristics are the result of environmental, or ecological, variables as opposed to internal ones, such as disease.)

The captive specimens exhibited cranial morphology dramatically different from that of wild specimens, especially a clear broadening or flattening of the skull (Meers 74). Interestingly, other ecophenotype Crocodilian species are characterized by this phenomenon as well. Cuban crocodiles (Crocodylus rhombifer), for instance, also appear to have exceptionally flat skulls in captivity compared to those from a normal wild condition of a dorsoventrally thick skull (Meers 74).

What factors are responsible for this morphological change in the skull of the captive-bred American alligator? Meers implicates biomechanical stress as a leading factor. Indeed, bone remodeling is known to be a product of biomechanical stress and strain. In his 1917 experiment involving captive lions, Hollister found modifications of morphology in lions similar to the ones Meers found decades later in alligators: relatively short, broad snouts, and relative stability near the orbits. Hollister attributed this distinct morphology to differences in the hunting and feeding process between wild and captive lions. Similarly, the simple fact that captive alligators are usually fed diets of nutria or dead fish, and very rarely any live prey, implies a lack of biomechanical stress, which likely affects normal crocodilian morphology (Meers 80).

Meers's argument for biomechanical stress as the primary cause of the captive alligator's ecophenotype finds further support in the sculpting of the skulls themselves. Earlier studies illustrated that the sculpting or texture of Crocodilian crania was likely adaptive--for strengthening a relatively flat skull in response to stress. This indicates that having to hunt in the wild was a significant source of stress for alligators.

Another possible factor in the development of this ecophenotype involves the dramatically different growth of wild alligators compared to that of their captive counterparts. In order to encourage maximum growth in a short period of time, captive alligators are usually fed very well, throughout the year. Wild alligators, on the other hand, must rely on hunting as their only means of feeding. Wild alligators hunt at night, the young feeding on insects and small crustaceans, and the adults eating a variety of animals, including snakes, turtles, birds, and muskrats. However, wild alligators eat little or nothing during their winter hibernation. Therefore, captive alligators are generally larger than their wild counterparts. Accordingly, Meers notes:

> The accelerated growth seen in captives from this practice could easily affect growth patterns of the skulls, and perhaps account for my earlier observation that skulls from captives are smaller than in wilds of nearly equal body mass, suggesting that crania cannot match the growth rate of the body. (Meers 82)

Morphology and Releasing
Captive-Bred Alligators

Whatever the causes of a distinct captive-bred alligator morphology, one consequence of this distinct ecophenotype is that captive-bred alligators have trouble surviving in a wild environment after they are released. Specifically, they die before they can adequately adapt their feeding behavior to their new environment. Meers recommends that release of alligators into the wild, which is necessary to conserve the species, be done in a way that minimizes the effects of captivity on the released animals. Meer recommends specific measures to minimize the effects of captivity on alligators that are destined to be released into the wild. He suggests, for example, that matching the growth rates of these captives to that of local wild populations would help their adjustment to the wild. Also, feeding live prey to captive alligators would produce biomechanical stresses similar to those encountered by wild alligators.

Conclusion

By means of its extraordinary adaptive capabilities, the American alligator has been able to survive, and thrive, for millions of years in its natural environment. But morphological changes that occur during captivity, although providing insight into these adaptations, pose a danger to the survival of the species. If the recommendations of Meers and others are implemented, and if, through further research, scientists can come to fully understand the morphological processes of captive-bred specimens, perhaps we can prevent the specific processes that impede the alligator's ability to survive when released into the wild.

Works Cited

Clark, J.M. "Phylogenetic Relationships of the Crocodylomorph Archosaurs." Unpublished diss. University of Chicago, 1986.

Coulson, T. "Some observations on the Growth in Alligators." London: N.p., 175 (1972): 315-335.

Elsey, R.M. "Growth Rates and Body Condition Factors of <u>Alligator Mississippiensis</u> in Coastal Louisiana Wetlands: A Comparison of Wild and Farm Released Juveniles." <u>Comparative Biochemical Physiology</u> 103A(4) (1992): 667-672.

Lele, S. "A New Test for Shape Differences When Variance-Covariance Matrices are Unequal," <u>Journal of Human Evolution</u> . N. d.: n. pag.

Meers, Mason B. "Three-dimensional Analysis of Differences in Cranial Morphology Between Captive and Wild Alligators," Unpub. 1996.

Rootes, W. "Growth Rates of American Alligators in Estuarine Palustrine Wetlands in Louisiana." <u>Alligator Journal</u> 14 (1992): 489-494.

(A+) This paper examines the environmental problems of acid rain and acidification by
employing three of the term-paper angles listed in Chapter 1. Specifically, it *defines*
terms, describes a *process*, and provides a *cause-and-effect* analysis. Notice that
although the student seems to come to the subject with a definite point of view and a
critical tone, she refrains from inappropriate moralizing or preaching. (APA style)

THE PROCESS OF LAKE ACIDIFICATION

Environmental pollution may seem like a recent phenomenon,
but it has existed since life began on this planet. Pollution can
be described generally as "any physical, biological, or chemical
change in [air or] water quality that adversely affects living
organisms or makes [that air] or water unsuitable for desired uses"
(Krauntz, 1994). The only difference between pollution in earlier
ages and in our modern time is that the earth had more time to
cleanse itself naturally during earlier ages, when there were fewer
inhabitants.

Today we no longer give the earth the opportunity to cleanse
itself naturally. When our modern-day factories emit pollutants
into the air, they set into motion a complex and potentially
devastating chain of environmental events that result in mass
destruction, death, and environmental damage that the earth will
spend thousands of years to repair. The following discussion traces
one particular such chain of events: acid rain and acidification.

What Is Acid Rain and What Causes It?

Acidic deposition, or acid rain, as it is commonly known,
occurs when chemical-laden emissions react in the atmosphere with
water, oxygen, and oxidants to form various acidic compounds. These
compounds then fall to the earth in either dry form (such as gas
and solid particles) or wet form (such as rain, snow, and fog). In
the United States, sulfur dioxide, which is emitted primarily by
coal-burning electric power plants, is the dominant cause of acid
rain. Nitrogen oxide emissions also play a role in the formation
of acid rain and are significant in the formation of ground-level
ozone as well. Electric utility plants account for about 70% of

annual sulfur dioxide emissions and 30% of nitrogen oxide emissions in the United States. More than 20 million tons of each of these two pollutant types are emitted into the atmosphere each year.

The natural acidity of rain water is increased by the presence of sulfur dioxide and nitrogen oxide, atmospheric pollutants originating mainly from fossil fuel combustion. These compounds are likely to be carried by winds over long distances, and away from their urban, mining, thermoelectric power plants, and industrial emission sources. During rainfall the acidic pollutants are washed out as sulfuric and nitric acids over vast areas and may affect pristine areas located hundreds or thousands of miles away from the point of origin (Shafer & Lanza, 1995).

What Are the Direct Effects of Acid Rain?

Aside from its impact after it has been assimilated by soils, lakes, and streams, acid rain results in a variety of problems. First, it causes forest degradation, as trees that once were nesting sources for countless winged creatures have become defoliated. Tree damage is particularly extensive at high elevations. For example, defoliation along the high ridges of the Appalachians to the Great Smoky Mountains is quite obvious, especially among red spruce trees above 2,000 feet in elevation.

Second, acid rain creates human health problems. For example, respiratory ailments such as emphysema and asthma are far more prevalent in areas that experience high levels of acid rain than in areas that do not. Air concentrations of acid aerosols (tiny droplets of sulfuric acid derived from sulfur dioxide emissions) pose an especially high health risk.

Third, acid rain contributes to the corrosion of metals and deterioration of stone and paint in buildings, statues, and other structures of cultural significance. These structures also become dirtier more quickly (Bartol & Bergen, 1992). Finally, acid rain does aesthetic damage. Air concentrations of sulfur and nitrogen species degrade visibility in large parts of the country, including our national parks, adversely affecting our citizens' enjoyment of these parks.

What Geographic Areas Are Most Susceptible to Acid Rain?

Three factors determine the extent to which a region is at risk as a result of acid rain. The first is the proximity to source areas: major cities where oil refineries and sulfur-burning coal plants are located. The second is the amount of rainfall; wet and humid regions are at higher risk than dry ones. The third, and least obvious, factor is the type of soils that dominate the area. Certain soils, particularly crystalline layers and noncarbonated sedimentary rocks, are considered to be more sensitive to acid precipitation than other soil types (Shafer & Lanza, 1995).

What Happens After Acid Rain Mixes with Water?

The two types of acid rain pollution--air pollution and water pollution--are inextricably linked. Harmful acid rain occurs because of contaminants in the sky. When acid rain falls to the ground or into lakes, ponds, and streams, the water becomes "acidified," which means that it becomes much more acidic than normal. The acidification of soil and water can result in no less than the usurpation of the equilibrium of life, amounting to a "reign of terror that chews up the life blood of plant, mammal and aquatic life" (Poore, 1993).

Acidification of water is a far more serious matter than acidification of soil, for two reasons. First, water is everywhere. It is stored in the form of oceans, lakes, and rivers, which cover more than two-thirds of the earth's surface. Water is also stored in polar ice caps and glaciers, in subsurface groundwater, and in the atmosphere (as vapor and droplets). Second, water is the single most efficient solvent on earth; in other words, it absorbs (holds) almost any nutrient or pollutant. As a result, nearly any pollutant can potentially end up in the water (Bouton & Stegeman, 1993).

Acidification is generally most acute in small bodies of water--lakes and ponds--that rest atop soil and that has only a limited ability to neutralize acidic compounds. Yet ground water is also surprisingly susceptible to acid rain. Ground water is precipitation that does not evaporate or run off into a river but percolates through the soil and permeable rocks until it is held back by an impermeable layer of rock or clay. This percolating process is also called "infiltration." The constant rising and falling of the water table and the fact that infiltrated water generally stays in the ground for a long time help ensure--under normal conditions--a high degree of purification (Krautz, 1994). In fact, until very recently ground water had been thought of as being a standard of water purity in itself. Under normal circumstances this is true; however, once ground water becomes acidified, the purification process can take many thousands of years (Krauntz, 1994).

What Is the Impact of Acidification on Plant and Animal Life?

The damage that acidification of water can cause can be startling. Acidification of water adversely affects aquatic organisms most directly. The number of species of fish, algae, zooplankton, and bottom-dwelling organisms starts to decrease when the pH of a lake drops under 6.0, long before a lake is deemed to be wholly acidified. Most planktonic algae, higher plants, and animals cannot survive if the pH drops too far below 5.0. Acidification of small lakes and ponds can result in a pH level as low as 3.0--a level comparable to that of vinegar--which is lethal for almost any fish or aquatic plant (Abrams, 1996).

Streams are as susceptible to damage from acid rain as are lakes. Approximately 580 of the streams in the mid-Atlantic coastal plain are acidic. In New Jersey, a state people often lampoon as being a "toxic accident," more than 90% of the streams are acidic. More than 1,350 of the streams in the mid-Atlantic highlands are acidic, and streams in the mid-Appalachians are also undergoing increasing acidification. Many streams in that area have already experienced trout losses due to the rising acidity (Krautz, 1994).

In some sensitive lakes and streams, acidification has completely eradicated fish species, such as the brook trout, leaving the bodies of water barren. Reproduction in sensitive species such as salmon and trout is affected by pH levels below 6.0 (Bouton & Stegeman, 1993). In fact, hundreds of the lakes in the Adirondacks of upstate New York have acidity levels indicative of chemical conditions unsuited for the survival of any fish species:

> The mountain air of the Adirondacks is notably clean and
> fresh. Most lakes and rivers are clear and unpolluted.
> However, due in large measure to acid rain from industrial
> areas in the East and Midwest, more than 200 higher elevation
> lakes are totally devoid of fish life. (Viscome, 1992)

In fact some of the lakes at the highest elevations don't hold any form of life. "Sadly, dead lakes and streams often appear clear and beautiful" (Shafer & Lanza, 1995).

Aquatic life is not the only type of life adversely affected by acidification. For example, the high-acid conditions of spring run-off coincide with the most vulnerable periods of the life cycle of amphibian species, such as frogs, toads, and salamanders, which breed in pools formed by a mixture of meltwater and spring rains (Philips, 1991). As the lake becomes less and less able to support life, mammals and birds that rely on the lake as a food source become endangered. As more species of plants and animals succumb to acid waters, the structure of a lake's web of life weakens and collapses (Shafer & Lanza, 1995).

Despite the devastating impact of acidified water on most animal and plant species, some species of insects and other aquatic animals actually thrive in acidic water, and "such hardy species may be found in far greater numbers where their natural enemies have died out" (Bouton & Stegeman, 1993). Certain plants also tolerate acidification. Water lilies, for instance, appear to be unaffected by moderately acidified water. Yet, although some species may survive or even thrive under acidic conditions, so many others are lost that the ecosystem as a whole becomes impoverished and collapses.

Conclusion

Acid rain damages forests, building materials, human-made structures, and human health. Even more devastating, however, once it reaches the ground, acid rain kills aquatic life as well as animals that depend on that life for food. Eventually, the earth may cleanse itself of the harmful acids that end up in our water. But the cleansing process can take thousands of years. It is important to understand the causes, process, and the consequences of acid rain so that society can take appropriate steps to prevent the short-term fallout.

References

Abrams, R., & Abrams, D. (1996, February). Environmental degradation. Colliers Encyclopedia, p. 9.

Bartol, C., Bergen, G., et al. (1992, October). Treating the earth as home. Nature Alert, p. 9.

Bouton, D., & Stegemann, E. (1993, September). Endangered and threatened fishes of New York. Conservationist, 48, 14.

Krautz, J. (1994, September). Poisoning the fountain of life: Fresh water pollution and its consequences. Contemporary Review, 265, p. 144.

Phillips, J. (1991, April). Fallen trees and acid lakes. Focus, 41, p. 25.

Poore, P., & Everitt, B. (1993, April). Enviro education. Garbage, 5, p. 26.

Prescott, L. (1994, April). Pollution solutions. Ranger Rick, 28, p. 20.

Schafer, R., & Lanza, P. (1995, April 1). Acid rain. All Hands, p. 29.

Viscome, L. (1992 May). The Adirondack park: One of a kind. Conservationist, 46, p. 8.

Williams, W. D. (1996, November). What future for saline lakes? Environment, 38, p. 12.

In this paper, the student explores the pros and cons of competing theories about what caused the extinction of dinosaurs. The organization is classic and effective: The student presents the theories in a logical sequence, and then closes with insightful observations about the present status of the debate and about its broader significance for science and humanity. (MLA style, with *Works Consulted* list)

THE CONTROVERSY OVER DINOSAUR EXTINCTION

Theorists have offered a variety of explanations for extinction of the dinosaurs. The two prevailing views are the comet theory and the habitat theory. According to the comet theory, the dinosaurs were extinguished in a relatively short time, as the result of a cataclysmic comet strike. The habitat theory states that gradual changes in climatic conditions and topography over a much longer time period were responsible for the depletion of the dinosaurs' food sources and in turn for their starvation and extinction. Other less prevalent but regionally accepted explanations include large-scale flooding, a global epidemic, and volcanoes.

The Comet Theory

The comet theory is based largely on the research of geologist Walter Alvarez, who first asserted it in the late 1970s (Cerveny 13). Essentially, the theory suggests that dinosaur extinction was a direct and immediate consequence of a catastrophic asteroid impact (Cerveny 13). The central argument of the theory, embraced by a wide segment of the scientific community, is that the large comet or asteroid strike on the Yucatan Peninsula resulted in such rapid and dramatic weather changes that the dinosaurs could not survive for more than a few weeks (Werner 2). Proponents argue that as an immediate result of the strike, which would have occurred between the Cretaceous and Tertiary periods over 65 million years ago, atmospheric conditions were drastically altered by wildfires, dust clouds, the spread of debris, and the resulting change in chemical composition of the atmosphere--all of which blocked the sunlight (Cerbeny 15). The result was a smoky, toxic environment that few mammals, if any, could survive for more than a few hours, if even a few minutes (Werner 2).

Over the years, theorists, writers, and illustrators have painted a vivid, apocalyptic picture of the final hours of the dinosaur. As one writer described it, the global atmospheric and climate changes made the earth appear as if "a living hell, a dark, burning, sulfurous world where all the rules governing survival of the fittest changed in minutes. The dinosaurs never had a chance" (Cerveny 13). Imagine an almost-tropical climate with lush vegetation changing suddenly into giant landslides, monstrous earthquakes, and especially the creation of a large, flaming plasma tunnel, which resulted from the near-vacuum created in the atmosphere upon impact of the asteroid (Cerveny 14). Imagine burning, molten rock spreading quickly, the atmosphere filling with smoke and vapors.

Arguments and Evidence Supporting the Comet Theory

For many years, theorists could not determine where the strike might have occurred and, therefore, whether the strike was of the right age or large enough to cause devastation so widespread as to result in the extinction of a vast variety of species: essentially the largest segment of mammalian life on earth during that time. Recently, however, scientists have uncovered several important pieces of physical evidence that strongly support the comet theory. At Chicxulub, Mexico, on the Yucatan peninsula, Dr. Alan Hildebrand and other scientists uncovered a variety of geological and topographical evidence that seems to corroborate the comet theory (Campbell 8).

First and foremost among the evidence was what everyone already knew about: a 110-mile-wide crater that suggests a meteorite as large as 6 miles across striking at a force equal to "10,000 times the strength of the world's entire nuclear arsenal simultaneously detonated" (Werner 2). Such an impact might cause the kind of worldwide atmospheric disruption required by the comet theory. Second, the crater sits on top of a limestone bed, leading Hildebrand and others to assert that when the meteorite struck, it vaporized the limestone into carbon dioxide, resulting in rapid temperature declines followed directly by greenhouse-effect warming (Werner 2). Third, Hildebrand found large amounts of specific debris and the outer space metal iridium in the Chicxulub crater: more concrete empirical evidence to support the Alverez comet theory (Campbell 8; Werner 2).

Some scientists also point to Hildebrand's discovery of an enormous number of fossilized dinosaur remains at the crater site as further evidence supporting the comet theory. However, this additional evidence would seem to prove only that this meteor killed these dinosaurs, and not that the impact of this meteor was responsible for the total extinction worldwide.

Arguments Against and Evidence Undermining the Comet Theory

Not all evidence at Chicxulub serves to support the comet theory. Most notably, the topographical data and pattern of debris strongly suggests that the asteroid struck Chicxulub obliquely-- that is, at an angle--in a northerly direction (Mestell 22). If this indeed was the case, the destruction and environmental disruption probably would have been limited to the Northern Hemisphere. Yet dinosaur extinction was a worldwide phenomenon, not limited to one region or to one hemisphere.

Also undermining the comet theory is the fact that comet theorists disagree among themselves as to what sudden atmospheric changes would have occurred after the strike and how these changes killed the dinosaurs. For example, some comet theorists have argued that the clouds produced as a result of the impact caused darkness and cold that the dinosaurs could not withstand, whereas others have argued that extinction resulted from the widespread fire and extreme heat resulting from the asteroid.

Morell and Kerr point out that the several months of darkness that probably occurred as a result of the asteroid impact should not in itself have resulted in the perishing of the dinosaurs, because dinosaurs were generally cold adapted. Also, other climate-sensitive creatures besides dinosaurs actually survived the asteroid aftermath, suggesting that perhaps climatic changes were not as widespread or as problematic as the comet theorists maintain (Morell & Kerr 1518).

The Loss-of-Habitat Theory

Because the comet theory is problematic on several grounds, many scientists think that the asteroid impact and the extinctions coincided by chance (Morell & Kerr 1519) and that another explanation is needed. Proponents of the loss-of-habitat theory have as their ally the scientific principle that the simplest explanation is usually the correct one. Their claim is that dinosaur extinction resulted from the same process that has caused extinction of many other species: the loss of habitat, which generally means loss of a habitable environment and/or a viable food source.

Empirically, this argument is strongly supported because loss of habitat is responsible for the extinction of thousands of animal species every year, especially insects. The argument also makes sense theoretically. The earth's large population of dinosaurs surely required vast amounts of vegetation for basic subsistence, and any one of a number of climate changes, such as a regional drought, could by itself over an extended time period have easily devastated the dinosaur population, at least in one region. Even a minor climatic change, if widespread enough and if prolonged for hundreds of years, could have completely destroyed the dinosaur population. Moreover, loss of habitat almost always results in susceptibility to disease and to a competitive process among species members, both of which serve to reduce the population.

Other Theories: Hybrids and Volcanoes

Although the comet theory and habitat theory each have merit, many believe that neither adequately accounts for the total extinction of dinosaurs. Some have offered a hybrid explanation, by which the comet probably played a contributing role, and some other series of changes--either related or unrelated to the comet but occurring around the same time--also contributed to the dinosaur's demise.

For example, perhaps the climatic and topographic changes that were problematic for the dinosaurs occurred not only as a result of the asteroid but also because of powerful volcanic eruptions, and regional extinction of certain species occurred first (Anonymous 394). Scientists have challenged the supposition that the metallic and "shocked" quartz that has been attributed to the asteroid are the result of the asteroid; they argue that the same properties are found in elements collected from volcanic eruptions, and that the impact of this process would have had a greater long-term affect that would have resulted in the worldwide extinction of dinosaurs (Anonymous 394).

Conclusion

Despite all the discord among the scientific community about what really caused dinosaur extinction, scientists agree on a few basic points: (1) a comet or an asteroid struck the Yucatan coast during the same geological time period in which the last of the dinosaurs disappeared 65 million years ago, between the Coruscates and Tertiary periods; (2) the projectile was approximately 6 miles in diameter, and it created a 110-mile-wide crater; and (3) the strike of the asteroid resulted in vast climatic changes. But this is as far as the consensus goes.

Whether the immediate topographical, geological, and atmospheric changes were severe enough to exterminate the dinosaurs immediately, or whether instead the impact was merely one of many events over a long period of time that eventually led to the demise of the dinosaur remains a contested issue. For scientists, the importance of understanding how such a strong and viable population could have been wiped out in a relatively short amount of time goes beyond the dinosaurs themselves. This particular scientific investigation is helping to define a process for evaluating the history and development of other species (including birds) as well. It is also helping to define a process for understanding the impact of cataclysmic events in general, the impact of the loss of habitat in general, and the implications of these issues for humans.

Works Consulted

Anonymous. "Telling It Big: Everyone Loves a Good Story, Especially with a Cunning Twist." <u>New Scientist</u> Aug. 1997: 3+.

Anonymous. "Counterpoint in Impact Debate." <u>Science News</u> 21 Jun. 1986: 394.

Budiansky, Stephen. "How Dumb Was the Dinosaur, Anyway?" <u>U.S. News & World Report</u> Jul. 1997: 66+.

Campbell, Wayne. "The 'Smoking Gun' of Dinosaur Extinction." <u>Canadian Geographic</u> Jan.-Feb. 1993: 8.

Cerveny, Randy. "The Day the Dinosaurs Died." <u>Weatherwise</u> Jul.-Aug. 1998: 13+.

Hecht, Jeff. ". . . But Soviet Crater Complicates the Picture." <u>New Scientist</u> 30 Mar. 1991: 14.

Mestel, Rosie. "New Angle on a Killer?" <u>Earth</u> Apr. 1997: 22+.

Morell, V. and Kerr, R. "How Lethal Was the K-T Impact?" <u>Science</u> 17 Sep. 1993: 1518+.

Rukavina, I. and Daneman, M. "Integration and Its Effect on Acquiring Knowledge about Competing Scientific Theories from Text." <u>Journal of Educational Psychology</u> Jun. 1996: 272+.

Werner, Lou. "Filling in Cosmic Holes." <u>Americas</u> (English Edition) Sep.-Oct. 1992: 2+.

(A+) This paper discusses a specific theory in geology known as plate tectonics. Notice how the discussion moves from basic, simple ideas to more complex, technical ones. This is a great organizational device for term papers. Notice also the student's use of two of the term paper angles listed in Chapter 1: the *competing-theories* approach and the *cause-and-consequences* approach. (MLA style, with *Works Consulted* list)

PLATE TECTONICS

The theory of <u>Plate tectonics</u> , originally termed <u>continental drift</u>, involves the movement of the various plates that together form the earth's surface. The theory was born of a variety of random observations by geologists during the latter half of the nineteenth century. In the 1880s, geologist Eduard Suisse distinguished two types of continental margins. The Atlantic type consisted of an abrupt truncation of former mountain belts and rifting structures; the Pacific type was characterized by parallel mountains, lines of volcanoes, and frequent earthquakes. Around the same time, geologist James Hall observed that sediments in mountain belts were 10 times thicker than those in continental interiors. A mid-ocean ridge that was later shown to circle the globe was first spotted in the nineteenth century.

Based on observations such as these, in the early twentieth century the theory of plate tectonics began to take shape. Geologist Alfred Wegener, between 1908 and 1912, led the way by tying together earlier observations into a cohesive theory, which he called the <u>theory of continental drift</u>. Wegener's basic premise was simple enough: The continents were actually floating plates, which over the course of millions of years drift away from one another, and then eventually collide again. Wegener's claim that continental plates sail along the ocean like icebergs was later disproved, of course, but other findings over the next few decades would lend considerable credence to his basic premise.

With the advent of sonar technology during the 1920s, it became possible for scientists to map the topography of the entire ocean floor. Although it wasn't until the 1960s that the entire ocean floor was been mapped in detail, scientists noticed early on a most striking topographical detail: a continuous ridge running across the ocean floor and, in serpentine fashion, traversing the entire globe. Through sophisticated carbon dating techniques, geophysicists determined that the ridge is actually new ocean crust created from below, and that as this crust is created, the surface on either side of the ridge moves away to make room for it. This new evidence provided important empirical support for the plate tectonic theory, since it proved that the various regions defined by the regions are indeed moving away from, yet at the same time toward, one another.

Geologic Manifestations of Plate Tectonics

Most people today know that the shifting of the earth's plates is responsible for earthquakes, which occur along the edges of the plates. Deep-seated earthquakes occur when one plate is forced into a deep mantle beneath another. Shallower earthquakes occur when one plate is dragged sideways alongside another. But plate tectonics is also responsible for many of the earth's most striking geologic features, including many mountain ranges, volcanic islands, and even seas.

Plate tectonics explains how most of the earth's largest mountain ranges were formed. Just as the continents split apart, they also collide from time to time. When continents collide, they both occupy the leading edge of converging plates, and because both are too light to sink into the earth's mantle, one plate pushes up onto the other, and a mountain range is born. The Himalayas were formed by this process; the Indian plate is pushing up into the Eurasian plate (Blanchard).

Eurasian plate tectonics were responsible for a variety of geographic phenomena in that area. For example, the Hercynian Mountain Range resulted from a collision between Africa-South America and North America in the late Carboniferous period 300 million years ago. It contains a series of folds believed to be associated with two subduction zones that migrated to the west. The Ural Mountains were formed when the north European and Kazakhstan plates collided, but the uplift occurred much later because of the east-west compression during the Permian period.

Plate tectonics also explains how certain volcanic islands are formed. The Hawaiian Islands are the result of a series of plumes, which are columns of exceptionally hot material that rise from the earth's core and through the earth's mantle. The plumes are stationary, and the plates and continents move above them. As a result, after one volcano has been formed, the plate on which it sits will move away from the column, which then melts into a new spot on the same or another plate. A new volcano forms, and the old one becomes inactive. Another work of nature, Yellowstone National Park, is a caldera that formed from the explosion of a volcano that had formed over the Yellowstone plume. Island-ocean collision can explain the formation of Japan, considered a mature island-arc. The subduction of the Pacific plate produced a series of stratovolcanoes along the eastern margin of the island and a paired metamorphic belt underneath the island (Manooch). This type of collision is quite rare.

Another type of collision, ocean-ocean collision, result in the formation of seas, as in the Molucca Sea region. One subduction zone dipped beneath the surrounding region, and another subduction, dipping east and converging into the same region, rendered the first inactive. The two subduction zones collided, causing two regions of the nearby arc to form a larger one, the Mindanoa arc.

Competing Theories about Plate Tectonics

Although plate tectonics is a relatively new area of science, geologists generally agree with the basic notion that shifting plates indeed cause continents to drift apart and collide, and cause the geological features described earlier. However, scientists have been unable to determine with certainty why the plates move in the first place. At present, there are three prevailing theories.

The first two theories involve temperature--more specifically, temperature differences. According to the first of these two theories, plate movement occurs when the earth's upper mantle is powered simultaneously by the cold surface of the plate and by the heat generated in the earth's center (Blanchard). The energy from the core can travel along the plumes that form from the center to the surface, driving the once-inactive plates along the earth. The plates must also be pushed away from spreading centers, pulled down into trenches, or dragged along by the friction of convection. However, this force cannot exceed the tensile strength of the plates, or they would break off into many smaller pieces.

The key to a second plume-centered theory is the heated material that rises through these columns. According to this version, plumes form hot spots within or below mantle layers. As heat migrates upward through the mantle layer, it diffuses outward into the surrounding, much cooler, material. The added heat makes the material less dense, and it too starts to migrate upward, slowing as it strays from its heat source.

The two plume-centered theories, although new, already have their critics, some of whom have drawn on the same basic principles to arrive at entirely different conclusions. The most prominent critic is Luckert, who has developed an alternative theory, which he calls expansion tectonics. Luckert credits the shift in continents not to natural movement but rather to planetary expansion. According to Luckert, the diameter of earth 160 million years ago was only 60% of its current diameter. Most of the planet was covered with land, which would break apart to form the continents we know today. Only when the earth expanded did ditches develop to form deep oceans instead of the shallow seas that existed at the time.

In his video, Luckert shows how the continents fit together like a puzzle and how the rifts that began during the Jurassic period opened to form the oceans. Unlike the other theories, which propose random shifting, his theory shows continents breaking apart from the heat pressure that expanded the planet (Luckert). The most significant period of change would have been the Eocene period, some 55 million years ago, when most of the displacement occurred and when the continental plates most clearly broke apart.

But can Luckert's expansion tectonics explain the formation of mountains and valleys? Luckert claims so, through several phenomena. First, tensile folding occurs as the planet expands, and longitudinal tension increases. The folds pull along the flank and crack open the bottoms of synclines for magma to intrude. Flanging occurs when a continent is displaced from its substratum by earth expansion; one retains its original curvature, and the other decreases. The continental crust sinks at its center and passes excess surface area to its outer edges. This would explain why many mountain ranges tend to appear along coasts, and flat valleys tend to appear inland--as they do in the North American continent.

Conclusion

To understand plate tectonics is to appreciate that our planet as we know it today was not formed overnight, and the mountains, valleys, islands, and seas that exist today were the direct result of specific, identifiable physical processes. Yet even as plate tectonics sheds light on what were once topographical and geological mysteries, the forces behind the process still remain a mystery.

Works Consulted

Blanchard, Donald L. "The ABC's of Plate Tectonics." Available online at home.earthlink.net/~dlblanc/tectonic/ptABCs.html. Accessed November 21, 1997.

John, Brain S, and David E. Sugden. <u>Glaciers and Landscape: A Geomorphological Approach</u> London: Edward Arnold Publishers LTD., 1976.

Luckert, Karl L. "Expansion Tectonics." Videotape based on lectures at the 1996 GSA Convention. Lufa Studio, NTSC norm. Two-tape set, 1996.

Manooch, Charles Samuel, IV. "Tectonics of the Eurasian Plate." Available online at wcuvax1.wcu.edu/~cm900/sam.html. Accessed November 21, 1997.

16

PSYCHOLOGY

Moral Development

Are Freud's Theories about Repressed Memories Valid?

The Placebo Effect

This paper compares the opposing theories of two researchers regarding moral development. It also discusses the critique of a scholar who studied and commented on the existence of an empirical relationship between those two theories. This paper demonstrates excellent organizational skills, an understanding of the topic at hand, and a maturity of writing style; in short, it's a prototype A+ psychology term paper. (APA style)

MORAL DEVELOPMENT

In 1976 Lawrence Kohlberg published a revolutionary theory. His theory identified six stages of moral development, where each stage was a product of biological maturation as well as increasing social experience. However, Kohlberg's theory was strongly criticized by many, including Carol Gilligan, an educational psychologist who specializes in personality development in young girls. According to Gilligan, Kohlberg studied only the moral development of males. Even though his theory was purported to extend to both sexes, Gilligan noted that females were relatively insignificant in his model. Therefore, Gilligan developed a new theory, one that compared the moral development of males to that of females. In her model, Gilligan defined two moral orientations. Each orientation was specific in matching one of the sexes.

Walker et al. (1987) examined the findings of both Gilligan and Kohlberg. In an attempt to find the true meaning of moral development and differentiate between Kohlberg's moral stage model and Gilligan's moral orientation model, Walker studied 80 family triads' responses to several separate issues. Beyond both Kohlberg and Gilligan's findings, Walker wanted to explain even more in depth what conditions might be responsible for an individual's moral orientation. Walker also attempted to deal with some issues left unresolved by previous studies.

Kohlberg

Kohlberg's theory states that moral development in humans occurs in distinct stages, "representing six modes of 'justice structures' within which adolescents tend to organize their social world" (Linn, 1991, p. 59). The first stage, exhibited by young children, is the preconventional stage. During this stage, children view right and wrong in terms of what serves their needs.

Following the preconventional stage, the next important stage in human development, according to Kohlberg, is the conventional stage. It is generally reached when the transition is made from childhood to adolescence. Linn wrote, "with progress in moral stage, the adolescent is believed to be more sensitive to the morality of particular circumstances as his or her judgment becomes free of personal and situational constraints" (Linn, 1991, p. 60). The individual becomes less self-centered in terms of morality, viewing what is right based on what parents and society deem acceptable. In addition, the individual looks at intention as well as outcome when judging other people (Macionis, 1995, p. 62).

Finally, the postconventional stage is reached as the individual begins to compare the morality of society with more abstract ethical principles. He or she realizes that what society deems legal may not be morally right (Linn, 1991, p. 62).

Critical Analysis of Kohlberg

Kohlberg's theory divides moral development into identifiable stages. Many of the same criticisms made of Kohlberg were made of researchers such as Piaget, who also studied stages of development in humans. For instance, it remains unconfirmed whether this theory applies to individuals of all societies or of just our own (Macionis, 1995, p. 132). In addition, it is believed that many people don't reach the final stage of moral development as Kohlberg describes it, which, in essence, is complete autonomy.

The primary criticism with Kohlberg's findings was that his research was based wholly on boys. He then made the mistake of generalizing his findings to all of society. Carol Gilligan took exception to Kohlberg's methodology and set out to explain the issue of the "portrayal of real-life dilemmas, those of females in particular" (Linn, 1991, p. 62). She characterized Kohlberg's flaw as "typical of social science, which uses the behavior of males as the norm for how everyone should act" (Macionis, 1995, p. 132).

Gilligan

Carol Gilligan set out to systematically compare the moral development of females and males. She argued two moral orientations, concluding that males and females have different processes of moral reasoning. In particular, she claimed that the first orientation "is that of justice (leading to equality), and the other is that of care (leading to connection and attachment)" (Linn, 1991, p. 63). She went on further to describe the first orientation as relating to males, attributing the latter orientation to females. Gilligan asserted that this discrepancy in moral orientation is due to the way in which a child is raised.

Rule-based male reasoning is considered, according to Gilligan, morally superior to person-based female thinking. She attributed this to the fact that males have long been subjected to impersonal applications of rules in the workplace, whereas women have had more of a concern for attachment as wives, mothers, and caregivers.

One critique of Gilligan's work regards the source of differences in orientation she documents between males and females. The critique is based on Gilligan's assertion that differences in orientation are due to cultural conditioning. According to this view, men and women will become more alike as time goes on--as women enter the workplace and men begin taking more responsibility in childrearing (Macionis, 1995).

Walker's Critiques

Walker and his colleagues (1987) were interested in studying the hypotheses of both Kohlberg and Gilligan. They discussed three issues in their article titled "Moral Stages and Moral Orientations in Real-Life and Hypothetical Dilemmas": (1) hypothetical versus real-life moral reasoning, (2) moral orientation, and (3) moral stages and moral orientation.

Kohlberg's theory is based almost entirely on hypothetical dilemmas, which have no social or historical context outside the specified circumstances (Linn, 1991). According to Kohlberg, the use of such hypothetical dilemmas is advantageous because they are highly conflictual and therefore are ideal for "testing the limits." Furthermore, hypothetical dilemmas allow an individual to consider a question without the impediment of preconceptions or prejudices. Some critics, however, feel that the exclusive use of hypothetical dilemmas is limiting. Principally, these dilemmas may contain issues that are either inapplicable or unfamiliar to certain individuals.

Another approach is to use real-life dilemmas in interpreting moral orientation. This is the approach Kohlberg and others took in researching prison inmates, and in another study involving high school students. In both cases the standard dilemmas elicited much higher moral scores than the real-life dilemmas (Walker et al., 1987). However, other research has contradicted Kohlberg's results. In 1975 Haan conducted a study of a much broader sample population and found that the real-life dilemmas usually resulted in a higher score than the hypothetical ones. Walker et al. pointed out that in all the previously mentioned studies, "the real-life dilemma was always one raised as an issue by the researchers, not the subjects" (p. 843). Therefore, the results may not be justified. Instead, Walker et al. suggested that researchers should probe the families and use "actual" real-life family dilemmas in their studies.

According to Kohlberg's model, there should be no significant difference in a subject's response between hypothetical and real-life dilemmas. Walker et al. wrote, "Kohlberg's strict moral stage model posits that each stage represents a holistic structure, implying that individuals should be relatively consistent in their moral reasoning across varying contexts" (p. 843).

Regarding the second issue, moral orientation, Walker et al. simply defined Gilligan's moral orientation model. They wrote, "the bias and limited perspective on morality that Gilligan believed was inherent in Kohlberg's approach led her to conclude that females' moral development was being down-scored in his system" (Walker et al., 1987, p. 844). Walker et al. concluded this discussion of this issue by suggesting the use of a larger and more representative sample than was used in the both Kohlberg's and Gilligan's studies.

The final issue Walker et al. discussed is the relationship between moral stages and moral orientation. They argued that the relation, if in fact there exists one, should be determined. In addition, they asserted that the extent to which the relationship exists should be empirically documented (Walker et al., 1987).

Concluding Remarks

The past few decades have seen extreme controversy in the field of moral development. Kohlberg's theory of moral stages has been criticized because of its confined basis of a male population. Gilligan, in turn, realized this generality and proposed her own theory defining two distinct moral orientations. Each theory has both its strengths and weaknesses, which Walker et al. enumerated. Walker et al. then suggested improvements that would correct for the weaknesses, such as using a larger, more representative sample population for future studies in this area.

Regarding Kohlberg's theory, several criticisms come to mind. First, it seems that most people, when not directly suffering the consequences of a decision or an action, would not be as inclined to do what is morally right. It is easy to see why answering questions pertaining to a hypothetical dilemma, or even a real-life dilemma that an individual doesn't actually face, might give false results. Furthermore, men and women clearly have different moral structures. As Gilligan points out, women are more concerned with relationship issues, whereas males are concerned with rights and justices.

In conclusion, a combination of both Kohlberg's and Gilligan's theories seems to be the best model. Kohlberg's assertion of stages of development combined with Gilligan's conclusion that there are two separate orientations would most aptly describe the path of an individual's moral development.

References

Linn, R. (1991). Sexual and moral development of Israeli female adolescents: Perspectives of Kohlberg and Gilligan. <u>Adolescence,</u> <u>26</u> (101), pp. 58-71.

Macionis, J. (1995). <u>Sociology</u> (5th ed.). Englewood Cliffs, NJ: Prentice Hall.

Walker, L., et al. (1987). Moral stages and moral orientations in real-life and hypothetical dilemmas. N. p., pp. 842-858.

(A+) This paper examines Sigmund Freud's theory about how repressed memories affect behavior, the theory's influence on practitioners and theorists, and recent challenges to the theory's validity. The student does a good job providing a clear overview of a very complex subject within the 1,200-word limit imposed by her instructor. (APA style)

ARE FREUD'S THEORIES ABOUT REPRESSED MEMORIES VALID?

Our ideas today about how repressed memories can affect one's behavior are rooted in the theories of Sigmund Freud, who also developed the concepts of id, ego, and superego. Freud's theories about repression have been widely applied and even popularized during the twentieth century. In fact, more recent theories about personality seem to implicitly embrace Freud's. At the same time, however, a number of cogent challenges to Freud's repression theory, the most recent coming from another scientific field, call into question its validity.

Freud's Id and Ego, and the Concept of Repression

According to Freud, the id is all of the individual's primitive emotional strivings, urges, or impulses; and although the id is considerably potent, these impulses can be controlled by the ego. Freud maintained that during childhood the ego gains and maintains its control mainly by repression, which renders and keeps these id impulses unconscious. Repressing these id impulses prevents them from coming into play as the individual matures through experience (Sanford, 1966). Sanford also noted, however, that repression is not inevitable, and that when an individual does not repress childhood impulses, these impulses either are modified to accord with experience and with the demands of reality, or find modes of expression that are harmless or perhaps even socially valuable (Sanford).

Early followers of Freud closely linked Freud's psychoanalytic concept of repression as a defense mechanism to his idea of an unconscious mind. The unconscious mind was construed by early Freudians as a supersensitive entity whose perceptual alertness and memory bank surpassed those of the conscious mind. A chief function of the unconscious mind was to screen and monitor memories and perceptual inputs, thereby inhibiting anxiety-arousing stimuli from breaking through the unconscious mind to the conscious one, or from the outside world to consciousness. Just as the conscious mind was believed capable of deliberately (consciously) inhibiting events by suppression, so the unconscious mind was considered capable of inhibition or cognitive avoidance at the unconscious level by repression (Mischel, 1971).

Freudian repression depended on an ego threat, such as a basic threat to self-esteem, and not just to unpleasantness. So in reality, the human mind employs the repression mechanism for events such as chronic child abuse or other emotional or physical trauma, and not for minor or infrequent events.

The Pervasive Influence of Freud's Repression Theory

Practitioners after Freud embraced his repression theory and popularized it to an extent that Freud and his contemporaries never suspected (Ofshe & Watters, 1993, p. 4). By the 1970s Freud's ideas about the unconscious mind and repressed memories had become a powerful and pervasive phenomenon, not just among psychoanalysts but also in popular culture--as an integral part of "pop" psychology. The pervasive influence of Freud's ideas about id, ego, and repression can be seen not only in its popularity among prac- titioners and laypeople but also in subsequent theories about personality development. Psychologists differ on whether they believe cognitive avoidance or an effort to avoid painful thoughts actually includes the unconscious defense mechanism of repression (Mischel, 1971). Nevertheless, theorists after Freud seem to have incorporated his notions into their own theories--even into their terminology.

Eugene T. Gendlin wrote on the repression paradigm, noting how personality theorists after Freud, such as Rogers and Sullivan, were greatly influenced by Freud's ideas about repression. Gendlin noted striking areas of agreement among the theories. The individual's early family relations inject certain values by which the child is loved only if he feels and behaves in certain ways, and experiences that contradict these demands are "repressed" (Freud), or "denied to awareness" (Rogers), or "not me" (Sullivan). Later, when the individual encounters experiences of this contradicting sort, the individual must either distort them or remain totally unaware of them. For, were the individual to notice the contradictory experiences, he or she would become intolerably anxious. The ego (Freud), or self-concept (Rogers), or self-dynamism (Sullivan) thus basically influences awareness and perception. This influence is termed "resistance" (Freud), or "defensiveness" (Rogers), or "security operation" (Sullivan). Regardless of which term is used, all three theorists seem to rely on the same basic concepts to explain a great deal of individual behavior (Gendlin, 1964).

Recent Challenges to Freud's Repression Theory

Despite the ubiquity that Freud's repression theory seems to have achieved, various experts have challenged the validity of Freud's repression theory, on a variety of grounds. One such challenge comes from Freud himself and is well supported by empirical evidence. Richard Ofshe and Ethan Watters pointed to substantial empirical evidence which shows that applying Freud's repression theory often results in "recovered memories" that turn out to be false. Freud himself admits to obtaining false memories of sexual abuse from his patients. In fact, these false memories led Freud to speculate that in many cases these "memories" are actually a patient's sexual instincts expressing themselves through the patient's unconscious mind (Ofshe & Watters, 1993).

A second challenge to Freud's repression theory actually turns the first challenge on its head. Specifically, there appears to be no empirical evidence to affirmatively support the theory. Freud's concept of repression has been applied in different ways by the mental health community for nearly a century. Yet all claims by practitioners seem to amount to nothing more than unsubstantiated speculation, tied to other Freudian concepts and speculative mechanisms. The only support for repression is in the nature of anecdotal evidence contributed by psychoanalysts who presume the existence of the repression mechanism. Even leading psychoanalytic theoreticians have recognized that the concept of repression is a "meta-psychological" principle rather than a testable hypothesis about human behavior (Ofshe & Watters, 1993).

A third challenge to Freud's repression theory comes from those who argue that what appears to be repression can readily be explained in other terms. One notable example is Mischel's criticism (1971) of the 1950 Zeller experiment, which involved the paired-associate learning task of associating nonsense syllables. Three days after Zeller's initial experiment, both experimental and control subjects relearned the same material, and they performed similarly. Immediately thereafter, they took a block-tapping test. The experimental subjects were led to believe that they had done badly on this test, thus threatening their egos, whereas the control subjects were led to believe that they had done well. Three days later, both groups again performed the initial learning task, and the experimental subjects actually did perform more poorly than they had earlier, suggesting that they had repressed their memory of performing the task three days earlier. This time, however, the experimental group was told that they had done well. Then both groups performed the learning task yet again, and the difference between the performance of the two groups was negligible. These results suggested to Zeller that the ego now allowed repressed memory of learning the task to surface to the conscious mind (Mischel, 1971).

Zeller's experiment would seem to lend credence to Freud's repression theory. But Mischel (1982) pointed out:

> Whenever a measure of retention of material is inferred from the speed with which it is relearned, it becomes impossible to separate the role of original learning from that of

remembering. Differential recall of material has been shown
to stem from differences in initial learning and covert
rehearsal of the material, at least under some conditions.
(p. 359)

Mischel pondered whether Zeller's findings were really a result of
repression, and concluded that rather than show repression they
might show only poorer learning caused by emotional upset and
disorganization. In other words, Zeller's subjects may simply have
learned less because they became disorganized or unmotivated, and
then learned more when they were relieved of their stress.

A final threat to Freud's repression theory comes not from
psychoanalytic theorists but from the biochemistry research laboratory. According to an article in <u>The Journal of the American
Medical Association</u> ("Biology," 1994), biology may have something
to do with repressed memory. Research indicates that psychological
stress alters memory storage in the brain. Repression usually
serves to hide long-term abuse during one's childhood. However,
such long-term abuse creates chronic stress that can impair
activity in the brain's hippocampal region, which is thought to be
critical in learning and memory, according to Robert M. Sapolsky,
Ph.D., an associate professor of neuroscience at Stanford
University School of Medicine ("Biology," 1994).

Conclusion

In sum, Freud's popular repression theory is now under attack
from several fronts. First, no reliable empirical evidence can
support it. Second, psychoanalysts generally admit that they have
blindly accepted the theory, that their anecdotal evidence proves
nothing, and that Freud's hypothesis was untestable. Third, behavior
that appears to show repression can be explained in other terms,
terms that hard scientific evidence now seems to corroborate.

Whether Freudian psychoanalysis will fall out of favor among
practitioners in the future is not certain. What is likely,
however, is that Freud's repression theory will continue to be the
subject of debate across academic and scientific disciplines, and

that further advances in biochemical research will shed additional light on how the human brain remembers--or fails to remember.

References

Biology enters repressed memory fray. (1994, December 14). <u>The Journal of the American Medical Association,</u> pp. 272, 1725.

Gendlin, E. T. (1964). A theory of personality change. In P. Worchel & D. Byrne (Eds.), <u>Personality change.</u> New York: Wiley.

Mischel, W. (1971). <u>Introduction to personality.</u> New York: Holt, Rinehart and Winston.

Ofshe, R., & Watters, E. (1993). Making monsters. <u>Society, 30,</u> pp. 4-16.

Sanford, N. (1966). <u>Self & society: Social change and individual development.</u> New York: Atherton Press.

This paper examines the placebo effect, its effectiveness, and its uses among physicians. Notice that the student begins with a careful and thoughtful definition of the term (not just a simple dictionary definition), so that the reader is clear from the start as to what the term means. This can be a highly effective approach to opening a term paper. (APA style)

THE PLACEBO EFFECT

The placebo effect has been defined as "an improvement in one's [physical] condition that occurs after taking a pill or undergoing a treatment with no obvious or demonstrable medical value" (Rubin, 1993, p. 78). Dr. Michael Stefanek, director of adult psychology at the University of Maryland School of Medicine, explained the placebo effect this way:

> "It may have a lot to do with our expectations or hope. We may expect to get some benefit from a treatment and might, even if it has no known physiological reason to work. If I have a cold and take some vitamins and really expect that to help, then I may go about my regular routine of exercise and work. And following that routine might actually help me to recover. Another factor is that taking a medicine, even one not shown to be effective, might decrease our anxiety. Since we are taking some action to improve our health, we feel more in control." (Stutz, 1997)

But Rubin's and Stefanik's definitions are too limiting because the placebo effect does not necessarily result only from placebos; that is, one can experience the placebo effect without taking medicine or receiving specific treatments. A better definition, then, must encompass changes in condition instigated by suggestive qualities of <u>any</u> healing intervention--not just by physiologic or pharmacologic properties (Letvak, 1995). According to Letvak, a placebo effect can be obtained "without any specific effort--and without a tangible placebo . . . The effect probably results from a complex interaction of psychological, physiologic, and sociocultural factors" (1995, p. 93). In short, the placebo effect is any outcome of the mind convincing the body that it is being helped.

The Significance of the Placebo
Effect as a Therapeautic Tool

Many studies support the general thesis that the placebo effect is real. One group of researchers, for example, studied 6,931 people who had had treatments that were later thoroughly discredited. Forty percent reported "excellent" improvement and 30% "good" results (Rubin, 1993). Massachusetts General Hospital also conducted a placebo study. One group of surgical patients received visits from the anesthesiologist the day before, whereas another group had long conversations with the anesthesiologists, who sat at their bedside, held the patients' hands, and reassured them that they would get as much pain medicine as they needed after the operation. The patients in that second group required only half as much painkiller after the surgery and were discharged almost three days earlier (Vernick, 1994).

Many other scientific studies have confirmed the validity of the placebo effect, showing on average that about a one-third of patients improve when given a placebo (Vernick, 1994). Various researchers have found that anywhere from 10% to 70% of patients given a placebo show improvement for a wide variety of symptoms and conditions--including coughing, seasickness, dental and postoperative pain, angina, migraine, and ulcer pain. The percentage showing improvement seems to vary depending primarily on the type of symptom or condition ("The Power," 1994).

Can a placebo affect a person's condition negatively as well as positively? The University of California, Berkeley Wellness Letter (1994) reported that, surprisingly, about 10% of people given a placebo report side effects normally associated with a chemically active drug, and others even experience withdrawal symptoms when they discontinue the placebo ("The Power," 1994). If this report and the studies it cites are credible, the implications are significant. The fact that individuals receiving placebos experienced unpleasant outcomes as well as pleasant ones suggests that the placebo effect is more than the result of "positive thinking"--a way of coping with a disorder; it goes to the disorder itself, facilitating the healing process, even if that means discomfort or pain for the individual.

The Placebo Effect as a Healing Mechanism

All the studies and statistics cited above involve alleviation of pain or discomfort, rather than actual healing (or curing) of a physiological disorder. This observation brings to mind an important question: Is the placebo effect limited to unmeasurable, therapeutic outcomes such as pain and depression, or has it been shown to provide measurable or observable healing as well?

As a threshold matter it should be noted that just because an individual responds to a placebo doesn't mean that the health problem is not genuine. Pain patients with documented tissue damage, for example, have received significant pain relief from placebos (Stutz, 1997). As for whether the placebo effect extends to observable and measurable outcomes, it is necessary to make a further distinction. At least one study has suggested that placebos can improve certain involuntary functions. Thomas Archer and Carl Leier of Ohio State University studied 24 patients who had taken part in heart failure treatment trials. Fifteen had received a placebo, and nine got no placebo and no active drug. They found that heart function improved significantly only in the placebo group (Rubin, 1993). The results of the Archer-Leier study should not be surprising, however, because the study involved heart function, an involuntary bodily function like body temperature and breathing rate. It is common knowledge that a human mind sufficiently trained and disciplined can indeed control these functions through conscious will.

Still at issue, however, is whether the placebo effect operates to heal (cure) physiological problems such as tissue damage, tumors, lesions, and fractures. It is important to distinguish between two types of placebo effects: a therapeutic effect that helps the individual (patient) to feel well, but does not necessarily cure the individual, and a genuine healing (curing) effect. It is striking that there are no credible studies to support the claim that the power of the mind can heal such physiological disorders. All supporting evidence is purely anecdotal. Testimonials abound, of course, and they involve all manner of panaceas, from faith healing to witchcraft, and so on. For example, a Filipino woman with lupus returned to her native village after drug treatment in the United States had failed to help her. A witch doctor removed a curse, and three weeks later, all the woman's symptoms were gone. The parents of a boy in chemotherapy rubbed a bogus magic mixture on his head and told him his hair would grow back. Although it did, when they stopped using the concoction his hair fell out again (Vernick, 1994). Without the benefit of controlled study, there is no way to evaluate such claims. They are, therefore, of little practical use to the serious researcher.

Use of the Placebo Effect Among Physicians

The placebo effect is by no means a modern-day discovery, as these provocative words by Plato suggest: "'A lie is useful only as a medicine to men. The use of such medicine should be confined to physicians'" (Plato's The Republic qtd. in Letvak, 1995, p. 93). Healers have recognized the placebo effect for many centuries. Long before antibiotics, laser surgery, and gene therapy, doctors depended on placebos to mobilize their patients' self-healing powers. When combined with soothing words, hope, and enthusiasm from a doctor, treatments of no known therapeutic utility--among them, lizard's blood, crushed spiders, and live leeches--proved to be genuinely therapeutic (Vernick, 1994).

According to Letvak (1995), many physicians today use the placebo response, unwittingly or not. They show care by carefully listening to the patient and being alert to physical and verbal responses. Letvak recommends to doctors that they assess their patients' perceptions of the medical system and their expectations of their doctors. Patients' attitudes and educational background often influence their treatment. The placebo effect, says Letvak, is stronger when the doctor shows confidence in the plan. He recommends that doctors tell their patients they believe the treatment will be helpful (Letvak, 1995).

An experiment in therapeutic touch under way at the Birmingham Burn Center of the University of Alabama may be the placebo effect in action, according to Skeptical Inquirer. One hundred thirty-one burn patients participated in the study in either a therapeutic touch or a sham group. Not all of the subjects remained the full six days. The authors criticized the study, and properly so, pointing out the distinction between the placebo effect and an "actual" effect:

> What if the mimic TT [therapeutic touch] practitioner feels compassion for the burn patient and accidentally performs actual TT? Since the human 'energy field' (presumably manipulated by TT) cannot be objectively quantified, there is no independent means to assess when manipulation is occurring. (Scheiber, 1997)

The authors concluded that the greatest lesson to learn from the study was the necessity for a true control group in addition to a sham and treatment group.

Scientists and physicians today generally agree, then, that the placebo effect is very real and can be very useful if it is used to make the power of the mind work for, not against, the patient. But are physicians careful to distinguish between therapy and healing when it comes to the placebo affect? Some physicians, including surgeons, claim not only a therapeutic effect but also a healing effect. Surgeon Bernie Siegel, author of Love, Medicine and Miracles, asserts:

> "The placebo effect can not only lessen the pain from a tumor, it can make the tumor disappear. I believe that physicians

should be incorporating more of the placebo effect--and patients' self-healing powers--into the care they provide. Personally, I will never let a patient go hopeless. I will always use something as a placebo." (Siegel qtd. in Vernick, 1994, p. 217)

Concluding Remarks

Despite the growing acceptance and use of the placebo effect by the medical community, it would seem that physicians would be more vocal about advocating its use. But, as Rubin told <u>U.S. News & World Report</u> (Rubin, 1993): "I think physicians have always been embarrassed by the notion that people get better when they're given dummy pills or dummy treatments." Perhaps what Rubin meant is that the medical community feels threatened by a growing awareness among laypeople that many of its treatments and prescriptions are unnecessary. The placebo effect makes the physician feel less important, less needed, and perhaps less legitimate.

References

Bower, B. (1996, Aug. 24). New pitch for placebo power. <u>Science News, 150,</u> p. 123.

Letvak, R. (1995). Putting the placebo effect into practice. <u>Patient Care, 29,</u> p. 93. Online. InfoTrac.

Rubin, R. (1993, November 22). Placebos' healing power. <u>U.S. News & World Report,</u> p. 78.

Scheiber, B. & Selby, C. (1997). UAB final report of therapeutic touch--An appraisal: University of Alabama at Birmingham Burn Center. <u>Skeptical Inquirer, 21,</u> p. 53. Online. InfoTrac.

Stutz, C. (1996, December 13). Dr. Michael Stefanek on the placebo effect. <u>Baltimore Jewish Times.</u> Online. Electric Library.

The power of hope. (1994, September). <u>The University of California, Berkeley Wellness Letter,</u> p. 3.

Vernick, S. (1994, July 1). Placebo power! (Healing properties of placebos). <u>Cosmopolitan,</u> p. 217. Online. Electric Library.

17

RELIGIOUS STUDIES

Prelude to Christianity: Hellenic and Hellenistic Religion and Philosophy

Handsome Lake and the Iroquois Religious Revival

Martin Luther on Faith and Free Will

This student covers a great deal of ground, greater than is generally advisable for a term paper. But the stated intent is an overview, and that is what has been delivered. Always be sure what your professor is asking for. This paper has no thesis, and does not go into deep research. Ask yourself (better yet, ask your professor) what is wanted. An overview, a research paper, and a thesis are very different requests. Don't confuse them, because if you do, your A+ paper may only get a C. (APA style)

PRELUDE TO CHRISTIANITY: HELLENIC AND
HELLENISTIC RELIGION AND PHILOSOPHY

This paper is not an attempt at anything more than an overview to set the stage for more detailed study of individual religions and philosophies of the Eastern Mediterranean, including Christianity, that were influenced by the Greeks.

Hellenic and Hellenistic

Although the terms <u>Hellenic</u> and <u>Hellenistic</u> are often used interchangeably to mean the spread of Greek culture throughout the ancient world, with respect to the religions and philosophies that began in the Greek region we can distinguish them. Most often, the term <u>Hellenistic</u> is used to describe the culture that flourished in the remains of Alexander's empire after his death; that usage is preserved here. In this paper, the term <u>Hellenic</u> refers to the religion and mythology of the classic, or Homeric, Greek historical period, dating from the time of Homer's <u>Iliad,</u> which gives a picture of early Greek religion.

This early Greek religion evolved from a blend of Achaean, Dorian, Minoan, Egyptian, and Asian elements. This period can also be called Olympic, referring to the pantheon of gods that ruled from Mt. Olympus. These gods derived from all the cultures that comprised the Minoan-Mycenean civilization. After about 500 B.C., this classical period gave way to the era of civil strife between the various city-states, and a series of mystery religions arose in prominence, although their seasonal festivities were celebrated as far back as 1400 B.C. During this strife-filled period, certain gods from the Olympic pantheon also became dominant over the rest, especially Dionysius and Apollo. Increasing monism, or the search for one principle or deity, gave rise to the rational thought of Greek philosophers who placed the spiritual path of knowledge above those of the warrior, the monk or ascetic, the magician, or the lover (Godwin, 1991).

Alexander "The Great"

The spread of Hellenic culture was initiated by Alexander, son of Philip II of Macedonia. Philip's kingdom of Macedonia dominated the Greek world; but his son defines the term "boundless ambition." Alexander conquered the vast Persian Empire between 336 and 323 B.C., and ushered in a new era that injected Greek culture and religion into the East and led to its admixture with a variety of native religions. Alexander did far more than encourage the building of Greek-style cities in the newly conquered lands. He cemented his rule not by imposing Greek ways, but by maintaining existing structures and bureaucracies so long as they swore allegiance to him. Then he went a step further and used marriage to intertwine the cultures and make potential enemies into relatives. He not only married a Persian woman, but required his soldiers to marry the Persian women they had taken up with. And he encouraged the integration of Persian religions, such as Zoroastrianism, with Greek practices.

With Alexander's death in 323 B.C., the empire was divided into three parts: Macedonia and Greece (ruled by the Antigonids); Egypt (ruled by the Ptolmies); and Palestine, Asia, and Asia Minor (ruled by the Seluecids). The next 300 years, which saw a tremendous amalgamation and spread of old and new religions and philosophies around a Greek core, can be termed the Hellenistic era.

The Olympian, or Hellenic, Era of Greek Religion

During this period, an array of superhuman gods ruled from Mt. Olympus, representing the native Aegeans of the Greek region, Minoans from Crete, and the Aryan invaders of the second millennium

B.C. The invaders followed a religious imperative that might be called the "path of the warrior" (Godwin, 1991, pp. 11-16), and had Zeus as their sky father god, Demeter as the earth mother, and Hestia as the virgin goddess of hearth and home. Hera, who became Zeus' wife under the new arrangement, and Hermes, the swift messenger god, were Aegean, and Rhea was a Minoan goddess, from a culture that was egalitarian and matricentric. Others came from Ionia (Apollo), Cyprus (Aphrodite), and Thrace (Dionysius and Ares). The patriarchal religion of the invaders made the male gods dominant, but the female gods had their own powers. Myths and legends were arranged and rearranged until these gods had familial relationships with one another, with Zeus as the head (Foot Moor, 1992). By the time of Homer, the pantheon was in charge of natural forces, but never equal to these forces because their powers were limited by the concept of fate, an irresistible force of destiny.

Not surprisingly, considering their diverse origins, these gods quarreled among themselves and resorted to all sorts of trickery, involving humans in their designs and thus intervening in human destinies. What sometimes seems to be an Olympian soap opera detailing the very human frailties of the gods also served as behavioral examples and warnings to the people. It does not seem accidental that the offspring of jealous Hera and powerful Zeus would be Mars, the god of war. War is the predictable outcome of mixing jealousy and power. The gods were immortal, but not all-powerful or always present (Foot Moor, 1992). The fact that even the gods were limited in their abilities and controlled by the fates served as a warning to humans of their far greater limitations. The lesson of story after story told by the Greeks is that overweening pride or <u>hubris</u> would bring the downfall of even the greatest of men.

Religious Practice

Greek religious practice at this time followed a variety of forms. The various deities were mainly called on to represent certain city-states, which they favored in wars and protected as guardians. Public ceremonies for these gods were aimed at keeping the city free from plague, conquest, or poverty. These became the occasions for great religious festivals where citizens and foreigners congregated. The gods were the subjects of great feats of art and architecture during the Golden Era of Greece (Foot Moor, 1992).

Throughout this era, however, other religious practices existed alongside this official state religion. Peasant farmers and shepherds continued magical or animistic practices aimed at propitiating spirits of the home or nature (Godwin, 1981) and these continued far into the Hellenistic and Roman eras, with local variations. In addition, mystery religions, always in the region, began to gain adherents as the power of the Olympians waned during increasing civil strife. These generally focused on oracular divination, regeneration, and the afterlife.

The Eleusinian Mysteries, in existence since at least the eighth century B.C., were perhaps the most widely practiced. Secrecy was so well maintained in these mystery cults that scholars still do not know exactly what initiates experienced, but the purpose of the initiations was twofold. At the lower level, information was imparted about the nature of higher worlds to large groups of people. At the higher level of the Great Mystery, smaller numbers of initiates were brought into direct contact with the beings of these higher worlds (Godwin, 1991). Unseen forces that affect humankind were represented in the vegetable world by pomegranates, corn, and poppies (this was seen as the mediator between heaven and earth), in ceremonies that profoundly affected the initiates. Among the information imparted in the Lesser Mystery was the heliocentric theory (the understanding that the earth revolves around the sun) which would have, at that time, profoundly shifted a person's view of the cosmos. Centuries later, fearing the effects of such a shift, the Christian Church was to reject both Copernicus and Galileo for precisely this "mystery."

Religion Begets Philosophy

Some of these mystery cults, such as the one dedicated to Dionysius, god of wine and pleasure, created such excesses that reactions were formed by other cults to Apollo and Pallas Athena, celebrating moderation, justice, and legalism. Out of the same "path of knowledge" grew the quests of philosophers such as Pythagoras (570-470 B.C.), Socrates (469-399 B.C.), and Plato, (429-347 B.C.), all of whom sought to combine spirituality, science, and human mental powers. The focus now became one of training the mind. The means of training the mind varied, but often combined intuition through a guide (or daemon--one's guardian spirit), Egyptian mysticism, and rational, logical enquiry. Plato sealed the ultimate doom of the Homeric pantheon with his establishment of an abstract quality of Absolute Good, to which even the gods were subject (Godwin, 1981).

These philosophies arose in response to many of the religious excesses and confusion during this era. Cynics followed Diogenes (c 372-287 B.C.), emphasizing self-sufficiency, limited desires, and a contemptuous attitude toward luxury or social convention. Zeno (c 335-263 B.C.), leader of the Stoics, identified reason with virtue, stressing an ascetic disregard for misfortune. The Epicureans searched for individual happiness through lives of moderate pleasure (Dougherty, 1998). Both Stoics and Epicureans believed the soul did not last beyond bodily death (Godwin, 1981).

This life of the mind and the pursuit of rational logic with its restraint of emotions contrasted sharply with the intense personal and emotional involvement of the mystery religions that remained popular among the common people.

Religious Trends and Practices
During the Hellenistic Era

Greece became an empirical power rather than a conglomerate of city-states, and Greek culture was exported throughout the world through Alexander and the three empires that followed his death. But as we have discussed, the flow of ideas went both ways, and a long period of active cross-cultural fertilization occurred. In the Ptolemaic empire, Egyptian and Greek practices intermingled. Long before Alexander, Egyptians had introduced their gods into commercial cities along the Mediterranean, and Isis became popular in Greece (Foot Moor, 1992). But this process of intermingling was greatly expanded during Ptolemaic times. The Ptolemies were successors of the Pharaohs, and thus claimed divinity themselves, representing the Imperial Cult of religion, whereby the ruler is the embodiment of a god on earth (Godwin, 1981). They had a vision of a religion that would unite the two races (Foot Moore, 1992). Sarapis, the Egyptian version of the Greek god of the underworld, Hades, was with Isis at the center of this new cult, which rapidly spread throughout the Greek world. A temple was built to Sarapis at the foot of the Acropolis in Athens.

Merchants carried the worship to Italy, and by 150 B.C. Isis was a commanding religious figure at Pompeii. There was a temple to Isis in Pompeii at the time of the volcanic eruption in 63 B.C. (Foot Moor, 1992). Among the Romans there was some serious resistance, however:

> Not only were the mysteries offensive to Roman religious and moral susceptibilities, they were the cult of a hostile political power as well. On a number of occasions the mysteries were legally proscribed and the temples of Isis torn down. (Sheler, 1992, p. 58)

But the appeal of Greek ways and the use of Greek teachers and businesspeople continued in Rome. And as Rome gained political control of the Mediterranean, the political associations of the cults disappeared and general acceptance followed.

At the same time, Zoroastrianism, imported from the Persian section of the empire, also played a powerful role. The philosopher Pythagoras is said to have been Zoroaster's pupil. This religion was dualistic and based on ancient Mithraism, where Ahura-mazda the Supreme Lord of Light contended with the Dark Lord Ahriman in a "perpetual state of warfare between the ultimately good and the ultimately evil" (Godwin, 1981, p. 13).

Christianity: A Seed Sprouts in Hellenistic Soil

The Hellenistic era also saw the rise of Christianity, first as an offshoot of Judaism, and later as a growing religion of its own. Hellenistically oriented Jews, such as Paul and the martyr Stephen, used Greek language and culture to advance the spread of the new religion to many centers in the Hellenistic world after being persecuted by those who saw them as Jewish heretics (Sheler, 1992). St. Paul's letter to the Corinthians is said to have been written to combat Greek philosophies of Cynicism with his own Hellenistic adoption of Stoic ideas (Fitzgerald, 1997). The charismatic experiences of the very earliest followers of Christ are connected to the mysteries; and the mythos has much in common with Mithraism. The Hellenistic connections to early Christianity are broad, and may lead to Jesus himself.

Recent excavations have demonstrated that Nazareth, where Jesus grew to manhood, was a trading city, with Greeks, Romans, Phoenicians, and Jews living side by side. It was into this melting pot of cultures and ideas that Jesus was born, and in the midst of these people he began his mission among the Jews. So before embarking on a study of Christianity, it makes sense to look carefully at the context of its birth, and at the influence of Hellenistic culture on both Jesus and his followers.

References

Dougherty, J. P. (1998, January). Western creed: Western identity. The World & I, p. 328.

Fitzgerald, J. T. P. (1997, April). Paul on marriage and celibacy: The Hellenistic background of 1 Corinthians 7. Book reviews. The Journal of Religion, pp. 289-190.

Foot Moor, G. (1992). History of religions. Book Chapters, Electric Library. Available at www.elibrary.com.

Godwin, J. (1981). Mystery religions in the ancient world. San Francisco: Harper & Row.

Sheler, J. L. (1992, April). The first Christians. U.S. News & World Report, pp. 58-71.

(A+) This student details a religious movement in the context of historical events and uses the historical chronology to allow the story to unfold as the details are presented. The student's attitude is analytical and detached, but respectful of all sides. Some would dispute the student's use of the term "Indians," which is intermixed here with "Native Americans." The student seems to have chosen familiar readability over political correctness; but you should be aware of your professor's attitudes on issues such as this one. (MLA style)

HANDSOME LAKE AND THE IROQUOIS RELIGIOUS REVIVAL

> [Every People should pursue the same path in] the process of society from the barbarous ages to its present degree of perfection . . . a love of exclusive property [would be] a happy commencement of the business [of civilizing the Indians]. (Secretary of War Henry Knox, 1789, qtd. in Wallace, A. 218)

The views of Henry Knox were not unusual in his day. Despite the fact that George Washington had attempted to implement a fair policy for the Native Americans of what was then the West, the cultural differences were too great to easily bridge, and the values too different to prevent clashes between the white and red men (Hewitt 215). Of the whites that came among the Indians and attempted to bridge the gap, the Quakers were by far the most accepted and successful. But despite the good intentions of the Quakers and the willingness of many Indians to cooperate with them, not all went well.

A Weak and Divided Iroquois Nation

The Iroquois believed in a Master of Life, also called the Maker of Things, who had been the first being on earth and had commanded men to love one another and live in peace. For some 200 years the Iroquois League uniting five tribes had lived in peace with each other, if not always with their neighbors. Their society was solidly based on old traditions, and the political system was so well constructed that it served as a partial blueprint for the U.S. constitution (Wallace, P. 25).

The American Revolution had split the Iroquois as it had the colonists; but whereas the colonies emerged stronger and more united, the Iroquois emerged divided, weak, and unsure of their place in the new political order. The powerful Mohawks had sided with the British and lost. Americans poured into the Mohawk Valley as the once-mighty Mohawks retreated into Canada (Hewitt 175-190).

With the league in tatters, many Iroquois looked to the victorious whites and did what their culture had often done: learn from their former enemy and absorb some of what made them strong. They accepted the idea that the religion of the whites was powerful medicine, and were not generally opposed to recognizing such medicine. For example, when the Iroquois League was at its height, a group of Woodland Sioux too small to defend itself joined the League and their powerful neighbors, the Seneca (one of the five Iroquois tribes). The band of Woodland Sioux was so small that within a few generations its language had disappeared and the tribe had merged with the Seneca. But for hundreds of years the Seneca continued to hold the ceremonies of that band, and honor the medicine of their gods. Just as the band had merged with them, so had the religious responsibilities (Morgan 250).

Seneca Cornplanter

One of the greatest proponents of the acquisition of white technology following the Revolution was the Seneca Cornplanter, who sent his children to college and encouraged the adoption of many white practices. Cornplanter had exchanged letters with President Washington, and had asked for a technical aid program. Washington responded, but the program met with limited success, and afterward the government turned to religious denominations for this service. Cornplanter met with the Quakers in Philadelphia and welcomed their help. The Quakers were dedicated and helpful, and do not appear to have attempted to force their beliefs on the Indians; but it is clear that this was not the attitude taken by the majority of whites (Hewitt 180). The quotation at the beginning of this paper is illustrative of what was certainly the majority position.

A Quaker named Henry Simmons, with two companions, arrived in the village of Cornplanter in May 1798 and set up a demonstration farm and later a school (Hewitt 187; Wallace, P. 94). The Quakers were generally accepted, but an important ingredient was missing: self-pride. For all their gentle ways, the Quakers were still monogamous Christians who were coming to present a system that in the end did not allow room for the gods and heritage of the Iroquois. It must have been difficult for the once-proud Iroquois to throw away their age-old culture as though it were inferior to the white culture; to do so would be to lose all pride in their race and themselves.

Handsome Lake

Cornplanter had a half-brother, Handsome Lake, who had once been a representative on the Great Council of the League, but in 1799 he could best be described as one of the many town drunks. On June 15 of that year, Cornplanter was brought the not-unexpected news that Handsome Lake was dying. When Cornplanter arrived at Handsome Lake's house, his niece told him that her father had called out "So be it!" from inside his house, and then walked out the door and collapsed. There was no perceptible heartbeat or breathing, and the body was becoming cold, so Handsome Lake was assumed to be dead. However, when the body was being moved into the house, a warm spot was discovered on his chest. The warm spot spread, and two hours later, he opened his eyes. Upon awaking, Handsome Lake told of a vision he had, a vision that was destined to play a crucial role in the future of the Iroquois (Wallace, P. 185).

Handsome Lake's Vision

Handsome Lake said that he heard his name called, and left his house. Outside he saw three men dressed in fine ceremonial clothes. They told him that they were sent by the Maker of Things to visit him and help him from his sickness. He was told to go to the strawberry festival, which began the next day, and report what the Maker of Things wanted things to be like on Earth. If he did not preach the message, he would be buried in a hot, smoking place. The message was contained in four "words" that summarized the evil practices of men, about which the Maker of Things was sad and angry. The four evil words were whisky, witchcraft, love magic, and abortion-sterility medicine. People guilty of these things were to admit their wrongdoings, repent, and never sin again. Those who committed small sins were to confess in public; the moderate sinners to Handsome Lake in a ritual; and the great sinners alone to the Great Spirit. It was also said that the strawberry festival was always to be held as tradition dictated, and that all the people were to drink the berry's juice. Men were not to drink alcohol, even in private, for the Great Spirit knew not only what people were doing, but what they were thinking as well. The messengers left, with the promise to return.

The people were gathered together and the vision was related to them. Henry Simmons was present, and reported that the vision had a profound effect on the audience. He was so moved that he asked to speak to the council, and did so in praise of Handsome Lake's teachings. On the night of August 7 he had another vision, in which he was to be taken along with the spirits if he wished. In the morning he dressed in his finest clothes, called in Cornplanter, and told him not to dress him for burial even if he appeared to be dead. After a while he said that he was going, but would return, and fell into a trance in which his arms and legs were cold, his body warm, and his breathing imperceptible. He is reported to have stayed in this trance for 7 hours (Wallace, P. 185).

The "Sky Journey"

The vision Handsome Lake described upon awakening is called the Sky Journey. In it Handsome Lake, led by a guide who carried a bow and arrow and was dressed in sky-blue clothes, walked up the Milky Way (which descended from the South Sky) and on which the entire human race was seen striving toward heaven. Along the way were descriptions of men and women who represented the good and bad in humans. At the gates of heaven they met George Washington, sitting on the veranda of a house, with his dog. He was the good white man who had told the then-friendless Iroquois to return to their homes and live happily "as long as the sun shines and the waters run for [you] are an independent people." Washington came closer to heaven than any white man (heaven was reserved for Indians). They also met Jesus, bearing nail scars on his hands and feet. Jesus said that his people had slain him in their pride, and that he would not return to help them "until the earth passes away." Jesus told Handsome Lake to inform his people that they would become lost if they followed the ways of the white man (Wallace, A. 24).

There was a fork in the road, where a narrow path led to heaven, and a wide road led to hell. The path to heaven was filled mostly with children; but a repentant woman was also seen on the road, and it was explained that each human was given three chances to repent. Handsome Lake was then given a tour of hell, being shown the punishments of the evil, and then given a tour of heaven, where he met his dog and Cornplanter's daughter, who expressed sorrow that her brother did not agree with and take the advice of his father. This referred to more than a domestic squabble. Cornplanter's son Henry was educated in Philadelphia, and held the whole of Indian culture in contempt. He felt that the best course was to reject the past totally and in effect become a white man. The guide then reminded Handsome Lake that the Great Spirit sees and knows all, and warned him that unless the people mended their ways and thought more about the Great Spirit and performed the White Dog Ceremony, a great sickness would come on the village (Wallace, A. 22).

Handsome Lake's Religion: Built on Familiar Ground

The religion that Handsome Lake was developing was not radically new. It revived many old traditions and customs, making it familiar to the people. It took the most appealing and useful aspects of its major competitor, Christianity, and tied them to established Indian beliefs, so that the adoption of new ideas could be viewed as coming from Indian, not Western, tradition. An example is the idea of conflict between the forces of good and evil.

Before the coming of Christianity, Native Americans had no concept of the heaven and hell described by Handsome Lake in his Sky Journey (Morgan 322; Wallace, A. 22). But the Iroquois creation myth included the conflict between the Maker of Things and his evil brother (Morgan 322; Wallace, P. 205). Thus it was easy for Handsome Lake to say that this struggle was continuing, to develop the good/evil--heaven/hell concept, and to do so without straying too far from traditional beliefs. Also, Handsome Lake often mentioned four spirits that guided him. The people could easily relate these to the Four Winds of the old religion. The changes in names was easy to accept, too, for the Iroquois themselves often assumed new names to correspond with significant events in their lives (Hewitt 175).

Handsome Lake attacked the Western idea of private property, which had never been a part of Indian culture except in the case of certain sacred objects, such as a man's war club (Morgan 122; Wallace, A. 212). He also attacked the traditional medical societies, saying that by their restricted membership, they had in effect made private property out of their ritual. Their secret meetings, which were often livened with alcohol, made him fear witchcraft. He finally compromised, allowing the societies to hold their rituals, but without the use of alcohol and only on the great feast days under the supervision of the "Faithkeepers," where all the people could see and benefit from the ceremonies (Wallace, A. 215).

Within a year, Handsome Lake had converted most of the Iroquois to his religion, and for a time he assumed an unprecedented position of power in the tribe (Wallace, A. 12). At his death, his teachings were solidly entrenched and remain prevalent among the Iroquois (Wallace, P. 185). The result was to restore self-confidence to his people, end much of the alcoholism that was rampant among them, and by reuniting his people, he made it possible for them to more effectively cope with their problems, both political and social (Wallace, A. 22).

Conclusion

Handsome Lake's revival is a classic example of how religion can and has been used to effect massive social reform. Such events should serve notice to those who believe that all religions are the false and useless beliefs of men and women with weak intellects. Handsome Lake was clearly a shrewd and practical man when he was sober. He had after all been one of the two Seneca representatives (The Keepers of the Western Door) on the Great Council of the Iroquois League. The Great Council was an institution with a history at that time of more than 200 years, as long and distinguished as our senate is today. And the council had executive, legislative, and judicial powers in one body (Morgan 134). Handsome Lake would not have been chosen had he not been an able politician. But it is not fair to assume that Handsome Lake simply used religion as a tool without truly believing what he taught. All accounts indicate that he sincerely believed in his mission. He can only be judged by what he accomplished for his people.

Works Cited

Hewitt, J. N. B. "Legend of the Founding of the Iroquois League." American Anthropologist Apr. 1892: 175+.

Morgan, Lewis H. League of the Iroquois. Rochester, NY: Sage & Brother, 1851.

Wallace, Anthony F. C. The Death and Rebirth of the Seneca. New York: Knopf, 1970.

Wallace, Paul A. W. The White Roots of Peace. Philadelphia: U of Pennsylvania Press, 1946.

This paper is a doctrinal analysis of how Martin Luther reconciled two seemingly contradictory aspects of his theology. The instructor's assignment required that the student refer only to Luther's writings, and not to any other sources. Notice that the student refers explicitly to Luther only occasionally, to avoid excessive repetition. (MLA endnote style)

MARTIN LUTHER ON FAITH AND FREE WILL

Martin Luther's discussion of the question of free will revolves around his central concern of upholding the absolute sovereignty and omnipotence of God. Also related to this concern, and intimately involved with the question of free will, is Luther's theory of justification. These two aspects of Luther's thought--his emphasis on the omnipotence of God and the nature of justification--make it necessary for him to deny free will in man. However, this denial of free will does not contradict Luther's understanding of the freedom of a Christian. In fact, the freedom of the Christian requires the denial of free will.

God is the absolute sovereign of the universe; he completely controls everything that happens. This is fundamental to Luther's thought, and it is from this vantage point that he views the question of free will. Because God is omnipotent, there is no room for chance in the operations of the world. God's will decides and controls everything:

> His will is eternal and changeless, because his nature is so. From which it follows, by resistless logic, that all we do, however it may appear to us to be done mutably and contingently, is in reality done necessarily and immutably in respect of God's will.[1]

Thus even though it might appear to men that they act of their own free volition, it must be understood that in fact they do everything of necessity according to God's will. For if men could do anything of their own free will, God's eternal and changeless will would be contradicted and God's omnipotence would be denied. To

preserve the nature of God, Luther denies that man has any free
will at all:

> God foreknows nothing contingently, but . . . He fore-
> sees, proposes and does all things according to His own
> immutable, eternal and infallible will. This bombshell
> knocks "freewill" flat, and utterly shatters it; so that
> those who want to assert it must either deny my bomb-
> shell, or pretend not to notice it, or find some other
> way of dodging it.[2]

Luther is also concerned with establishing that God can be
trusted. To be able to trust God, it is necessary that God have
complete control in all matters, for if anything could happen apart
from his will, then he could not be trusted in everything. This
becomes extremely important in the context of salvation, for God
has given the promise of salvation in the gospel. Here again, man
must be denied free will, for if he had free will he could do
something contrary to God's will, and then God could no longer be
trusted to fulfill his word:

> For if you hesitate to believe, or are too proud to
> acknowledge, that God foreknows and wills all things,
> not contingently, but necessarily and immutable how can
> you believe, trust and rely on His promise?[3]

Luther illustrates this question of trusting God with the incident
of the hardening of Pharaoh's heart. If Pharaoh had had the
freedom to respond to the plagues that God set on him by turning
away from his persecution of the Israelites, God would not have
been truthful to the Israelites in saying that he would harden
Pharaoh's heart.

These two aspects of the knowledge of God--that he is omnipotent and trustworthy--achieve their greatest significance for man
in terms of salvation. Because God is the only author of salvation, men must understand him and the nature of his salvation, or
they will be entirely lost. It is for this reason that Luther is

so concerned with refuting Erasmus' notion of free will. For if men do not understand what their powers are and what God's powers are in matters pertaining to salvation, they cannot live a godly life. The notion that man has free will is a very dangerous idea: "But this false idea of 'freewill' is a real threat to salvation, and a delusion fraught with the most perilous consequences."[4]

So Luther proceeds to analyze man's will in the context of its powers relating to salvation. Man's will, because of its corruption, can do no good of itself. Man's will is captive either to the will of God or to the will of Satan. Man is powerless to do anything to effect his salvation, Only with grace can the will ever do any good. "Hence, it follows that 'freewill' without God's grace is not free at all, but is the permanent prisoner and bond-slave of evil, since it cannot turn itself to good."[5]

Because man's will is so completely bent toward evil, it would be impossible for anyone ever to be saved if salvation depended on works. Thus it becomes clear that Luther's doctrine of salvation develops directly from his notion of the absolute omnipotence of God and its corollary denial of free will. Everything happens of necessity, by the power of God's will, and therefore man can have no free will because he is compelled and not free in any of his actions.

This will of man, however, is fallen and corrupt and is capable of only evil. Even though God sustains all actions in men, they can still do only evil. God pushed Pharaoh further into evil not because God made Pharaoh evil, but because Pharaoh could only move in that direction. Because man can do nothing good on his own, it would be impossible for him to attain salvation if salvation depended on works, "by the power of 'freewill' none at all could be saved, but every one of us would perish."[6] However, God has given the promise of salvation through Jesus Christ. Because God can be trusted, it is certain that this promise is indeed valid. But because salvation cannot come by works, as man's will is totally corrupt, it follows that salvation must come by God's grace alone. It is by God's grace that a Christian can have faith, and it is by faith alone that the Christian can be saved.

If the will of man is so corrupt and able to do only evil, and if its power is nil without the grace of God, what is meant by the freedom of a Christian? The freedom of a Christian does not lie in his ability to do what he chooses, or to freely dispose of his actions, because he does all things by necessity. Rather his freedom consists in a freedom from works. Luther draws the distinction between the inner and the outer man. The inner man is the soul, and it is to this man that freedom is given with the gift of grace. It is a spiritual freedom which makes the heart free from all sins, laws, and commands:

> The believing soul by means of the pledge of faith is free in Christ, its bridegroom, free from all sins, secure against death and hell, and is endowed with the eternal righteousness, life and salvation of Christ its bridegroom.[7]

The outer man would correspond to the fleshly man who must live in the world. This freedom Luther is speaking about does not apply to him because he must perform works in his relations with his neighbors. He always strives to do good works out of his love for God, but he is free from the burden of thinking that he can be justified by these works. "Our faith in Christ does not free us from works, but from false opinions concerning works, that is from the foolish presumption that justification is acquired by works."[8]

It should be clear by now that the enslaved will and the freedom of a Christian do not refer to the same thing, and that Luther does not contradict himself by holding both. That man can do no good is a function of his corrupt and enslaved will; thus his will can do nothing to effect his salvation. However, the freedom of a Christian lies precisely in a freedom from the necessity to do any works at all in order to be saved. The freedom of a Christian does not mean that now his will is free to turn only to good works, but rather that he has no need of works. Even in a

Christian the will is not always turned toward good, but God no longer counts this against him.

The enslaved will and the freedom of faith, instead of being contradictory, actually imply each other, so that both must be held together. If a Christian who has faith begins to think that he can gain salvation by doing good works, or if he thinks his will is free to do good works, he will lose his faith and his freedom:

> A Christian is free from all things and over all things
> so that he needs no works to make him righteous and
> save him, since faith alone abundantly confers all these
> things. Should he grow so foolish, however, as to
> presume to become righteous, free, saved and a Christian
> by means of some good work, he would instantly lose
> faith and all its benefits.[9]

It is important for a Christian to understand that he does not have free will, for if he does not understand this, he might try to attain salvation by his works, and in the very process he would be lost. Thus the freedom of a Christian in faith requires the negation of free will, for if he had free will, he would lose his faith.

If free will is denied, there must be a means to salvation that is not dependent on works. This is the case because God has given the promise of salvation in the gospel. And because God can be trusted, there must be a way of attaining this salvation. Because salvation cannot come by works, because the will is not free, it must come by the grace of God alone, freeing the Christian from the need to do any works at all. The denial of free will then implies the fact of faith and the freedom of a Christian.

Endnotes

[1] Martin Luther, "The Bondage of the Will," <u>Martin Luther</u>, ed. John Dillenberger (Garden City, NY: Doubleday & Company, Inc., 1961) 181.

[2] Luther, "Bondage" 181.

[3] Luther, "Bondage" 184.

4 Luther, "Bondage" 189.

5 Luther, "Bondage" 187.

6 Luther, "Bondage" 199.

7 Martin Luther, "The Freedom of a Christian," <u>Martin Luther</u>, ed. John Dillenberger (Garden City, NY: Doubleday & Company, Inc., 1961) 61.

8 Luther, "Freedom" 81.

9 Luther, "Freedom" 64 ff.

18

SOCIOLOGY

Sociological Explanations for Criminalization of Drug Use in Canada

Cities in North America: Decline of the Urban City

Hispanic and Asian-American Values

The Contemporary Suburb: A Response to Fishman's Technoburb

This paper examines and critiques various sociological explanations for Canada's drug policies. This paper illustrates that it is perfectly appropriate to approach your topic with an implicit point of view, as long as you justify that point of view with incisive criticism and cogent arguments, as this student has done. Also, notice that in the final paragraph the student suggests potential avenues for further research—an excellent way to conclude a term paper. (APA style)

SOCIOLOGICAL EXPLANATIONS FOR
CRIMINALIZATION OF DRUG USE IN CANADA

Since the Opium Act of 1908, drug laws in Canada have been concerned with the protection of individuals from the adverse effects of many different drugs, and the protection of society from individuals consuming these substances. However, much of the research in social policy as it relates to these laws, and the effects of these laws, has been quite critical (for example, Alexander, 1990; Blackwell & Erickson, 1988; Boyd, 1991). The overwhelming criticism of Canada's drug laws by these social policy researchers is that the laws do nothing to stop or even prevent the use of drugs by Canadians, and in some instances these laws do more harm than good to both the individual and to Canadian society.

Were these social policy researchers simply independent, academic researchers, the federal government's propensity to ignore them while refining and creating drug laws might be justified. However, many of these researchers have been in the field for many years, and are employees of such organizations as the Addiction Research Foundation (an agency of the government of Ontario, and the largest treatment and research center in North America), and the Canadian Centre on Substance Abuse, an arms-length policy organization of the federal government, created under "Canada's Drug Strategy" (Fischer, 1993). Most recently, in opposition to the passing of Canada's newest drug law (Bill C-7), the Addiction Research Foundation's president told the Senate:

> For a law to actually work, it should meet three tests. It
> must be effective, accepted and equitable. It should not

cause more problems than it's trying to prevent. Will C-7 meet these three tests? The research evidence suggests that for the most common illicit drugs, it will not. (Kendall, 1995, p. 4)

Why, then, do legislators continue to battle drug abuse by creating laws that criminalize drug use? Various psychological and sociological explanations have been offered. The scope of this paper is necessarily limited to examining three prevailing sociological explanations: (1) the conflict theory, (2) social constructionism, and (3) status politics and moral entrepreneurship.

The penultimate objective of this paper is to point out the merits of each theory and the problems with each theory. This paper's ultimate objective, however, is to show, by way of the inadequacies of the sociological theories, that a more fruitful avenue of inquiry should embrace the notion that illicit drug use is very much a moral issue, and that morality remains at the heart of the reasoning, at least implicitly, behind treating the use of drugs as a criminal issue.

The Conflict Theory

The conflict theory explanation of drug policy is based, at a most general level, on the examination of conflict between dominant and subordinate groups in society (Giffen, et al., 1991). This aspect of conflict theory assumes, however, that the dominant and subordinate groups are more or less homogenous in nature. Most research in the field of drug policy recently, however, deals with power being located in "institutional structures in society (economic, governmental, religious, etc.)" (Giffen et al., 1991, p. 10), which does not presuppose homogenous groups.

The flexibility of conflict theory in defining opposing groups in society has resulted (for better or for worse) in the freedom for social policy theorists to define many different opposing interests. Some researchers (most notably Johns, 1991) have argued that drug laws tend to unfairly affect minorities and the poor. Johns argued that the "War on Drugs" performs functions that benefit the dominant group, which, in different cases has been the government, pharmaceutical companies, and alcohol and tobacco companies. For example, a focus on the War on Drugs during the Reagan and Bush administrations focused public attention on drug use as a cause, rather than a symptom, of the plight of the poor in a wealthy society. As well, Johns believed that a focus on the War on Drugs also took attention away from the greater harm to society and individuals that tobacco, alcohol, and even pharmaceuticals cause, to the benefit of the companies involved in the marketing of these legal drugs.

Social Constructionism

In studying social problems, social scientists fall roughly into two camps: the objectivists and the constructionists. Objectivists argue that what constitutes a social problem is the scientifically measurable harm a condition does to human life or human well-being (Goode & Ben-Yehuda, 1994). Constructionists, or subjectivists, on the other hand, argue that it is the "degree of felt public concern over a condition or issue" that defines that condition as a social problem (Goode & Ben-Yehuda, p. 88). Although constructionists may look at the objective factors in judging the severity of a condition, they typically seek to point out the difference between the public perception of a problem and its objective seriousness. Constructionists point out that there may even be social problems that have no objective basis: A good example of this would be the persecution of witches (Goode & Ben-Yehuda, 1994).

According to Goode (1991), when U.S. President Reagan and his wife Nancy declared the War on Drugs in 1986, many social policy researchers asked "Why?" and "Why now?" Self-reported drug use had been on a steady decline in the decade leading up to the declaration, and there seemed to be no objective justification for announcing a War on Drugs. For example, since the first drug laws in Canada and the United States, deaths and illness resulting from licit drug use (particularly tobacco and alcohol) have been far more numerous than they have been for illicit drug use (Boyd, 1991; Goode, 1991). Further, Alexander (1990) pointed out that "a large body of careful research shows that recreational use of illicit drugs, including marijuana, cocaine, and heroin, does not lead to addiction or other harm for the majority of users" (p. 64).

Thus, constructionists might conclude that harsh jail sentences, increased police powers, lessened personal rights and privacy, and the like have all come about largely as an over-reaction to the actual problems that are caused by illicit drug use. It should be noted that Goode (1991) found some objective basis for a renewed focus on drug abuse (most prominently in rising numbers of heavy users of cocaine and crack cocaine). As a result, Goode concluded that even though the social problem of drug abuse in the late 1980s was "constructed," it was based, in part, on objective factors that shouldn't be ignored by social constructionists.

Moral Entrepreneurship and Status Politics

The concepts of moral entrepreneurship and status politics are closely linked, and are themselves closely linked with the construction of social problems. Each of these two concepts requires that one person (in the case of the moral entrepreneur) or any segment of society (in the case of status politics) attempt to create rules that others must follow. In doing so, the rules define who is deviant in a society and who is not.

The societal creation of rules by an individual can be attributed to the work of a moral entrepreneur (Boyd, 1983). Moral entrepreneurs can also enforce rules that they feel some people are willfully breaking yet for which they are not being sufficiently punished (Goode & Ben-Yehuda, 1991). Boyd (1983) pointed out that individuals, and not groups or social institutions, can be thought of as moral entrepreneurs (p. 260).

The concept of status politics accommodates rule-making and rule-enforcing groups as well as individuals. Status politics deals well in cases where there are few tangible gains to be made by the dominant group. The gain, rather, is symbolic, in which a particular life-style (the one of the dominant group) is embodied in legislation, whether it is enforceable or not (Giffen, et al., 1991). An example of this is the legislation that added marijuana to the list of banned drugs in 1923 in Canada, even though little, if any, marijuana was currently in the country. That symbolic gain here was the legislation of a life-style which was disagreeable to the "problem" that U.S. law enforcement officials were reporting they were having with marijuana at the time.

Critiques of the Three Sociological Theories

The three theories of prohibition discussed above share remarkably similar elements. They all envision an agent, or a group of individual (and like-minded) agents, engaged in the active creation of a code of conduct that ultimately benefits themselves in some way, hinders the activities of another group, or both. However, each theory has certain problems, which are often not fully dealt with.

In the case of conflict theory, society is often simplified to the point where any one group with interest in the prohibition of drugs (whether the group be governmental, pharmaceutical, or legal drug companies) may be labeled as an actively dominant group. This implies a rather loose definition of the dominant group, resulting in a possible mislabeling of the members of a group. As well, the actions of the public at large are often trivialized or ignored, as are the actions of the oppressed group.

Similarly, although social constructionism often identifies the dominant members involved in influencing social policy, it often fails to determine the mechanism through which public opinion may be molded. Although there is plenty of evidence to support the idea that the drug problem (and the "solutions" to it) constitutes a social construction, we would have to admit that it is a superbly constructed one, even if we are unsure how exactly it was constructed. In other words, if social constructionism implies a link between those doing the constructing and the general population, how is that link made? How can it be broken? There may be answers to that question (the media may be a key factor; see Hagan, 1980), but the mechanism through which conditions get "made" into social problems is unclear.

Finally, both theories of status politics and moral entrepreneurs suffer from many of the same problems: lack of specificity regarding the agents involved, lack of describing the mechanism through which public or community thought may be changed, and sometimes even the guessing of the motives of those involved.

However, it should be noted that despite the lack of a strict adherence to the "explanation" of drug prohibition through the use of these theories, they have fairly good explanatory power, and good prediction value as well. For example, with these theories we can both explain why the owner of a large alcohol company (Miller Beer) in the United States contributes to the Partnership for a Drug-Free America organization (an anti-drug group in the United States, most famous for its egg and frying pan depiction of a "brain on drugs"), and predict that it will continue to do so in the future (Johns, 1991).

Concluding Remarks

None of the three sociological theories examined above adequately explain the mechanisms involved in the Canadian government's continuing prohibitionist drug policies. Moreover, all three theories seem to ignore morality as a contributing factor in the criminalization of drug use. Perhaps it is this factor--an appeal to people's morality--that serves in many cases as the link between the general population and the dominant groups, status politicians, and constructors of social problems.

A potentially fruitful area for further research, then, might be to explore how morality has come into play in the enactment of drug laws, either in Canada or elsewhere, and to survey other possible approaches to dealing with problems associated with drugs--approaches that do not rely on criminalization or on moralistic judgments.

References

Alexander, B. K. (1990). <u>Peaceful Measures: Canada's Way out of the</u>
<u>'War on Drugs.'</u> Toronto: University of Toronto Press.

Blackwell, J. S., & Erickson P. G. eds. (1988). <u>Illicit Drugs in</u>
<u>Canada: A Risky Business.</u> Scarborough: Nelson Canada.

Boyd, N. (1982). The dilemma of Canadian narcotics legislation: The
social control of altered states of consciousness. <u>Contemporary</u>
<u>Crises 7,</u> pp. 257-269.

Boyd, N. (1991). <u>High society: Legal and Illegal Drugs in Canada.</u>
Toronto: Key Porter Books Limited.

Fischer, B. (1991). Maps and moves. <u>The International Journal of</u>
<u>Drug Policy, 5</u>(2), pp. 70-81.

Giffen, P. J., Endicott, S., & Lambert S. (1991). <u>Panic and</u>
<u>Indifference. The Politics of Canada's Drug Laws. A Study in</u>
<u>the Sociology of Law.</u> Ottawa: Canadian Centre on Substance
Abuse.

Goode, E. (1991). The American drug panic of the 1980s: Social
construction or objective threat? <u>The International Journal of</u>
<u>the Addictions, 25</u>(9), pp. 1083-1098.

Goode, E., & Ben-Yehuda N. (1994). <u>Moral Panics: The Social</u>
<u>Construction of Deviance.</u> Cambridge, MA: Blackwell.

Hagan, J. (1980). The legislation of crime and delinquency: A
review of theory, method, and research. <u>Law & Society Review</u>
<u>14</u>(3), pp. 603-628.

Johns, C. (1991). The war on drugs: Why the administration
continues to pursue a policy of criminalization and enforcement. <u>Social Justice, 18</u>(4), 147-165.

Kendall, P. (1995). A Response to Bill C-7 Controlled Drugs and
Substances Act by Perry Kendall, President and CEO, Addiction
Research Foundation to The Standing Senate Committee on Legal
and Constitutional Affairs. Ottawa: Addiction Research
Foundation.

Ⓐ⁺ This student discusses the decline of urban cities in North America by first providing some background information, examining two North American cities to better define specific problems, and finally, proposing alternatives to preventing further decay. But the student concludes by taking a risk—he acknowledges the possibility that the entire approach of the paper and of the available sources is wrong, and proposes an insightful potential solution. It is an admission of partial failure, but that failure is shared by civic leaders everywhere. What is more important here is that the student has kept the big picture in focus, and is going beyond the intellectual confines of his present sources to seek a solution. (APA style)

CITIES IN NORTH AMERICA: DECLINE OF THE URBAN CITY

Urban Decline: Historical Background

The evolution of cities in North America is no different from that in any other part of the world. Cities have emerged because of their proximity to natural resources, primarily water power, coal, ores, and seaports. The urbanization process began during the Industrial Revolution, which began in Europe in the 1700s and found its way to America by 1850. The growth of the manufacturing industry lured the masses with the creation of jobs, and the improved methods of transportation--most notably boats, canals, and railroads--enabled cities to receive food from all parts of the world in exchange for the goods they provided. The influx of immigrants to America during the mid-nineteenth century also added to the burgeoning urban population.

The economic boom that nurtured the growth of these cities also had a downside. These large concentrations of people created sanitation, transportation, and housing problems; and the diverse cultural mixes fueled increases in violent crime. Slums with boundaries drawn along ethnic lines emerged, and the quality of living amid these overcrowded conditions began gradually deteriorating.

Urban decay escalated during the Great Depression of the 1930s, and U.S. President Franklin D. Roosevelt shrewdly recognized the need to address the problems before they reached "the point of no return." He created a federal agency, the Public Works Administration, to specifically deal with urban issues and to provide much-needed funding for road repairs and bridge construction. The resulting creation of jobs reduced the massive unemployment that was crippling the nation's economy; but just as importantly, it was a visible sign that the U.S. government was doing what it could to assist the people. Despite its ambitious agenda and initial success, the PWA and its sister programs of the New Deal were not enough to cure urban ills. But they helped, they gave hope, and they bought time until the buildup to World War II brought an end to the Depression.

Author and urban scholar Jon C. Teaford divided post-Depression urban history into three distinct time periods. The first period encompasses the 1940s and early 1950s, and was defined by the retaliation of businesses, urban planners, and city governments against urban decline. In Teaford's view, they devised mostly superficial urban commissions comprising mostly elitist former government officials and retired businessmen, who created grandiose plans aimed at polishing the tarnished image of cities. The second phase, in the 1950s through the late 1960s, marked extensive federal government involvement in renewal programs, climaxed by President Lyndon Johnson's elaborate Great Society answer to FDR's New Deal, specifically designed to "fight the war" on urban poverty.

Like Teaford, T. Sugrue, writing in the <u>Journal of Urban History</u>, had a jaundiced view of attempts at urban relief. His view of the third time period (beginning in the 1970s and continuing to the present) charted a recession of federal government funding for city programs. Further, he described the emergence of mayors with high ambitions collaborating with private land developers "to preach the 'gospel of urban hype' and exaggerated urban improvements for political gain" (Sugrue, 1996). According to Sugrue, planners, in whose hands much of the urban revitalization programs were placed in the 1960s and 1970s, regarded the decline of cities "largely as a physical rather than a social problem" (Sugrue, 1996). They believed that blight was the main cause of urban decay. Cities were unattractive and harbored disease, and the scenery was little more than a succession of dilapidated buildings. The natural solution, in their opinion, was to "beautify" urban areas through modern architecture. If this view is accurate, urban planners are guilty of oversimplifying the problems facing cities.

Sugrue believed that federal housing legislation also concentrated mostly on eliminating urban "blight," but proved to be largely unsuccessful. Federally funded public housing programs were credited with eliminating slums, but the neighborhoods that replaced them fared no better than the slums. Government-financed community grants to encourage inner-city homeowners to upgrade their houses were somewhat successful, but the improvements were primarily cosmetic and did little to bring people back to the city; instead, they began relocating to the suburbs in ever-increasing numbers in the early 1970s (Sugrue, 1996).

To better understand the problems facing North American cities, case studies of two cities are examined, and although each is unique in its own way, the problems they face are remarkably similar.

Montreal: Canada's Crown Jewel

Montreal was once the jewel in Canada's crown of economic prosperity. One of Canada's first industrialized cities, Montreal's production depended largely on the textile industry. The pinnacle of this French-Canadian city was reached in 1967, when the world was mesmerized by its charm in Expo 67. At this time, Montreal was paving the way for urban development in North America, and was being described as "the most powerful cog in Canada's economic engine" (Canada, 1996). As the 1970s arrived, Montreal was beginning its decline. Its industrial sector had not expanded beyond textiles and began being undercut by competition from other markets. With its economic base eroded, Montreal's businesses began failing in succession, creating a staggering unemployment rate that remains the largest of any city in North America.

As if sensing economic ruin, Montreal's island population began deserting to the suburbs in droves. In the period between 1972 and 1991, its population decreased by 260,000, while the suburbs grew by over half a million. A Canadian political columnist summed up the situation as follows:

> Families with children, a house, and a steady income are at the core of any city; they are the ones who care about the school system and how a city is run. But, Montreal is gradually becoming a place of extremes: well-off dink (two-income households with no kids) condo-owners co-existing with a larger group of increasingly poorer tenants (<u>Canada,</u> 1996).

Montreal, essentially, has no middle class, for the people who would comprise that class left for the lower taxes and larger variety of services promised by the suburbs.

Businesses have also followed the middle-class migration to the suburbs. The loss of a major employer, CP Rail, to its new headquarters in Calgary was a devastating blow to an already shaky economy. As yet another sign of its plummeting economic fortunes, the Bank of Montreal's chairman of the board has speculated that perhaps the time had come to move the corporate office elsewhere, and change the company's name (<u>Canada,</u> 1996).

The relocation of industry is reflected in Montreal's mass transit system. Because there are fewer city dwellers, there are fewer people using public transportation. The majority of the newly transplanted suburbanites are commuting to their jobs in the city, and the increased traffic is wreaking havoc on Montreal's bridges and roadways. The city, already crippled by a massive loss of income, is now faced with mounting highway repair costs (<u>Canada,</u> 1996).

With the economic base shrinking, the tax burden is concentrated on the dwindling number who have remained in the city. Montreal's business taxes have ballooned, to become the third highest in North America. This serves to increase the city's downward spiral. With the province's desire to establish a separatist government, the highest murder rate in Canada, and the population expected to drop off by another one-third by the year 2031, the future prospects for Montreal are, unfortunately, rather bleak. It has been, perhaps, most appropriately described as "a doughnut city--empty at the centre" (Canada, 1996).

From Top to Bottom: The Fall of New Haven

New Haven, Connecticut, is not a city of the immense size of Montreal. However, it is experiencing similar urban decline. It is one of the oldest cities in America, and since World War II, has experienced a significant downturn. As early as 1948, Yale University's college community was experiencing problems of housing overcrowding. People began moving to the outskirts of town in numbers that were hardly significant at first. Ethnic subcultures also began to emerge that made no attempt at assimilating with the rest of the community. According to author Raymond Wolfinger, "What you noticed was a certain obsessiveness among ethnic groups to remain separate" (Minerbrook, 1992).

However, the one strong link remaining in the chain that bound New Haven's people together as a community was a strong economy. At that time, New Haven was a center of industry, responsible for the employment of 60% of all area workers. At its economic peak in 1954, manufacturers employed 33,000 people, all of whom were city residents. Even the corporate presidents lived in New Haven, so they had not only a professional stake in the city's progress, but a personal one as well.

Ironically, while the city was reaching its economic climax, the wheels of social unrest and decline were already being set into motion. In the period between 1929 and 1947, no new schools were built, and the civic leaders unwisely chose not to take advantage of the federal government's Public Works programs. Rather than send their children to rundown schools, middle-class families chose instead to send them to private schools. Private school enrollment jumped from 14% to 23% within a 20-year period (Minerbrook, 1992). The overcrowding problem that began shortly after World War II escalated, and by 1950, 14% of urban dwellings lacked sufficient plumbing.

By the 1960s, the suburbs began attracting both people and jobs away from New Haven. Suburban tax incentives and financing of home mortgages for veterans turned out to be too attractive for many families to ignore. More than 12,000 long-time residents left New Haven and took both their money and their skills to suburban areas, where the population grew by 120,000 people (Minerbrook, 1992).

At this same time, the black population more than doubled, as African-Americans relocated from the South in hopes of securing better incomes. Thus began a period of racial strife in New Haven that exists to this day, as the economic disparity between blacks and whites has widened. In predominantly white neighborhoods, annual household incomes increased 20% in the years 1980 to 1988. However, in the heavily black and Hispanic populated areas, median income dropped 46% (Minerbrook, 1992).

Today, New Haven ranks fifth in poverty in the nation, with the living standards of 22% of its residents below the poverty level. In 1988 only 32% of New Haven residents were earning what would be considered middle-level incomes (Minerbrook, 1992). Furthermore, New Haven has the highest number of AIDS cases in the state of Connecticut, an astonishing 20%. It also records the highest infant mortality rate of any city in America (Minerbrook, 1992). This is certainly not the picture to be featured in the brochures describing the city that houses one of the most hallowed learning institutions in the world.

Is There an Answer?

What, if anything, can be done to curb the urban decay that claims both medium and heavily populated cities? In 1992, it was reported that only 12% the total U.S. population lived in big cities, whereas more than 50% was ensconced in the suburbs

(Crocker, 1992). Skyscrapers are still being built, and new or remodeled architectural marvels are still cropping up in business districts. This does little to solve the problems of unemployment, homelessness, and crime shared by all urban areas.

In the cases of Montreal and New Haven, because their cultural and learning institutions provide thousands of jobs to transplanted suburbanites, shouldn't the suburbs lend a hand in bailing them out? The U.S. federal government, once so active in the affairs of its cities, has been noticeably silent since the era of Reaganomics of the early 1980s. Presidents Reagan and Bush did little to aid the shared plight of cities, and Bill Clinton has done little more than either of his predecessors.

Quite simply, the urban areas of North America can no longer handle these problems alone. Government loans are certainly not the answer, as they are merely a temporary solution and the problems created by mounting debts will force people to leave rather than remain in the cities. Without strong economies in the urban cores, there is little hope that the future of North American cities will be any more promising than the present (Minerbrook, 1992).

Conclusion

Because the flight of the middle class is the hallmark of decline, it would seem that programs which lure a significant number of middle-class residents back into the cities either through tax breaks or investment incentives are in order. Tax schemes currently favor those who move into suburbs where distances are greater, transport infrastructures are expensive, sewers go farther to serve fewer people, and other costs are similarly affected. Because the suburbs are often controlled by separate governments from the cities, perhaps it will be necessary for state, province, or federal governments to find ways to reverse this trend and make it economically attractive to live where services are consolidated and less expensive. But to entice the middle class back, the cities will have to provide safe streets and good schools, jobs, transportation, and recreational facilities.

There does not seem to be any silver bullet that will solve all these problems. Cleaning up blight alone did not work. Pouring in money did not work. In any case, the problem has gone so far that without some kind of economic program spearheaded by the national governments of both the United States and Canada, cities in North America have little chance of surviving the next millennium. The money simply is not presently in the cities themselves.

Upon reflection, this paper and most of the available sources and studies on urban areas have focused on the failures of cities. Perhaps this approach is backward. Perhaps we should spend more time and money studying the successes, wherever we find them, and look for what they have in common. Studying failures has not provided the answers.

References

Crocker, C. (1992, May 9). "Doomed to burn?" <u>Economist</u>. Available Online at www3.elibrary.com/search/getdoc [1997, May 21].

The doughnut city. (1996, March 1). <u>Canada and the world back-grounder</u>. Available Online at www3.elibrary.com/search/getdoc [1997, May 21].

Glaab, C., & Brown, T. (1976). <u>A history of urban America</u>. New York: Macmillan.

Minerbrook, S. (1992, November 9). "Why a city alone cannot save itself." <u>U.S. News & World Report</u>. Available Online at www3.elibrary.com/search/getdoc [1997, May 21].

Schweke, W. (1995, September 1). "Making comparative advantage work for economic opportunity." <u>Review of black political economy</u>. Available Online at www3.elibrary.com/search/getdoc [1997, May 21].

Sugrue, T. (1996, September 1). "More than skin deep". <u>Journal of urban history</u>. Available Online at www3.elibrary.com/search/getdoc [1997, May 21].

This paper compares Hispanic-Americans and Asian-Americans in terms of family, gender roles, and workplace. The paper also discusses the roles of both cultures in the United States today, as well as providing the student-writer's personal reactions. What sets this paper apart is that the student goes further and asks the less common and less politically correct question of what is lost in the rush to cultural identity, while avoiding the strident emotional extremes into which this issue often leads students. (APA style)

HISPANIC AND ASIAN-AMERICAN VALUES

Differences between ethnic groups in the United States have always been a subject of concern. Whenever there has been a significant influx of immigration, opposition has cropped up, as have claims that despite the fact that every wave of immigrants in the past has assimilated over time, this group will not, and they are therefore not "good Americans." This was said about the Irish in the mid-nineteenth century, about the Slavs in the early twentieth century, and about the Japanese in the 1930s; today Hispanics are the target.

The "melting pot" theory holds that with more time and generations in the United States, the ethnic groups will lose their unique character and become more assimilated. Indeed, this has been the case for most ethnic groups. It does not mean that all of the "old" culture is lost, nor does it mean that acceptance and equality in society will happen quickly, easily, or equally for all incoming cultures. Certain groups have clung to ways of thinking, feeling, and acting that differentiate them from mainstream American culture. This is especially true of those who maintain the religious affiliation of their original homeland (Comatosh, 1998). But it is also important to look at the other side of the coin. When Nikita Khruschev came to the United States, he was taken to visit many parts of the country to see the breadth of American culture, and his response was to ask Lyndon Johnson, "How do you get them to be all the same?" (Comatosh, 1998).

Although U.S. citizens are tuned to the unique qualities of recent immigrants, most second-generation Americans can be spotted as Americans by any European or Asian in a moment. This is not as true of Americans moving to Asia or South America. The United States was founded on an idea, a theory of how people should be governed and govern themselves, not on a race or a creed. <u>American</u> is not a racial or cultural identity: It is a state of mind. It is not monolithic, and it is always moving (often influenced by waves of immigrants), but nonetheless it does exist and is obvious to people from other parts of the world (Comatosh, 1998).

Studying individual groups is useful insofar as it makes us aware of the common values that individuals share with other members of their ethnic group and those that are shared with the broader culture. Two groups, Hispanic-Americans and Asian-Americans, are especially prominent in the United States today. Perhaps the most intriguing question in the study of these groups is how the values of these groups compare to one another.

Hispanic-Americans are not a single monolithic culture in the United States. Similarly, no culture is inclusive of all Asian-Americans. However, certain recurring value trends appear when studying individuals from the same ethnic backgrounds.

Family and Gender Role Comparison

One place where value trends manifest themselves is in family and gender roles. The adoption of traditional family and gender roles is more common among Hispanics than among other groups (Vazquez-Nuttall, 1987). Hispanic culture dictates that men should be "strong, authoritative, and dominant," and women should be "gentle, submissive, obedient, and homebound" (Comas-Diaz, 1988).

Hispanic families tend to be large; in fact, Hispanics have the highest fertility rate of any ethnic group. Sociologists attribute this to two main factors. Principally, Hispanic culture places a high value on children. Also, the Catholic Church's ban on contraceptives discourages many Hispanic couples from using birth control.

Many Hispanic families adhere to the belief that the needs of the child come before the needs of the adult. Children are taught

that cooperation rather than competition is a goal of social-
ization. In addition, Hispanic families typically place more
emphasis on harmony within the family than on material acquisition.

Asian-Americans also value traditional family and gender
roles. Filial piety, originally a Chinese cultural principle that
has spread to other Asian cultures, refers to traditional patterns
of social relations (Chu, 1985). Such patterns define specific
roles for men and women, and demand duty and obligation to the
family from all its members. Many Asian families consist of a
mother, who cooks and cleans at home, and a father, who is responsible for earning money and providing for the family. Sons are
expected to take care of the elders, carry on the family name,
and meet all the obligations of family leadership. Daughters are
obligated to be submissive and obedient. Deviation from these
traditional roles brings shame, not only to the individual, but to
the entire family.

Workplace Comparison

Another place where value trends appear is in the workplace.
U.S. workers have always been heterogeneous. These differences are
exemplified by the comparison of Hispanics and Asian-Americans.

Hispanics tend to value the expression of warmth and caring
between people; this holds true at the workplace (Cacas, 1995).
Furthermore, there is a general belief that cooperation is better
than competition. Hispanic workers value affectionate and personal
relationships with their business associates.

Asian-Americans, on the other hand, tend to be more task
oriented. Asian-American workers value the ability to toil and
sacrifice for one's company. These conflicting values often cause
problems when Hispanics and Asians conduct business together. The
Asian task-oriented approach, for example, may be misunderstood
by Hispanics as cold and uncaring. Likewise, the Hispanic caring
and personal approach may be misunderstood by Asians as weak and
irresolute.

Hispanics and Asians in the United States Today

Both of the ethnic groups discussed in this paper have values that tend to conflict with those of the mainstream U.S. culture. These conflicting values have the potential to cause problems. Both ethnic groups also have certain values that are consistent with the values of American culture. These values have the capacity to help ethnic groups flourish in American society; however, they can cause problems of their own. This was true, too, of earlier waves of immigrants (Comatosh, 1998).

As stated earlier, Hispanics value cooperation over competition. This idea contradicts many commonly held beliefs of U.S. culture; Americans believe competition is paramount. This creates problems for Hispanics, especially in the job market. Hispanics who do not effectively compete may have trouble getting jobs, particularly high-paying white-collar jobs. In one study, Hispanic police officers in a big-city department were found to have excellent records as "beat cops," but showed far less interest in testing and applying for management roles above the rank of sergeant--positions that would take them off the streets. They were therefore less represented in higher ranks than would be expected and hoped (Comatosh, 1998).

Asian-Americans share the U.S. ideal of competition. This enables them to get better jobs with higher pay than Hispanics. For this reason Asians are often considered a "model minority" (Steinberg, 1981). Yet this model minority status creates its own distinct problems. Many other ethnic groups feel that Asians are taking "their" jobs. As a result, Asians are often detested by other ethnic groups, sometimes resulting in hate crimes. Filmmaker Spike Lee addressed this issue directly in his film <u>Do the Right Thing.</u>

Both Hispanic and Asian-American women share the burden of a traditional female gender role. This contradicts the modern U.S. female gender role, in which it is common for a woman to be independent and work outside the home. Asian and Hispanic women often have trouble adapting to modern gender roles while still remaining true to their ethnicity. This raises a question: Should American citizens be true to their ethnicity or to their own desires as individual citizens in a democratic society where everyone is supposed to have their own inalienable and individual right to life, liberty, and the pursuit of happiness?

Changes in My Own Attitudes

Studying the values of both the Hispanic and Asian-American ethnic groups has helped me see the differences between the truths about these ethnic groups and the stereotypes associated with them. I now see that although most stereotypes have a root of truth, they are not necessarily true themselves.

It is popular today to see the change in ethnic images as a positive step where oppressed minorities are now able to celebrate their history and live in their own culture. As a result of this research I feel more open-minded about other ethnic groups. I have a new-found respect for, and understanding of, both the Hispanic and Asian-American cultures. But I have also come to the disturbing conclusion that much of what has happened is just as much a loss of what it means to be an American as a discovery of ethnic roots. Whereas in the past we celebrated the ties that bound us together, now we are celebrating the things that set us apart. The first led to discrimination. The second may lead us to a racial and ethnic separation even more destructive. Mexicans and Guatemalans have no interest in becoming Koreans or Japanese. The opposite is true as well. My research leads me to believe that the melting pot that uses both to create something new while honoring the old is perhaps not such an outdated ideal after all.

References

Cacas, S. R. (1995, Dec. 12). Office politics: Report explores diversity issues in the workplace. Asian Week.

Chu, G. (1985). The emergence of the new Chinese culture. In Wen-Shing, T., & Wu, D. (Eds.), Chinese Culture and Mental Health. San Diego, CA: Academic Press.

Comas-Diaz, L. (1988). Cross-cultural mental health. In Comas-Diaz, L., & Griffith, E. (Eds.), <u>Clinical Quidelines in Cross-Cultural Mental Health.</u> New York: Wiley.

Comatosh, W. (1998). "What is an American?" Unpublished dissertation. University of California, Los Angeles.

Morrison, J., & Zabusky, C. F. (1993). <u>American Mosaic: The Immigrant Experience in the Words of Those Who Lived It.</u> Pittsburgh, PA: University of Pittsburgh Press.

Steinberg, S. (1981). <u>The Ethnic Myth: Race Ethnicity and Class in America.</u> Boston: Beacon Press.

Vazquez-Nuttall, E., Romero-Garcia, I., & de Leon, B. (1987). "Sex roles and Perceptions of Femininity and Masculinity of Hispanic women: A review of the literature." <u>Psychology of Women Quarterly, 11,</u> 409-425.

This paper presents opposing perspectives on the changing suburban economy and culture. Notice that the student organizes this paper around two opposing camps—one supporting the thesis of a sociologist name Fishman, and the other (the "detractors") criticizing his thesis and providing alternative views. (APA style)

THE CONTEMPORARY SUBURB:

A RESPONSE TO FISHMAN'S TECHNOBURB

In his works <u>Bourgeois Utopias: The Rise and Fall of Suburbia</u> and "Megalopolis Unbound," Robert Fishman (1989, 1990) argued that we are currently seeing the development of a new kind of city, the technoburb, which sharply contrasts with the suburban development of the 1960s and 1970s. Fishman contented that the rise of the technoburb, a result of technological development and the insurgence of technology-based businesses surrounding major metropolitan areas, was significantly different from the rise of the earlier suburban regions, and that the new technoburb bears little in common economically or culturally with the suburb from which it emerged. Although other theorists, such as Sharpe and Wallock (1994), agreed with Fishman's supposition that differences could be explained from a sociological and evolutionary perspective, they refuted the central message of Fishman's works, asserting instead that these same communities demonstrated characteristics similar to their ancestral suburbs. In order to understand Fishman's argument and the challenges to it, it is necessary to consider the views of a number of sociologists, historians, and urban planners as they relate to the transformation of the suburbs.

Fishman's Argument for a Distinct Technoburb

In "Megalopolis Unbound," Robert Fishman (1990) pointed out that architects, sociologists, and urban planners all have acknowl-edged the same sociological phenomenon--a recent change in the American landscape--which they describe by way of various terms, including edge city (also utilized by Garreau, 1992), sprawl, spread city, and others, all of which suggest the extension of urban regions outward to what were once described as suburban and even rural areas. Growth in the suburbs, including the influx of businesses, increasingly diverse populations, and changes in the economic base of these communities, have all led to the view either that these suburbs are simply swollen and unable to function or that a process of wiping out the distinction between the city and the suburb is currently under way (Fishman, 1990).

Fishman contended that neither of these claims is actually true, but that instead a new kind of city, the technoburb, is emerging. The technoburb, claimed Fishman, is distinguishable both from the city and from suburban communities in that it is based primarily in the "amenities of technological civilization" and the extension of technology-based businesses into communities on the fringe of larger urban centers (Fishman, 1990). Fishman asserted further that the transformation of these regions has occurred to such an extent that there are few similarities between the technoburb and their ancestral suburbs.

Fishman is not the only theorist who has argued that the transformation of the suburban regions through the insurgence of technological amenities and technology-based companies has transformed suburbs into technoburbs. Other theorists, including Garreau (1989) and Muller (1981), have suggested that the basic structure of the suburb as a segment of an urban center has clearly changed, and that suburbs have been reshaped in the process of striving for their own autonomy.

Garreau (1989) traced the development of the suburb and of individual and identifiable subcultural components of the suburb, and then used these components to demonstrate that the suburbs have developed many of the very components that define a city. Garreau observed that suburban communities have delineated themselves from their urban centers socioeconomically, culturally, and ethnically. Suburbs are no longer simply places where individuals who work in the city live and commute from for their employment in the industrial centers. As more and more businesses have moved outside the city for land opportunities, less expensive operational costs, and

greater availability of office and industrial space, the development
of the suburbs as small but distinguishable "urban" communities has
led to what Garreau characterized as the basic components for the
end of the suburb. Now in its place is a separate urban subculture--
akin to Fishman's autonomous suburban landscape.

Mark Gottdiener and George Kephart (1991) also argued for the
creation of separated urban centers within what were once suburban
regions, suggesting that urbanization of the suburbs has resulted in
the creation of distinguishable central metropolitan areas that are
not necessarily connected in any way other than in their substantial
urban centrality. Muller (1981) also recognized that the changes
in the suburban landscape have resulted in the development of a
multiplicity of urban centers, and that the autonomy of the central
city in what were once suburban centers clearly distinguishes the
change that has occurred as well as differentiating one suburban
center from another.

Fishman's Detractors

The foregoing observations all lend support to Fishman's
thesis that a truly distinct entity--with its own center, autonomy,
and identity--has emerged from our suburbs. But several theorists
disagree, and maintain instead that the emerging urban development
in suburban regions is still rooted in, even connected to, the
foundations of suburban culture. Margaret Marsh (1990), for
example, argued that what appears to be a new technoburb is actually based in an autonomy central to the denizens of the original
suburban landscape. But Marsh's claim is dubious on two grounds.
First, it seems a contradiction because it would be this same
autonomy that distinguished the older suburbs from the urban center
in the first place. Second, Fishman did not claim that the suburbs
were ever autonomous, but to the contrary, that they were dependent
on their common urban center.

In more direct contrast to the views of Fishman, Jean Gottman
(1990) argued that these new suburban communities are not actually
fully distinguishable, primarily because they have yet to establish

their autonomy, and therefore their own separate and delineated economic and sociological culture. Gottman pointed out that the key cultural characteristics of Fishman's new and distinct technoburb simply cannot be decoupled from those of the earlier suburban culture.

Like Gottman, Baldassare (1986) recognized a nexus between Fishman's technoburb and its ancestral suburb that undermines Fishman's argument for a truly autonomous suburban region. In addition, Baldassare pointed to job markets and to the availability of industry as evidence of a continued connection between suburban and urban communities.

Sharpe and Wallock (1994) challenged a different aspect of Fishman's argument--that the economic conditions of the suburbs have reached a "critical mass" resulting in greater similarities between the suburbs and the urban centers and the necessity and inexorable push for separation and autonomy. According to Fishman, with increasing industrial development and influx of high technology comes the creation of a demographically distinct population and the development of an economic center. Fishman asserted that the delineation of the technoburb from its suburban base is the direct result of these processes.

Although Sharpe and Wallock (1994) recognized the central arguments of Garreau, Muller, and Fishman, at the same time they recognized a nexus between the new technoburb and the old suburb-- as defined by Marsh, Baldassare, and Gottman. Sharpe and Wallock claimed that the suburb, in any incarnation, will always embrace its original, underlying economic and social culture--at least to some extent. They asserted that although the current transformation of the suburban landscape might appear to be the emergence of something quite new and distinct, this metamorphosis is actually just a stage in the evolution of the suburb--and not a change in its fundamental foundation.

Summary

Although Fishman's perspective on the development of the technoburb finds considerable support among sociologists, it has been met with credible challenges as well. The Fishman camp sees a new technoburb with its own cultural identity and economic autonomy in sharp contrast to the suburb from which it emerged. Fishman's detractors see instead a new suburban center but with clear and strong ties to the culture and economy of the old suburb--in other words, another stage in the evolution of the suburb.

Apart from the impact of the new technoburb on the economy and culture of the former urban center, its cultural impact on its own denizens leads one logically to ask an important sociological question: Is a sudden decline in, or even demise of, suburban culture that is supplanted just as suddenly by a new culture healthy for the society, even if it is healthy for the economy? Normative issues such as this one might serve as fruitful areas for further research and investigation.

References

Baldassare, M. (1986). Trouble in Paradise: The Suburban Transformation in America. New York: Columbia University Press.

Fishman, R. (1989). Bourgeois Utopias: The Rise and Fall of Suburbia. New York: Basic Books.

Fishman, R. (1990, Winter). Megalopolis unbound. Wilson Quarterly, 14, 28.

Garreau, J. (1992). Edge City: Life on the New Frontier. New York: Anchor.

Gottdiener, M., & Kephart, G. (1991). The multinucleated metropolitan region: A comparative analysis. In Kling, R., et al. (Eds.) Postsuburban California: The Transformation of Orange County Since World War II. Berkeley: University of California Press.

Gottman, J., & Harper, R. (1990). <u>Since Megalopolis: The Urban writings of Jean Gottman.</u> Baltimore, MD: Johns Hopkins University Press.

Marsh, M. (1990). <u>Suburban Lives.</u> New Brunswick, NJ: Rutgers University Press.

Muller, P. (1981). <u>Contemporary Suburban America.</u> Englewood Cliffs, NJ: Prentice Hall.

Sharpe, W., & Wallock, L. (1994, March). Bold new city or built-up 'burb? Redefining contemporary suburbia. <u>American Quarterly,</u> <u>46</u>(1), 1-30.

19

TECHNOLOGY AND SOCIETY

This well-documented paper explores the scientist's social responsibility by focusing on the philosophy and activities of physicist Edward Teller, who helped develop the atomic and hydrogen bombs. The paper's endnotes demonstrate that in researching the topic, the student dug deep into a variety of primary sources, thereby earning her A+ grade. (MLA endnote style)

THE SOCIAL RESPONSIBILITY OF SCIENTISTS:

A LOOK AT EDWARD TELLER

Since the dropping of atomic bombs on Japan more than a half century ago, a dialogue has developed among people both inside and outside the scientific community, about whether and to what extent scientists bear responsibility for the ways their discoveries and inventions are used. Bertrand Russell stated that it is impossible in the modern world for a scientist "to say with any honesty, 'My business is to provide knowledge, and what use is made of the knowledge is not my responsibility.'"[1] On the other hand, Edward Teller, one of the physicists who created the atomic bomb, argued that the only responsibility of scientists is to discover new knowledge, and that what is to be done with that knowledge is simply not their responsibility.

But Teller's ideas seem inconsistent with his own actions, since he was intimately involved both in formulating and implementing U.S. defense policy before, during, and after World War II. But there is another element in Teller's view that might explain this inconsistency, an element developed not as much in his writings as in his actions: the notion that Western scientists have a responsibility to preserve democracy by lending their expertise to the building of successively more advanced weapons, which will provide a strong defense for democratic nations against their totalitarian neighbors.[2] Yet this notion seems directly opposed to the position of many other scientists: that the uses of science for destructive purposes is immoral and irresponsible.

Teller's views and his actions are worthy of close examination, not only because they help us to understand the social and political dynamics that led to the proliferation of nuclear weapons, but also because they provide insight about the general debate over the social responsibility of scientists--a debate that is sure to continue far into the new millennium.

Edward Teller's Ideas About a Scientist's Social Responsibility

In 1979, Teller told The New York Times:

> The job of a scientist is to do science, maybe to apply it, and then, if he is capable of doing so, to explain what he has found. To feel responsible for what is in nature, or to feel responsible for having increased the capability of people to accomplish something--such feelings are completely misplaced.[3]

Teller developed this position in a series of lectures delivered at the University of Missouri in 1961. In the first of these lectures, Teller freely admitted that the rapid advancement of science has made the planet an extremely dangerous place to live. But he rejected the popular notion that scientists "should now find the means to rescue us from our superabundance of power"[4] "and that the scientist is morally responsible for the fruit of his labor."[5] According to Teller, the call for social responsibility among scientists is in reality an assertion that scientists alone should decide what is to be done with scientific knowledge; in other words, that we should be governed by scientists.

To support his argument, Teller drew on the anti-democratic image of Plato's Republic, in which all power is to be exercised by a small number of philosopher-kings, or guardians, who bear some resemblance to our idea of scientists. Such a government, Teller asserts, would be dangerous for the country because rule by any elite group, including scientists, would subvert and destroy democracy and lead to an autocratic state with absolute power over the people. "That is the government by philosopher kings. This may become the government of scientists if ever the modern Republic is realized."[6] Another danger of such an autocracy, claimed Teller, lies in the fact that scientists are not trained to make social decisions, but rather to solve narrowly defined puzzles for which definite and recognizable solutions can be found. Political decisions, on the other hand, are almost always based on incomplete and insufficient information. And "more than anything, politics calls for feeling and compromise--things that the scientist in his narrow field has no occasion to practice."[7]

In short, Teller equated the idea of scientists' social responsibility with government by scientists, and dismisses the idea as unworkable at best and probably destructive to the society. But he also dismisses any claim that scientists have any social responsibility at all. For Teller the only real responsibility of a scientist

> is to find out what he can about nature. It is his responsibility to use new knowledge to extend man's power over nature. He is the creator of new tools, more fantastic than those described in the tales of the thousand-and-one nights of Arabia.[8]

Along with a responsibility to discover new knowledge is the responsibility to explain this knowledge in clear, simple, and understandable terms. But for Teller the scientist's responsibility ends here.

Teller's Actions Belied His Own Philosophy

In contradiction to his philosophy about a scientist's proper role, Teller in fact became a significant participant in the process by which the new atomic physics was used. He was an active proponent of nuclear power generation and other commercial uses for nuclear explosions. He was closely involved with the initiation of the Plowshare Program in 1957, which marked the beginning of the application of nuclear technology to peacetime uses. In 1968 he co-authored a textbook on the constructive uses of nuclear explosives,[9] and he wrote on this topic extensively for the popular press as well.[10]

Even more telling than his involvement in peacetime and commercial applications of nuclear physics was Teller's involvement

in its military application. Teller has been frequently characterized as the "father of the hydrogen bomb." U.S. News & World
Report described Teller in 1963 as the man regarded as "most
responsible for the fact that the U.S. was first to develop a
hydrogen bomb."[11] But this does not mean simply that he developed
the technology used to make the bomb. Not only was Teller perhaps
the program's prime catalyst, he was one of its leading proponents;
in fact, some described Teller as obsessed with the program. He
contributed to the increasing dependence of the United States on
super-destructive weapons as its major means of defense. In doing
so he had stepped out of the narrow role of a scientist who merely
discovers and describes new knowledge, a role that Teller himself
defined.

Teller's zeal about seeing the H-bomb program through to
completion is evident in his relationship with scientist J. Robert
Oppenheimer, who became Teller's nemesis during the H-bomb project.
Oppenheimer vehemently objected to the program, on three counts:
(1) it was not morally right to build a weapon of such unlimited
destructive power; (2) there was no urgent need for it as there
had been with the atomic bomb project, and (3) it would lead to
the U.S. dependence on weapons of mass destruction for its defense.
Oppenheimer's opposition resulted in the withdrawal of his U.S.
government security clearance in 1954, and Teller's testimony
against Oppenheimer at his security clearance hearings was largely
responsible for the result of the hearings.

Teller's influence on U.S. defense policy continued through
the 1960s, 1970s, and into the 1980s. He strongly opposed the
Partial Test Ban Treaty of 1963,[12] and helped formulate the U.S.
cold war strategy, which relied heavily on a retaliatory capacity
so great that it posed a threat to the survival of the human race.
In the 1980s, President Reagan's new "ideology of defense"--the
"Star Wars" initiative, as it is popularly known--was really a bid
to retain scientific expertise for the requirements of war. Once
again, Teller was at the center, aiding the Reagan administration

not only in developing the Star Wars technology, but also in articulating the underlying ideology. In 1982 <u>The New York Times</u> reported that "Edward Teller, the nuclear physicist widely credited with inventing the hydrogen bomb, visited President Reagan at the White House recently to give him an idea for another revolutionary weapon."[13] In fact, in a 1983 article in <u>The New York Times</u>, where several scientists were cited as criticizing an anti-missile defense as either technically unworkable or strategically dangerous, Teller was the only scientist mentioned by name who supported the administration's plan.[14] Curiously, just after President Reagan first unveiled the Strategic Defense Initiative in a 1993 public speech, the White House issued a disclaimer that "Edward Teller, the physicist, had no involvement whatsoever in President Reagan's speech last month calling for a futuristic missile defense system."[15]

It seems clear that Teller's own activities ran contrary to his notion of a disinterested scientist whose primary aim is to discover and explain new knowledge. In his biography, Teller's comments about the Oppenheimer case might shed some light on his ideas about his own "social" responsibility: "What the Oppenheimer case did to me was to make out of me a micro-politician"--by which he means someone who must become involved in the daily dealings of politics--and that he "had believed, and I still believe, that a physicist should be a physicist and not a politician, but I did become a politician, and I became one in self-defense."[16] But Teller's explanation is unconvincing because he had been active politically before the Oppenheimer case, during the hydrogen-bomb program.

Concluding Remarks

Bertrand Russell, quoted at the beginning of this paper, noted also that science "has from the first had an intimate and sinister connection with war."[17] For Russell, scientists have a deep responsibility because they know their knowledge could "fall into the hands of men and institutions devoted to utterly unworthy objects."[18] And many scientists agree. Physicist Marvin Goldberger put it this way: "When we become involved in areas that have a clear and unmistakable implication for destruction, I don't see any way we can walk away from our responsibilities.[19]

Teller, on the other hand, might walk away from this "responsibility," for he has said about his own activities, "For years, I have tried to counteract the consequences of neglecting military technology in the United States."[20] According to Teller, Franklin Roosevelt inspired him to turn science to the service of war:

> For the first and only time, I heard Roosevelt speak. He talked about the responsibility of the scientist. "If the scientist . . . in the free world will not help make weapons, then freedom will cease to exist." I felt that Roosevelt was speaking to me . . . at the end of [the speech], my mind was made up and I [have not] changed my mind since.[21]

In the end, Teller had a strong sense that it is the obligation of science to preserve democracy against all threats, and that discharging its duty included using science to gain military advantage. He was inspired by Roosevelt to "help make weapons" to save democracy. He certainly labored assiduously in the first task; it remains for history to decide what he contributed to the latter goal.

Endnotes

[1] Bertrand Russell, "The Social Responsibilities of Scientists," Science 131 12 Feb. 1960: 392.

[2] See, for example, Edward Teller, "The Human Rights Movement: Providing for Peace," The Center Magazine (Jan.-Feb. 1985: 22-26.

[3] The New York Times, 2 Jul. 1979: B7.

[4] Edward Teller, The Reluctant Revolutionary, the Paul Anthony Brick Lectures, 3rd Series. (Columbia: U of Missouri Press, 1964) 11.

[5] Teller, _Reluctant_ 12.

[6] Teller, _Reluctant_ 16.

[7] Teller, _Reluctant_ 20.

[8] Teller, _Reluctant_ 21.

[9] Edward Teller, Wilson K. Talley, Gary H. Higgins, and Gerald W. Johnson, _The Constructive Uses of Nuclear Explosives_ New York: McGraw-Hill, 1968.

[10] For example, see Edward Teller, as told to Allen Brown, "How Nuclear Blasts Can Be Used for Peace," _Reader's Digest_ May 1959: 108-110.

[11] _U.S. News & World Report_, 2 Sep. 1963: 12.

[12] See Jeffrey Marsh, "Science and Defense Policy," _Commentary_ Apr. 1977: 67-70, for a discussion of Teller's role in defense decisions.

[13] _The New York Times_, 18 Oct. 1982: A1.

[14] _The New York Times_, 25 Mar. 1983: A8.

[15] _The New York Times_, 29 Apr. 1983: D2.

[16] Stanley A. Blumberg and Gwinn Owens, _Energy and Conflict: The Life and Times of Edward Teller_, (New York: G.P. Putnam & Sons, 1976) 378f.

[17] Russell, "The Social Responsibilities of Scientists," 391.

[18] Russell 392.

[19] Marvin Golberger, quoted in _A Is for Atom, B Is for Bomb_, WGBH Transcripts (Boston: WGBH Educational Foundation, 1980): 12.

[20] Edward Teller, _The Bulletin of the Atomic Scientists_, Apr. 1983: 43.

[21] Edward Teller, quoted in _The Bulletin of the Atomic Scientists_, n.d.: 24.

This student discusses the uses, benefits, and ethical issues of genetic engineering in agriculture and medicine. This is a good example of a paper where the research was done entirely on the Internet. Given the topic's timely nature, this makes sense. However, it generally makes no more sense to ignore traditional resources than it does to ignore what is available online. Students should be aware that professors look at references to see how thoroughly a student has researched the material. (APA style)

THE CONSEQUENCES OF GENETIC ENGINEERING

Genetic engineering in agriculture has been employed on a widespread basis for nearly three decades (C.R.G., 1997). Farmers have been planting hybrid grain crops, such as corn, soybeans, and wheat, with the purpose of increasing their crop yields. Fruits, vegetables, and flowers have also been genetically engineered to produce products that have longer shelf lives, more appealing color, better flavor, and more diversity. Agricultural scientists have been able to alter the genetics of living organisms to prevent viral and bacterial infestations of plant life. More recently, technology has allowed researchers to isolate, experiment with, and alter genes in higher-level animals and humans. The ethical issues, as well as the potential environmental consequences, of genetic engineering are staggering. The purpose of this paper is to examine a few of the issues and concerns as they relate to the biotechnology of genetic engineering.

Genetic Engineering in Agriculture

Genetic engineering is a field of research that receives public funding as well as funding from the private business sector (Ho, 1997). Antoniou (1996) best described the science when he stated that "Genetic engineering (transgenics) allows the isolation, cutting, joining and transfer of single or multi-genes between totally unrelated organisms circumventing natural species barriers" (p.3). As an example, he wrote, "transgenic tomatoes and strawberries are under development which contain the anti-freeze gene from arctic fish" (p.3).

In 1994 the FDA approved the sale of the Flavr Savr Tomato, marketed under the brand name McGregor's Tomato (C.R.G., 1997). It was the culmination of a $95 million research project which isolated a gene that contains enzymatic coding to affect the ripening process in tomatoes. By altering this gene, the tomato can remain on the vine for an extra five days, and maintain freshness and firmness during shipping. The financial implications of developing such a product are obviously attractive to those in the business world. However, one of the ways in which the company, Calgene, intended to benefit from the development of the product was to take advantage of the longer shelf life after harvesting. Because the length of time that the tomatoes will remain fresh has been extended, the product can be shipped from farther away, outside the United States, where pesticide and labor laws are not as strict as they are domestically. Calgene also created a variety of cotton to better resist the effects of Bromoxynil, a pesticide shown to cause birth defects in animals that is also categorized as toxic to human genetic development (Lane, 1997).

The alteration of genetics in the agricultural industry is appealing from a financial standpoint. However, many concerned scientists have expressed their distress over the effects of genetic engineering in a variety of domains, including the ecosystem, and possible effects on human health and welfare. S.A.G.E. (Students for Alternatives to Genetic Engineering) pointed out that "plant and animal species have evolved over millions of years," naturally without the help of humankind (1997, p. 2). Their concern lay in the fact that genetically altered, living organisms are being released into the environment and might mutate and reproduce, despite assurances from researchers that this will not happen.

But in documented cases, transference to other species has occurred. Genes inserted into canola to increase the plant's resistance to herbicides have appeared in certain weeds closely related to the canola plant, creating a weed that is also more resistant to herbicides. Genetic testing conducted in a strawberry field resulted in the transfer of the altered gene to nearby wild plants, up to 50 meters surrounding the field containing the newly cultivated plants. Lane (1997) reported that 40% of all biotech field tests in the United States involve the development of herbicide-tolerant crops. Many crops have been engineered with protein genes that resist viruses. Viral genes inserted into plants could give rise to new strains of viruses that would be devastating to other organisms in the environment. Lane went on to state that "genetically engineered organisms pose great risks to ecosystems, since they can become dynamic living parts of them" (p. 6).

Opponents of genetic engineering are concerned about a potential domino effect from the transfer of altered genes to other species. Relatively unpredictable results of genetic engineering could alter the ecological relationships between naturally occurring bacterial organisms in the soil. In turn, plant life, insects, and animals could be affected. The effect could continue up the food chain, affecting wildlife, habitats, and eventually the entire ecosystem.

On the other hand, proponents of genetic engineering have claimed that the benefits of such research could be great (Ho, 1997). Benefits include the possibility of feeding the hungry with genetically modified crops better able to resist pests, thereby increasing yields. Also, the potential of developing strains of bacteria and plants that can degrade toxic waste and digest contaminants in the environment are currently being researched.

S.A.G.E. (1997) has addressed potential risks to health and the environment presented from the production and consumption of genetically engineered foods identified by scientists outside the biotech industry. A few of the most significant risks noted include the emergence of new toxins and allergens in foods and increased contamination of the earth's water, food supply, and environment

due to increased use of chemicals on crops. The accelerated contamination could increase the incidence of reproductive problems,
birth defects, and certain types of cancers. In this argument,
S.A.G.E. expanded its argument beyond genetic engineering as such
to include any chemical use on crops. More to the point was the
risk of accidental introduction of defective genes into the gene
pool that could cause a type of genetic pollution.

Genetic Testing in Medicine

In the past 5 years, more than 50 tests have been developed
to predict a human's potential for predisposition to genetically
transferred diseases (S.A.G.E.). Hundreds of tests are available
today, including tests for cystic fibrosis, muscular dystrophy,
fragile X syndrome, Huntington's disease, Lou Gehrig's disease,
and Tay Sachs. The information could prove to be invaluable for
medical diagnosis and treatment, but the concern that the information gathered could be taken out of context is real.

Documented cases of genetic discrimination have surfaced,
primarily by insurance companies. In a 7-year-old boy who was
tested, a gene predisposing him to a certain type of heart disease
was identified. Even though the child's condition was controlled by
medication, his parents' insurance company refused coverage of any
required medical treatment relating to his heart problems on the
basis that it was a preexisting condition since he had the gene
since birth (C.R.G., 1997). In another instance, a woman whose
medical records were legally obtained by a life insurance company
contained a doctor's notation that her father had been diagnosed
with Huntington's disease. The insurance company denied coverage
due to this genetic "tag." The uncertainty that research in genetic
testing will lead to treatment or cures for certain diseases raises
the question of whether the testing is worth the consequences of
discrimination based on the results of testing (C.R.G., 1997).
That this issue has become a focus of debate outside the scientific community is evidenced by its being the central issue in a
Broadway play: Johathan Tolin's <u>Twilight of the Golds.</u>

Summary

The field of biotechnological science is rapidly expanding. The advancements made in the past two decades have opened new discussions on the legal, ethical, and moral considerations of altering naturally occurring genes. These discussions are far behind the progression of the science. The implications and consequences of genetic engineering in the ecosystem are continually emerging, however. As technology and knowledge of genetics continue to grow, so do the concerns about how far we should go.

This paper does not even touch on the legal question of patenting of genetic research, nor the recent successes in animal and human cloning. It appears that humankind is not yet prepared to deal with the rapidly accelerating legal, moral, and ethical ramifications of genetic engineering. The positive consequences of transgenics could have an effect on world hunger and medicine. However, the question of who will decide how far to go in applying genetic technology is a question that is not likely to be answered anytime soon.

References

Antoniou, M. (1996). Genetically engineered food--panacea or Pandora's box? Available at home1.swipnet.se/~w-18742/ mianart1.htm.

C.R.G. (Council for Responsible Genetics), (1997). Consumer alert: FDA approval of flavr savr tomato paves the way for genetically engineered foods. Available at www.essential.org/crg/ consumeralert.html.

C.R.G. (1997). Position paper on genetic discrimination. Available at www.essential.org/crg/gendisc.html.

C.R.G. (1997). Preventing genetic discrimination: A call for action. Available at www.essential.org/crg/prevent.html.

Ho, M.W. (1997). Genetic engineering: The unholy alliance. Available at home1.swipnet.se/~w-18742/mahounho.htm.

Lane, M.F. (1997). Excerpt from: Land-speed-trials: winners and losers in the biotechnical race. Available at home1.swipnet.se/~w-18742/ecolrisk.htm.

S.A.G.E. (1997). Allergens, health and environmental risks. Available at www.sage-intl.org/health.html.

S.A.G.E. (1997). Environmental risks. Available at www.sage-intl.org/genetic.html.

A⁺ This student makes extensive use of a device that gets many students in trouble: the rhetorical question. Here, however, the use is appropriate, for the stated goal of the paper is to explore the *questions* that technologies raise for society. Another device is the comparison of two critical essays with very different perspectives on the issue. This student does not simply parrot their views; their essays are the centerpieces of a broader discussion. (MLA style)

THE INFLUENCE OF MODERN TECHNOLOGY: BEYOND GOOD AND EVIL

Is technology good or evil? Who benefits from it? Emanuel Mesthene and John McDermott are two scientists who debate the virtues and vices of the technology age. Both may agree that technology is here to stay, but hold divergent views on its application in society. In any case, hardly anyone can debate that technology has a grip on the modern world. This paper is an attempt to first define what technology is, and then explore some of the questions it raises for society.

What Is Technology?

The term <u>technology</u> is strongly associated with the application of science to the widespread solution of technical problems. Many scientists view technology as a continuum that stretches from very basic scientific research, through applied research to diverse social, economic, and political implications (DeVore 23).

Technology includes important social, political, and ethical aspects that could constitute a distinct discipline, separate from math, science, engineering, and so on. It has also been suggested that because technology has its own knowledge and structure, its study should be similar to how one would organize the study of any other discipline, such as algebra or physics (DeVore 24). However, DeVore believed that while technological knowledge may have the appearance of a formal discipline, it is in truth a "qualified form of knowledge" (24).

In DeVore's view, technology draws from formal knowledge, such as that found in the sciences and math, but it does so selectively and in response to specific applications. It is inter- disciplinary in its use of formal knowledge (DeVore 25). The study of technology also includes its own abstract concepts, theories, rules, and maxims. Unfortunately, like other disciplines, it offers opportunity for analysis that "loses its meaning and identity" in the attempt to justify the study:

> A considerable proportion of technological knowledge is prescriptive and tacit, and difficult to codify and generalize. The form as well as the complexity of technological knowledge is related to the kind and level of technological activity. Isolated from activity and removed from the implementing context, much of technological knowledge loses its meaning and identity (McGinn 180).

What's the Purpose of Technology?

More directly, what is the point of technology? Is it an end in itself? Perhaps it is, for a very persistent feature of human history or anthropology is innovation. We might say that what makes a human being distinctively human is the tendency or drive to change things--to invent.

Is there a purpose to technology? If so, what is that purpose? profit? social justice? individual freedom? saving time and labor? All have been suggested, but it is reasonable to think of all these possibilities as side benefits that are only rarely the genuine intent. Technology is a way to an end. Many of the reasons stated may be driving forces, but at the moment of innovation, some concrete problem--not an abstract goal--is most often the focus of the innovator. And viewing historical innovations, we might miss the point entirely from our distance.

Think of how much sooner the Egyptians would have built the pyramids with modern technology, and think of the backbreaking work that so many would have been spared. But then, think of all the jobs that would have been lost. Cheops kept 25,000 people employed for 25 years or so, and many historians view it as an early public works employment program. And remember that there is no "pyramid building technology" as such. To have the technology would mean to have an entirely different society, and that society would probably have no interest in building a pyramid. Changes in society go hand-in-hand with changes in technology.

Some say that technology knows no compassion. It's not human lives that count in this view, but how one can profit. The bottom line is that technology is cost saving, and concern about the time it saves relates only to dollars and cents. In this Marxist scenario, progress in technological terms means more money for the capitalists in a system, but may inadvertently serve the less wealthy or middle class, which is the biggest consumer of technology, spending hard-earned money on technology's gadgets and services. Karl Marx defined "true" progress as "social" progress. He believed that technological development could not achieve the peace and absence of turmoil that would bring social progress to the masses, even as a side effect.

Mesthene's View

Emanuel Mesthene's essay "The Role of Technology in Society" made the important point that every new technology offers both new opportunities and new problems, simultaneously and inseparably. Some people focus on the opportunities, some focus on the problems, and some say "Big deal! Been there, done that, no problem!" (p. 66-67).

Going beyond Mesthene's "good and evil" view, a third way might be added. Technology also induces change by creating a certain frame of mind, an openness to change, a willingness to look for novel solutions to old problems, and even a willingness to see problems to which we used to be blind. Mesthene might respond that this easily led to a kind of blindness, an inability to see that anything but change (or technology) may hold the answer to a problem. Think of technology as a person on life support for a long period. After a while it's easy to become overly dependent and fail to recognize alternative ways for self-sustenance. This discussion could go on forever, but the essential point is that technology, for better or worse, increases our choices.

As Americans, we value choice. Are there not something like 266 television channels to choose from on satellite dishes? Are there not hosts of package deals companies invent to entice would-be consumers to purchase goods or services? How many life insurance plans, for example, or bank savings programs does a person have to choose from these days? Telephone companies bombard the airwaves with "choices." The American marketplace is filled with them. Simplicity is definitely a thing of the past. But although we may not like the offerings, the choice remains ours.

Choice goes with concepts of freedom and human rights; perhaps it should not be surprising that science and technology have gone furthest in precisely those nations that value such things. Mesthene claims that: "society has at least as much at stake in the efficient utilization in technology as in that of its natural or human resources" (69).

Mesthene defined technologies as tools in the general sense, "the organization of knowledge for practical purposes" (70). This definition is quite inclusive and helps present technology as pervasive both now and in the past. Why are we more concerned today than in the past about the effects of technology? Many of our technologies are more powerful and more quickly apparent and have more lasting (even irreversible) effects on both humans and the environment. Many feel that such effects should be prevented or stopped. But technology is so intertwined with society that to undo one technological advancement is to dismantle them all: an unrealistic proposition.

It's been suggested that in light of the El Niño effect, a program to systematically cut back on the number of automobiles on the highway wouldn't be a bad idea. But think of the adverse effect this would have on the petroleum, construction, and auto services industries alone. Pulling cars off the road might be a great symbolic move to start saving our planet, but embarrassingly impractical in our world of reliance on metal fabrications powered by carbon-powered technology. The "anti-technology camp" would say that these industries represent billions of dollars--and that it's easy to see that any political inspiration to curtail automobile production and mobility for the sake of the planet or any other cause would be stopped dead in its tracks.

Despite such a cynical view, Mesthene noted that technology can change our values (71). It makes old goals (e.g., infant survival) more easily attainable, and it brings previously unattainable goals within reach (e.g., organ transplants). In short, there is a good side to technology. But there is also a tendency to say that if we can do something, we should do it. As technology increases and life becomes more complex, choices also become more complex. The pressure this creates in the individual and social institutions is enormous. And many people do not deal well with change.

McDermott's View

This brings us to McDermott's essay, "Technology: The Opiate of the Intellectuals." The article raises some strong points in an attempt to refute Mesthene. It reflects a pervasive distrust of government and military, and in technology because so much of it is linked to the military (McDermott 82-84). The Internet, for example, has been around for the masses for just a few years. However the military was experimenting with it back in the 1950s and 1960s, and began using it in earnest in the 1970s, almost 20 years before this technology was available to the public. Indeed, McDermott chose to define technology in terms of control, hierarchy, and expense, using as his prime example a particularly foolish military activity called program bombing (83). He definitely seems to be one of those people whom Mesthene said focus only on the problems. Inadvertently, he used an excellent argument against himself in describing how the Internet would not have existed had the military not created it.

It is interesting to consider another related example McDermott might have used: computers. In the late 1960s, computers meant mainframes, decks of cards for input, hierarchies of white-coated technicians, limited access, a sense of mystery, almost a religious or mystical air to it. But just a few years later, when the first personal computers (PCs) hit the market, the story changed dramatically. Are computers instruments of control by some elite hierarchy? Or are they instruments of individual empowerment and freedom? Does the history of the development of PCs and the Internet support McDermott or Mesthene?

Conclusion

I must side with Mesthene in this dispute. The control of fire gave us cooking, heating, and arsonists. The spear allowed man to feed his family and kill his neighbors. The wheel allowed us to transport goods and choke the roads with cars. Technology itself is neutral. It is a physical possibility that exists, whether we have knowledge of it or not. It is the uses we put it to with our free will that gives it a moral dimension.

Works Cited

DeVore, P. W. "Introduction to Transportation Technology." In J. R. Wright and S. Komacek, eds., <u>Transportation in Technology Education</u> 41st yearbook, Council of Technology Teacher Education. Columbus, OH: Glencoe, 1992: 1+.

McGinn, R. E. "What Is Technology?" <u>Research in Philosophy and Technology</u> New York: Simon & Schuster: 179+.

McDermott, J. "Technology: The Opiate of the Intellectuals." <u>Technology and the Future</u> (Reprinted from <u>The New York Times Review of Books</u>) 31 Jul. 1969: 77+.

Mesthene, E. G. "The Role of Technology in Society." In A. H. Teich, ed., <u>Technology and the Future</u> New York: St. Martin's Press, 1979: 66-76.

(A⁺) The style of this paper is distinctively journalistic. Notice that sentence fragments are used occasionally for impact. Be sure your instructor will accept this sort of approach before you write a paper in this style. Note that although the style of this paper is somewhat informal, because the paper is packed with information, including personal interviews, an informal style is acceptable. (MLA style)

THE BEST PIECE OF WORK (APOLLO 13, APRIL 11-17, 1970)

A 50-cent switch had a single, simple mission: to turn off the power to the heater in an oxygen tank when it got warm enough. Just once it failed to do that. The result was a tremendous explosion that left three American astronauts sitting in a dying capsule shorn of its supply of electricity, drinking water, and oxygen on a "non free-return orbit" that would take them on a quick trip around the moon and then on a long, long trip into deep space.

Thus began America's first in-space disaster and paradoxically, NASA's finest hour: the flight of Apollo 13. Most people know of Apollo 13 from the movie. But this paper is really about how the great technological achievement of the twentieth century may well have been not in the machines that took us to the moon, but in the response to this disaster. Men and women rose above their training, their plans, and their preparations to accomplish something that after years of working together, they discovered they were prepared to do. It is also about how quickly we forget the risks taken in the name of technology and progress while taking for granted the gifts:

> There will be risks, as there are in any experimental program, and sooner or later, inevitably, we're going to run head-on into the law of averages and lose somebody. I hope this never happens, and with NASA's abiding insistence on safety, perhaps it never will, but if it does I hope the American People won't feel it's too high a price to pay for our space program. None of us was ordered into manned space flight. We flew with the

knowledge that if something really went wrong up there, there wasn't the slightest hope of rescue.

We could do it because we had complete confidence in the scientists and engineers who designed and built our spacecraft and operated our Mission Control Center and training network. It was they who made Gemini the success it was, and I'm proud and happy that we who flew Gemini missions didn't let them down.

Now for the Moon.

--Lt. Col. Virgil I. Grissom, Seabrook, Texas, January, 1967 (Grissom, Introduction)

The Right Stuff

One month after speaking these words, "Little Gus" Grissom, the second American to fly in space--and the first human to leave our planet twice--burned to death in a flash fire inside an Apollo capsule on Pad 34 at Cape Kennedy, with fellow astronauts Ed White and Roger Chaffee. America didn't see it on television as it did the Challenger accident, but the country was shocked. Americans knew Gus Grissom. He was one of the original seven astronauts; he had "the right stuff." His partner Ed White had thrilled the world with his walk in space. Now they were dead, and America wasn't prepared for it. After only 15 flights in space, we had been lulled into forgetting what a dangerous undertaking spaceflight still was. Less than a year before, Vladimir Komorov had been killed when Soyuz 1's parachute failed, but in those times, that only made us feel superior, not mortal.

When Apollo 13 took off (only three years after the fiery reminder on pad 34 took the life of Gus Grissom and his companions), the media was apathetic, and so were the American people (Kranz). And so on Monday, April 13, 1970, nobody was watching the televised program being sent to earth from Apollo 13 because the networks weren't interested. Local Houston television wasn't even covering it when Command Pilot Jim Lovell closed the program:

This is the crew of Apollo 13 wishing everybody there a nice evening, and we're just about ready to close out our inspection of Aquarius (the lunar lander) and get back for a pleasant evening in Odyssey (the main capsule). Good night.

It wasn't a good night. It was a very bad night. Just after signing off from the television program that nobody watched, Jim Lovell was told to turn on a certain fan:

Thirteen, We've got one more item for you, when you get a chance. We'd like you to stir up your cryo tanks (Mission Report 128).

In the Silent Vacuum of Space

The fan inside an oxygen tank was turned on, and for more than a minute two wires that had become bare during ground testing arced and shorted. The nickel-steel alloy could withstand 900 pounds of pressure per square inch, but the arcing wires warmed the liquid oxygen in the still full tank (Mattingly). A physics degree isn't required to guess what happened next. There was no sound in the vacuum of space when the tank exploded and blew out the whole side of the service module; but the crew felt and heard the ship shudder. Telescopes on earth saw a shining cloud of gas where there had been only a speck.

Commander Jim Lovell looked at Fred Haise, a practical joker, who was coming through the tunnel from the lunar lander; but his expression said "Not me!" (Lovell). A moment later the warning alarm went off and voltage dropped on Main Bus B, one of two central power circuits. They were headed for deep space at 15,000 miles per hour, but the voices of Lovell and Swigert were calm and businesslike in the now-famous exchange:

Lovell: I believe we've had a problem here.

This is Houston. Say again please.

Swigert: Houston, we've had a problem. We've had a MAIN BUS B UNDERVOLT.

Houston: Roger, MAIN B UNDERVOLT (Mission Report 130)

On the ground, the controller who monitored systems data saw his whole panel go red. He thought something must have gone wrong with his console (Kranz). He couldn't imagine anything that would cause everything he saw at once, and when everything goes, where do you start trying to track down the problem? "What in hell is going on up there?" came two minutes later when the other shoe fell:

> Houston, we've got a MAIN BUS A UNDERVOLT now, too (Mission Report 134).

There was no quick, shattering end as with Challenger. Instead, an astronaut's horror story unfolded bit by bit. Oxygen is used in spacecrafts not only for breathing, but also to feed electric fuel cells, which provide power for the ship, and whose by-product is the supply of water, which is used not only for drinking, but also to keep the computers from overheating. Everything is backed up; there are three fuel cells and two oxygen tanks, but the explosion blew out all the plumbing, and the oxygen from the good tank was lost as well. The service module where the explosion occurred also contained the rocket motor that was supposed to put them back into earth orbit, and butted up against the heat shield. The astronauts could not risk using the rocket motor, which might have blown up, and had no way of checking the heat shield; if it had been damaged, they were likely to burn up on re-entry even if they managed to get back to earth (Kranz).

Four Long Days

For four long days the world waited in horrified amazement as problem after problem was solved, while Jim, Jack, and Fred flew the tiny lunar lander Aquarius back to Earth. To understand fully how Apollo 13 was saved, we have to look more closely at the team on the ground. Who were these people?

They Grew Up Together

Just as Columbus depended on his crew, so did the astronauts. But the crew wasn't on board with the astronauts. And that ground crew was something special. These were the people (mostly men at that time) who had created their jobs. Often hired right out of university graduate labs in their early 20s, they were the best and the brightest. They also held few preconceptions of what was possible. They worked together, they learned together, and they grew up together as engineers managing the system they had created for 10 years through Project Mercury, and then Gemini, and now Apollo. They knew not only their jobs, but every strength and weakness, every quirk of personality and streak of genius of the 16 controllers on their team as well as those on the other teams (Kranz).

There were four teams in those days: White, Maroon, Black, and Gold. They rotated on a regular basis as a flight progressed. The flight director was the conductor of this technological symphony, sitting in the center of the back row in the theatre-like control room. There were four screens at the front of the room with data, maps, and pictures that everyone could refer to. In front of each controller were monitors and panels for data, keyboards, and a square panel with 16 buttons, one for each controller. By pushing those buttons, they could listen in or join in on any conversation in the room or any conversation another controller was having with some point around the world. A huge recorder running 6-inch tape separately recorded every loop of what was being heard and said at any given moment. The flight director would sometimes be listening to all 16 loops at once. Listening to his "orchestra," he could instantly pick up a sour note--a change in vocal pitch or a word that signaled trouble (Kranz).

When Gus Grissom spoke of his complete confidence in those who "operated our Mission Control Center and training network," this is what he was talking about. Not only did the astronauts have to trust the controllers, but the controllers had to trust each other, for when their shift was over, they had to be able to leave their posts and know that the next two teams would keep it all together until they returned the following day. Most of all, this applied to Gene Kranz, the #1 flight director. The problems involved in the last orbits and landing of Apollo 13 were so great that he pulled his White team completely offline into a duplicate control room upstairs to prepare for the landing. Glynn Lunney (Black team flight director) was in charge of keeping everyone alive and getting them back so that there could be a landing.

A Technological Work of Art

From all accounts, ego was submerged during the next 4 days, and the polished organization developed in the past 10 years didn't rise to the moment; it simply became superfluous as inspired improvisation took over. Fluid groupings formed, merged, and dissolved as necessary to solve problems and then everyone moved on (Lunney, Mattingly, Kranz). In the heat of the moment they had raised their craft to a technological work of art: splendid varia-tions on a well-rehearsed theme. And that team expanded outward from the control room to Building 35, where hundreds of engineers from suppliers such as Grumman had onsite teams of their own, and from there around the country. About 35,000 people made up the network (Kranz). Some fellow in Los Angeles had to get up in the middle of the night, go down to his factory, and pee in a plastic bag his company had made for another purpose to see if it was strong enough, since the urinal wasn't working and they had to have someplace . . . (Brooks 267).

A "Successful Failure"

After nearly 4 days of this, 135 hours since liftoff, the crewcut, bull-necked, 32-year-old Gene Kranz put on his "lucky" white vest, took over from Glynn Lunney, and brought his White team back on for the last shift. Lovell and his crew had flown the tiny Aquarius (with 20 tons of mangled service module and the powerless Columbia still attached) back to the earth. Now they jettisoned the service module and for the first time saw how much damage had been done as it drifted away. "There's one whole side of the spacecraft missing!" Lovell reported in amazement--"The whole panel is blown out almost from the base of the engine"

(Mission Report 125). That news brought everyone's thoughts back to the heat shield. They lined themselves up perfectly on the tiny window in the atmosphere that provided safe entry only if the heat shield was intact. Then, just an hour before hitting the atmosphere at nearly 25,000 miles per hour, Jim, Jack, and Fred climbed into the dead capsule Columbia, used the air pressure in the connecting tunnel to gently separate them from Aquarius without changing their now-ballistic course, and came down almost on the deck of the aircraft carrier Iwo Jima while the world watched it live, (and for the first time in color) on their televisions. After 142 hours, 54 minutes, and 41 seconds, Apollo 13 had landed safely less than a mile and a half off target (Mission Report 325). President Nixon called Jim Lovell. "Our mission was a failure," said Lovell, "but I like to think it was a successful failure" (Brooks 402).

Just as the technology of musical instruments led to the possibility of the symphony orchestra with its complex and sophisticated music, the technology of spaceflight led to the communal work of technological art that brought Apollo 13 home. It was too complex to be planned; and the response required rising above and beyond training to improvisation. It was a moment in time where humans had brought themselves, with immense effort and expense, equal with their own level of technology. For a brief space of time, the organization approached the level of organism, acting as a united whole. It was indeed a rare moment.

The Best Piece of Work

The twentieth century will be remembered as the time when the human race first broke the bounds of earth and reached toward the stars. And these are the men and women who did it. Certainly the glory is shared by many, and certainly the heroes would not have been heroes had the opportunity not presented itself. But they placed themselves where the action was, they were prepared, and in that moment they delivered or, in the case of some astronauts, died trying. Flight director Glynn Lunney found himself and Gene Kranz in _Time_ magazine and ticker-tape parades. He had been an engineer, a test pilot, and for nearly 20 years a controller and flight director. By 1980, 10 years after the Apollo 13 mission, he had concluded overall direction of the Apollo-Soyuz project, and now had responsibility over all payload decisions for the upcoming shuttle program. But he was still only 43 years old. He puffed thoughtfully on a cigar the size of Havana during an interview in his huge corner office looking out at Galveston Bay in the distance. The peak of his "official" career was still ahead. But for the past couple hours, his thoughts had been on Apollo 13. He was silent for a minute, faraway. Then Lunney lowered his cigar, leaned very close to his interviewer, and said: "Pat, that's the best piece of work I've ever done--and what's more, it's the best piece of work I'll ever get a chance to do."

Works Cited

Brooks, Courtney G., James M. Grimwood, and Loyd S. Swenson, Jr. _Chariots for Apollo: A History of Manned Lunar Spacecraft_. Washington, D.C.: Scientific and Technical Information Branch, NASA.

Grissom, Virgil I. _Gemini: A Personal Account of Man's Venture into Space_. New York: Macmillan, 1968.

Kranz, Gene. Personal interview (1995).

Lovell, James. Personal interview (1995).

Lunney, Glynn. Personal interview (1995).

Mattingly, Ken. Personal interview (1995).

National Areonautics and Space Administration, Office of Manned Space Flight. _Apollo 13 Mission Report MSC-PA-R-70-7_. Washington, DC: NASA, 1970.

NOTES FOR AN A+ TERM PAPER

NOTES FOR AN A+ TERM PAPER

NOTES FOR AN A+ TERM PAPER

NOTES FOR AN A+ TERM PAPER

NOTES FOR AN A+ TERM PAPER

NOTES FOR AN A+ TERM PAPER

NOTES FOR AN A+ TERM PAPER

NOTES FOR AN A+ TERM PAPER